CW00336115

WOMEN AND AUSTERI

Austerity has become the new principle for public policy in Europe and the US as the financial crisis of 2008 has been converted into a public debt crisis. However, current austerity measures risk losing past progress towards gender equality by undermining important employment and social welfare protections and putting gender equality policy onto the back burner. This volume constitutes the first attempt to identify how the economic crisis and the subsequent austerity policies are affecting women in Europe and the US, tracing the consequences for gender equality in employment and welfare systems in nine case studies from countries facing the most severe adjustment problems.

The contributions adopt a common framework to analyse women in recession, which takes into account changes in women's position and current austerity conditions. The findings demonstrate that in the immediate aftermath of the financial crisis, employment gaps between women and men narrowed — but due only to a deterioration in men's employment position rather than any improvements for women. Tables are set to be turned by the austerity policies which are already having a more negative impact on demand for female labour and on access to services which support working mothers. Women are nevertheless reinforcing their commitment to paid work, even at this time of increasing demands on their unpaid domestic labour.

Future prospects are bleak. Current policy is reinforcing the same failed mechanisms that caused the crisis in the first place and is stalling or even reversing the long-term growth in social investment in support for care. This book makes the case for gender equality to be placed at the centre of any progressive plan for a route out of the crisis.

Maria Karamessini is Professor of Labour Economics and Economics of the Welfare State at Panteion University of Social and Political Sciences, Greece. She is also Director of the Centre for Gender Studies at the University. She has published extensively on labour market issues, employment and social policy, gender inequalities in paid work and equality policy.

Jill Rubery is Professor of Comparative Employment Systems at Manchester Business School, UK. She is also founder and Co-Director of the European Work and Employment Research Centre. She has published widely on comparative employment systems, gender equality and labour market segmentation.

Routledge IAFFE Advances in Feminist Economics

IAFFE aims to increase the visibility and range of economic research on gender; facilitate communication among scholars, policymakers, and activists concerned with women's well-being and empowerment; promote discussions among policy makers about interventions which serve women's needs; educate economists, policymakers, and the general public about feminist perspectives on economic issues; foster feminist evaluations of economics as a discipline; expose the gender blindness characteristic of much social science and the ways in which this impoverishes all research, even research that does not explicitly concern women's issues; help expand opportunities for women, especially women from underrepresented groups, within economics; and, encourage the inclusion of feminist perspectives in the teaching of economics. The IAFFE book series pursues the aims of the organization by providing a forum in which scholars have space to develop their ideas at length and in detail. The series exemplifies the value of feminist research and the high standard of IAFFE sponsored scholarship.

WOMEN AND AUSTERITY

The economic crisis and the future for gender equality

Edited by Maria Karamessini and Jill Rubery

Routledge
Taylor & Francis Group

LONDON AND NEW YORK

First published 2014
by Routledge
2 Park Square, Milton Park, Abingdon, Oxon OX14 4RN

Simultaneously published in the USA and Canada
by Routledge
711 Third Avenue, New York, NY 10017

Routledge is an imprint of the Taylor & Francis Group, an informa business

British Library Cataloguing in Publication Data
A catalogue record for this book is available from the British Library

Library of Congress Cataloging-in-Publication Data
Women and austerity : the economic crisis and the future for gender equality / edited by Maria Karamessini and Jill Rubery.
  pages cm
Includes bibliographical references and index.
ISBN 978-0-415-81536-9 (hardback) – ISBN 978-0-415-81537-6 (pbk.) –
ISBN 978-0-203-06629-4 (e-book) 1. Women–Employment–United States.
2. Women–Employment–Europe. 3. Sex discrimination against women–United States.
4. Sex discrimination against women–Europe. 5. United States–Social policy–21st century. 6. Europe–Social policy–21st century. 7. Global Financial Crisis, 2008–2009.
I. Karamessini, Maria. II. Rubery, Jill.
HD6095.W671962013
331.4094—dc23   2013004286

ISBN: 978-0-415-81536-9 (hbk)
ISBN: 978-0-415-81537-6 (pbk)
ISBN: 978-0-203-06629-4 (ebk)

Typeset in Bembo
by Cenveo Publisher Services

MIX
Paper from
responsible sources
FSC
www.fsc.org   FSC® C013604   Printed and bound by CPI Group (UK) Ltd, Croydon, CR0 4YY

CONTENTS

FIGURES

TABLES AND BOXES

Tables

Box

ACKNOWLEDGEMENTS

This edited volume is the outcome of original scientific work presented by the authors in two international symposia on 'Women, Gender Equality and Economic Crisis'. The first symposium was held in Athens on the 1st and 2nd December 2011 and the second in Reykjavik on the 21st and 22nd April 2012.

The Athens symposium was organized by the Centre for Gender Studies of the Social Policy Department of Panteion University of Social and Political Sciences, which is directed by Maria Karamessini. The event was hosted and funded by Panteion University. The Reykjavik symposium was organized by Thora Kristin Thorsdottir in collaboration with EDDA – Centre of Excellence, at the University of Iceland, and sponsored by: ASÍ – Icelandic Confederation of Labour; BSRB – Federation of State and Municipal Employees; Equality Council; Ministry of Education, Science and Culture; Ministry of Finance; Ministry of the Interior; Ministry of Welfare; SA – Confederation of Icelandic Employers; SLFÍ – Association of practical nurses; STRV – Reykjavik's Municipal Employees' Association; and VR – The Commercial and Office Workers' Union. Both the Greek and the Icelandic symposiums were supported by two Manchester research centres – the Manchester Fairness at Work Research Centre and the European Work and Employment Research Centre. We are grateful to all these funders and to all discussants and paper-givers at these events.

We are incredibly grateful to Thora Thorsdottir not only for organizing the excellent Iceland conference and securing the funding for that conference but also for preparing the manuscript for us for submission to the publishers, a task undertaken with extreme dedication and attention to detail.

We would like to thank Rob Langham and Natalie Tomlinson from Routledge for their very positive support for this book project from the beginning. Routledge also republished Jill Rubery's original edited book on *Women and Recession* in 2010, which in part sparked the idea of a follow-up volume.

Our intellectual debts are many and various but we would like to thank first of all the original contributors, to the first volume on *Women and Recession* in 1988 edited by Jill Rubery. In that first publication Jill worked particularly closely with Jane Humphries and Francesca Bettio. Francesca, apart from Jill, is the only author from the original volume also to contribute to this book and her chapter draws on her work as lead co-ordinator for the European Union's expert groups on gender, employment and gender equality (EGGE, ENEGE). We, the current volume editors, along with many of the contributing authors, have participated in the past and/or currently as members or co-ordinators of these networks. Our own work has been much enriched by the opportunity to work with so many gender and employment experts from so many countries.

This brings us last but not least to our thanks to the authors of this volume who have eagerly participated in the symposiums and the book project. Their long research experience and expertise on gender issues in the fields of employment and social policy have been valuable. We all share concerns for the future of gender equality as a social goal in the light of the shift in political and policy priorities since the onset of the global economic crisis and the adoption of austerity measures. These are not only threatening women's hard won employment gains but also the welfare and employment protections that provide essential support for socially progressive gender equality objectives. The main hope of the editors of this volume is to revitalise interest in gender equality as a central principle that needs to be at the core of any plan to move beyond the current negative policy prescriptions that are dominating this current phase of austerity.

CONTRIBUTORS

Randy Albelda is a Professor of Economics at the University of Massachusetts Boston and former Vice-President of the International Association for Feminist Economics. Her research and teaching focuses on economic policies affecting low-income women in the US. Her co-authored books include *Glass Ceilings and Bottomless Pits: Women's Work, Women's Poverty* and *Unlevel Playing Fields: Understanding Gender Inequality and Discrimination.*

Ursula Barry is a Researcher and Lecturer at the School of Social Justice, University College Dublin, Ireland, specialising in gender, equality and public policy. She is the author of a wide range of research reports and articles on economic and social policy, gender and equality issues in Ireland and is the Irish representative on the EU Network of Experts on Gender Equality (ENEGE) and a Senior Expert on the EU Socio-Economic Network on Non-Discrimination. Ursula is the editor and contributor to *Where are we now – new feminist perspectives on women in contemporary Ireland* (New Island publishers, Dublin 2008).

Francesca Bettio is Professor of Economics at the University of Siena, Italy. Her main areas of expertise are in labour and gender economics as well as population economics. Her research interests range from fertility and female labour market participation – including wage differentials, discrimination, and labour market segmentation – to the economic analysis of the family, of care work and, recently, of international female migration and sex work. She has a long record of collaborating with the European Commission as an expert on female employment, and she is currently lead co-ordinator of the European Network of Experts on Gender Equality (ENEGE).

Marina Capparucci is Professor of Economics at La Sapienza University of Rome, Italy. She teaches labour economics and labour market policies. Her main fields of research include economics of education and training, wage determination and wage distribution, labour market segmentation, welfare and employment. She is the author of numerous journal articles, reports and books, including a 2010 book on *Labour Market and Income Policies. Theoretical models and the reform processes* (in Italian). She has also recently published on European employment models, including flexicurity, regional disparities, and labour market effects of migration.

Pauline Conroy is a graduate of University College Dublin and the London School of Economics. She has worked with the European Commission on gender and anti-poverty issues, with the Council of Europe on women outworkers in Europe and with the International Labour Organisation on disability rights in employment. She was the first editor of the European Commission's *Annual Report on Equal Opportunities between Women and Men* and has co-authored (with Helen O'Leary) a study of indebtedness among low-income families in Ireland: *Do the Poor Pay More?*

Virgínia Ferreira is a Professor of Sociology at University of Coimbra, a member of the EU's Network of Experts on Gender and Employment (EGGE) and on Gender Equality (ENEGE) and a founding member of the Portuguese Association of Women's Studies. Her teaching and research focus on sociology of work and employment, sociology of gender relations and gender equality policies. She recently published the edited book: *A Igualdade de Mulheres e Homens no Trabalho e no Emprego em Portugal: Políticas e Circunstâncias* (Equality of Women and Men in the Employment System in Portugal: Policies and Circumstances).

Mária Frey is a Professor at the Institute for Human Resources of the Corvinus University, Budapest. Her main areas of research are employment policy, labour market and equal opportunities for men and women. Between 2008 and 2011, she worked as national expert in the EU Network on Gender and Employment and, in 2012, became a member of the EU's Network of Experts on Gender Equality (ENEGE).

Elvira González Gago is an economist specialising in employment, social cohesion and regional policies. She is Spanish member of the SYSDEM network of researchers on labour market issues and of the EU's Network of Experts on Gender Equality (ENEGE) and also a member of former EGGE and EGGSI networks since 2008. She has directed projects for the European Commission and for Spanish institutions, such as the Ministry for Labour and Social Services and Equality and the employment departments of various Spanish regions. She has provided technical assistance on the National Plan for Equal Opportunities between Women and Men and on the Special Plan against the Gender Pay Gap.

Maria Karamessini is Professor of Labour Economics and Economics of the Welfare State and Director of the Centre for Gender Studies at Panteion University of Social and Political Sciences (Athens). She has directed many research projects including the first Graduates' Survey in Greece and has been a member of all the European Commission expert groups on Gender and Employment since 1997 (EGGE, EGGSIE and currently ENEGE). She has recently published two articles on the gender impact of economic crises: 'Labour market impact of four recessions on women and men in Greece: comparative analysis in a long-term perspective' (*Social Cohesion and Development* 7(2), 2012) and 'Strukturkrise, Schocktherapie und Gender in Griechenland' (in Ingrid Kurz-Scherf and Alexandra Scheele Hrsg. *Macht oder ökonomisches Gesetz?* 2012).

Tiziana Nazio is a Lecturer in Sociology at the University of Turin and Affiliate Fellow of the Collegio Carlo Alberto. She is author of *Cohabitation, Family and Society*, Routledge 2008. Her research focuses on female employment and family formation from a comparative perspective; she has participated on a number of EU projects including most recently 'WORKCARE – Social quality and the changing relationship between work, care and welfare in Europe' (2006–08). She was principal investigator of the ESRC-funded project 'Are storks striking for a contract renewal? Childbirth under changing employment, family and welfare arrangements' (2006–08) at Nuffield College, Oxford University.

Jacqueline O'Reilly is Professor of Comparative Employment Relations and Human Resource Management at the University of Brighton Business School in the UK. She is Director of the Centre for Research on Management and Employment (CROME) and is a Leverhulme Major Research Project Fellow (2009–12). She previously worked at the Wissenschaftszentrum Berlin; and at UMIST, Manchester. She has held a Jean Monnet Fellowship at the European University Institute, Florence and has studied at L'Observatoire Sociologique du Changement, Paris and Nuffield College, Oxford. In 1998 she co-edited *Part-time Prospects* with Colette Fagan.

Diane Perrons is Professor in Economic Geography and Gender Studies at the Gender Institute, London School of Economics and a member of the UK Women's Budget Group. She researches the social implications of economic restructuring and increasing inequality, paying attention to work organization and the social reproduction of daily life. Her most recent book is on *Gender, Migration and Domestic Work: Masculinities, male labour and fathering in the UK and USA* (with Kilkey, Majella and Plomien, Ania 2013).

Ania Plomien is a Lecturer at the Gender Institute, London School of Economics and Political Science and a member of the UK Women's Budget Group. She investigates the relationship between institutional structures and gender relations and outcomes in the context of transition, particularly in Central Eastern Europe and at the European Union level. Her most recent book is on *Gender, Migration and Domestic Work: Masculinities, male labour and fathering in the UK and USA* (with Kilkey, Majella and Perrons, Diane 2013).

Anthony Rafferty is a Lecturer in Employment Studies at Manchester Business School, University of Manchester and member of the Fairness at Work Research Centre (FairWRC) and European Work and Employment Research Centre (EWERC). His research covers issues of equality and diversity in the labour market, labour force analysis, and social and labour market policy. Recent publications cover topics such as the equality impact of the economic crisis, the labour market impact of welfare reform, gender differences in job quality in Europe, and ethnic penalties in graduate level employment.

Jill Rubery is Professor of Comparative Employment Systems at Manchester Business School and founder and Co-Director of the European Work and Employment Research Centre. She has published widely on comparative employment systems, gender equality and labour market segmentation. Her 1988 edited book *Women and Recession* was republished in its original form by Routledge in 2010. Between 1990 and 2007 she co-ordinated the European Commission's Network of Experts on Gender and Employment (EGGE). Recent publications include *European Employment Models in Flux* (jointly edited with Gerhard Bosch and Steffen Lehndorf 2009) and *Welfare States and Life Transitions* (jointly edited with Dominique Anxo and Gerhard Bosch 2010). In 2006 she was elected a Fellow of the British Academy. She is an Associate Editor of *Feminist Economics*.

Marcelo Segales Kirzner has a Master's in Regional Economics and researches and consults on evaluation, labour market policies, young workers' situation, social inclusion and gender perspective. In particular he has examined flexicurity and other European employment policies and has specialized in the assessment of the Spanish National Reform Programme including employment, health and other social policies with a gender-sensitive perspective. He has taught regional economics, labour and macroeconomics at a public university in Seville, Spain.

Mark Smith is an Associate Professor and Director of the Doctoral School at Grenoble École de Management, France. His research interests focus on gendered labour market outcomes including working conditions, working time management, work–life integration and the impact of employment policy in different country contexts. He is a co-coordinator of the European Commission's ENEGE network. He has co-authored a number of books, book chapters and journal articles including *Gender and the European Labour Market* (with F. Bettio and J. Plantenga, forthcoming 2013 with Routledge).

Thora Kristin Thorsdottir is a research associate of the Social Research Centre and a PhD student in sociology at the University of Iceland. Her PhD project concerns the effects of drastic economic fluctuations on the gender division of labour. She has published on work–life balance in Iceland in recession and recovery, on the gender division of labour in Iceland and gender differences in welfare state attitudes. Previously she was an adjunct at the University of Akureyri where she taught research methods and statistics. In addition she has taught courses on research methods at the University of Iceland as a part-time lecturer since 2007.

Alina Verashchagina is a Post-doctoral Research Fellow at La Sapienza University of Rome, Italy. She holds a PhD in economics from the University of Siena, Italy. She was a member of the co-ordinating team of the EU Expert Group on Gender and Employment (EGGE) between 2008 and 2011 and is currently a member of the core expert group of the European Network of Experts on Gender Equality (ENEGE). Her principal research interests are economics of education and economics of gender within the broader framework of labour economics. She has co-authored journal articles and book chapters, as well as reports on fiscal systems and female employment in Europe, gender segregation, elderly care and the labour market impact of the current crisis.

Paola Villa is an economist and Full Professor at the University of Trento. She is the author of numerous studies on labour economics with particular reference to internal labour markets; labour market regulations and deregulation; gender in the labour market; fertility; labour market performance; youth. She is an expert on gender studies and equal opportunities policies in a comparative perspective. She has an extensive record of experience advising the European Commission in the field of gender equality and gender mainstreaming and since 2008 has been a member of the co-ordinating team and Italy's national expert for the European Commission Expert Advisory Group on Gender and Employment (EGGE) and the newly formed European Network of Experts for Gender Equality (ENEGE).

PART I

Developing the analytical framework

1

INTRODUCTION – WOMEN'S VULNERABILITY TO RECESSION AND AUSTERITY

A different crisis, a different context

Maria Karamessini

Main aims and structure of the book

This edited volume on *Women and Austerity* has three main aims. The first is to identify the impact of the current global financial and economic crisis and the subsequent sovereign debt crisis on women relative to men, particularly its effects on gender equality in the employment and welfare systems of advanced economies. The second is to improve our understanding of women's vulnerability to recession and the policy responses to it in the light of their increased integration into employment and the evolution of gender regimes and contracts since the last major recession in the US and Europe. Both of these strands are developed to provide a framework for considering the challenges that the current structural economic crisis poses for further advancement towards gender equality in advanced societies. Identifying and discussing these challenges is the third and final aim of the book.

Our inquiry is limited to North America and Europe. A distinctive aspect of the current crisis in this part of the globe, compared to previous recessions since 1973, is its significant effect on services, in which the greatest share of female employment is concentrated. This effect is associated with the intensity and duration of the current crisis but also with austerity policies which have been and/or are being implemented to counter the impact of the crisis on public finances. In the US, employment in services contracted by 2.2 per cent between 2008 and 2010. Contraction has been much greater in the European countries hardest hit by the crisis, such as the Baltic States, Iceland, Ireland, Greece and Spain. Austerity policies, especially in the countries that have been or are being implementing fiscal consolidation packages and plans, have largely contributed to this outcome through their direct impact on public sector employment and their recessionary effect. These policies are also responsible for public sector pay freezes and reductions, cuts in social expenditure and welfare state reforms that have different implications for women and men. Given that the public sector and social transfers and services have been key for women's economic integration and access to protected employment and good quality jobs from the Second World War onwards, austerity represents a major challenge for gender equality.

Five years after it officially began in the US, the current crisis – widely referred to as 'the Great Recession' – is not yet over since its structural causes have not been tackled. Until now, the advanced core of the world economy has been most affected. Although significant state intervention in the initial phase avoided collapse of the financial system and recessionary spirals, recovery in 2010 and 2011 was weak in most advanced economies while it was very strong in many emerging and developing ones.

Recovery in the advanced economies has further weakened in 2012, mainly due to a sharp slowdown of the Euro area, which is experiencing a politically induced second recessionary dip. EU institutions have opted for fiscal consolidation to address sovereign debt crises in the periphery of the Eurozone and curb the continuing rise in sovereign debts elsewhere. They promote a coordinated imple-mentation of austerity policies and structural reforms in labour and product markets and the welfare state by all EU Member States. There is now considerable internal pressure also on the US federal government to engage in a decisive reduction of the public deficit, as illustrated by the political negotiations over fiscal adjustment between President Obama and the Republicans after the November 2012 elections. Austerity is expected to have negative effects not only on demand for female labour but also on access to services that support women as carers, thereby often compelling them to substitute for cutbacks through increasing unpaid domes-tic labour. The policies in the EU are commonly being enacted without reference to the notion of gender mainstreaming, despite commitments to this principle by the EU from 1995 onwards. This book discusses the gender dimensions of policy responses to the crisis during all its phases. It places, however, particular emphasis on the austerity and fiscal consolidation policies taken to include both immediate or short-term demand restricting measures and longer-term structural and institu-tional reforms under employment, income and social policies.

To interpret the longer-term impact of these policies on gender equality we also need to explore the second and related main aim of the book, that is to develop an updated framework for understanding women's vulnerability to recession and aus-terity drawing on Jill Rubery's classic edited volume *Women and Recession*, published in 1988 and republished in 2010 as a Routledge classic. This volume contributed not only to the understanding of long- versus short-term trends in women's employ-ment, by analysing the different roles of gender segregation in the labour market and the different degrees of women's integration into wage work in the US, France, Italy and the UK but also related women's employment to different configurations of the state and family in these four OECD countries. This latter approach provided a comparative analysis of employment in relation to welfare states before the explo-sion of work on comparative welfare systems in the 1990s and beyond.

The above framework provides the starting point for this collection but it is updated in three important respects: firstly in relation to the nature of the crisis and the context in which austerity policies are being enacted; secondly in relation to the impact that twenty years of further integration of women into wage employment may have had on the gender contract and on associated responses to recession and changes in labour demand; thirdly in relation to the potential for the current austerity programmes to constitute a turning point, particularly in European social models, which could roll back the increasing support for working families across Europe in the past decades, even in countries where this support was clearly inadequate before the crisis. The framework developed in 1988 took as an underlying hypothesis that there was likely to be a longer-term upward trend in women's employment integration supported by a developing welfare state, even if these tendencies might be suppressed in periods of recession or by interludes of economic and political policies aimed at cutting back the welfare state. The current context raises the possibility of long-term retrenchment even in welfare systems that are still underdeveloped and may also reveal potential for a general trend away from gender equality rather than simply delayed progress.

To consider these issues this book brings together a wealth of expertise on gender, employment and welfare state systems. The first part provides two conceptual papers, one by Rubery on the framework for analyzing women in austerity, and another by O'Reilly and Nazio on the changing gender contract. The second part includes a comparative paper on developments in women's labour market position in Europe during the crisis (Bettio and Verashchagina) and nine country case studies. The selected cases include the US (Albelda) that was at the origin of the crisis, two countries that were at the heart of the initial financial crisis (Iceland (Thorsdottir) and the UK (Rafferty and Rubery)) and one strongly affected by it (Hungary (Frey)) and the five countries that triggered and foment the ongoing Eurozone crisis (Greece (Karamessini), Ireland (Barry and Conroy), Portugal (Ferreira), Spain (Gago and Segales Kirzner) and Italy (Verashchagina and Capparuchi)). The third part of the volume consists of two chapters dealing with policy issues and a concluding chapter. Villa and Smith deal with developments in the gender equality goal within the EU employment policy during the crisis and the chapter by Perrons and Plomien is on why the goal of gender equality needs to be integrated in alternative projects for developing more inclusive and equitable routes out of the crisis. The concluding chapter (Karamessini and Rubery) then draws together the key arguments and evidence developed in the book to consider the future prospects for gender equality.

Women's position pre-crisis

Apart from the 1988 edited volume by Rubery[1] on how in the US, UK, France and Italy the economic structure, labour market institutions, family organization and the welfare state jointly shaped the experience of women during recessions in the 1970s and 1980s, most of the English language literature on advanced countries has in practice only dealt with the experience of US women, focusing particularly on the impact of business cycles and crises on the variation of the gender gap in the unemployment rate (Milkman 1976; Lynch and Hyclak 1984; Seeborg and DeBoer 1987; Miller 1990; Goodman *et al.* 1993). However, in the 1990s and 2000s, an important literature emerged on the impact of economic crises on women's labour market outcomes, fertility and well-being in many newly industrialized and developing countries (see review by Sabarwal *et al.* 2010). Moreover, feminist economists have strongly criticized the social costs, gender dimensions and macro-economics of IMF economic stabilization and structural adjustment programmes imposed on these countries, which have been accused of gender blindness and male bias (Elson 1995; 2002; Beneria 1999).

In practice, many of the central issues to emerge from the literature on emerging and developing economies are common to those identified as salient for advanced economies. These are also the central issues covered in this book, namely employment segregation by sex and its influence on job losses, added/discouraged worker effects, and the impact of the crisis on social infrastructure and services, social reproduction and women's unpaid work. There are though three important sets of differences between the two groups of countries that call for different research questions. Firstly, in advanced economies women are predominantly concentrated in services not in manufacturing or agriculture and their integration in formal paid employment is much higher, with the share engaged in the underground economy and informal work much lower. Secondly, the welfare state and safety nets are much more developed, while being residual or non existent outside the advanced countries. Thirdly, in the latter, compared to other parts of the globe, the challenges to traditional gender roles, family models and the gendered division of labour posed by feminist movements, women's changing aspirations and public policies have been much stronger.

However, the pre-crisis gender regimes of advanced economies also varied greatly and these differences in the gendered pattern of paid and unpaid work could be attributed to variation along similar dimensions. Over recent decades all these economies have tended to experience an apparently irreversible integration of women into paid work, more continuous female activity patterns and a decisive shift away from the male-breadwinner family model towards a dual earner/adult worker model. However, national variation in the historical pattern of women's integration in paid employment and construction of the welfare state and in gender contracts have still generated significant country differences as well as intra gender variations in women's labour market integration, including participation, location in the employment structure, relative pay and social rights. This variation also applied to the spread and configuration of the gender specialized dual earner/adult worker family model (Lewis 2001; Lewis *et al.* 2008; Daly 2011).

Table 1.1. shows that, in 2007, among our nine countries, women's integration in paid employment ranged from very high (Iceland) to very low (Italy, Greece, Hungary) while the incidence of temporary employment among women ranged from very extensive (Spain and Portugal) to unimportant (US, UK, Hungary). The female part time rate was very low in Hungary, Portugal and Greece but very high

TABLE 1.1 Women's integration in paid work and family models in selected European countries and the US 2007

			%	
	Employment rate (15–64 years)	Temporary employment rate*	Part time employment rate*	Dual earner couples**
Greece	47.9	13.1	13.7	55.7
Hungary	50.9	6.8	4.2	64.7
Iceland	81.7	13.6	24.8	90.2
Ireland	60.7	9.5	34.9	62.2
Italy	46.6	15.9	31.2	58.7
Portugal	61.9	23.0	8.7	70.1
Spain	55.5	33.1	20.8	61.9
UK	66.3	6.4	37.2	76.7
USA	65.9	4.2 (2005)	17.9	66.2
EU-21 average	58.5		28.7	
OECD average	57.2	12.9	23.8	

* Percentage of dependent employment. ** Proportion of all couples with at least one partner working; only for the USA, proportion of all married couples with at least one spouse working.
Source: First column: Eurostat, European Labour Force Survey (online database); second and third columns: OECD. Stat (data extracted on 21 Oct 2012); fourth column: calculated from Bettio and Verashchagina (this volume), Table. 4.2, and US Department of Labor, Bureau of Labor Statistics: www. bls.gov/news.release/archives/famee_05302008.htm

in the UK, Ireland and Italy. The dual earner family model was the most common model in all nine countries, but the male breadwinner model remained widespread in Greece, Spain and Ireland. Iceland, the UK and Portugal were the countries with an indisputable predominance of the dual earner family model and the lowest occurrence of male breadwinner couples. However, the great majority of women partners in Portugal – higher even than in Iceland – worked full time, while in the UK a very large proportion worked part time.

Nature and origins of the economic crisis

The story of the crisis is now well known. The bursting of the housing bubble in the US in 2007 and the fall of Lehman Brothers in 2008 caused the near collapse of the global financial system. This triggered the deepest and most protracted global economic crisis after 1929 and the second major crisis that the US has exported to the world. The banking crisis, credit crunch and deleveraging of households led to the global economic contraction of 2009 while the financial rescue of banks by the states, the fall in tax revenues and the rise in expenditure on unemployment benefits produced by the recession and the implementation of fiscal stimulus plans swelled public deficits and debts. The deterioration of public finances in a context of short supply of funds in financial markets set the stage for sovereign debt crises in the most indebted countries.

There is a wide consensus among scholars that the 'failings' of the financial sector and markets are at the heart of the current crisis (see for instance Krugman 2009 and Stiglitz 2010). The removal of national restrictions to capital mobility and financial deregulation, the globalization of financial markets, the emergence of a non-regulated shadow banking system, and the oversupply of funds and liquidity is a trend that started from the US after the breakup of the International Fixed Exchange-Rate System in 1971. This trend was followed by the other advanced economies and then extended to the transition (to capitalism) economies of Eastern Europe and Russia and many newly industrializing and developing countries through conditional financial aid by the IMF and other lenders or EU integration. Global financial markets and international capital flows have been responsible for currency and financial crises all over the world since the 1980s, of which the current is the most global, the largest and the deepest.

Beside the indisputable role of financial capital in triggering the global crisis there are other structural determinants. Leading economists have identified a major underlying cause in the global imbalances built up by the structural transformation of the world economy in the past decades, namely the decisive shift of competitive advantage in manufacturing from 'the West' to Asia and the conversion of the advanced economies into services economies (Stiglitz 2010). This analysis complements that on financial deregulation and globalization, since the US has deliberately opted for financing its growing trade deficit over the past decades by mass capital inflows from oil-producing and export-led growth countries with balance-of-payments surpluses (Varoufakis 2011). It is these inflows that have in fact fuelled the financialization of the US economy, its housing and stock exchange bubbles and the skyrocketing of the financial speculation of Wall Street in the global financial markets.

Growing income inequalities in the US and most advanced economies have also been put forward by many scholars as a structural cause of the crisis, but this thesis has provoked controversy. In their review of the debate, Atkinson and Morelli (2011) summarize Stiglitz's hypothesis in the following way: the households in the lower part of the distribution experienced stagnating incomes and were stimulated to borrow in order to improve their standard of living. Unsustainable borrowing led to default and this undermined the viability of over-exposed financial institutions. Taking a radical perspective, Harvey (2010) argues that, in the last twenty-five years, capital disempowered labour and kept wage growth below productivity gains. The resulting demand problem and the gap between labour's earnings and consumption expectations were bridged by increasing household indebtedness. Similarly, but adding a global perspective, Seguino (2010) contends that growing inequality both within and between countries is the hidden cause of the crisis or, at least, one of the factors that precipitated it. The gap between wage levels and productivity growth and the rise in the share of national income going to 'rentiers' were the main determinants of rising inequality. On the other hand, the great majority of economists reject these arguments or remain completely silent on the issue. Krugman (2012) recognizes that inequality is a great problem, but notes that we still do not know exactly how or by how much rising inequality has contributed to the financial crisis. Some feminist scholars such as Walby (2009) have also argued that the principles underlying the aims and goals of institutions of financial governance are gendered; and gender inequalities in the governance of the financial architecture are part of the cause of the crisis. The common thread here is that the causes of the financial crisis are to be looked for in the wider power relations of society and not simply in narrow issues such as form of financial regulation.

Whatever the differences in existing views on the structural character and causes of the current crisis, it has become evident that consumption-driven growth patterns based on huge private and public debts, an extreme financialization of the economy and an unregulated financial sector were unsustainable. In other words, the neoliberal model of capitalism has definitely lost its credibility.

Recession experiences and policy responses

Although the interconnectedness of financial markets diffused the crisis rapidly from the US to the other parts of the world, this occurred on different time scales, with different intensity and followed different patterns, according to regional and national specificities in both transmission mechanisms and in their pre-existing economic imbalances. For instance, in Europe, the global crisis has seriously destabilized the Eurozone with a series of sovereign debt crises that erupted in its periphery (Greece, Ireland and Portugal). In so doing, it has brought to the fore all the weaknesses of the project of European integration, that is not only the lack of financial management mechanisms for the Euro but also the deep structural flaws in the constitution of the single currency, the growing polarization between the industrialized North and the increasingly deindustrializing South and the absence of a European-wide development strategy (Aglietta 2012).

The nine countries selected as case studies for this book differ with regard to their recession experiences and policy responses. Although the global crisis originated in the US, the recession was less deep there than in most of the other eight countries in 2008–9 because of the huge fiscal stimulus package of around 5.5 per cent of GDP in 2008 that was adopted in order to avoid the 'real' economy going into freefall. In Spain, the UK and Portugal discretionary stimulus measures in 2009–10 were equivalent to 3.2 per cent, 2.4 per cent and 1.7 per cent of 2008 GDP respectively (European Commission 2010). Conversely, in Italy and Greece the few fiscal measures taken in 2009 to stimulate economic activity were offset by demand-restricting measures of equivalent size, while Iceland, Hungary and Ireland initiated fiscal consolidation in 2008. Iceland and Hungary did so under IMF Stand-by Agreements signed in November 2008. Ireland implemented five consolidation packages between mid-2008 and 2010 with a total net-deficit reducing impact of 9 per cent of GDP in 2008–10 in order to offset the negative impact on public finances of enormous capital injections into Irish banks (European

TABLE 1.2 Recession and fiscal policy in selected European countries and the US 2007–2012

	2007	2008	2009	2010	2011	2012*
			GDP growth (%)			
Greece	3.0	−0.2	−3.3	−3.5	−7.1	−6.0
Hungary	0.1	0.9	−6.8	1.3	1.6	−1.2
Iceland	6.0	1.3	−6.8	−4.0	3.1	2.1
Ireland	5.2	−3.0	−7.0	−0.4	1.4	0.4
Italy	1.7	−1.2	−5.5	1.8	0.4	−2.3
Spain	3.5	0.9	−3.7	−0.1	0.4	−1.4
Portugal	2.4	0.0	−2.9	1.4	−1.7	−3.0
UK	3.5	−1.1	−4.4	2.1	0.9	−0.3
USA	1.9	−0.4	−3.5	3.0	1.8	2.1
EU–27	3.2	0.3	−4.3	2.0	1.5	−0.3
		Government deficit (% of GDP)				
Greece	−6.5	−9.8	−15.6	−10.7	−9.4	−6.8
Hungary	−5.1	−3.7	−4.6	−4.4	4.3	−2.5
Iceland	5.4	−13.5	−10.0	−10.1	−4.4	−2.8
Ireland	0.1	−7.4	−13.9	−30.9	−13.4	−8.4
Italy	−1.6	−2.7	−5.4	−4.5	−3.9	−2.9
Spain	1.9	−4.5	−11.2	−9.7	−9.4	−8.0
Portugal	−3.1	−3.6	−10.2	−9.8	−4.4	−5.0
UK	−2.7	−5.1	−11.5	−10.2	−7.8	−6.2
USA	−2.8	−6.4	−11.9	−11.3	−10.1	−8.5
EU–27	−0.9	−2.4	−6.9	−6.5	−4.4	−3.6

* Forecasts.
Source: European Commission, European Economic Forecast, Autumn 2012. Data for 2007 and for Iceland come from the Statistical Annex of European Economy, Spring 2012.

Commission 2011, p. 15). Despite the implementation of fiscal consolidation, the general government balance as a proportion of GDP turned from a 0.1 per cent surplus in 2007 into a 30.9 per cent deficit in 2010 (Table 1.2).

The transmission mechanisms of the crisis differed by country, although the financial institutions of all European countries suffered from their exposure to toxic derivatives bought from American banks and the credit crunch that followed Lehman Brothers' failure. Being the closest to the American financial model, with the heaviest reliance of their economies on a deregulated and globalized financial sector, the UK and Iceland were the countries that were hit hardest by the initial financial crisis. The crisis in the UK started in mid-2007 with bank runs, but was contained by financial rescues and recapitalization by the state at the cost of an increase in sovereign debt. Iceland's oversized banking sector, which had developed an enormous cross-border activity and taken on high leverage and risk, crashed in

October 2008 when financial markets realized the risk and pulled their money out. The devaluation of the Icelandic krona by 80 per cent in 2008 produced an upsurge in the foreign-currency denominated debt that represented about 70 per cent of the business sector's debt and 20 per cent of that of households, while the take-over and recapitalization of banks by the state led to a spectacular rise in sovereign debt (Table 1.3). Similarly, the crisis in Hungary also started in autumn 2008 with a capital flight from its banking sector which had borrowed heavily internationally to offer loans in foreign currency to households and firms. Capital flight caused the devaluation of the forint which increased the private and sovereign debt in foreign currency and forced the government to request financial help from the IMF to secure external financing.

Ireland and Spain succumbed to the crisis not because of the foreign activities of their banks but due to the bursting of their enormous domestic housing bubbles, although Ireland had built a far more globalized and deregulated financial sector in the 2000s and had extended financialization of the economy more than Spain, following the neoliberal model of capitalism. In both countries state intervention saved banks and, in the Irish case, also bond-holders and thereby turned private debt into public debt. The size of the bailout in Ireland was equal to 29 per cent of GDP over the period 2009–10, thus leading to a skyrocketing of sovereign debt and a request for external financial assistance. In November 2010 a loan agreement was signed by Ireland with the IMF, Eurozone countries, UK, Sweden and Denmark, which is conditional on the implementation of an economic adjustment programme including a three-year fiscal consolidation plan. Some months earlier – May 2010 – Spain had made a strategic U-turn with the announcement of a fiscal consolidation plan

TABLE 1.3 Household and sovereign debt in selected European countries and the US in 2007 and 2010

	Household debt-to-income ratio (%)		Sovereign debt-to-GDP ratio (%)	
	2007	*2010*	*2007*	*2010*
Greece			107.4	145.0
Hungary	50.3	68.4	67.1	81.4
Iceland			28.5	93.1
Ireland	196.9	202.6	24.8	92.5
Italy	57.0	65.1	103.1	118.6
Spain	129.9	127.8	36.2	61.2
Portugal	126.8	130.1	68.3	93.3
UK	151.8	143.1	59.0	80.2
USA	137.6	124.4	67.5	99.1
EU-27			59.0	74.8

Source: For sovereign debt: European Commission, Statistical Annex of European Economy, Spring 2012. For household debt: Eurostat database (EU Member States) and OECD, Economic Outlook No. 91 - Table 18 (USA).

alongside labour market reforms. This coincided with the decision of the newly formed coalition government in the UK to accelerate the switch from fiscal stimulus to austerity in order to eliminate the 'structural' public sector deficit.

Greece and Portugal were relatively spared by the initial financial crisis and the first phase of the economic crisis, but became protagonists of the sovereign debt and Eurozone crises in its second phase. Greece was the first country to be attacked by financial markets at the end of 2009 when it needed to refinance its very high sovereign debt, a large proportion of which was held externally. The sovereign debt-to-GDP ratio was the highest in the EU before the crisis and further deteriorated in 2008 and 2009 due to recession and the operation of automatic stabilizers, since the fiscal policy stance was neutral. In May 2010 Greece signed a loan agreement with its Eurozone partners and the IMF that required a huge fiscal consolidation effort in the first three years of implementation (2010–12). After proceeding to the restructuring of its sovereign debt held by private creditors in March 2012, Greece signed with the same lenders a second loan agreement meant to fund the recapitalization of the Greek banking system and the prolongation of fiscal adjustment. Before the crisis, Portugal's sovereign debt was nine percentage points above the EU-27 average. It rose sharply between 2008 and 2010 due to fiscal stimulus and the operation of automatic stabilizers. Financial market speculation on the dissolution of the Eurozone, even after Greece's and Ireland's bailouts and the rise in the interest rates on Portuguese sovereign bonds, obliged the government to sign a financial bailout agreement with the Eurozone partners and the IMF in May 2011 and pursue a three-year severe austerity plan. The non-achievement of fiscal targets for 2012 raised fears that Portugal would need new loans like Greece and led to a one-year extension of the adjustment period.

Like Greece and Portugal, Italy was not directly hit by the financial crisis but experienced a large decline in economic activity in 2008–9 due to the substantial contraction of industrial production and exports. The Italian government did not implement a fiscal stimulus package but the 'Cassa Integrazione Guadagni', a wage-guarantee fund for laid-off workers who maintain their employment status, operated as a powerful automatic stabilizer of demand and economic activity recovered along with export markets in 2010 amidst a general recovery of growth in the advanced economies. Italy was also spared in the first one and a half year of the sovereign debt and Eurozone crises, because its sovereign debt as a proportion of GDP was huge but only a small share was held externally. It was only after the sovereign debt crisis had engulfed Greece, Ireland and Portugal in summer 2011 that the risk of contagion also menaced Spain and Italy. After two years of relatively modest fiscal adjustment which had, nevertheless, significantly curtailed social expenditure, Italy was the last of the peripheral countries of the Euro area to adopt an austerity plan in August 2011 and a second plan in December 2011 intended to ensure a balanced budget by 2013.

Italy, Ireland, Iceland and Hungary were the countries that experienced the deepest recession in the first phase of the economic crisis (2008–9) while Greece and Portugal have been the hardest hit by the sovereign debt crisis and the return to austerity policies in the second phase (2010 onwards). Having opted first for fiscal stimulus and quantitative easing and then for soft fiscal adjustment, the US has not only attenuated the intensity of the recession in 2008–9 but also experienced a strong recovery in 2010 at 3 per cent growth rate, stronger than in the EU on average (Table 1.2). The UK, Italy, Hungary and Portugal also experienced positive growth in 2010 but at 2.1 per cent or less. In 2011 and 2012 only the US continued to have positive growth in both years at 1.8 and 2.1 per cent respectively, apart from Iceland that bounced back from earlier declines to register growth rates of 3.1 and 2.1 per cent respectively. In mid-2012 the Euro area and EU entered a second recessionary dip; the fall of economic activity over 2012 being forecasted at -0.4 per cent and -0.3 per cent respectively (Table 1.2).

Fiscal consolidation is aimed at reducing government deficits and debt accumulation. Several indicators are used by international organizations to monitor progress, all presenting strengths and weaknesses. The simplest one is the general government primary balance, i.e. total general government revenue minus total general government expenditure excluding interest payments.[2] A primary deficit decrease reduces the net borrowing needs and debt accumulation by the general government while primary surpluses can reduce sovereign debt if used to pay interests and principal. Table 1.4 shows that, between 2009 and 2012, Greece, Ireland, Portugal, the UK and Spain have achieved the greatest fiscal consolidation measured by the improvement of the primary balance as a proportion of GDP. Hungary, Italy and the US recorded the smallest change. Iceland lies in-between the two groups of countries. Its primary deficit certainly rose to 10.2 per cent of GDP in 2008, but this was mainly due to the injection of public monies in the rescue of the

TABLE 1.4 Primary balance of general government* in selected European countries and the US as percentage of GDP

	2009	2012	2009–2012 (change in p.p.**)
Greece	−10.5	−1.4	9.1
Iceland	−3.4	1.9	5.3
Hungary	0.1	1.6	1.5
Ireland	−11.9	−4.4	7.5
Portugal	−7.3	−0.5	6.8
Spain	−9.4	−3.3	6.1
Italy	−0.8	2.6	3.4
UK	−9.5	−3.0	6.5
USA	−9.4	−5.5	3.9
EU-27	−4.2	−0.6	3.6

* Total general government revenue minus total general government expenditure excluding interest payable. ** p.p.= percentage points.
Source: European Commission, European Economic Forecast. Autumn 2012. Data for Iceland come from European Commission, Statistical Annex of European Economy. Spring 2012.

financial system. This one-off expenditure was not repeated in 2009 and the primary deficit fell to 3.4 per cent of GDP that year. According to the latest European Commission forecasts, the Icelandic government will have achieved a primary surplus of 1.9 per cent of GDP in 2012 (Table 1.4).

Finally, in 2012 the US exhibited the highest borrowing needs (including for interest payments on debt), as measured by the general government deficit as a proportion of GDP, among the nine countries of our sample. In the same year, Ireland, Greece, the UK, Spain and Portugal remained those with the highest general government deficit-to-GDP ratio among the remaining eight European countries (Table 1.2), in spite of their relatively greater fiscal consolidation effort.

Austerity and challenges for gender equality

Since Greece's near default at the beginning of 2010, sovereign debt crisis has been proclaimed by the EU, the OECD and the IMF as the top threat for any single member state while the elimination of public deficits through fiscal consolidation is the top priority of economic policy. The dominant discourse conceals though a series of important issues. First, a rising sovereign debt does not necessarily imply a looming sovereign debt crisis while public deficits stimulate economic activity, and thus may actually improve public and private debt sustainability. Second, in the overwhelming majority of countries the origin of high sovereign debts is not the state but banks. Thus cuts in public sector jobs, services, investment and welfare states may not only be socially damaging and unfair, making citizens pay for the failures of global financial capital and the enrichment of the upper classes but may also hamper achievement of long-term economic and social goals. Third, in all major crises the financial, fiscal and economic aspects are intertwined. Hence stagnation of economic activity or recession induced by austerity policies increases the household debt-to-income and sovereign debt-to-GDP ratios, thus exacerbating and not resolving the financial and fiscal crises. Last but not least, austerity undermines women's progress towards equality in paid work and economic independence and may provoke an ideological backlash favouring a return to traditional gender roles and backward-looking gender contracts. These last issues that are related to the central theme of this volume are discussed in detail by Rubery and O'Reilly and Nazio in the next two chapters of this first part of the book.

Notes

1   The other contributors to this volume were Francesca Bettio, Patricia Bouillaguet-Bernard, Annie Gauvin, Jane Humphries, Marilyn Power, Roger Tarling and Jill Walker.
2   The main strength of this indicator is that it is straightforward and calculated on the basis of raw data. It is, though, affected by the business cycle and extraordinary one-off fiscal measures which distort measurement of the real fiscal consolidation effort. More sophisticated indicators of fiscal consolidation are the 'cyclically adjusted primary balance' and the 'structural balance'. For definitions and data, see IMF Fiscal Monitor (2012).

However, these indicators are based on a great number of country-specific subjective assumptions, making comparability across countries problematic.

References

Aglietta, M. (2012) *Zone Euro: Éclatement ou Fédération*, Paris: Éditions Michalon.

Atkinson A. B. and Morelli, S. (2011) 'Economic Crises and Inequality', *Human Development Research Paper* 2011/06, United Nations Development Programme, available at: http://hdr.undp.org/en/reports/global/hdr2011/papers/HDRP_2011_06.pdf (accessed 16.1.2013).

Benería, L. (1999) 'Structural Adjustment Policies', in J. Peterson and M. Lewis (eds) *The Elgar Companion to Feminist Economics*, Cheltenham, UK, and Northampton, USA: Edward Elgar.

Daly, M. (2011) 'What Adult Worker Model? A Critical Look at Recent Social Policy Reform in Europe from a Gender and Family Perspective', *Social Politics*, 18(1): 1–23.

Elson, D. (1995) 'Male Bias in Macro-economics: The Case of Structural Adjustment', in Diane Elson (ed.) *Male Bias in the Development Process*, 2nd edn, Manchester: Manchester University Press.

——. (2002) 'The International Financial Architecture – A View from the Kitchen', *Femina Politica – Zeitschrift fur feministische Politik-Wissenschaft*, 11(1): 26–37.

European Commission (2010) *Public Finances in EMU – 2010*, European Economy 4/2010, available at: http://ec.europa.eu/economy_finance/publications/european_economy/2010/pdf/ee-2010-4_en.pdf (accessed 16.1.2013).

European Commission (2011) 'The Economic Adjustment Programme for Ireland', *European Economy Occasional Papers* 76/2011, Directorate General for Economic and Financial Affairs, European Union, available at: http://ec.europa.eu/economy_finance/publications/occasional_paper/2011/pdf/ocp76_en.pdf (accessed 16.1.2013).

Goodman, W., Antczak, S. and Freeman, L. (1993) 'Women and Jobs in Recessions: 1962–92. Gender Differences in Job Losses Less Common in Recent Downturn', *Monthly Labour Review*, 116(7): 26–35.

Harvey, D. (2010) *The Enigma of Capital and the Crises of Capitalism*, London: Profile Books.

IMF Fiscal Monitor (2012) 'Taking Stock: A Progress Report on Fiscal Adjustment', *World Economic and Financial Surveys*, Washington D.C.: International Monetary Fund.

Krugman, P. R. (2009) *The Return of Depression Economics and the Crisis of 2008*, New York: WW Norton & Co.

——. (2012) *End This Depression Now!*, New York: WW Norton & Co.

Lewis, J. (2001) 'The Decline of the Male Breadwinner Model: Implications for Work and Care', *Social Politics*, 8(2): 152–169.

Lewis, J., Cambell, M. and Huerta, C. (2008) 'Patterns of Paid and Unpaid Work in Western Europe: Gender, Commodification, Preferences and the Implications for Policy', *Journal of European Social Policy*, 18(1): 21–37.

Lynch, G. J. and Hyclak, T. (1984) 'Cyclical and Noncyclical Unemployment Differences among Demographic Groups', *Growth and Change*, 15(1): 9–17.

Milkman, R. (1976) 'Women's Work and Economic Crisis: Some Lessons of the Great Depression', *Review of Radical Political Economics*, 8(1): 71–97.

Miller, J. (1990) 'Women's Unemployment Patterns in Postwar Business Cycles: Class Difference. The Gender Segregation of Work and Deindustrialization', *Review of Radical Political Economics*, 22(4): 87–110.

Rubery, J. (ed) (1988, reissued 2010) *Women and Recession*, London and New York: Routledge & Kegan Paul.

Sabarwal, S., Sinha, N. and Buvinic, M. (2010) 'How Do Women Weather Economic Shocks? A Review of Evidence', *Policy Research Working Paper* 5496, The World Bank, Poverty Reduction and Economic Management Network, Gender and Development Unit. Available at: http://www-wds.worldbank.org/external/default/WDSContentServer/WDSP/IB/2010/12/07/000158349_20101207080622/Rendered/PDF/WPS5496.pdf (accessed 16.1.2013).

Seeborg, M. and DeBoer, L. (1987) 'The Narrowing Male-Female Unemployment Differential', *Growth and Change*, 18(2): 24–37.

Seguino, S. (2010) 'The Global Economic Crisis, its Gender and Ethnic Implications and Policy Responses', *Gender and Development*, 18(2): 179–199.

Stiglitz, J. E. (2010) *Freefall. America, Free Markets, and the Sinking of the World Economy*, New York: WW Norton & Co.

Varoufakis, Y. (2011) *The Global Minotaur. America, the True Origins of the Financial Crisis and the Future of the World Economy*, London: Zed Books Ltd.

Walby, S. (2009) 'Gender and the Financial Crisis', paper for UNESCO Project "Gender and the Financial Crisis". Available at: http://www.lancs.ac.uk/fass/doc_library/sociology/Gender_and_financial_crisis_Sylvia_Walby.pdf (accessed 16.1.2013).

2

FROM 'WOMEN AND RECESSION' TO 'WOMEN AND AUSTERITY'

A framework for analysis

Jill Rubery

The relationships between gender, recession and austerity must be considered as historically and societally specific. Gender relations have evolved over time but following country-specific paths and the impact of the recession and austerity programmes will depend on both the form and the robustness of gender relations in a specific country context and on the particular form that the recession and austerity programmes take in interaction with wider labour market, social and political institutional arrangements. This focus on institutions, including, following Martin (2004), gender relations as an institution, immediately distances the framework adopted here from the current dominant but opposing frameworks used within mainstream economics and policy analysis to understand the relationship between gender relations and the wider economy. These alternate between a perspective that treats women universally as essentially carers first and thereby permanently in a state of contingent and temporary participation in the labour market work and the more optimistic scenario which regards discrimination as only a residual legacy linked to a past where institutional arrangements did indeed dominate, as opposed to the present where the market ensures the triumph of meritocracy and the even treatment of individuals, whatever their gender. The former approach sees women as the natural candidates to bear the burden of the downturn in demand but may well overestimate the scope for reversing women's integration into employment. The latter perspective focuses on the rate of progress towards closing gender gaps and glosses over the need for women to defend their existing gains and resist reversals in equality or the emergence of gender inequality in new forms.

The institutionalist approach adopted here instead links the analysis to both cyclical and longer-term change in national employment and social models and to the social construction of gender relations within a specific institutional and political context. Furthermore, it identifies gender as both a relevant variable in assessing the outcomes of change but also as a factor that may shape the specific path of adjustment to recession and the sovereign debt crisis. That is, gender relations are both an input into and an outcome of the national model and the associated adjustment process. This gender mainstreaming of the analysis of social and economic change also allows for variations in the impact of recession by gender across countries and social groups, according to the interactions between gender relations, institutions and the chosen adjustment mechanisms. The analysis utilizes some of the new terms that have been developed to explain incremental institutional change (Streeck and Thelen 2005) and considers how the continued co-existence of competing ideologies with respect to women's roles can give rise to variable outcomes, depending on the extent to which emergent ideologies of equality are pushed aside by the far from dormant ideologies of subordination and difference. The framework thus puts in question the predictions of a modernist linear progress towards equality while at the same time regarding the changes over recent decades as long term and not readily or easily reversed.

The organization of the chapter is as follows. In the first section we explore frameworks for understanding the cyclical effects of recession on job loss, labour supply and public policy. The second section considers the specificities of the current recession, taking into account both the evolving and changing position of women and the specific nature of recession and the subsequent political responses. This provides a context for considering in the third section the extent to which the current recession and austerity programmes can be expected to constitute a critical juncture in the evolution of gender relations and the types of institutional changes that may ensue.

Analysing women's economic position: a review of frameworks

Gender differences in vulnerability to recession and austerity derive from differences in women's position, relative to that of men's, in the job structure, in the family and the welfare economy. However, while these differences in position will shape possibilities and likely outcomes we also need to consider how these likely outcomes may be modified by the behaviour of social actors, including employers, trade unions and the government.

Men and women are differently positioned in the job structure and the pattern of gender segregation can provide insights into why recession and austerity may have differential impacts by gender (Rubery 1988). At a basic level, gendered impacts can be anticipated because of differences in the playing out of the recession by sector, occupation or employment contract. Gender differences in labour market position may be due to both exogenous factors, that is where sex-typing of jobs is relatively independent of economic conditions, and to endogenous factors, that is where, for example, a concentration of women in the most precarious jobs reflects women's perceived position as less committed or less advantaged workers. The latter type of jobs have been labelled buffer jobs, that is numerically flexible labour intensive jobs that facilitate adjustment of labour input to demand changes (Bettio 1988). While the allocation of women into these types of jobs may be regarded as related to their position in the family system, there are different views on the factors that account for the share of buffer jobs in the economy. For some, the persistence of low skill and low value added jobs is attributed to the differential impact of technology (Doeringer and Piore 1971). Some feminist scholars offer an alternative explanation where the crowding of women into separate segments lowers incentives to use innovation and technology to convert these jobs into stable high value added jobs. Poor job quality may be thus an outcome of an available labour supply for low wage work (Bergmann 1986). Women may react to poor job quality by being more unstable workers than might be the case if they were able to access jobs with better employment conditions (Felstead and Gallie 2004).

Sex-typing of jobs is not confined to these buffer-type jobs and may be related to other 'stereotypical' characteristics of women (England 2005), ranging from their caring roles in the family, their assumed greater altruism associated with an apparent preference for public service jobs or their deemed suitability for posts requiring attractive or people-oriented service and administrative staff. Segregation, even though based on stereotypes, may protect women against job loss by shielding them from competition from men (Milkman 1976; Bettio 2002) and by placing women in protected sectors. Segregation also reduces employers' scope to use women as a flexible buffer or as a cheap labour substitute in male-typed jobs. Indeed, results from earlier work found that greater cyclical volatility for women was primarily confined to a number of manufacturing industries and was not found either for employment as a whole or in sectors where women's employment share was low, where women primarily may have been undertaking administrative tasks that in this time period may have been regarded more as fixed overheads (Humphries 1988; Rubery and Tarling 1988).

While the prevailing pattern of segregation is likely to influence the initial employment shakeout, the disturbance to companies' profits and cost structures as a result of the downturn in demand may induce employers to initiate or to accelerate programmes of longer-term restructuring and employment changes, with consequences for the pattern of gender segregation. Women's availability at lower wages than equivalent men may provide incentives for longer-term processes of substitution and restructuring within previously male-dominated occupations. Reskin and Roos (1990) identified processes of substitution and changes in occupational and gender hierarchies in the US (see also Crompton and Sanderson 1990 and Grimshaw and Rubery 2007 for the UK). Either whole occupations may become feminized or new divisions within an occupation may emerge, with women concentrated in the lower status areas. In these studies substitution was induced more by labour shortage or new technological possibilities than by downturns in demand. However, although substitution may be easier in times of labour shortage, when employers begin to hire after a major downswing, there may be an enhanced imperative to reduce costs that could induce processes of substitution. Furthermore, to the extent that the substitution may take place through outsourcing to lower cost providers, this could occur even in a context of job destruction. This form of substitution may be between higher paid and lower paid women, for example through outsourcing of public sector jobs to private sector companies, rather than between men and women. To the extent that recession leads to downgrading of wage and employment expectations of men, the outcome could also include some men moving into female-type jobs, even at the same wage levels as women.

This review suggests that while segregation is key to understanding gender differences in impact, these gender differences will also vary across groups of women and men (Rubery 1988). Some women may provide a flexible reserve in buffer jobs but so will men, particularly in sectors where women are not significantly represented. The age, class and nationality of buffer groups will also vary, with young men and migrants particularly vulnerable as buffer groups in the current crisis (see Bettio and Verashchagina this volume). Some women and some men are likely to be employed in occupations or sectors that are protected from cyclical volatility, although the protected sectors may vary over time and according to the nature of the recession (see below). And some may enter new jobs that provide direct or indirect substitutes for higher paid core jobs. These different roles will affect different labour force groups and sectors and at different stages in the business cycle. The importance of these different processes can also be expected to vary both by recession and by country, according in particular to the prevailing gender regime.

The gender impact of recession is also likely to reflect differences between the positions of men and women in relation to the family economy and to the welfare system. These differences include not only the material and work relationships, such as contribution to family income, to caring work and access to benefits and public services but also social norms with respect to the appropriate and expected gender roles. Women's presumed distinctive characteristics as carers first and labour force participants second have underpinned the notion that women may act as either a voluntary or involuntary labour reserve (Bruegel 1979; Rubery and Tarling 1982). The notion of a flexible reserve that can be mobilized to supplement or to act in competition with the core labour force links to Marx's general notion of a reserve army with floating and latent components. However, the presumption of labour supply flexibility now informs more of the debate in mainstream economics on labour market flexibility. This literature regards women as contingent and intermittent participants, that is as outsiders to the labour market and who will consequently be negatively affected by employment protection legislation protecting insiders (Bertola et al. 2002; 2007; OECD 2006). As outsiders, women, along with others such as younger people, are argued to be vulnerable to unemployment in a recession and to long-term exclusion if regulation reduces job vacancies. Moreover, Bertola et al. (2007) hypothesize that trade unions take advantage of women's contingent commitment to paid work to push up wages and employment protection above competitive levels in those sectors where the labour displaced will not become openly unemployed but will willingly take up non-wage work activities. Displaced women are assumed to take up childcare full-time, on the presumption that women across developed countries are always carers first and workers at best second.

This approach takes the position of women as common across countries and time, such that gender simply becomes a dummy variable in cross country analysis (for a critique see Figart 2005; Rubery 2011) while more institutionalist and feminist research has tended to stress the path dependency of women's relationship to the waged labour market (Pfau-Effinger 1993; 1998), influenced both by the pattern of employment opportunities and the constitution of women's roles in welfare and economic regimes as primarily wives, mothers or workers (Sainsbury 1996). Path dependency suggests that even if it would be convenient for capital, the state or for unemployed men if women could be reabsorbed back into the family economy in periods of job shortage, this is unlikely to be feasible if their integration into wage employment has induced changes in the family economy and in social norms related to the gender division of labour that are not readily reversible (Humphries and Rubery 1984). Domestic labour may no longer be able, for example, to act as an effective supplement to wage income where mass-produced commodities have become cheaper than home production. The notion of relative autonomy of social reproduction (Humphries and Rubery 1984) provides a frame-work for exploring under what conditions one might anticipate any rolling back or reversal of women's integration into and commitment to wage employment. This approach calls for an analysis of the role played by the state, in the form of the tax and welfare systems, in shaping work incentives on the one hand or childcare support on the other. However, the logic of the relative autonomy approach is that women's participation over time may move from contingent to permanent, such that even a major retrenchment of welfare support may not lead to voluntary withdrawal if dual earner patterns have become embedded in social norms and in household finances and consumption patterns. Any reversal may also have a sig-nificant negative impact on aggregate demand and potential for growth in con-sumer-led capitalism. The extent to which women withdraw, voluntarily or involuntarily, may take on particular importance in the current recession due to the absence of other mechanisms of adjusting labour supply as opportunities for early retirement or dependency on disability benefits are being cut rather than expanded. The need to reduce open unemployment for political reasons in a period of recession may encourage the cutback of support services for working parents but while the cutbacks undoubtedly cause problems they will not necessarily induce women's full withdrawal.

Although the state may not be able to readily reverse or manipulate women's labour market participation, there is no doubt that public policy has had significant impacts on the long-term development of women's employment integration, within and between countries. These effects are both long term, linked to the path-specific evolution of welfare, employment and gender regimes and, more recently, linked to the relatively widespread positive developments in state-sup-ported equality policies across Europe including the UK (Ray et al. 2010; Waldfogel 2011). These more recent developments, which to some extent suggested a process of convergence of public policy, were spurred on by the policy arguments that women's employment had a positive role to play in boosting employment rates in an ageing Europe (Lewis *et al.* 2008, see also Villa and Smith this volume). Similar arguments were developed to argue a business case for more female friendly retention strategies such as work-life balance options or stronger gender equality policies in order to extend the utilization of female talent. These arguments were always context specific and importantly focused only on the economic benefits to the neglect of both the social justice arguments (Noon 2007) and on the need for rights to work not to be interpreted as obligations to work regardless of care provision (Lewis and Giullari 2005). The key issues raised by the recession and the follow-on austerity measures include first the extent to which social actors, including the government, employers and trade unions, will revert to prioritizing male employment at times of jobs shortage. A second key issue is whether the legacy of the focus on women's integration into employment may take different forms for different groups; for example, for those dependent on state benefits, the outcome may still be a focus on wage work and integration at the expense of rights to care while those who could be supported within the family may be encouraged to return to full-time caring.

This review of the factors shaping gender effects through demand side, supply side and policy change has already identified a number of key areas where both the specifics of the gender regime and the specifics of the crisis and the policy response can be expected to impact on the actual outcomes. It is to a consideration of these specifics that we now turn.

Post-2008 recession and austerity: the gender implications in context

To restate the cliché – more often than not forgotten in economic analysis – context is all. Four types of context are relevant here: first, the historical development of the gender regime; second, recent trends in gender relations and gender-related policy; third, the origins and pattern of the 2008 financial crisis; and fourth, the subsequent emergence of the sovereign debt crisis and the political context in which responses are being made.

To turn first to the gender regime context, it is well known that there have been distinct paths of development of gender regimes, reflecting the different process of exclusion and integration of women in the productive economy, the different institutional arrangements in the labour market and the different evolutions of family and social systems including gender relations (Orloff 1993; Pfau-Effinger 1993; 1998; Stier *et al.* 2001). Furthermore, while there are clusters of different gender regimes, giving rise to notions of types or typologies, there are also within these clusters major exceptions and subtle nuances that may provide different contexts for understanding responses to recessions. For example, although Sweden, Finland, Norway and Iceland can lay claim to fit a Nordic or Scandinavian group model based on a distinct adult worker form of gender relations supported by public services, there are significant differences between the actual Swedish, Norwegian, Finnish or Icelandic models, manifest in for example the extent and form of part-time work or in policies with respect to the form of childcare support (Elligsæter and Leira 2006, see also Thorsdottir this volume). Likewise, although there is an apparent Southern European model where a strong family system and high employment regulation is associated with low female participation, Portugal does not fit the model as it has one of the highest shares of full-time female employment despite sharing many other characteristics of the Southern model including the low incidence of part-time work (Tavora 2010, see also Ferreira this volume). Neo-liberal economies such as the US and the UK also differ in significant respects with US women more likely to work on a full-time basis than women in the UK despite even lower levels of support from public services. Eastern European countries share a common legacy of high female integration but differ in the extent to which alternative ideologies, associated for example with a resurgence of religion, have affected attitudes to women's work post the political change.

Recent years have seen some challenges to these differences in patterns of female integration and in associated employment and social models as there has been an almost universal trend towards more women in higher education, more women in employment and consequently greater frequency of dual earner households. These changes in behaviour have also been by and large increasingly supported by a spread of parental leave and childcare arrangements, supported to some extent by the state. There have also been changes in the pattern of family formation, although these have taken on different forms according to the social model (Anxo *et al.* 2010a; 2010b); to oversimplify, in some countries the main effects had been a decline in fertility – particularly in the southern countries – while in others the more dominant trend has been towards children born outside marriage. This implies a general decrease in children born inside marriage, with the main variant whether it is an acceptable social norm to have children outside of marriage. Overall, however, this also constitutes a decline in women's acceptance of their traditional role to have children within the institution of marriage, a behavioural change which is also likely to reflect a reduced willingness among men to commit to marriage and also to children. The key question for this book is how this apparent convergence towards a greater and more long lasting integration of women into wage employ-ment, supported by more welfare services, and facilitated by reduced fertility, is likely to affect responses to the recession. Here we would hypothesize, in line with the notion of the relative autonomy of social reproduction argument, that the changes that have taken place over the past two decades or so in family formation, the household economy and in social norms and attitudes are sufficiently profound and embedded to be resistant to cyclical policy changes. Nevertheless, the degree of embeddedness varies and resistance may be weaker where the move towards dual earner models is more recent and where there is more evidence of the co-existence of competing models or competing ideologies or social norms with respect to women's roles and behaviours.

The impact of recession by gender obviously depends on the context in which recession occurs, through which transmission mechanisms and sectors. The crisis that started in 2007–8 had different immediate effects across countries due to a range of factors, including, to name but a few, the importance of the financial sector, the reliance of the country's demand on construction and the associated property boom, the impact of the crisis in the country's key export markets and the government responses to the downturn (through fiscal and financial policy and through measures to stabilize employment). Applying this approach to understanding potential differences across countries, we can hypothesize that where the main effect of the crisis was indirect, through changes in demand levels, then it was mainly manufacturing and construction that took the immediate hits, areas which in most countries, though not all, are male dominated (CEC 2010: chart 9). The fall out from the financial sector had a more mixed gender effect, although more women appear to occupy buffer-type jobs in the finance sector (Rubery and Rafferty 2013). To the extent that the rest of private services have been affected in a second round, as a consequence of job loss first in finance, manufacturing and construction, the full impact on women's employment can be considered to have been delayed. Moreover, governments have been more likely to provide temporary help to high profile manufacturing and construction sectors in the form of support for short-time working or additional assistance to those made redundant than in private services and retail[1]. The initial recession path was held to primarily affect men due to the destruction of male-type jobs, though the effects may have been modified in some countries such as Germany by short-time working measures (OECD 2009; 2010). However, the second round impacts are now being felt across the service sector, thus changing the focus from a male- to female-dominated recession, at least in some contexts. Of course the groups that are most immediately affected by the jobs shortage are the new entrants, mainly young people, both male and female, and those who have been made redundant; but there is another less visible group that may also be affected, namely women in prime age who have taken temporary breaks from employment to care for children but who may face major problems of re-entry.

The economic crisis that has engulfed the world since 2008 is not a standard deficient demand crisis but instead is a debt crisis that started with banks and individual indebtedness, based on asset bubbles, but where that debt has now been transferred to sovereign states. The markets that created the debt and the bubbles are now questioning the ability of states to finance it, thereby reducing the ability of states to act as the financers and employers of last resort. The economic recession can thus not be divorced from the current fiscal and sovereign debt crisis which has led most countries to retreat quickly from the fiscal stimulus policies adopted immediately when the crisis began. Instead their focus is now on trying to reduce the deficit by fiscal tightening. While those policies are clearly in many cases worsening rather than resolving the debt crisis, the development of an alternative strategy requires global action and leadership which is lacking. Thus, whatever the merits of the policies, in most countries citizens face significant cutbacks in public expenditure with consequences for both jobs and for public services and benefits.

These austerity policies clearly have the potential to shift the burden of adjusting to the debt crisis back on to women as they have most to lose from cutbacks to both services and public sector jobs.

There are a number of important features of this sovereign debt crisis which may have particular implications for the gendering of outcomes. First of all, in some contexts the fiscal deficits are being blamed not on private indebtedness and bailouts but on public sector profligacy and the presence of an overpaid, bureaucratic and essentially unproductive sector and workforce. Given women's predominance in many countries in public sector work, this approach is potentially converting women's public sector jobs from high social value to low social value or from productive to unproductive jobs. Second, the public sector is no longer a stabilizing but more a destabilizing influence on the economy, contributing to rather than offsetting jobs cuts, at least in some countries. Third, the alternatives to public services are often unpaid family services, with direct implications for women's unpaid labour.

The severity and spread of the debt crisis, the emergence in many OECD countries of right-leaning governments and the lack of global leadership to lead us out of this crisis provides a context in which the outcomes of this crisis could well turn out to provide a significant turning point for both gender relations and employment and welfare arrangements in European and OECD societies more widely. There is therefore a need to consider how this current crisis could lead to significant forms of institutional change. Institutional change both impacts on and is influenced by gender relations and it is to potential scenarios for institutional change that we now turn.

The current crisis as a critical juncture: the potential for long-term institutional change in gender relations, employment and welfare systems

The current crisis is far from simply a standard downside of a business cycle and is likely to lead to far reaching social and economic change. We need therefore new frameworks for analysing both the potential impact of this critical juncture on the path of gender relations and likewise the influence of prevailing gender relations on the specific policy responses adopted to deal with the crisis and sovereign debt problems.

If we regard gender relations as socially constructed and therefore subject to change, we can draw on recent debates on institutional change in varieties of capitalism to start this process. It is worth noting that the varieties of capitalism literature has in fact largely excluded gender from the scope of socially constructed institutions; (for a critique see Mandel and Shalev 2009). Instead, gender is largely absent from and treated as independent of the institutional arrangements at the heart of the varieties of capitalism; where gender issues are addressed the essential characteristics of gender relations are treated as universal, not as socially constructed

(Estévez-Abe *et al.* 2001; Estévez-Abe 2005; Soskice 2005). In contrast we follow Martin (2004) in insisting that gender is a social institution:

> While 'traditional' institutions like the family, economy, and polity are accepted as 'distinctly social' in character…., gender is not. Gender is reduced by many scholars and by popular culture to biology – genes, hormones, morphology – and psychology in ways that deny its sociality and susceptibility to social construction. Thus, insistence on gender's collectivity, sociality, and fluidity are required to make the case for its institutional status. Attention to its collective character and historical and geographical variations will, I believe, affirm its susceptibility to human agency and its changes and variations over time.
>
> *(Martin 2004: 1262)*

Among the frameworks we have outlined so far, the one that relates most closely to theoretical debates on institutional change is the concept of relative autonomy of social reproduction. Under this approach gender relations are socially constructed and relatively enduring but also subject to mediated influence from change in other institutions including the production, welfare and family systems. To provide more detailed analysis of these mediating influences, it is useful to draw on some of the key concepts that have been developed to explore both incremental and more disruptive forms of institutional change within national models.

A particularly useful approach for understanding institutional change, developed by Crouch and Keune (2005) to explain the ease with which Thatcher changed the institutional climate in the UK, is to recognize the presence of competing or conflicting ideologies within an institutional environment, thereby providing latent resources that can be mobilized to support quite radical institutional change. In the Crouch and Keune example, Thatcher could draw on internal support from the City of London to bring about the dominance of neoliberalism against the established Keynesian and pluralist establishment. Applying this approach to gender relations requires taking explicit account of the presence of multiple and contradictory ideologies underpinning gender relations. In particular the ideology of greater equality is likely to co-exist with ideologies of essential difference and/or subordination to the interests of men. These contradictory values may even be held by individual women (Fortin 2005) and the dominance of one view may change over time to fit more with their experience (Kroska and Elman 2009). Thus, even where there appears to be an emerging dominant ideology of greater equality, there is still potential for the revival of more conservative ideologies. Moreover, there is scope for divergence in ideologies between the political and the domestic domains as well as between groups and between genders. This also has resonances in gender studies where there is now recognition of multiple femininities and multiple masculinities, for example by Connell and Messerschmidt (2005) on hegemonic masculinities where the authors call for recognition of 'social struggles in which subordinated masculinities influence dominant forms' (op.cit.: 829). In this work gender ideologies are constantly being reconstructed to fit new conditions and under influence from multiple rather than singular social norms.

Adopting this approach allows for a more open perspective on the meaning of path-specific development, where there are multiple internal resources on which to draw and where political choices at critical junctures are key in shaping the actual path of development followed (Djelic and Quack 2007). In short, path dependency does not imply historical determinism. Instead, as Crouch (2005a) has argued, social actors, in shaping the next phase of development of a social model, are likely to draw on a range of societal resources, potentially including discarded or dormant institutions and ideologies. This process of institutional bricolage may be influenced by struggles between competing gender ideologies such that no linear or smooth process towards the adoption of a gender equality ideology, without contradictions or reversals, can be anticipated.

This more open approach to the path of institutional change is also in line with arguments that challenge the more functionalist versions of varieties of capitalism. In these approaches synergies and complementarities between institutional domains are assumed to exist and to shape and limit the path of change, thereby reducing the focus on the possibility or likelihood of tensions and conflicts between different institutional domains (Howells 2003). Moreover, Crouch (2005b) has pointed out that even the notion of complementarity has multiple meanings: in some countries institutions in one area provide compensation for gaps in another area, while in others the institutional arrangements work in the same direction and are more synergistic than compensatory. Where one institutional domain is compensatory the complementarity may have arisen by chance rather than as an outcome of common ideologies or social norms and practices across domains. In a period of rapid change this chance development of compensatory arrangements may break down. Indeed a non-functionalist approach to institutional change has to recognize the likelihood that the forces acting on institutional domains may vary in form and intensity, leading to the potential for mismatch to emerge over time. Gender relations have probably experienced more sustained change than other institutional domains, resulting in many countries in an increasing mismatch between the form of gender relations as practised by citizens and the form of gender relations embedded in welfare states and labour markets. This disjuncture can be expected to continue under the crisis and there may be no effective mechanisms at work to bring the institutional domains back into synergistic or compensatory relations.

In addition to acknowledging the possible influence of both competing ideologies and tensions between domains in shaping responses to the current crisis, we can mobilize some of the tools developed for classifying and exploring processes of incremental institutional change (Streeck and Thelen 2005) to hypothesize about the form of institutional developments at this critical juncture. Here we draw on the notions of a) *displacement,* where over time subordinate institutional arrangements may increase in importance and displace traditional arrangements; b) *conversion,* where a policy or institution may take on different meanings and functions as circumstances change; c) *drift*, where compliance with an institution may lapse as conditions change.

This range of tools enables us to develop some speculative hypotheses on the scenarios with respect to gender relations that could emerge under a prolonged and unresolved financial and fiscal crisis, resulting in persistent job shortage and associated with major reductions in public expenditure. We are interested here in the two-way interactions between gender and other institutional arrangements, where institutional changes reshape the form of gender relations and the form of gender relations influences the path of institutional change in the labour market and welfare system.

To consider first the impact of the crisis on the constitution of labour supply, a key issue is whether the emerging gender egalitarian ideology gives way to a revival of a more conservative ideology of women as homemakers and carers. This potential *displacement* of an emerging dominant ideology may be more plausible where there are strongly competing ideologies and where these ideologies are both embedded in social policy. Two examples can be found, in Germany and Austria, where the egalitarian and the conservative models seem to be operating side by side (Anxo *et al.* 2010a; Mairhuber 2010 – see Box 2.1). In such cases the balance between the two ideologies may change in a recession, even though full displacement is unlikely. Conversely, change in the dominant ideology is less likely where there is a relatively strong or enduring egalitarian ideology, reinforced by the continuous and often full-time integration of women into wage work, such as occurred in France, Finland or Sweden (Pfau-Effinger 1993; 1998; Lewis *et al.* 2008; Anxo 2010; Erhel *et al.* 2010).

BOX 2.1 CONFLICTING GENDER IDEOLOGIES: THE CASES OF GERMANY AND AUSTRIA

Germany provides an example of a social model where the ideology of greater gender equality has been grafted on to a system which still retains the deeply embedded characteristics of a strong male breadwinner welfare state. The latter element is reflected in its income splitting tax system which provides a major subsidy to stay at home spouses and the growth of the mini jobs system, where there are major tax incentives to take up very short-time or low paid part-time jobs. The more recent developments, based more around the Swedish adult worker model can be attributed both to the influence of the old East German model of women in full-time work and to concerns about the fertility rate in Germany, particularly the low fertility of higher educated women who seemed to be choosing work over family (Lewis *et al.* 2008). These new developments can be traced to around 2001 (Lewis *et al.* 2008) when incentives were introduced for mothers to return to work after one rather than the maximum three years of parental leave. This was followed in 2006 with increased childcare places for under threes and in 2007 by a shortening of parental leave to 12 months (14 if the other parent takes at least two months of the leave) but paid at a much higher rate – two-thirds previous earnings (67 per cent) – (with a minimum of €300 and a maximum of €1800 per month). These policies recognize that women may now want to combine work and family, not trade them off as in the traditional strong male breadwinner model but the government has been unwilling to contemplate reforming the male breadwinner welfare state at a time when male breadwinners are facing losses from the reforms to unemployment and pension systems and from the erosion of collective bargaining (Anxo *et al.* 2010a).

Austria provides an example where the election of a conservative right-wing government led to the reversal of policies associated with women's integration into employment but also where there is evidence of at least some partial resistance among women to these efforts to turn them back into family dependants. The Austrian policy regime was already based on long parental leaves, limited childcare and engagement in part-time work when, in 2002, following the resurgence of a more conservative ideology, there were clear policy efforts to encourage women to stay home. A new universal childcare benefit extended the benefit period to 30 months while the latest date by which mothers could return to a guaranteed job remained at 24 months. However, the conservative family ideology has not fully dominated the policy domain as subsequently some elements of this policy approach were reversed with options to take the childcare benefit at a higher rate for a shorter period and with some progress made on rights to reduce working hours and to return to full-time work once children are older, although the eligibility conditions for these rights may reduce their impact (Anxo *et al.* 2010a; Mairhuber 2010).

The ideology of women as the homemaker and care-giver may be applied selectively; for example in the UK, there is evidence of disincentives being introduced and state support being dismantled for mothers to work when there are young children where the mothers are in couple households. However, a different approach is taken where there is no male partner, so that lone parents, mainly mothers, are being required to seek work even when the children are very young, in order to avoid the state taking on responsibility for family income provision. This policy area also provides an example of a case where there may be a *conversion* of apparently progressive policies prior to the recession into more oppressive and coercive policies for a specific group. Thus the focus on women's right to integrate into wage employment which dominated policy debates in the 1990s and 2000s may be converted into a policy which stresses not the right to work but the obligation to work combined with a reinforced lack of a right to care unless supported by a partner.

Institutional *drift* could occur if the economic calculus changes significantly such as to induce non-compliance with a social norm. Changes to the costs of higher education in countries such as the UK could in principle lead to *drift*, that is a movement away from compliance with the social norm established over recent decades that participation in higher education is determined by academic criteria not by differences in life chances by gender. Women now account for more than half of university students such that decisions to invest in education by parents and by individuals do not seem to have been strongly influenced by differential access to high paid jobs over the lifecycle. However, if employment prospects decline and other countries follow the UK lead requiring students to fund their education, some women or indeed their parents may redo the calculus and decide against the investment. This would reverse one of the major social changes over recent decades.

However, the response to these changing conditions is not predetermined and indeed in the UK's case the share of female students has continued to rise in 2012, the first year of the higher fee levels. This could be explained not only by women's higher expectations and aspirations being enduring and not easily reversible but also by the reduced certainty and prospects for young men. Women may feel less certain that they could, even if they so wished, rely on male partners to gain jobs providing sufficient income. Enhanced uncertainty could reinforce women's commitment to education and employment, even in a context in which the benefits from education for women over the lifecourse are likely to be significantly reduced due to their lower earnings and more intermittent participation, while funding the same level of fees. Again, however, the specifics of the institutional arrangements may be critical as any unpaid loans will be written off after thirty years so that actual risks for individual women for the present are thereby reduced. In short, the economic calculus is changing in different directions so that the outcome on dominant institutional arrangements is unclear.

If we turn to the possible impact of gender on the institutions in the labour market we can find a potential example of *displacement*, where the so-called standard employment relationship (SER) (Bosch 2004) is no longer the dominant employment institution. Instead it may be displaced by the panoply of non-standard or flexible arrangements that have grown alongside the integration of women into the labour market and which, particularly in relation to part-time work, have been associated with the diversification of labour force groups (Vosko 2010). This growth of non-standard employment has already facilitated the displacement of certain aspects of the SER in some contexts, particularly the move to abolish pay for unsocial hours and the decline in job protection for those on standard contracts (Rubery 1998). The prolonged recession could take this a stage further if the norm for employment moved closer towards a spot contracting system, at least for the less powerful groups, including the majority of women and some men.

Already in the UK the standards at the bottom of the private sector labour market are being used as the benchmark for what can be considered reasonable employment conditions, with anyone paid better or given greater security, as in the public sector, regarded as too privileged. These minimum private sector labour market standards are arguably reflective of the conditions under which disadvantaged or discriminated groups can be expected to work. The initial argument for more flexible floors to the labour market, made for example by the OECD *Jobs Study* (1994), was to allow those with low productivity to price themselves into work. Now there is a process of *conversion* taking place, with these low standards becoming a benchmark or a norm for all. In this sense women, against their own wishes and interests, may act as a reserve army of labour by providing a benchmark for companies to use to reduce employment standards. Paradoxically, notions that gender difference is a thing of the past may facilitate the generalization of apparently neutral but poor employment standards.

Another *conversion* of an institution that may take place applies to public sector employment, as this is converted from a quality to a cost-focused employer, in response to the notion that it is public sector employment that is the drain on taxpayers and the cause of the crisis. This would have direct implications for the quality of women's employment experience but also for public services, as in the US, where high quality staff are difficult to recruit and retain in public services due to the low value attached to public sector employment in both material and ideological terms (Donahue (2008) quoted in Hutton (2011)). However, nation states in Europe may be hoping that the general downgrading of employment opportunities may enable them to continue to recruit and retain women in the public sector or even in some countries in outsourced and even lower paid private sector employment.

The current and deepening recession and debt crisis may thus yet prove to be a critical juncture resulting in significant changes in institutional arrangements in labour markets, welfare and family systems that bring about a reshaping of gender relations. However, there is no simple way to predict the outcomes unless one takes a non-institutional view of gender, such that outcomes will be dependent upon biological differences rather than on the actions of social actors in reshaping and reconstructing the social institution of gender. The social institution of gender relations is also likely to shape the pattern of change and development in institutions but in varying ways, reflecting the differences in gender regimes between countries. In discussing pressures for change we need to allow for processes of resistance as well as compliance or simple economic adjustment. Resistance may take different forms; women, for example, may be resistant to attempts to revitalize non-egalitarian ideologies, resulting in increased commitments to education and employment or reduced fertility. Men may be resistant to being pressured into employment arrangements associated with women, for example into part-time work, even if these pressures are reinforced by the carrot of in-work benefits or the stick of threatened benefit removal if such jobs are turned down. Not only may individual men feel that this form of work does not fit with their social identity but there may also be concerns over the potential impact of this normalization in that it may result in a lowering of employment standards for all.

While the actual outcome is unknown it is hard to predict a positive scenario under current political conditions unless the economic crisis becomes a catalyst for progressive political change. Yet, in discussing the impact of the crisis for gender relations, it becomes clear that critical junctures are not only about choices between progressive and regressive policies but also about different scenarios of regression, for example towards either greater exclusion from wage employment or towards potentially more inclusion but through a levelling down of employment standards. This outcome would contrast with the expectations that equality would involve upwards equalization with men. Within and between these various scenarios there is clearly much scope for conflict among men and women. However, it is also the case that the interests of men and women coincide as well as conflict. For example, both sexes have an interest in preventing the downgrading of employment conditions as this outcome may provide a new lower standard against which men's employment may also be compared. Likewise, at the household level both sexes have an interest in strategies to protect the household against unemployment and poverty, which may well include the development of strong dual earner households so that there is some buffer to household finances if one of the partners becomes unemployed. Thus the important issue at this critical juncture is to identify sources of solidarity and common interests among the sexes, a process which is in fact facilitated by recognizing and identifying potential sources of conflict and difference among the sexes, instead of treating the crisis as either gender neutral or inherently biased against men. The importance of establishing common ground across the sexes is raised by the danger that the current crisis is changing the role of the state (Rubery 2013) from an agent that in principle promotes gender equality to one that may reverse gender equality gains made over recent decades. This agency may work through cuts in social services and associated reversals of policy to support women's employment, through changes to the amount and quality of public sector employment and through specific tax and benefit policies designed to encourage women to quit the labour market or to take on highly flexible and low paid employment.

Conclusions

This overview of frameworks for analysing the effects of the financial crisis and the austerity programmes on the position of women in the labour market has considered both the shorter-term effects and the potential for this critical juncture to induce significant institutional change, possibly in unanticipated directions. The openness of the frameworks presented reflects the identification of potential but opposing tendencies in both gender relations and in labour market organization. In gender relations there is the strong evidence over recent decades of long-term and persistent change in both women's aspirations and labour market activities and in the associated organization of the family economy and relations. The long-term secular change, however, coexists with continuing processes of discrimination and non-egalitarian ideologies, which could still emerge in some contexts to challenge this secular trend. There is also an openness about predictions with respect to labour market trends, as the crisis and austerity measures could be anticipated to lead to processes of exclusion of women as contingent workers on the one hand, but equally on the other hand to inclusion, but through processes of substitution that may facilitate a levelling down of labour standards. The most likely outcome is that these alternatives will co-exist with mixed outcomes for employment prospects. Thus there may be some increase in the number of women who are inactive due to problems of lack of public services and job opportunities, coexisting both with some improvements for some women in career opportunities and chances relative to men and some increase among women in employment in precarious and debased terms and conditions of employment. The different gender ideologies will also have an uneven impact, with the rise of conservative ideologies more likely in some countries and contexts than others. However, even within a society the multiple ideologies may be mobilized to women's disadvantage but in different ways and different contexts. For some women the issue will be that they have not achieved a right to work, but for others, particularly those dependent on benefits, the issue is more likely to be that they have not achieved a right to care.

Furthermore, the future prospects for women are being particularly challenged by the nature of the crisis and the associated austerity measures. The public sector has played a crucial role in providing women with employment, with professional career opportunities and with higher minimum standards at the lower end of the job ranking. All of these advantages are being challenged by the austerity cuts. Women are also the most dependent on public services to enable them to work and are the group most likely to have to provide the services that are cut from public provision through their unpaid labour.

Overall, although the outcome may not be uniformly negative, the likelihood is that the next years will not only bring some severe hardship to women but also potentially call into question some of the cornerstones of women's progress over recent decades, including even their rights to education and the option of public services as a substitute for domestic labour.

Note

1 See Brenke *et al.* 2011 for an analysis of the concentration of short-time work in manufacturing and in industrial services in Germany.

References

Anxo, D. (2010) 'Towards an Active and Integrated Life Course Policy: The Swedish Experience' in D. Anxo, G. Bosch and J. Rubery (eds) *Welfare State and Life Stage Transitions: a European Perspective*. Cheltenham: Edward Elgar.

Anxo, D., Bosch, G. and Rubery, J. (2010a) 'Shaping the Life Course' in D. Anxo, G. Bosch and J. Rubery (eds) *Welfare State and Life Stage Transitions: a European Perspective*. Cheltenham: Edward Elgar.

—— (eds) (2010b) *Welfare State and Life Stage Transitions: a European Perspective*. Cheltenham: Edward Elgar.

Bergman, B. (1986) *The Economic Emergence of Women*. New York: Basic Books.

Bertola, G., Blau, F. and Kahn, L. (2002) 'Labor Market Institutions and Demographic Employment Patterns', *NBER Working Paper, No. 9043*, Cambridge, Mass., July. Available at: http://www.nber.org/papers/w9043 (accessed 19.12.2012).

—— (2007) 'Labor Market Institutions and Demographic Employment Patterns', *Journal of Population Economics*, 20: 833–67.

Bettio, F. (1988) *The Sexual Division of Labour*. Oxford: Clarendon Press.

—— (2002) 'The Pros and Cons of Occupational Gender Segregation in Europe', in *Canadian Public Policy*, XXVIII, Supplement 1.

Bosch, G. (2004) 'Towards a New Standard Employment Relationship in Western Europe', *British Journal of Industrial Relations*, 42(4): 617–36.

Brenke, K., Rinne, U. and Zimmerman, K. (2011) Short-Time Work: The German Answer to the Great Recession IZA (The Institute for the Study of Labour) Working Paper series DP No. 5780. Available at: http://papers.ssrn.com/sol3/papers.cfm?abstract_id=1871560## (accessed 19.12.2012).

Bruegel, I. (1979) 'Women as a Reserve Army of Labour: A Note on Recent British Experience', *Feminist Review*, 3: 12–23.

CEC (Commission of the European Communities) (2010) *Employment in Europe*, Luxembourg.

Connell, R. and Messerschmidt, J. (2005) 'Hegemonic Masculinity: Rethinking the concept', *Gender and Society*, 19(6): 829–59.

Crompton, R. and Sanderson, K. (1990) *Gendered Jobs and Social Change*. London: Unwin Hyman.

Crouch, C. (2005a) *Capitalist Diversity and Change*. Oxford: OUP.

—— (2005b) 'Three Meanings of Complementarity' in 'Dialogue on "Institutional complementarity and political economy"', *Socio-Economic Review*, 3: 359–63.

Crouch, C. and Keune, M. (2005) 'Changing Dominant Practice: Making Use of Institutional Diversity in Hungary and the UK', in W. Streeck and K. Thelen (eds) *Beyond Continuity: Institutional Change in Advanced Political Economies*. Oxford: Oxford University Press, pp. 83–102.

Djelic M.L., and Quack, S. (2007) 'Overcoming Path Dependency: Path Generation in Open Systems', *Theory and Society*, 36: 161–86.

Doeringer, P.B. and Piore, M.J. (1971) *Internal Labour Markets and Manpower Analysis*. Massachusetts: Heath Lexington.

Donahue, J. (2008) *The Warping of Government Work*. Harvard: Harvard University Press.

Elligsæter, A. and Leira, A. (2006) *Politicising Parenthood in Scandinavia: Gender Relations in Welfare States*. Bristol: The Policy Press.

England, P. (2005) 'Gender Inequality in Labor Markets: The Role of Motherhood and Segregation', *Social Politics: International Studies in Gender, State and Society*, 12(2): 264–88.

Erhel, C., Lima, L. and Nicole-Drancourt, C. (2010) 'From Selective Exclusion Towards Activation: A Life Course Perspective on the French Social Model', in D. Anxo *et al.* (eds) *The Welfare State and Life Transitions*. Cheltenham: Edward Elgar, pp. 208–30.

Estévez-Abe, M. (2005) 'Gender Bias in Skills and Social Policies: The Varieties of Capitalism Perspective on Sex Segregation', *Social Politics*, 12(2): 180–215.

Estévez-Abe, M., Iversen, T. and Soskice, D. (2001) 'Social Protection and the Formation of Skills: A Reinterpretation of the Welfare State', in P.A. Hall and D. Soskice (eds) *Varieties of Capitalism: The Institutional Foundations of Comparative Advantage*. Oxford: Oxford University Press, pp.145–83.

Felstead, A. and Gallie, D. (2004) 'For Better or Worse? Non-standard Jobs and High Involvement Work Systems', *The International Journal of Human Resource Management*, 15(7): 1293–316.

Figart, D. (2005) 'Gender as More Than a Dummy Variable: Feminist Approaches to Discrimination', *Review of Social Economy*, LXIII (3): 509–34.

Fortin, N. (2005) 'Gender Role Attitudes and Labour Market Outcomes of Women Across OECD countries', *Oxford Review of Economic Policy*, 21(3): 417–38.

Grimshaw, D. and Rubery, J. (2007) *Undervaluing Women's Work*. Equal Opportunities Commission, Working Paper Series No. 53. Available at: http://www.equalityhumanrights. com/uploaded_files/equalpay/undervaluing_womens_work.pdf (accessed 03.05.2013).

Hirsch, D. (2011) *Childcare Support and the Hours Trap: The Universal Credit*, Resolution Foundation and Gingerbread. Available at: http://www.resolutionfoundation.org/ media/media/downloads/Childcare_and_the_hours_trap_under_Univeral_Credit.pdf (accessed 19.12.2012).

Howells, C. (2003) 'Varieties of Capitalism: And Then There Was One?' *Comparative Politics*, 36(1): 103–24.

Humphries, J. (1988) 'Women's Employment in Restructuring America: The Changing Experience of Women in Three Recessions', in Rubery, J. (1988) (ed) *Women and Recession*. London: Routledge, pp. 12–40.

Humphries, J. and Rubery, J. (1984) 'The Reconstitution of the Supply Side of the Labour Market: The Relative Autonomy of Social Reproduction', *Cambridge Journal of Economics*, 8(4): 331–47.

Hutton, W. (2011) *Fair Pay in the Public Sector*, London: HM Treasury. Available at: http:// www.hm-treasury.gov.uk/indreview_willhutton_fairpay.htm (accessed 19.12.2011).

Kroska, A. and Elman, C. (2009) 'Change in Attitudes about Employed Mothers: Exposure, Interests, and Gender Ideology Discrepancies', *Social Science Research*, 38: 366–82.

Lewis, J. and Giullari, S. (2005) 'The Adult Worker Model Family, Gender Equality and Care: The Search for New Policy Principles and the Possibilities and Problems of a Capabilities Approach', *Economy and Society*, 34(1): 76–104.

Lewis, J., Knijn, T., Martin, C. and Ostner, I. (2008) 'Patterns of Development in Work/ Family Reconciliation Policies for Parents in France, Germany, the Netherlands, and the UK in the 2000s', *Social Politics: International Studies in Gender, State and Society*, 15(3): 261–86.

Mairhuber, I. (2010) 'Transitions in Female and Male Life Course: Changes and Continuities in Austria', in D. Anxo, G. Bosch and J. Rubery (eds) *Welfare State and Life Stage Transitions: a European Perspective*. Cheltenham: Edward Elgar.

Mandel, H. and Shalev, M. (2009) 'Gender, Class and Varieties of Capitalism', *Social Politics*, 16(2): 161-81.

Martin, P.Y. (2004) 'Gender as a Social Institution', *Social Forces*, 82(4): 1249–273.

Milkman, R. (1976) 'Women's Work and Economic Crisis: Some Lessons of the Great Depression', *Review of Radical Political Economics*, 8(1): 73–97.

Noon, M. (2007) 'The Fatal Flaws of Diversity and the Business Case for Ethnic Minorities', *Work Employment and Society*, 21(4): 773–84.

OECD (1994) *The Jobs Study*. Paris: OECD.

—— (2006) *Employment Outlook*. Paris: OECD.

—— (2009) *Employment Outlook*. Paris: OECD.

—— (2010) *Employment Outlook*. Paris: OECD.

Orloff, A. (1993) 'Gender and the Social Rights of Citizenship: The Comparative Analysis of Gender Relations and Welfare States', *American Sociological Review*, 58(3): 303–28.

Pfau-Effinger, B. (1993) 'Modernisation, Culture and Part-Time Employment: The Example of Finland and West Germany', *Work, Employment and Society*, 7(3): 383–410.

—— (1998) 'Culture or Structure as Explanations for Differences in Part-time Work in Germany, Finland and the Netherlands?', in C. Fagan and J. O'Reilly (eds) *Part-Time Prospects; Part-Time Employment in Europe, North America and the Pacific Rim*. London: Routledge, pp. 177–98.

Ray, R., Gornick, J. and Schmitt, J. (2010) 'Who Cares? Assessing Generosity and Gender Equality in Parental Leave Policy Designs in 21 Countries', *Journal of European Social Policy*, 20(3): 196–216.

Reskin, B. and Roos, P. (1990) *Job Queues, Gender Queues*. Philadelphia: Temple University Press.

Rubery, J. (ed.) (1988, reissued 2010) *Women and Recession*. London: Routledge.

—— (1998) 'Part-time Work: A Threat to Labour Standards', in J. O'Reilly and C. Fagan (eds) *Part-Time Prospects: Part-Time Employment in Europe, North America and the Pacific Rim*. London: Routledge, pp. 137–55.

—— (2011) 'Towards a Gendering of the Labour Market Regulation Debate', *Cambridge Journal of Economics*, 35(6): 1103–126.

—— (2013) 'Public Sector Adjustment and the Threat to Gender Equality' in D. Vaughan-Whitehead (ed.) *Public Sector Shock*. ILO and Edward Elgar, forthcoming.

Rubery, J. and Rafferty, A. (2013) 'Women and Recession Revisited', *Work, Employment and Society*, forthcoming.

Rubery, J. and Tarling, R. (1982) 'Women in the Recession' in D. Currie and M. Sawyer (eds) *Socialist Economic Review*. Manchester: Merlin Press.

—— (1988) 'Women's Employment in Declining Britain', in J. Rubery (ed.) *Women and Recession*. London: Routledge.

Sainsbury, D. (1996) *Gender, Equality, and Welfare States*. Cambridge: Cambridge University Press.

Soskice, D. (2005) 'Varieties of Capitalism and Cross-National Gender Differences', *Social Politics*, 12(2): 170–79.

Stier, H., Lewin-Epstein, N. and Braun, M. (2001) 'Welfare Regimes, Family-Supportive Policies, and Women's Employment along the Life-Course', *The American Journal of Sociology*, 106(6): 1731–760.

Streeck, W. and Thelen, K. (2005) *Beyond Continuity: Institutional Change in Advanced Political Economies*, Oxford: Oxford University Press.

Tavora, I. (2010) 'Understanding the High Rates of Employment among Low-educated Women in Portugal: A Comparatively Oriented Case Study', *Gender, Work and Organisation*, 19(2): 93–118.

Vosko, L. (2010) *Managing the Margins Gender, Citizenship, and the International Regulation of Precarious Employment*, Oxford: Oxford University Press.

Waldfogel, J. (2011) 'Family-friendly Policies', in P. Gregg and J. Wadsworth (eds) *The Labour Market in Winter: the State of Working Britain*, Oxford: Oxford University Press.

3

CHALLENGING THE BALKANIZATION OF GENDER CONTRACTS

Jacqueline O'Reilly and Tiziana Nazio

Introduction: the balkanization of labour markets and the social contract legacy

The balkanization of labour markets refers to the institutional rules that established unbridgeable boundaries between non-competing groups in the labour market (Kerr 1954). Writing at the nascence of the standard employment contract, associated with lifetime employment and seniority pay, Kerr was referring to the rules governing skills and wage setting arrangements for workers in internal labour markets (Reich 2009). These rules excluded workers with non-standard employment contracts from this 'sheltered sector, and confined [them] to the residual competitive secondary sector' (Rubery 1978: 19). Kerr suggested that governments could do little to challenge the rights of insiders, but they could make the rules of entry more equitable by placing outsiders on a more equal footing in competing for vacancies.

Since the post-1960s civil rights movement and an extended period of heightened industrial conflict there have been attempts to remove, or at least diminish, these inequalities. This is evidenced by legislative initiatives to reduce gender and racial discrimination, to encourage and integrate part-time and temporary employment, increased access to pension entitlements, childcare provision, leave arrangements and flexible working for both parents (O'Reilly 2003; Lewis *et al.* 2008). Since 2000 equality rights and discrimination law have been institutionalized across Europe, although the impact of this has varied among countries (Krizsan *et al.* 2012).

Concurrently, since the economic crisis of the 1970s, we have also witnessed the continued erosion of traditional employment rights and benefits in terms of entitlements, pay and pensions. But rather than diminishing the differences between non-competing groups in the labour market, the barriers between insiders and outsiders remain and are being reinforced (Rueda 2005; Standing 2011; Emmenegger *et al.* 2012). The pernicious consequences of insecurity have had an impact on traditional core workers, as well as expanding the flexible secondary labour market. These developments illustrate what Polanyi called the 'double movement', involving both the destructive marketization of the standard employment contract and simultaneous attempts to develop measures of social protection.

However, the evidence for growing 'precarization' or the 'insecurity thesis' has been contested (Heery and Salmon 2000). The extent and severity of this is also mediated by different institutional contexts (Blossfeld *et al.* 2005). While some forms of insecurity have increased, other workers have benefited from an expansion of job opportunities and an increase in job tenure, at least up until 2008 (Auer and Caze 2003; Doogan 2009). The traditional boundaries between dual labour markets, described by Kerr, were becoming increasingly fuzzy as the legacy of previous recessions unfolded in terms of new job opportunities, the quality of working life and changing contractual relations around work (Supiot 2001). Grimshaw and Rubery (1998) argued for an integrated analysis of both internal and external labour markets in which the boundaries between the two are regarded as more permeable than in traditional segmentation theory.

Humphries and Rubery (1984) called for a more holistic perspective to understand the interrelationships and relative autonomy of the spheres of economic production and social reproduction, without assuming a complementary fit between them. This approach illustrated how women's availability for paid work varied across countries. This was because the 'rules of the game' were shaped by the different institutional provisions governing the organization of the sphere of social reproduction, for example in the organization of care, schools and consumption (O'Reilly 1994; O'Reilly and Fagan 1998; Rubery *et al.* 1999; Blossfeld and Hofmeister 2006; Rubery this volume). The competing demands on mothers' time in paid work and unpaid caring have created 'work-life conflicts' (McGinnity and Whelan 2009). These in turn have raised significant societal problems related to the changing structure of employment and job opportunities, declining fertility, the aging demographic profile and the limited provision of care services across the generations (Saraceno and Keck 2010; 2011).

In the decade preceding the 2008 global financial crisis, labour market policy and welfare reform debates were often framed in terms of 'contractualism' and the need for a 'new social contract' (O'Reilly and Spee 1998; Cappelli 1999; Crouch 1999; HMSO 1999; Supiot 2001; Esping-Andersen 2002; Lewis 2002; Bosch 2004). Criticism of the post-war social contract was based on the inequity of rights and entitlements being linked to employment status that no longer corresponded to the reality of contemporary work. As mothers increasingly work for pay, and as marriage and fertility rates decline, reformers are forced to address the inconsistencies and gendered inequalities emanating from the post-war social contract or, as Humphries and Rubery (1984) argued, the disharmony between the spheres of economic production and social reproduction.

From a socio-economic and legal perspective, Vosko (2011) illustrates how vary-ing solutions to these conflicts have developed both between countries as well as between different socio-economic groups. She suggests these produce a range of new forms of the 'gender contract' to manage paid work and care. This suggests that a plurality of gender contracts can co-exist, even within the same society, which could be seen as reflecting the balkanization of labour markets Kerr originally referred to. Gottfried (2013) questions the limitations of contractualism and the concept of a gender contract arguing in favour of a 'reproductive bargain' as a better way to capture these changes. In reviewing these debates we ask how useful they are in helping us understand the consequences of austerity for gender equality, or whether we might expect to see a new form of balkanized labour markets and gender contracts.

The sexual contract: ubiquitous masculine domination

The story of the 'original' social contract in political philosophy was inherently based on a sexual contract, according to Pateman (1988). She argued that the intellectual fissure created by the polarized concepts of public and private in liberal democratic theory generates an unbridgeable segregation in power relations between men and women. Women are incorporated into a private sphere of civil society differently from men, who belong to the public world of 'freedom, equal-ity, rights, contract, interest and citizenship' (Pateman 1989: 4). The patriarchal individuals of the original fraternal social contract were men, legitimizing their 'male sex-right' over women establishing a 'fraternal social contract'. The pre-contractual conditions of contract were based on the ascribed and subjugated sexual status of women to the private sphere.

The exclusion of women from the original social contract was, according to Rousseau, because they lacked a sense of justice; they were ruled by emotions and incapable of a moral, rational capacity to act as required of public institutions (Rousseau 1911: 332). Rationality and sentimentality were diametrically opposed. The family generated particularistic bonds. Participation in public institutions required suppressing private interests in the pursuit of universalistic goals of justice. Women were less capable than men of harnessing their natural sexual passions, in part because of their biological role as mothers, and their attachment and responsi-bility to the particularistic interests of the family. According to Pateman, Hegel argued that women pervert the universal property of the state into a possession and ornament for the family: 'In a world presented as conventional, contractual and universal, women's civil position is ascriptive, defined by the natural particularity of being women' (Pateman 1989: 51–2).

Exposing the sexual nature of the original social contract uncovers the ideologi-cal presuppositions that are inherent in the political philosophy underpinning contemporary democratic institutions. Pateman argued that this analytical frame-work can inform our understanding of 'real life' contracts, as found in marriage, employment, prostitution and surrogacy 'contracts'. These are examples of how the male sex-right is established in the public sphere. The property negotiated in these contracts is 'the property that individuals are held to own in their persons' (Pateman 1988: 5).

However, Fraser (1997) posited that a husband's power over his wife is not purely a matter of a master-subordinate model, even though lower earnings over the life cycle and rising divorce rates make women more vulnerable to poverty. Fraser proposed linking the socio-economic processes to what happens within marriage to provide a broader analysis of the dynamics of power than Pateman's appeal to the 'male sex-right'. The master-subordinate grid of interpretation is only one in competition with other models of intimate relations, such as 'companionate egalitarian heterosexuality' found in middlebrow mass culture. Today, gender, sex and sexuality are fraught, fragmented and contested, both within national cultures as well as within a globalized context; but Pateman does not sufficiently acknowledge these differences. Connell and Messerschmidt (2005) argued that 'hegemonic masculinity' is not a universal norm; it takes a variety of forms with a hierarchical status order that has been historically contested.

Fraser (1997) criticized Pateman's analysis for de-contextualizing the female worker by focusing on the employment relation in abstraction. Reducing capitalist employment relations to 'wage slavery' can be considered too severe, even if the employment relation implies domination and subjection. Fraser argued that women's earnings could actually confer some leverage outside the workplace by providing women with some autonomy and choices, important especially if they want to leave a marriage. For Fraser 'one must balance subordination in paid work against the potential for relative freedom from subordination outside it. The latter will vary with people's social location, as determined in part by their place in the gender division of unpaid labor' (Fraser 1997: 230). Even where Pateman argued that women can never be the same kind of workers as men, the formulation implies 'too seamless a fit between marital power and capitalist power, thereby missing the possibility of trade offs' (Fraser 1997: 230). Pateman's analytical grid is incapable of capturing these 'more abstract forms of social mediation and impersonal mechanisms of action coordination' (Fraser 1997: 230). Change is also always analysed through the interpretative grid of the sex-rights of men over women, producing an enduring master-subordinate model of analysis, thereby putting subordination, rather than exploitation at the crux of the wage-slave relationship and 'other person' property relationships. Exploitation can take many forms, and Pateman's analysis is only *one* possible interpretative lens.

More recently Pateman has argued that her approach is not essentialist or fatalist and is capable of understanding autonomy and agency (Pateman and Mills 2007). Her intention was to highlight 'that the sexual contract was integral to the historical changes that led to the consolidation of the modern state and its institutions… the logic of contractual argument was designed to show that an understanding of interconnecting, but neglected, ideas and political structures was central to any democratic transformation' (Pateman and Mills 2007: 227–8). Pateman's analysis and critique of the 'social contract' story, so central to understanding modern democratic institutions, indicates the deeply engrained nature of the public-private distinctions that still permeate our conceptualization of the individual, the citizen and equality, and the social context in which these identities are experienced and realized.

We may not ever achieve an equal society because of the dilemmas of trying to combine policies that acknowledge both similarity and difference, or the incompatible rationales governing the organization of the family and firm, or as Pateman argues the fissure of the public-private divide imposed by the original fraternal contract. But the way in which governments, organizations and individuals adapt to gender conflicts in these different spheres can have important consequences for the opportunities and rewards that women are able to access. Some women are clearly benefiting from progress up the occupational ladder, albeit at the cost of not becoming parents at all or limiting themselves to one child (Nazio 2008b). Other women, not willing to make these compromises, do not progress at the same rate, or may choose to drop out (Hewlett 2007). The choices around new forms of maternalism and employment are riven with class and ethnic differences (Dale and Holdsworth 1998; Duncan 2005). Women unable to have a rewarding labour market experience may reject the criteria for success and social status in the publically accepted sphere; some may 'choose' to focus on their families given the costs and quality of available care services, others may be forced into this role because of the lack of job opportunities. At the same time governments are making it more difficult for particular groups of women such as single parents to take the maternalist option (Orloff 2006). McRobbie (2007) and Adkins (2008) have argued that the evident differentiation of economically successful women creates a divide between 'top girls' and mothers: occupational success is based on a sexualized identity that requires 'successful' women to be young, free and childless.

The concept of a sexual contract unveils the essential public and private divide in managing and synchronizing 'work-life' balances and conflicts that are rooted in a longer philosophical tradition permeating democratic institutions and policy-making. However, Fraser's (1997) critique of Pateman's monolithic conception of a sexual contract provides us with a lever to look for contradictions and conflicts between these spheres. It also echoes the call from Streeck (2010) and Rubery (2011a) to understand how the recent crisis has brought long-term contradictions and conflicts between the spheres of social reproduction and economic production into sharper relief.

The gender contract: modernization through historical conflict

Examining how gender relations have changed over time is essential for understanding the current crisis and previous recessions (Rubery 1988 and this volume). Using an historical analysis Tilly and Scott (1978) highlighted how changes in the economic sphere and the political arena interact to shape different paths of women's integration into paid work. They illustrate how family organization changed historically in both France and Britain through the process of industrialization, modernization and new forms of regulation, but resulted in different forms and levels of female employment. Industrialization in France was slower and artisanal production persisted; women maintained a stronger full-time work role in family firms and minimum pay legislation covered women as well as men (Laufer 1998). In Britain, in contrast, industrialization was more rapid and extensive with the wholesale onslaught of the factory system. The resulting appalling working conditions led social reformers in Britain to push much more quickly for employment legislation to 'protect', and effectively exclude, women and children from intensive employment alongside men in the factories; but little was done to protect against gender differentiated pay systems.

Tilly and Scott's analysis highlights how the regulation and recognition of gender relations had a differential impact on the modernization, organization and definition of women's paid work. It also shaped who was included or excluded from employment and social protection. The legacies of these political decisions still influence present day formulations of gender conflicts, work-life balance policies and issues around gender equality in what Fouquet et al. (2002) have referred to as challenges to contemporary social contracts between the sexes in Europe.

Using the concept of a gender contract, Hirdman (1998) provides a historical critique of the role of trade unions in improving conditions for women in Sweden. The gender contract concept draws attention to power relationships between men and women in the gender system characterized by gender segregation and the dominance of the male norm. In Sweden modernization threatened the traditional gender system by creating a 'structural disharmony, a *de facto* gender conflict' (Hirdman 1998: 36). Gendered conflicts over which kinds of men and women had the right to vote, to be educated and to work were part of the process of modernization and democratization; if women were to be treated the same as men, which men and which women were to be included? Hirdman's analysis chronicles the changes in female integration into two main historical periods: the household contract (1930–60) and the individualistic contract (1960–90). The latter is further divided between the equality contract (up until 1975) and the move towards equal status contract (1975–90).[1]

The 'household contract' developed in Sweden (1930–60) as a result of concerns about demographic depopulation. Influential Swedish thinkers such as the Myrdals[2], argued for state intervention to encourage marriage, provide support for mothers and facilitate their employment. Their aim was to speed up female integration and the expansion of social reforms, to rejuvenate the stagnant Swedish economy. Nevertheless, traditional conceptions of gender relations survived: the 'woman problem' was now called 'family policy'. Welfare policies continued to be modelled around the male breadwinner with a professionalized modern housewife (Hirdman 1998: 40).

The articulation of, and solutions to, the gender conflict in Sweden during the 1930s onwards were framed in terms of dissimilarity between men and women, i.e.

how to manage women workers as mothers. The widely supported 'dual role model' expected women to work before having children, but to withdraw after childbirth with redistributive policies provided by the welfare state. Issues of similar treatment to men were not an area of contention at that time but later this led to tensions between integration and segregation, and divisions between mothers that worked and those that did not.

At the end of the 1960s the two-income family was considered the desired norm for long-term change by the social democratic government. The 'new social gender contract', according to Hirdman, in the second phase of welfare state development, was one between women and the state: the individualistic gender contract 1960–90. This removed political concern about the role of men in the domestic division of labour. Welfare policies in the form of day-care centres, individualized taxation (from 1971) and parental leave insurance (from 1974) enabled and rewarded working mothers. The result was a massive increase in women's labour force participation from 53 per cent to 86 per cent between 1970–90. Fertility rates remained high, and labour market participation improved women's economic citizenship; expectations were that women could participate like men. But, Hirdman argues, a 'special place' had been created for women workers with new forms of segregation such as part-time work in the public sector, and while women's political representation increased, female politicians tended to be in 'soft areas'.

The subsequent equal status contract (1975–90) temporarily 'resolved' the 'gender conflict' in Sweden through building the welfare state and creating new spaces and provisions for women. The move from an 'equality contract' to an 'equal status contract' reflected the failure of demands for similarity of treatment; the reality of segregation raised the issue of recognizing difference fairly (Hirdman 1998: 43). Equal status is now administratively integrated into organizations and negotiated by human resource and equality officers in companies, unions, political parties and government. Gender conflicts based on similarities have vanished, but conflicts around dissimilarities remain significant.

Reproductive bargains and the limits of contractualism

Despite the intuitive appeal of the language of contract, Gottfried (2013) argues that its over-legalistic terms of reference limit understanding of how agents negotiate productive and reproductive work. It also fails to sufficiently capture a broader conceptualization of gender relations which allows for both variations among different categories of women and men within the same society and for the on-going negotiation of these relations. Instead, Gottfried (2009: 2013) proposes using the concept of 'reproductive bargains', suggesting that:

> A bargain constitutes a hegemonic framework within which actors negotiate rules and rule-making. 'Bargain' implies a set of normative rules and institutions regulating interactions, self-conceptions, and social relations. This notion of 'bargain' not only implies a bounded agreement (structure) proscribing and

prescribing conduct (habitus), but also injects a dynamic notion of boundaries being made (agency).

(Gottfried 2013: 124)

Reproductive bargains include institutions, ideologies and identities associated with providing care. A variety of organizations can intervene to provide care on a paid or unpaid basis, including the family, the state, and the market, as well as non-governmental not-for-profit organizations. Normative rules govern the types of work available to different groups of women and men, and the different power resources affect their ability to negotiate the reproductive bargain (Gottfried 2013: 125–6).

Gottfried's proposition moves the debate from discussing work and care to distinguishing between productive and reproductive labour. Connolly and Whitehouse (2010: 8) suggest that 'the term reproductive labour is not necessarily coded as unremunerated or located with the private sphere'. Reproductive labour includes not only care provision, but health, education and consumption. This work can be paid or unpaid, in the formal or informal sector of the economy and organized in the private or public domain. Using these concepts builds on the argument of Humphries and Rubery (1984) about the need to integrate the spheres of social reproduction and economic production, but situates it in relation to the gender contract debates.

Connolly and Whitehouse (2010) also suggest that Gottfried's contribution moves the discussion from contract to bargain. Bargaining carries the connotation of on-going negotiations that captures the flux operating in contemporary labour markets and the growth of precarious employment. Gottfried's proposition is that the idea of 'reproductive bargaining' makes us more sensitive to the differentiated negotiations between different groups of women within the same society according to the kinds of resources they can draw on. It can also allow us to make comparisons between societies. And, it can provide a global perspective that takes account of immigration and international labour flows that supply demand for reproductive labour in the northern hemisphere.

But, whether the concept of a reproductive bargain is distinct from a gender contract approach, or whether it could provide an important contribution to these debates is not yet sufficiently clear. Looking back at the development of this concept based on the work of Pearson (1997), she argued that the 'reproductive bargain' is an implicit, and sometimes explicit, agreement of the organization of tangible benefits and responsibilities provided by the state for families and citizens. The concept was based on anthropological research surrounding the economic crisis in Cuba in the 1990s. The Cuban revolutionary 'reproductive bargain' provided work, food, utilities, health and educational infrastructure until the collapse of the Soviet Union. Attempts to fill the gap in public services required for social reproduction were made predominantly by women, providing what they could, unpaid and within the home. Other consequences were a dramatic decline in fertility rates; an expansion of employment and exchange in the informal and illegal economy; and loss of jobs for women in formal non-productive sectors, such as health and education, where the status and resources of these jobs diminished drastically. The messages from Pearson's study are salutary lessons that we could draw out to consider the possible implications for Europe today, albeit that the scale of economic development is so radically different. But they also indicate that the concept of reproductive bargains, as formulated by Pearson (1997), is not so far removed from the concept of a gender contract approach: both approaches provide an analysis of the impact of significant historical change in the way the 'social contract' operates and how it impacts on the immediate lives of women in these societies. Gottfried's contribution is to bring this concept of bargaining closer to the way individuals and households negotiate work-care options in a global labour market.

In sum, sexual contract theorists emphasized the ubiquitous reproduction of masculine domination inherent in the historical development of contemporary democratic institutions. Gender contract approaches have given greater weight to how gender relations vary significantly over time and place. This is as a result of modernization and the conflicts it generates in attempts to resolve incompatibilities between the organization of economic production and social reproduction. The concept of reproductive bargains shares some similarities with the gender contract approach from the macro social contract level. Gottfried's contribution attempts to locate the agency within these structurally defined spaces. She also seeks to identify how these negotiations are changing through global labour markets, and the different power relations that exist within economically rich societies. We now turn to examine how these debates can inform our interpretation of the current economic crisis on gender relations.

Consequences of austerity for emancipatory transformation

The current financial crisis and its consequences need to be seen as a particular historical form of social order (Streeck 2010), breaking with the post-war social contract. The idea of the market as a historically embedded and institutionalized social order draws on the work of Polanyi (1957). Based on the concept of a 'double movement', Polanyi argued that marketization destroyed traditional social relations through contractual market exchange; simultaneously new forms of social protection developed to contain the processes of commodification, but this also excluded particular groups from access to rights and resources. Fraser's (2011) critical evaluation of Polanyi, in the light of the economic crisis, has proposed that this 'double movement' should be understood as a 'triple movement'. The third dimension requires examining the emancipatory consequences of these transformations for disadvantaged groups in both the previous social order and the one that is emerging. Marketization disembeds traditional gender inequalities and reveals new emancipatory possibilities; but countervailing forms of protectionism against marketization generate new forms of exclusion.

Marketization has been associated with an increased precarization of non-standard employment where women are more likely to be employed, for example in mini-jobs that do not require social insurance contributions (Weinkopf 2009). Neo-liberal reforms are deconstructing the established social model in many countries (Bosch *et al.* 2009; Gallino and Borgna 2012). Concurrently, protective legislation introduced prior to the crisis extended parental and care leaves and increased childcare provision (Lewis *et al.* 2008). In the UK the National Minimum Wage provided pay protection at the bottom of the wage scale and a series of equal pay cases in the UK have successfully ruled in favour of the women plaintiffs (Deakin and McLaughlin 2012). While there is evidence of a double or even triple movement, the direction of this change is moving across a range of policy arenas and is not uniform or consistent.

Before the crisis, government responses to the conflicts created by new work-care challenges varied between countries, as well as between different institutions in the same society. Saraceno and Keck (2010 and 2011) illustrate how contradictory rationales for elderly care and childcare co-exist and are organized across a range of different government departments. Leira's (2002) analysis of policy reform of childcare services in Nordic countries illustrates this diversity of rationales and provisions. States have taken different paths to expand state-sponsored childcare services, strengthen fathers' rights to care or even introduce cash grants for childcare. But commonality was found in the move away, in all Nordic countries, from childcare being regarded as a 'woman's question' to becoming a gender-neutral question of 'family choice' around the organization of domestic and paid work. Leira argues that gender-neutral family choices combined with gender segregation in employment resulted in these policies still having gender-differentiated consequences: fathers were still less likely to take time out to care. Only where this was enforced as a 'take it or lose it' option were take-up rates higher for fathers. Leira suggests that neutralizing the policies into questions of family 'choice' removes their emancipatory potential and 'might serve to cement a new version of the gender contract by reinforcing the care of children as a special responsibility for mothers' (Leira 2002: 88). If there is a reproductive bargain taking place, it is not necessarily resulting in significantly greater equality.

The formulation of policy agendas is highly influenced by the shape of the political coalitions making these demands. Naumann's (2005) historical comparison of feminist movements in Sweden and West Germany illustrates the long-term impact of these differences. The 'gender conflict' in Sweden focused on the role of mothers as workers. In contrast, women's demands in West Germany were formulated in terms of a rejection of the traditional family, demands for autonomy over their bodies and abortion rights. The consequence of these demands had very different outcomes for policies to integrate mothers into paid work. Skocpol (1995) and Koven and Michel's (1993) analysis of maternalist political organizations have shown how these groups can shape the policy agenda in relation to identifying which women and mothers are considered deserving and less deserving of welfare and pension benefits. The constitution of different coalitions involved in the policy process defines whether women are treated as women, mothers, workers or working mothers, and what their entitlement and status should be. Transformative state feminism, according to McBride and Mazur (2010), is shaped by coalitions of women's social movements and associations and how this affects their integration into mainstream politics. However, there is not a simple trade-off between regime types and policy success. Policy subsystems are complex and do not conform to consistent patterns of regime types. Policy reform needs to first identify commonalities and differences across policy areas and their compatibility in supporting, for example, caring over the lifecycle.

Since 2000 there has been an extensive introduction of equality legislation and anti-discrimination institutions across Europe, and in some countries where they had never previously existed (Krizsan *et al.* 2012). The appearance of convergence, however, conceals the underlying complexity, variety and capacity of these initiatives. The multiplicity of institutions promoting equality has been influenced by regional norms and locally based political opportunity structures. Gender equality as a top political priority at the EU level appears to have fallen off the political agenda (Villa and Smith this volume). While there have been significant attempts to promote gender equality in a number of fields, 'work-life conflicts' around the organization of social reproduction remain pertinent. Rubery (2011a) argues that reforms in the past decade to deal with these gender conflicts has produced a hybridization of regime types in Europe and a politics of 'bricolage'.

Conclusion: Austerity as a catalyst for rethinking gender contracts and balkanization

Progress in gender equality has gone hand in hand with a continued balkanization of gender contracts within and between countries reflecting societal and class specific legacies of the integration of women into paid work. Differences before the crisis in the organization of work and care illustrated very distinct labour market trajectories across a spectrum from work-poor to work-rich households (Warren 2000; Gregg and Wadsworth 2011; Nazio and O'Reilly forthcoming). The consequences of austerity may work in a number of directions for different types of household. Rising levels of unemployment will increase the number of work-poor households where no one is in paid work (Gregg *et al.* 2010). Welfare measures to address this may bias towards encouraging traditional male breadwinner models of labour market participation (Ingold 2011). Households where both partners are working will be differentiated between those in part-time and full-time employment. Work-rich households with two full-time employees may well be divided between high earning professionals, and those who need to work out of economic necessity. In modified breadwinner households, with the mother working in marginal forms of part-time work, transitions to non-employment tended to be more common than transitions into a dual full-timer model (O'Reilly and Bothfeld 2002) even in the period before the crisis. In contrast, those with better quality part-time jobs were either able to maintain them, or to move into dual full-time earner households. These balkanized trajectories, evident before the crisis, are likely to become more entrenched as job opportunities diminish, and unless a more radical policy agenda to address these is implemented.

Contemporary radical propositions vary in the detail of how a public organization of the labour market could be achieved, but some of the core elements they often share are: 1) a re-conceptualization of security over the life cycle that is not dependent on time spent in paid employment; 2) an individualization of rights and benefits that do not reinforce traditional gendered household dependencies; and 3) a comprehensive review of the institutional provision of support services over the life-course. Examples of some proposals include extended 'social drawing rights' (Supiot 2001), transitional labour markets (Schmid 2008), a basic income (Standing 2011), or flexicurity (Wilthagen 1998). Rubery (2011b) has advocated the need to combine policies of inclusive labour markets with specific policies to empower women. Some of these proposals could be considered 'mildly utopian'. But Deakin (2000: 24) reminds us that:

> the process of institutional construction which culminated in the mid-20th century welfare state had begun half a century earlier amidst conditions of growing economic insecurity and the casualization of work under a 'globalized' trading regime, although it had different names then. That generation championed what Sidney and Beatrice Webb called the 'public organization of the labour market'. That aim must at times have seemed just as remote to that earlier generation as it sometimes appears to us today.

Deakin (2000) proposes an evolutionary perspective that can allow us to understand how the standard employment contract is changing. The blurring of employment statuses, the decline of trade unions and the diversification of the labour force has brought an end to relational contracting of the standard employment contract: employers' prerogatives are less curtailed and work has intensified; trade unions have moved from being co-regulators to monitors and enforcers of employee legal rights.

We might expect to see new coalitions of actors attempting to contain the destructive path of marketization that will challenge traditional status hierarchies. Some of this contestation will take the form of public demonstrations; other forms will be through lobby groups, unions, the courts and the practices of firms as they respond to the consequences of recession and their need to draw on a range of differently skilled workers either from home or abroad.

These challenges indicate how significant a modernization of the traditional social contract is required, not only for gender equality, but also to provide for the necessary improvement in skills, income earning potential and job growth. However, if the priority for gender equality is blinded out by austerity policies focused on budget deficit reductions, paying scant regard to the gendered consequences of these policies (Hogarth et al. 2009; TUC 2010; 2011; Sands 2012; Council of the European Union 2012), gender contracts are likely to become even more balkanized and entrenched. The value of a gender contract perspective in examining these developments is to directly draw attention to the gendered dimension at the base of how these rules governing the organization of production and social reproduction were both established and are still evolving.

Notes

1 A more recent discussion of differentiated policy responses to challenging the gender contract in Nordic countries has been provided by Leira (2002) for Nordic countries, by Puchacz (2010) for Sweden and by Fouquet *et al.* (2002) for the EU.[1]

2 Gunnar and Alva Myrdal were influential intellectuals in Sweden in the tradition of utopian philosophy but were also closely involved in pragmatic politics of the time (Hirdman 1998: 40). For them, questions about production and reproduction were not separate dichotomous fields, but formed part of an integrated package. At the time of the 1932 election of the SDP government, the Swedish trade unions supported the ideology of a male breadwinner family model with stay at home mothers. Two important strands opposing the adoption of this solution to this 'gender conflict' were, on one hand, radical theoretical Marxists who argued for the socialization of reproduction and, on the other, social engineers symbolized by Gunnar and Alva Myrdal who argued for policies to support mothers combine family responsibilities with paid work (Myrdal and Klein 1956).

References

Adkins, L. (2008) 'From Retroactivation to Futurity: The End of the Sexual Contract?', *NORA – Nordic Journal of Feminist and Gender Research,* 16(3): 182–201.

Auer, P. and Cazes, S. (2003) *Employment Stability in an Age of Flexibility: Evidence From Industrialized Countries,* Geneva: ILO.

Blossfeld, H.P., Klizjing, E., Mills, M. and Kurz, K. (eds) (2005) *Globalization, Uncertainty and Youth in Society,* London: Routledge.

Blossfeld, H.P., Hofmeister, H. (eds) (2006) *Globalization, Uncertainty and Women's Careers,* Cheltenham: Edward Elgar.

Bosch, G. (2004) 'Towards a New Standard Employment Relationship in Western Europe', *British Journal of Industrial Relations,* 42(2): 617–36.

Bosch, G., Lehndorff, S. and Rubery, J. (2009) *European Employment Models in Flux: A Comparison of Institutional Change in Nine European Countries,* London: Palgrave Macmillan.

Cappelli, P. (1999) *The New Deal At Work: Managing the Market-Driven Workforce,* Boston: Harvard Business School Press.

Connell, R.W. and Messerschmidt, J.W. (2005) 'Hegemonic Masculinity: Rethinking the Concept', *Gender and Society,* 19: 829–59.

Connolly, J. and Whitehouse, G. (2010) 'Understanding Women's Employment Patterns Within and Between Nations: An Assessment of Conceptual Frameworks', paper presented to The Australian Sociological Association. Available at: http://www.tasa.org.au/uploads/2008/12/Connolly-Julie_-Whitehouse-Gillian.pdf (accessed 03.12.2012).

Council of the European Union (2012) *Third Report on the Social Impact of the Economic Crisis and Ongoing Fiscal Consolidation,* in T.S.P. Committee (ed.) Brussels: Directorate-General Economic Affairs and Competitiveness DG G 2B. Available at: http://bookshop.europa.eu/en/the-social-impact-of-the-economic-crisis-and-ongoing-fiscal-consolidation-pbKE3112594/ (accessed 03.12.2012).

Crouch, C. (1999) *Social Change in Western Europe,* Oxford: Oxford University Press.

Dale, A. and Holdsworth, C. (1998) 'Why Don't Minority Ethnic Women in Britain Work Part-time?', in J. O'Reilly and C. Fagan (eds) *Part-time Prospects,* London: Routledge, 77–95.

Deakin, S. (2000) 'The Many Futures of the Contract of Employment', *ESRC Centre of Business Research Working Paper no. 191*, Cambridge. Available at: http://ideas.repec. org/p/cbr/cbrwps/wp191.html (accessed 03.12.2012).

Deakin, S. and McLaughlin, C. (2012) 'Equal Pay, Litigation Strategies, and the Limits of the Law', Paper presented to the ESRC Seminar 'What is Fair Pay?' University of Brighton, 9 November. Available at: http://www.brighton.ac.uk/bbs/research/esrc2012/ fairpay.php (accessed 03.12.2012).

Doogan, K. (2009) *New Capitalism? The Transformation of Work*, Cambridge: Polity Press.

Duncan, S. (2005) 'Mothering, Class and Rationality', *The Sociological Review*, 53(1): 50–76.

Emmenegger, P., Häusermann, S., Palier, B. and Seeleib-Kaiser, M. (eds) (2012) *The Age of Dualization: The Changing Face of Inequality in Deindustrializing Societies,* Oxford: Oxford University Press.

Esping-Andersen, G. (2002) *Why We Need a New Welfare State,* Oxford: Oxford University Press.

Fouquet, A., Gauvin, A. and Letablier, M.-T. (2002) *Des Contrats Sociaux entre les Sexes Différents Selon les Pays de l'Union Européenne*, Paris: Conseil d'Analyse Economique.

Fraser, N. (1997) 'Beyond the Master/Subject Model: On Carole Pateman's *The Sexual Contract*' in N. Fraser, *Justice Interruptus: Critical Reflections on the 'Postsocialist' Condition,* New York and London: Routledge, 225–35.

Fraser, N. (2011) 'Between Marketisation and Social Protection: Ambivalences of Feminism in the Context of Capitalist Crisis' Online lecture. Available at: http://www.crassh.cam. ac.uk/events/1536/ (accessed 03.12.2012).

Fraser, N. and Gordon, L. (1994) '"Dependency" Demystified: Inscriptions of Power in a Keyword of the Welfare State', *Social Politics: International Studies in Gender, State and Society*, 1(1): 4–32.

Gallino, L. and Borgna, P. (2012) *La Lotta di Classe dopo la Lotta di Classe*, Bari: Laterza.

Gottfried, H. (2009) 'Japan: The Reproductive Bargain and the Making of Precarious Employment' in L. Vosko, I. Campbell and M. MacDonald (eds) *Gender and the Contours of Precarious Employment*, New York: Routledge.

-- (2013) *Gender, Work and Economy: Unpacking the Global Economy*, Cambridge: Polity Press.

Gregg, P. and Wadsworth, J. (2011) 'Workless Households', in P. Gregg and J. Wadsworth (eds), *The Labour Market in Winter: The State of Working Britain*, Oxford: Oxford University Press.

Gregg, P., Scutella, R. and Wadsworth, J. (2010) 'Reconciling Workless Measures at the Individual and Household Level. Theory and Evidence from the United States, Britain, Germany, Spain and Australia', *Journal of Population Economics*, 23(1): 139–67.

Grimshaw, D. and Rubery, J. (1998) 'Integrating the Internal and External Labour Markets', *Cambridge Journal of Economics*, 22(2): 199–220.

Heery, E. and Salmon, J. (eds) (2000) *The Insecure Workforce*, London: Routledge.

Hirdman, Y. (1998) 'Social Policy and Gender Contracts: The Swedish Experience' in E. Drew, R. Emerek and E. Mahon, E. *Women, Work and the Family in Europe,* London: Routledge, 36–46.

HMSO (1999) *A New Contract for Welfare: Safeguarding Social Security*, in Department of Social Security (ed): HMSO Stationery Office Books.

Hogarth, T., Owen, D., Gambin, L., Hasluck, C., Lyonette, C. and Casey, B. (2009) 'The Equality Impacts of the Current Recession', *Equality and Human Rights Commission Research Report 47*, Manchester: EHRC.

Humphries, J. and Rubery, J. (1984) 'The Reconstitution of the Supply Side of the Labour Market: The Relative Autonomy of Social Reproduction', *Cambridge Journal of Economics*, 8(4): 331–47.

Ingold, J. (2011) 'An International Comparison of Approaches to Assisting Partnered Women into Work', *Department for Work and Pensions Working Paper No 101*, Sheffield: DWP. Available at: http://research.dwp.gov.uk/asd/asd5/rrs-index.asp (accessed 03.12.2012).

Laufer, J. (1998) 'Equal Opportunity between Men and Women: The Case of France', *Feminist Economics*, 4(1): 53–69.

Kerr, C. (1954) 'The Balkanisation of Labor Markets', in E.W. Bakke and P.M. Hauser (eds) *Labour Mobility and Economic Opportunity*, New York: MIT Press. Reproduced in Kerr, C. (1977) *Labor Markets and Wage Determination: The Balkanization of Labor Markets and Other Essays*, University of California Press: Berkeley and Los Angeles.

Koven, S. and Michel, S. (1993) *Mothers of a New World: Maternalist Politics and the Origins of Welfare States*, New York: Routledge.

Krizsan, A., Skjeie, H. and Squires, J. (2012) *Institutionalizing Intersectionality: The Changing Nature of European Equality Regimes*, Houndsmills Basingstoke: Palgrave Macmillan.

Leira, A. (2002) 'Updating the Gender Contract? Childcare Reforms in the Nordic Countries in the 1990s', *NORA – Nordic Journal of Feminist and Gender Research*, 10(2): 81–9.

Lewis, J. (2002) 'Individualisation, Assumptions About the Existence of an Adult Worker Model and the Shift towards Contractualism', in A.H. Carling, S. Duncan and R. Edwards (eds) *Analysing Families: Morality and Rationality in Policy and Practice*, London: Routledge.

Lewis, J., Knijn, T., Martin, C. and Ostner, I. (2008) 'Patterns of Development in Work/Family Reconciliation Policies for Parents in France, Germany, the Netherlands, and the UK in the 2000s', *Social Politics*, 15(3): 261–86.

McBride, D. and Mazur, A.G. (2010) *The Politics of State Feminism: Innovation in Comparative Research*, Philadelphia: Temple University Press.

McGinnity, F. and Whelan, C.T. (2009) 'Comparing Work-Life Conflict in Europe: Evidence from the European Social Survey', *Social Indicators Research*, 93: 433–44.

McRobbie, A. (2007) 'Top Girls?' *Cultural Studies*, 21(4): 718–37.

Myrdal, A. and Klein, V. (1956) *Women's Two Roles*, New York: Humanities Press.

Naumann, I.K. (2005) 'Child Care and Feminism in West Germany and Sweden in the 1960s and 1970s', *Journal of European Social Policy*, 15(1): 47–63.

Nazio, T. (2008a) *Cohabitation Family and Society: European Experiences*, London and New York: Routledge.

—— (2008b) *Are Storks Striking for a Contract Renewal? Childbirth under Changing Employment, Family and Welfare Arrangements: Full Research Report*, ESRC Available at: http://www.esrc.ac.uk/my-esrc/grants/RES-061-23-0127/read (accessed 20.05.2012).

Nazio, T. and O'Reilly, J. (forthcoming) 'Household Transitions in Europe' working paper available from the authors.

O'Reilly, J. (1994) 'What Flexibility do Women Offer? Comparing the Use of, and Attitudes to, Part-time Work in Britain and France in Retail Banking', *Gender, Work and Organization* 1(3): 138–49.

—— (2003) *Regulating Working Time Transitions in Europe*, Cheltenham: Edward Elgar.

O'Reilly, J. and Bothfeld, S. (2002) 'What Happens After Working Part-time? Integration, Maintenance or Exclusionary Transitions in Britain and Western Germany', *Cambridge Journal of Economics*, 26(4): 409–39.

O'Reilly, J. and Fagan, C. (1998) *Part-time Prospects: International Comparisons of Part-time Work in Europe, North America and the Pacific Rim*, London: Routledge.

O'Reilly, J., Nazio, T. and Roche, J. (2014) 'Compromising Conventions: Attitudes to Maternal Employment in Europe', *Work, Employment and Society*, forthcoming.

O'Reilly, J. and Spee, C. (1998) 'The Future Regulation of Work and Welfare: Time for a Revised Social and Gender Contract?', *European Journal of Industrial Relations*, 4(3): 259–81.

Orloff, A.S. (2006) 'From Maternalism to "Employment for all:" State Policies to Promote Women's Employment Across the Affluent Democracies', in J. Levy (ed) *The State after Statism*, Cambridge: Harvard University Press.

Pateman, C. (1988) *The Sexual Contract*, Cambridge: Polity Press.

—— (1989) *The Disorder of Women: Democracy, Feminism, and Political Theory*, Cambridge: Polity Press.

Pateman, C. and Mills, C. (2007) *Contract and Domination*, Cambridge: Polity Press.

Pearson, R. (1997) 'Renegotiating the Reproductive Bargain: Gender Analysis of Economic Transition in Cuba in the 1990s', *Development and Change*, 28(4): 671–70.

Polanyi, K. (1957) *The Great Transformation: The Political and Economic Origins of our Time*, Boston: Beacon Press.

Puchacz, K. (2010) *In the Search for Social Justice: Social Citizenship and the New Gender Contract. Case Study of Sweden*, Saarbrucken: Lambert Academic Publishing AG.

Reich, M. (ed) (2009) *Segmented Labor Markets and Labor Mobility*, Cheltenham: Edward Elgar.

Rousseau, J.J. (1911) *Emile*, translated by B. Foxley, London: J.M. Dent & Sons Ltd.

Rubery, J. (1978) 'Structured Labour Markets, Worker Organisation and Low Pay', *Cambridge Journal of Economics*, 2(1): 17–36.

—— (1988) *Women and Recession*, London: Routledge.

—— (2011a) 'Reconstruction Amid Deconstruction: Or Why We Need More of the Social in European Social Models', *Work, Employment and Society*, 25(4): 658–74.

—— (2011b) 'Gender and Regulation: The Use and Misuse of the Gender Equality Cause', Regulating for Decent Work Conference ILO, Geneva, July.

—— (this volume) 'Women and Recession: A Framework for Analysis'.

Rubery, J., Smith, M. and Fagan, C. (1999) *Women's Employment in Europe: Trends and Prospects*, London and New York: Routledge.

Sands, D. (2012) *The Impact of Austerity on Women. Fawcett Society Policy Briefing*, London: Fawcett Society.

Saraceno, C. and Keck, W. (2010) 'Can We Identify Intergenerational Policy Regimes in Europe?' *European Societies*, 12(5): 675–96.

Saraceno, C. and Keck, W. (2011) 'Towards an Integrated Approach for the Analysis of Gender Equity in Policies Supporting Paid Work and Care Responsibilities', *Demographic Research*, 25(11): 371–406.

Schmid, G. (2008) *Full Employment in Europe: Managing Labour Market Transitions and Risks*, Cheltenham: Edward Elgar.

Skocpol, T. (1995) *Protecting Soldiers and Mothers: The Political Origins of Social Policy in the United States*, Cambridge: Belknap Press.

Standing, G. (2011) *The Precariat: The New Dangerous Class*, London and New York: Bloomsbury.

Streeck, W. (2010) 'E Pluribus Unum? Varieties and Commonalities of Capitalism', *Max Plank Institute for the Study of Societies (MPIfG) Discussion Paper No. 10/12*.

Supiot, A. (2001) *Beyond Employment: Changes in Work and the Future of Labour Law in Europe*, Oxford: Oxford University Press.

Tilly, L. and Scott, J. (1978) *Women, Work and Family*, New York: Holt, Rinehart and Winston.

TUC (2010) *The Gender Impact of the Cuts, TUC Cuts Briefing*, London: TUC. Available at: http://www.tuc.org.uk/extras/genderimpactofthecuts.pdf (accessed 03.12.2012).

TUC (2011) *The Gender Impact of the Cuts – A Year on. TUC Cuts Briefing*, London: TUC. Available at: http://www.tuc.org.uk/tucfiles/163/GenderImpactofCutsrevisited.pdf (accessed 03.12.2012).

Vosko, L. (2011) *Managing the Margins: Gender, Citizenship, and the International Regulation of Precarious Employment,* Oxford: Oxford University Press.

Warren, T. (2000) 'Diverse Breadwinner Models: A Couple-based Analysis of Gendered Working Time in Britain and Denmark', *Journal of European Social Policy,* 10(4): 349–71.

Weinkopf, C. (2009) 'Germany: Precarious Employment and the Rise of Mini-jobs', in L.F. Vosko, M. MacDonald and I. Campbell (eds) *Gender and the Contours of Precarious Employment,* London and New York: Routledge.

Wilthagen, T. (1998) 'Flexicurity: A New Paradigm for Labour Market Policy Reform?' in WZB (ed) *WZB Discussion Paper FS I, 98-202,* Berlin. Available at: http://papers.ssrn.com/sol3/papers.cfm?abstract_id=1133924 (accessed 03.12.2012).

PART II

Recession and austerity: experiences in the EU and selected country cases

4

WOMEN AND MEN IN THE 'GREAT EUROPEAN RECESSION'[1]

Francesca Bettio and Alina Verashchagina

Introduction

At the time of writing (November 2012) about four and a half years have passed since the 'Great Recession' officially began in Europe. The recession is still in process, with the latest statistics having recently certified that the Eurozone entered a second output dip while employment in the EU as a whole is still hovering around bottom values since 2008. Any assessment of the impact of the recession is thus bound to be a provisional exercise. It is especially provisional from the gender and labour market perspective adopted in this chapter, since the second employment dip is being driven by the so-called fiscal consolidation of public budgets which is feared to disproportionately affect female labour but whose effects have not yet fully materialized.

Our main goal here is a stock-taking exercise of how recession and recovery – the crisis for short – impacted on labour market outcomes for men and women, and on gender equality in employment in Europe. Any such exercise, however, must rely on theory for interpretation. We shall accordingly review facts and theories with a primary interest in narrating facts and a parallel interest in gauging the adequacy of theories.

This interweaving of facts and theories is condensed into three headline stories. The first such story is about the downward levelling of the most important gender gaps in the labour market (with the exception of the gap in unpaid housework and care). These key developments raise questions about the role that occupational segregation has played in sheltering women's jobs and pay from the worst effects of the recession.

The second headline story is that the recession appears to have accelerated change in women's income role within households, frequently even turning them into the sole breadwinner. Important questions here concern the relevance of the so-called 'added worker effect' versus the 'discouraged worker effect', the reluctance of women to exit the labour market and disappear into inactivity.

The final story documents the demise of the buffer role myth as applied to the female labour supply and relies on a revised version of the segmentation hypothesis to identify the buffers of this crisis, young workers on temporary contracts, both women and men, and migrant workers, especially third country nationals.

Theories are briefly reviewed in the first section. Each of the three sections that follow discusses one headline story. The final section briefly concludes with some lessons that can be drawn from this crisis. These lessons concern the fruitfulness of the different theories when faced with the facts, the difference between those risks that were widely anticipated with regard to women's labour market position and those that actually materialized, as well as the need to revise conventional ways of measuring and monitoring progress in gender equality within the labour market.

Economic theory before this crisis

Economic theorizing about the gender impact of recession and recovery can be summarized into two oppositions. With respect to the behaviour of male and female labour supply, we have the added versus the discouraged worker effect. With respect to male and female employment trends, we have women acting as a buffer versus women as a group protected from volatility due to occupational segregation.

The added versus discouraged controversy dates back to the 'Great Depression' of 1929, but has regained the limelight in the so-called 'Great Recession' that we are currently experiencing. Aldrich Finegan and Margo (1993: 1) have summarized the arguments in contention:

> According to W.S. Woytinsky, the depression created a large population of 'added' workers, persons who entered the labour force when the head of the household was thrown out of work. Woytinsky suggested, however, that added workers would leave the labour force as recovery progressed in the late 1930s so that 'the number of jobs necessary to reduce unemployment … [was] less than the reported volume of unemployment would suggest'. Disagreeing with Woytinsky, Clarence Long asserted that the number of added workers was negligible compared with the number of 'discouraged' workers – 'persons who would enter the labour market only when unemployment began to fall […]'.

If the added worker effect prevails, women's behaviour is counter-cyclical, and results in increased activity (labour market participation) during a recession. If the discouraged worker effect is dominant, inactivity increases. In both cases it is workers' behaviour – that is, the supply side – that drives the outcome.

In alternative theorizing, employers' behaviour – the demand side – is deemed more important, and the focus is on employment and unemployment, rather than on flows to and from inactivity. The labour reserve or *buffer hypothesis* is a case in point. It is rooted in Marxian theory and, like the added/discouraged worker effect, posits a male breadwinner economy. The claim, however, is that women constitute a labour reserve that is pushed back by employers when demand slows down, and called out when demand is booming.[2]

The buffer role for women has been revisited by the proponents of the segmentation hypothesis. Here the important divide is not so much between male and female labour but rather between primary and secondary jobs. Women are confined to the secondary job segment, alongside ethnic minorities and other groups. Depending on the theoretical variant, the dividing line between primary and secondary is rooted in employers' reliance on 'internal market' rules for the workers they are interested in retaining – the skilled, primary segments – while unskilled, secondary segments face ruthless competition in an unregulated labour market (Doeringer and Piore 1971); or else it may rest on employers' tendency to hire women to do unstable jobs because they are socially more 'disposable' (Edwards *et al.* 1975) or on the unions' fight against de-skilling (Rubery 1978; Wilkinson 1981). The predictions common to all these variants are limited competition between and limited mobility across the segments, with the secondary segment playing a buffer role in a recession.

On the contrary, says the gender segregation hypothesis, female employment may be sheltered in a crisis (Milkman 1976). The core argument is that sex-typing of occupations is widespread, takes time to change and, where change takes place, it may result in re-segregation of new occupations rather than merely de-segregation of older ones. As a result the comparative volatility of female employment over the cycle is not determined a priori but is strongly affected by the sectoral and occupational patterns of employment losses and gains (Bettio 1988). Segregation also affects the gender pay gap in a recession as, for example, male wages may be higher (lower) than average in the most cyclically sensitive occupations and sectors, and vice versa.

It is tempting to dismiss all these hypotheses as 'obsolete'. One reason for possible obsolescence is the assumption of the male breadwinner economy that many of them share, especially the added/discouraged worker debate and the buffer role hypothesis. A male breadwinner economy no longer reflects reality. Moreover, unemployment benefits and other income cushioning provisions are now far more common during a recession than they were in the past, which may specifically weaken possible added worker effects particularly if there are elements of household means testing determining benefit levels. Also trade union membership is still male dominated, but less so than in the past,[3] and education and skill are no longer male prerogatives, with both developments detracting from the strength of the original segmentation theory. Last but not least, occupational and sectoral segregation still shapes the allocation of jobs to men and women, but much less so than in the 1960s or 70s.

Yet the hypotheses retain relevance. Consider gender income roles. In 2007, just before the recession set in, on average 70 out of 100 couples with at least one working-age partner were dual-earning in the 24 countries fearuring in the EU-SILC survey (see Table 4.2). While this can be read as the demise of the male breadwinner era, in the majority of dual-earner couples the woman's contribution is lower than her partner's (less than 45 per cent of the combined income of the couple), perhaps not so low as to qualify all these couples as 'one and a half earners', but low enough to qualify the female partners as 'secondary' earners (European Commission 2011a: Figure 3). Hence there are enough secondary earners and non-earners among women to allow for an added worker effect if the latter is redefined to encompass new entries into employment but also those working longer hours.

In regard to unemployment benefits, most European countries operate some income support schemes, but coverage may be selective or replacement rates low, depending on the country (see, among others, Figari *et al.* 2010). This leaves scope for the added worker effect (or for discouragement). In regard to occupational segregation, a long-term decline has been documented in most of the countries for which appropriate evidence is available (Bettio 2008). However, current levels are still high across European countries and the declining trend has apparently halted in the European Union as a whole over the past decade (Bettio and Verashchagina 2009). Hence segregation can still play a protective role.

The idea of segmentation has also come back in fashion as a tool for analyzing the repercussions of the present crisis. In recent theorizing, however, segmentation opposes 'protected' labour segments with 'unprotected' ones (Bentolila and Bertola 1990; Boeri and Garibaldi 2007). The basic idea is that if differential employment protection is granted, particularly against dismissal, the disparity in bargaining power between 'insiders' in a firm (tenured/adult/skilled workers) and 'outsiders' (younger/untenured/in need of training) can be reinforced by legislation. Women are sometimes included among the 'outsiders' because of their more frequent exits and entries into the labour market. But they are also part of the insiders, e.g. because they tend to be well represented among (tenured) public employees. When a downturn strikes, the groups with less employment protection are the natural candidates for a buffer role, men and women alike.

How do these hypotheses perform in the light of the current recession? In what follows we do not formally test each or even some of them, but the evidence we gather suggests that the segregation and the segmentation hypotheses remain fertile. By contrast, there has been sufficient change in women's income role and labour market integration to limit the occurrence of large added worker effects while definitely undermining the buffer role hypothesis.

The levelling of the gender gaps and the role of occupational segregation

Stylized facts about unemployment, pay, employment and unpaid work

In the first quarter of 2012 the male unemployment rate in the EU as a whole rose above the female rate in anticipation of the second dip in employment. Such reversal of the gender unemployment gap has occurred more than once since the crisis began, but each time this happened it attracted attention from the media because of the symbolic as well as the concrete message it conveyed. It may in fact be considered emblematic of the first headline story of this crisis, namely *the downward levelling of gender gaps*. Practically all the principal gaps were levelled downward – that in employment beside that in unemployment, but also the pay gap, the inactivity gap and the poverty gap. The basic facts are reported below.

Unemployment

Female unemployment was somewhat higher than male unemployment in the EU27 at the start of the recession in 2008 (7.4 per cent versus 6.4 per cent: see Figure 4.1) but proved to be stickier thereafter as it experienced a less sharp increase in the downturn compared to male unemployment but also slightly slower re-absorption where and when recovery set in. Hence the repeated reversal of the gender unemployment gap that we have just noted, including the latest episode

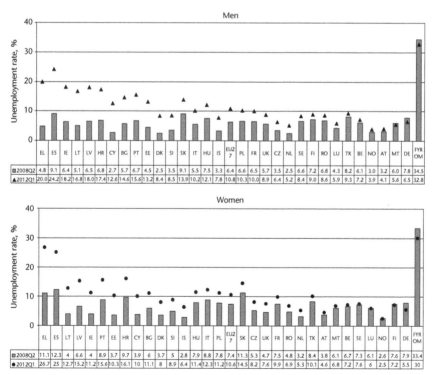

FIGURE 4.1 Unemployment rates by sex for the EU27 and 32 European countries 2008–2012

Note: countries are ordered by increase in unemployment.

Source: Eurostat data, own elaborations. Reproduced from Bettio *et al.* (2013: Figure 1.3).

at the time of writing when the rate for men reached 10.8 per cent as compared with 10.6 per cent for women (Figure 4.1).

The top ten countries for percentage point increases in unemployment from the onset of the recession are the same for men and women: Greece, Spain, Ireland, Lithuania, Latvia, Croatia, Cyprus, Bulgaria, Portugal and Estonia. In many of these countries output contractions were also among the largest. Although the vast majority of countries witnessed a greater increase for men, the exceptions are worth noting. In Greece, Malta, Romania and Turkey, unemployment among women grew more in percentage terms. While the impact of the recession was rather uneven in these countries, all of them score below the EU27 average for level of female employment. This sends out a warning that the crisis may have curtailed women's job opportunities more where these were lower to start with. At the same time, it also indicates that even in low-opportunity countries, women held on to the labour market rather than behaving as buffers. We shall come back to this last point later.

Employment

In Europe as a whole (EU27) male employment dropped earlier in the recession and faster. Between 2008 and 2012 (second and first quarter, respectively) men's employment rate went down from 73.3 per cent to 69.1 per cent. The fall in the female rate was more contained, from 59.2 per cent to 58.2 per cent. Again, country patterns differ. In no member state except Germany had the female or male employment rate recovered their respective pre-recession peaks by early 2012.[4] Also, a marked north-west versus south-east divide can be observed between i) countries showing signs of some recovery with respect to the lowest point reached in the first downturn ('trough' value); and ii) countries where employment never stopped declining[5] or declined again towards a second 'trough'. Nine countries belong in this second group as far as female employment is concerned – Bulgaria, Croatia, Cyprus, Greece, Denmark, Ireland, Portugal, Spain and the UK – the number of countries being higher for male employment (Figure 4.2).

Inactivity

Many more women than men were inactive before the crisis, and the disproportion remained throughout the crisis, but with a lower gender inactivity gap. As a combined result of employment and unemployment patterns, inactivity has risen among men as a result of the crisis and declined (slightly) among women. In early 2012 men had not yet regained their pre-recession rate of economic activity, while a slight increase had taken place for women.

For obvious reasons, it is the segment of the inactive comprising young men and women neither in education nor in training – the so called NEETs – that attracts policy attention. Again, the proportion of female NEETs in the population aged 15 to 24 was and remained higher than the corresponding proportion among men. It is nevertheless noticeable that, due to the rise in male inactivity, the opposite was

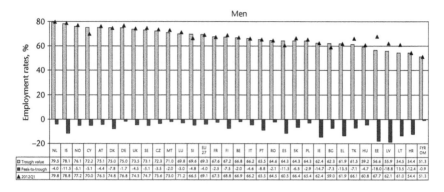

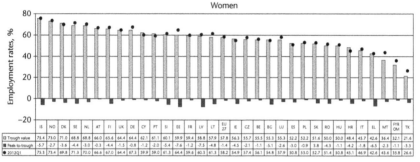

FIGURE 4.2 Peak-to-trough and trough-to-2012Q1 variations in employment by sex for the EU27 and 32 European countries

Note: sorted by the 'trough' value.

Source: Eurostat data, own elaborations.

true for 11 countries in 2010, the very depth of the crisis (Eurofound 2011: Fig. 3, p. 3).

Pay

Earnings decreased for men and women, because jobs were lost, hours were reduced (often as a job preserving measure), bonuses were cut or, more generally, because wage competition sharpened. In relative terms, however, female earnings decreased less and actual pay cuts were less common.[6] In 2010 the gender pay gap (GPG) in unadjusted form stood at 16.4 percentage points in the EU as a whole, down from 17.6 in 2007.[7]

The decline was observed in the majority of member countries. According to Eurostat data the unadjusted GPG went down between 2007 and 2010 in 16 out of 25 member countries for which data are available, with the largest reductions (between 3 and 5 per cent) in Lithuania, the Netherlands and Slovenia, moderate reductions in Denmark, Cyprus, Malta, Poland, Sweden, the Slovak Republic and the UK, and a less than 1 per cent decline in Belgium, France, Finland, Luxembourg, Romania and Spain. In four of these countries – the UK, the Slovak Republic,

Romania and Spain – a pre-recession declining trend is observable from 2002. According to national level data, however, the list of countries witnessing a decline in the unadjusted GPG is longer. National sources indicate a decrease for Norway[8] and for two countries for which Eurostat data are not available, Croatia and Estonia (Bettio *et al.* 2013: Table 2.2).[9]

Poverty

Income poverty is, and remains, more widespread among women, but in the two initial years of the recession (2008–9, the latest available) the increase was more or less equally shared, with men suffering marginally more. One reliable measure of income poverty for the purpose of comparisons over time is the at-risk-of-poverty-rate (ARPR) anchored at a fixed point in time; i.e. an individual is considered as poor if his or her income falls below the poverty line applied to a specific year in the past. Currently, Eurostat sets 2005 as the reference year. In the first two years of the crisis a considerable increase of the risk of poverty emerged in a number of countries (Bettio *et al.* 2013: Table 5.3). At the EU27 level, the ARPR grew by 1.7 per cent among women and by 2.3 per cent among men. Developments in severe material deprivation in the first two years of the crisis depict a similar picture[10]: women suffer from greater material deprivation and the crisis slowed down progress towards reducing it while also narrowing the gender gap. Again, there is considerable heterogeneity across countries.

A notable exception to the generalized tendency towards smaller gaps concerns *unpaid work*. Unpaid housework and care are likely to have gone up and women are likely to have shouldered the largest increase, with a consequent widening of the gender gap. Within the EU, household expenditure dropped between 2008 and 2009 in three categories of goods and services for which unpaid work may provide a good substitute: catering, goods and services for routine household maintenance, and outpatient services. Although the order of magnitude differs, the majority of countries that were experiencing recession in 2009 recorded lower purchases under these categories, thereby establishing the possibility of an increase in unpaid work. Selective support comes from time use surveys conducted before and during the crisis. In Italy, redistribution of unpaid work towards men and away from women was greater in the 1990s and early 2000s than it was between 2002/3 and 2008/9, which may reflect the fact that housework increased even at the beginning of the recession, and more so for women. Spain is also witnessing a tendency for unpaid work to be redistributed among the sexes, and the comparison between time use survey results for 2003 and 2010 is consistent with the possibility that the crisis slowed down progress in such redistribution. The evidence for Turkey is more conclusive. Based on the latest time use survey, unpaid work was forecast to rise during the recession, with the increase accruing disproportionally to women. Admittedly, however, the evidence remains slim, overall.[11]

How sectoral and occupational segregation matters

Across countries, exposure to the employment fallout of female and male workers differed primarily because of the sheltering role played by occupational and sectoral segregation. When the recession first struck, output and employment contractions were larger in those countries where industry, construction and selected financial branches were hit the most. Since women are consistently under-represented in these sectors, their comparative vulnerability was lower. In the jobless and uncertain recovery that followed, female employment was relatively sheltered by comparatively rigid demand in sectors like social and health care, or even education.

How solid is the evidence that employment segregation actually limited job losses for women? And did it also protect women's wages, thus contributing to the narrowing of all gender gaps? In what follows we garner some evidence in both respects.

Employment segregation and relative employment fallout

We first conduct a simple exercise to ascertain how strongly within-country gender differences in employment variations in the downturn correlate with the level of segregation. The higher the degree of protection that segregation affords female employment in a country, the larger the expected difference from male employment. Of course, the correlation is meaningful as long as patterns of sectoral segregation are similar across countries, which is broadly confirmed by recent research (Bettio and Verashchagina 2009).

For this purpose, employment vulnerability is measured by peak-to-trough declines in the employment rate in the downturn, and comparative vulnerability is defined as the difference between the decline in the male and in the female rates (Table 4.1, columns 1, 2 and 3). The cross-country correlation between the comparative vulnerability and the 2009 IP segregation index turns out to be equal to 0.50 for sectoral segregation and 0.40 for occupational segregation, with both values displaying statistical significance at the conventional 5 per cent level (Table 4.1). Although caution is demanded in assessing correlations, as they need not indicate causality, the results conform to the experience of past recessions when over-representation in certain service occupations and the public sector worked in favour of women in a number of countries (Rubery 1988).

Three important qualifications must be made which limit the significance of this result. The first is methodological and involves the distinction between cycle and trend. In any given employment branch or occupation, female employment may be protected because the underlying labour demand trend is strong enough to offset greater vulnerability to the cyclical swings or because the specific branch or occupation is intrinsically less exposed to cyclical swings; or both. The original hypothesis about segregation[12] focused on *cyclical* vulnerability, i.e. distinguished between cycle and trend whereas no such distinction is made here. This would require a more refined analysis that is outside the scope of this chapter.

TABLE 4.1 Employment vulnerability in the downturn for the EU27

Country	Employment peak-to-trough variations, MEN(1)	Employment peak-to-trough variations, WOMEN(2)	Absolute gender difference in employment peak-to-trough variations (3)=(1)–(2)	IP index of occupational segregation, 2009(4)	IP index of sectoral segregation, 2009(5)	Employment/output elasticity peak-to-trough, MEN(6)	Employment/output elasticity peak-to-trough, WOMEN(7)
AT	4.4	0.3	4.1	26.1	19.53	0.828	0.056
BE	2.0	1.1	0.9	25.5	19.58	0.469	0.258
BG	7.3	5.1	2.2	29.4	21.84	0.823	0.575
CY	5.1	1.2	3.9	29	19.72	1.707	0.402
CZ	3.5	2.1	1.4	28	20.69	0.594	0.356
DE	1.7	0.8	0.9	26.2	19.46	0.250	0.118
DK	7.8	3.6	4.2	25.5	19.71	0.964	0.445
EE	18.0	7.6	10.4	31.8	25.36	0.942	0.398
EL	13.5	6.5	7	22	16.02	1.345	0.648
ES	11.5	3.0	8.5	27	20.84	2.147	0.560
FI	7.5	4.4	3.1	29.3	24.15	0.726	0.426
FR	2.5	1.2	1.3	26	19.02	0.582	0.279
HU	4.7	1.1	3.6	28.4	20.84	0.564	0.132
IE	14.7	4.5	10.2	27	22.13	1.365	0.418
IT	4.6	1.8	2.8	24.4	19.76	0.654	0.256
LT	13.5	4.8	8.7	29.2	22.67	0.849	0.302
LU	3.0	2.6	0.4	23.7	16.48	0.384	0.333
LV	18.8	7.5	11.3	28.5	23.58	0.787	0.314

TABLE 4.1 Employment vulnerability in the downturn for the EU27. (*Continued*)

Country	Employment peak-to-trough variations, MEN(1)	Employment peak-to-trough variations, WOMEN(2)	Absolute gender difference in employment peak-to-trough variations (3)=(1)−(2)	IP index of occupational segregation, 2009(4)	IP index of sectoral segregation, 2009(5)	Employment/output elasticity peak-to-trough, MEN(6)	Employment/output elasticity peak-to-trough, WOMEN(7)
MT	2.0	2.3	0.3	23.4	16.35	0.437	0.503
NL	4.0	3.0	1	24.9	18.73	0.793	0.595
PL	2.9	0.9	2	26.2	20.62	6.924	2.149
PT	8.8	2.0	6.8	27.1	21.61	1.368	0.311
RO	2.1	4.3	2.2	23.1	17.26	0.243	0.498
SE	5.1	4.4	0.7	26.1	21.86	0.689	0.594
SI	4.8	5.4	0.6	26.1	18.53	0.503	0.566
SK	6.5	3.8	2.7	30.4	24.63	0.773	0.452
UK	4.5	1.5	3	24.7	19.47	0.717	0.239
EU 27	**4.0**	**1.4**	**2.6**	**25.8**	**19.83**	**0.706**	**0.247**
Correlation Columns 3 and 4	0.40						
Correlation Columns 3 and 5	0.50						
Correlation Columns 6 and 7	0.90						

Source: Eurostat data, own elaboration.

The second qualification is that, while the distribution of feminized and male-dominated jobs across sectors and branches ensured comparative employment stability at the aggregate, national level, this was not necessarily the case within each sector, branch or occupation. A case in point is manufacturing. In this male-dominated branch the overall employment declined across all member countries except Malta and Luxembourg between 2008 and 2012 (second and first quarter, respectively) as well as in the first downturn (2008–10, second quarter). In 15 of the member countries experiencing a decline, women lost proportionately more jobs during both periods.[13]

The third qualification is that segregation may matter for female (or male) employment within each country, but across countries national labour market specificities may play an important role. For example, if the response of male employment in a given country is much higher than EU average this is also likely to hold for female employment responsiveness, although the latter may be lower than the former. Employment responsiveness to output variations is measured by elasticity,[14] and Table 4.1 sets out peak-to-trough employment elasticities for men in column 6 and for women in column 7. The cross-country correlation between the two sets of elasticities is very strong (0.91) indicating that country effects may be large.

Employment segregation and relative pay for women

Unless we believe that wages are fully flexible, the fact that men lost comparatively more jobs than women need not necessarily lead to a relative fall in men's to women's hourly wages although this was what happened in practice.[15] Employment segregation may, in fact, institute a link between the two, for example if the female-dominated sectors that are shielded from the employment fallout are also those where gender disparities are weaker (and conversely). Available evidence indicates that segregation may have contributed to the narrowing of the GPG in some countries but not in others.

Three factors have contributed to the decline in the GPG: cuts in the non basic wage components of pay packets, sectoral segregation and policy-related developments such as ongoing programmes to reduce the GPG. Research using the EU-SILC survey for Belgium indicates that wage reductions typically originate from cuts to the more volatile component of pay packets, those 'extra' payments that include bonuses, premiums for overtime and the like. All these typically weigh more on men's pay and tend to be found more frequently in male-dominated employment sectors. Subjective evaluation by labour market experts in a variety of European countries supports the findings for Belgium.[16] Thus segregation may have eased the levelling downward of gender pay disparities, albeit indirectly.

In some instances segregation had a direct impact, one such case being Croatia. Here, the GPG would have declined by 0.2 points in 2009 had the sectoral distribution of employment remained the same as in 2008 (the start of the recession) whereas the actual decline totalled 0.6 points. The order of magnitude is inevitably small as the decline spans one year only, but the implication is that segregation accounted for the lion's share.[17] However, a different result was found for Belgium where the wage gap would have declined by 0.7 percentage points had the sectoral composition of employment remained unchanged from 2007; this is practically the same decline that actually took place. Further research is clearly needed to ascertain whether sectoral/occupational segregation had a significant, direct impact on the narrowing of the gender gap in other European countries.

Women's income role in this recession and the added versus discouraged worker effects

The second headline story coming out of the present Great Recession is that it is likely to accelerate transition to a co-primary income role for women. The critical numbers in the story are as follows. In 2007, just before the crisis struck, dual-earner couples accounted for 74.1 per cent[18] of all couples with at least one working-age partner in the 24 European countries included in the SILC survey (simple average). The pure 'male' breadwinner typology, where only 'he' earns, made up a little over one-fifth of the total (21 per cent), while female breadwinner couples accounted for a 4.9 per cent share. By (the end of) 2009, dual-earner couples had lost considerable ground (-5.1 per cent), mainly to the benefit of female breadwinner couples (+4.7 per cent), while male breadwinner couples more or less retained their share (+0.4 per cent). This shift towards female breadwinner couples was more pronounced in some of the countries worst and first hit by the crisis – mainly the Baltic countries (Estonia, Latvia and Lithuania).

To what extent do the additional female breadwinners represent added workers, i.e. new entries into employment of previously inactive women as opposed to working women who managed to retain their job while their partner lost his? In each country the loss in share of dual-earner households was very similar to the gain in share of female breadwinner households, suggesting that the second alternative is more plausible. However, added worker effects cannot be ruled out.

Qualified support for added worker effects comes from some research to investigate why inactivity went down for women in the EU27 while increasing for men (see section above). Thus the 2011–12 edition of *Labour Market Developments in Europe* (European Commission 2011b: Box 1.1.1, Table 2, p. 11) reported evidence of an added worker effect among married women with children, as the theory predicts, but the analysis was conducted at the EU level while confirmation would be needed at a country level for conclusive proof. Ghignoni and Verashchagina (2012) investigated the issue for Italy, but their results are mixed. They found that the added worker hypothesis holds for the Central and Southern regions of the country, but not for Northern regions where women's labour market participation is not too dissimilar from that of an average European woman. We may therefore speculate that an added worker effect has shown up at the aggregate European level primarily thanks to what happened in some low female employment countries. But the actual order of magnitude may be modest.

TABLE 4.2 Couples by partner's income role in 24 European countries, share of the total in 2009 and percentage change 2007–2009

Country	2009			2007–2009 (%)		
	Male bread-winner couples	Dual-earner couples	Female bread-winner couples	Male bread-winner couples	Dual-earner couples	Female bread-winner couples
AT	22.14	68.29	9.57	−5.95	−1.44	7.39
BE	19.49	75.54	4.98	−3.36	2.72	0.65
CZ	27.16	64.43	8.41	4.24	−7.67	3.43
DE	22.36	65.62	12.02	−1.87	−4.60	6.47
DK	11.25	81.37	7.31	3.77	−7.34	3.50
EE	20.95	66.10	12.94	3.43	−10.64	7.21
ES	30.40	63.28	6.33	−4.60	1.40	3.22
FI	12.67	76.79	10.53	3.36	−6.92	3.55
FR	16.34	74.21	9.45	−1.51	−3.09	4.60
GR	37.04	54.23	8.73	−5.36	−1.46	6.83
HU	27.06	60.20	12.74	1.40	−4.47	3.07
IS	8.96	86.30	4.74	1.05	−3.92	2.87
IT	35.86	53.76	10.38	−1.67	−4.97	6.64
LT	18.75	66.82	14.43	2.65	−10.23	7.58
LU	29.26	61.45	9.29	−1.89	−3.45	5.33
LV	20.69	65.73	13.58	6.61	−15.63	9.02
NL	18.15	75.21	6.64	−1.78	−1.61	3.49
NO	10.58	82.58	6.84	0.34	−2.30	1.96
PL	30.97	58.16	10.87	−0.51	−0.18	0.69
PT	25.14	63.17	11.69	0.16	−6.89	6.72
SE	10.67	80.05	9.28	1.97	−6.22	4.24
SI	16.41	72.15	11.42	3.36	−7.13	3.75
SK	19.53	72.59	7.87	3.69	−8.24	4.54
UK	20.75	67.98	11.27	2.34	−8.73	6.39
Simple average	21.4	69	9.6	0.4	−5.1	4.7

Note: Couples with at least one of the partners working.
Source: EU-SILC surveys for 2008 and 2010, own elaborations. Reproduced from Bettio *et al.* (2013: Table 1.3).

By positing a high unemployment scenario and by focusing primarily on married women with children, the original controversy of the added versus discouraged worker effects concentrated on two alternatives, that of non-active mothers entering the labour market as the husband lost jobs or income and that of employed mothers exiting the labour force out of discouragement as they lost their jobs. A third possibility, i.e. that married mothers would hold on to the labour market despite having become unemployed was not given much weight, arguably because it was believed that mothers were intrinsically less attached to the labour force.

We do not know of data proving otherwise for the current recession, but available evidence indicates that women in general showed no lower labour market attachment than men. Between 2008 and 2011, slightly more men than women (respectively 762,000 and 632,000) exited on the grounds of discouragement. As a result, the EU27 share of discouraged workers in the non-active population rose by 2 percentage points for men, and by slightly more than 1 point for women, although the starting value was, and remains, higher for the latter (Bettio *et al.* 2013: Figure 1.7). If labour market attachment had become stronger also among working mothers, this should further encourage revision of the original added/discouraged worker paradigm.

While full resolution of this issue must be left for future research, clear signs of labour market attachment on the part of women indicate in no uncertain terms that households tangibly perceived how important women's income has become to ensure all the members against the risk of poverty. On the strength of this perception we would venture that this crisis might be accelerating the long-term transition in women's income role from secondary to co-primary earners.

The demise of the buffer role myth for women

If female jobs are comparatively sheltered and women show no less labour market attachment than men, the buffer role can hardly fit the pattern of female employment. In fact, this recession has conclusively refuted the idea of women as a whole acting or behaving as buffers. The modern, European 'buffers' are male migrants, especially third country nationals, alongside young men and women in temporary employment. As we shall argue, the characteristics and behaviour of these groups are largely, though not entirely accountable within the modern debate on segmentation.

Starting with temporary employment, we find that in Europe (EU27) temporary employment is distributed fairly equally between men and women, with a slight prevalence of the latter: in the first quarter of 2012 men on temporary contracts reached 12.6 per cent of total male employment, while the figure for women was 1.1 percentage points higher (13.7 per cent). A modest gender gap also characterizes most member states, the exceptions being Bulgaria, Latvia, Lithuania and Romania (Figure 4.3).

During the downturn, a last-in-first-out principle prevailed, as firms chose to retain tenured employees and stopped renewing temporary contracts. As a consequence, the peak-to-trough share of male temporary employment declined from 13.7 per cent to 12.5 per cent in EU27, and a very similar contraction was recorded for the share of female temporary employment (from 15.2 per cent to 14.1 per cent). Declining shares mean, of course, that the downward swing was stronger for temporary workers. Uncertainty about recovery in some countries and protracted recession in other countries account for a mixed pattern after the first dip. At the EU level, there was a slight decrease in the share of temporary female employment, while substantial stability prevailed for men. By early 2012,

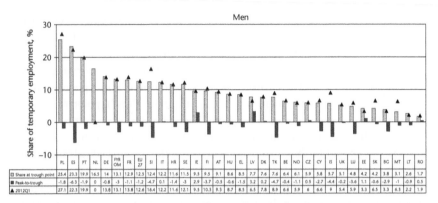

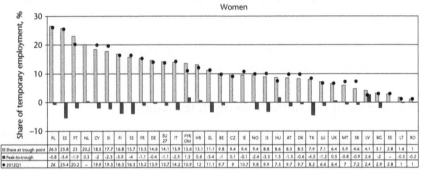

FIGURE 4.3 Temporary employment peak-to-trough change and 2012 values by sex for the EU27 and 32 European countries

Source: Eurostat data, own elaboration. Reproduced from Bettio *et al.* (2013: Figure 1.9)

the (small) gender gap had grown smaller than it had been in 2008, but the change is marginal (Figure 4.3).

It is well known that temporary employment is disproportionately concentrated among younger workers who have therefore been used to cushion the employment fallout among adult and older workers, in line with the predictions of the segmentation debate. Temporary employment may bring some advantages to young workers, including more opportunities to shop around for better jobs; however, this crisis added higher cyclical sensitivity to the list of disadvantages for this type of labour relation. For example, the average young worker on temporary employment in the EU experienced a wage penalty of 14.4 per cent in 2010 in comparison to a worker on an open-ended contract with similar characteristics. Moreover, his/ her chances of transiting to an open-ended contract were barely over one-third in the same year (34.6: European Commission 2012b: Table 2, p. 146).

In order to illustrate the age divide in employment vulnerability Figure 4.4 displays peak-to-trough losses in employment for young workers (15–24), adult workers (25–49) and older workers (50–64). To keep the figure simple, four country examples of different patterns are presented alongside the EU27 average: Estonia, Spain,

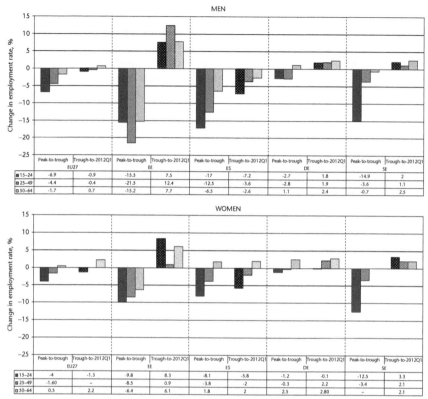

	EU27		EE		ES		DE		SE	
MEN	Peak-to-trough	Trough-to-2012Q1	Peak-to-trough	Trough-to-2012Q1	Peak-to-trough	Trough-to-2012Q1	Peak-to-trough	Trough-to-2012Q1	Peak-to-trough	Trough-to-2012Q1
15–24	-6.9	-0.9	-15.5	7.5	-17	-7.2	-2.7	1.8	-14.9	2
25–49	-4.4	-0.4	-21.5	12.4	-12.5	-3.6	-2.8	1.9	-3.6	1.1
50–64	-1.7	0.7	-15.2	7.7	-6.5	-2.6	1.1	2.4	-0.7	2.5

	EU27		EE		ES		DE		SE	
WOMEN	Peak-to-trough	Trough-to-2012Q1	Peak-to-trough	Trough-to-2012Q1	Peak-to-trough	Trough-to-2012Q1	Peak-to-trough	Trough-to-2012Q1	Peak-to-trough	Trough-to-2012Q1
15–24	-4	-1.3	-9.8	8.3	-8.1	-5.8	-1.2	-0.1	-12.5	3.3
25–49	-1.60	–	-8.5	0.9	-3.8	-2	-0.3	2.2	-3.4	2.1
50–64	0.5	2.2	-6.4	6.1	1.8	2	2.5	2.80	–	2.1

FIGURE 4.4 Peak-to-trough variations by workers' age group in the EU27 and selected countries

Source: Eurostat data, own elaborations.

Germany and Sweden. In Estonia the recession hit the labour market hard and quickly, but a sustained recovery has set in since; in Spain the repercussions of the recessions on employment were marked and no recovery was in sight at the time of writing; in comparative terms Germany hardly suffered from the recession, while in Sweden both the recession and the recovery have been comparatively moderate. Taken together these countries broadly cover the possible range of employment patterns in the Union in the course of the crisis. The figure bears out the finding that in Europe as a whole (i) the younger the worker the higher the employment losses during recession; and (ii) this age pattern is common to men and women, though less pronounced for the former.

One of the drivers of this age divide is the employment protection regime operating in some countries, as emphasized by the modern segmentation debate. Compare the pattern for Spain and Estonia. Spain, where the incidence of temporary employment is one of the highest in Europe (25.4 per cent for women and 22.3 per cent for men in 2012Q1), well illustrates the buffer role of young workers, male and female. In Estonia, however, the labour market is fully flexible for both young and older workers. This caused extremely high losses in the recession, but not primarily to the detriment of the youngest men. In fact, the worst hit groups were adult male workers, and the pattern for this country is repeated in other Baltic and Eastern European countries (Latvia, Bulgaria, Hungary and Poland). No clear picture emerges for countries with very contained losses such as Germany.

In order to fully explain why, unlike young workers, older employees were spared the worst effects of the downturn, a different and contingent development must be brought into the picture. Among men, and on average for Europe, job losses for workers older than 55 were relatively contained. Among older women employment has never stopped growing, though it slowed down as the crisis unfolded (see also European Commission, 2012a: Chart 4, p. 206). This growth is likely to reflect both the stronger labour market attachment of cohorts now entering the older age range compared to those who are exiting and also the rise in the pension age in several European countries in their efforts to curb public deficits.

For buffer-role-groups like young workers (male and female) the expectation is that employment recovery, too, should be more pronounced. However, in the vast majority of countries that are experiencing some consistent recovery after the first dip, employment gains up to the first quarter of 2012 are too uncertain and slim to yield any firm indication.

Like young workers, foreign workers tend to be over-represented in temporary employment, e.g. in construction. They are also over-represented in irregular employment, especially third country nationals who find it difficult to get or retain a regular work permit. On these and other grounds they are ideal buffer candidates. There is little doubt, in fact, that the most vulnerable group in this crisis is male migrants, and in a fairly consistent geopolitical order: third country nationals were the worst hit by job losses, followed by mobile male workers from within the Union, that is, male citizens of the Union working in a European country other than their own.

Figure 4.5 displays peak-to-trough variations for the set of countries featuring in the previous figure. In EU27, the peak-to-trough drop in the employment rate reached -5.2 percentage points among male, mobile, EU workers, and -8.6 percentage points among male migrants from outside the EU. By comparison, the figure for local (national) male workers is -3.8 percentage points. In 14 out of the 22 countries for which relevant data exist, the highest employment fallout was, in fact, for third country nationals (see Bettio *et al.* 2013: Fig. 1.14).

The pattern is rather different for female workers. Mobile women workers from within the EU have been by and large spared in the downturn. In fact, they proved less vulnerable to the recession than local women in EU27 as a whole. The converse holds for female migrants from outside the Union. It is conceivable that part of the explanation lay, again, with occupational and sectoral segregation combined with greater political pressure to 'regularize' migrant workers in sensitive, social care occupations. So called 'independent' female migration from Eastern Europe

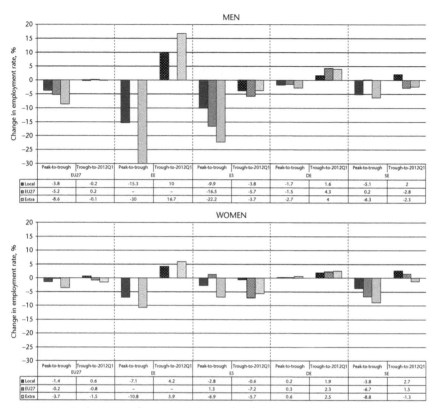

FIGURE 4.5   Peak-to-trough variations by workers' nationality in the EU27 and selected countries

Source: Eurostat data, own elaborations.

and from outside Europe has grown considerably over the past decades, filling shortages of local workers in service and care jobs, and in elderly care in particular (Morokvasic 2003; Bettio *et al.* 2006; Kofman and Raghuram 2007). Shortages of skilled and semi-skilled care workers were reported in several European countries just before the recession began (Bettio and Verashchagina 2009). Under pressure from households and institutions to secure care workers, South European governments have often given priority to these migrants when granting regular work permits. During the recession the growth in demand for elderly care workers may have eased rather than reversed. However, in the specific experience of Spain the employment rate of female migrants from within the EU has turned negative and very large since the first employment dip, possibly on account of fiscal consolidation (Figure 4.5).

The strength of labour demand for care workers may also contribute to explaining why, contrary to what old or modern theories of segmentation would anticipate, education and skill were no longer a comparative advantage for female workers in some countries during the downturn.

A common finding for previous recessions is that the less educated a worker is, the higher her/his risk of losing the job, and vice versa. In the current recession this holds for the 'average' EU male and female worker, but not for all workers or in all countries. For example, the average European worker with tertiary education was still comparatively shielded from dismissals, but not well-educated women in some Baltic and Mediterranean countries. In Estonia and Latvia, as well as in Italy and France, it was low-educated women who benefited from lower employment losses. Moreover, in countries where some recovery is under way, employment growth is often stronger among middle-educated women and men than it is at the top end of the educational range, although there are exceptions to this pattern (Latvia and Malta), and the order of magnitude is still too small for any safe conclusion to be reached (Bettio *et al.* 2013: Figure 1.13 and related discussion).

Conclusion: which lessons can we draw from this crisis?

Behind the bare figures and the technical jargon of segregation, peak-to-trough or added worker, the present crisis has brought real hardship to both men and women. This decries any attempt to conclude by drafting a final scoreboard where male and female workers compete for bearing the heaviest losses in employment, income or working conditions. We prefer to conclude by asking whether and how analysis of this crisis has taught us lessons that sharpen our ability to detect and counter old and novel gender disparities.

The first lesson we would draw is about discrepancy between expectations and outcomes. Initial evidence of a strong impact of the downturn on male employment was received by the American media and some academic circles as a novelty deserving coinage of terms such as a 'mancession' or 'hecession'. European reactions were less confrontational but the fact that the initial evidence ran counter to the fear of a disproportionate impact on women lessened the interest in the gender question. As a result perhaps the most serious long-term repercussion of this crisis with regard to women's and men's labour market positions is going unnoticed. By this, we mean the widening of geographical disparities and the real threat that a two-tier country system of gender equality may be emerging in Europe. As noted earlier, Bulgaria, Cyprus, Greece, Spain, Denmark, Ireland, Croatia and Portugal all experienced falling or stagnating female employment rates in the past four years. With the exception of Portugal and Denmark all these are countries with below average female employment from before the crisis. In all the so-called PIIGS countries,[19] (Portugal, Ireland, Italy, Greece and Spain), fiscal consolidation is having a much more severe impact on welfare provisions than in the rest of Europe, an issue which we disregarded in this paper but which is widely discussed in the rest of this book. What matters for the countries with considerable retrenchment in the welfare infrastructure or low and falling female employment, or both, is not so much how women are faring vis-à-vis men, but how much progress in women's labour market integration has been rolled back with respect to some desirable target.

An additional lesson we would draw concerns the adequacy of the conceptual tools that were inherited from economic theory. Initial fears of a disproportionate labour market impact on female workers may have been fed by theoretical stereotypes that we have seen to no longer fit women as whole: the buffer role and the discouraged worker role in particular. The strength of labour market attachment that women displayed and the importance that women's earnings took on during this crisis clearly indicate that women can no longer be sex-typed as socially disposable. We also reviewed evidence suggesting that some women may still fit the added worker typology but we can no longer expect this to be a dominant outcome. Finally, the segmentation and segregation hypotheses must be seen as complementing each other rather than excluding one another: we need to account for the fact that female employment as a whole was sheltered by segregation in the initial crisis period but also for the fact that atypical contracts confined young women to the overexposed employment segment, alongside young men.

The final lesson is about the challenge launched by this crisis to our understanding and measurement of gender equality. One of the headline stories to have emerged from the present recession is the levelling downward of gender gaps with regard to employment, income, poverty or working conditions, the one likely exception being the gender gap in unpaid work which may have widened. Before this happened there was widespread consensus that gaps capture the extent of gender equality and that narrower gaps indicate progress therein. Suffice it to mention that indices of gender equality mushroomed in the last fifteen to twenty years and most of them are based on gender gaps (Plantenga *et al.* 2012).

To gauge what is implied by the narrowing of gender gaps as a result of the recession we should consider again the case of the employment rate. Prior to the recession, ten member states were above the 65 per cent employment rate mark for women (15 to 64 years old), while the number was down to six in the most recent quarter as Estonia, Latvia, the UK and Slovenia slipped below. In the vast majority of member states, moreover, the target employment rate set by the Europe 2020 Strategy looks further away now than it did four years ago, particularly among women. Can this be called progress in gender equality only because men experienced a steeper fall in employment?

The problem clearly stems from the fact that gender gaps do not measure the distance between women's position and certain employment goals in some absolute sense but only relative to the position of men in a national context. When relative measures are used for comparisons over time they often produce paradoxical results. A similar issue arises, for example, if the conventional measure of poverty – the proportion of the population earning below the poverty line – is used to assess change over time. Should income fall for each single member of the population but more so for the rich, the poverty line would diminish and poverty would reduce! To solve the problem the value of the poverty line in a given year is chosen as the standard of reference and change is measured against this fixed standard (the resulting measure is the head count ratio 'anchored' at the chosen year). We could adopt a similar solution to measure change in gender disparities over time. For example, we could consider taking the difference between the current female employment rate and a target value (75 per cent for the 20 to 64 years old or some such value) and flank this indicator with the traditional gender gap measure. As with other topics that have been addressed in this paper, however, we must entrust this one to future research.

Notes

1 This chapter draws heavily on the joint EGGE–EGGSI report by F. Bettio *et al.* (2013). The report is based on the contributions from the national experts of the two networks and is available at http://ec.europa.eu/justice/gender-equality/document/index_en.htm. EGGE stands for 'European Network of Experts on Employment and Gender Equality Issues'; EGGSI for 'European Network of Experts on Gender Equality and Social Inclusion'. Both networks served the Gender Equality Unit which is now part of the EC Justice Division. While we gratefully acknowledge the support of the European Commission and the contributions of the national experts to the original report, the content of this chapter is our responsibility, including any mistakes.

2 The substitution hypothesis challenged such claim, arguing instead that the pressure to lower labour costs during recessions may give an incentive to employers to substitute women for men as women are secondary income earners, hence potentially cheaper (Gardiner 1976). Given that episodes of overt pay discrimination between male and female workers are much rarer now than in the 1970s when the hypothesis was first put forward, and given that it would have proven extremely difficult to garner recent evidence to substantiate the hypothesis, we do not discuss it in this paper.

3 Female representation is growing among union members and even exceeds men's in the UK due to the weight of the public sector (http://www.etuc.org/r/1368).

4 In Austria too this happened, but only for female employment.

5 In these cases the latest quarter available at the time of writing, 2012Q1, is considered as a trough point. This is the case for male employment in Ireland, Greece, Italy, Portugal, Croatia and FYROM, and for female employment in Greece and the UK (for details see Bettio *et al.* 2013: Appendix 1).

6 At least 20 per cent of male respondents to the European Social Survey (ESS) in the majority of the 17 countries surveyed reported having to take a reduction in pay in the period 2008–2010; for women, this happened in less than half of the countries surveyed (ESS data, round 5, year 2010, first release: 26.10.2011; http://*www.europeansocialsurvey.org/*).

7 The 2010 value is the latest available (Eurostat online series *tsdsc340*).

8 The discordance between Eurostat and national data for Norway stems primarily from the different sectoral coverage. See Bettio *et al.* (2013: footnote 33).

9 There is also evidence that the adjusted wage gap declined alongside the unadjusted gap, but only in the Slovak Republic (Piscová and Bahna 2011).

10 The severe material deprivation rate is the percentage of the population that cannot afford at least four of the following nine items: i) to pay their rent, mortgage or utility bills; ii) to keep their home adequately warm; iii) to face unexpected expenses; iv) to eat meat or proteins regularly; v) to go on holiday; vi) a television set; vii) a refrigerator; viii) a car; ix) a telephone.

11 For further details on developments in unpaid work see Bettio *et al.* (2013: chapter 3).

12 See Rubery (1988), in particular the chapters by Bettio, by Humphries and by Rubery and Tarling.

13 Eurostat data, online database, series lfsq_egan2. To illustrate using the EU27 figures, men's employment in manufacturing declined by 9.8 per cent over the entire period (2008 second quarter–2012 first quarter) and by 9.4 per cent over the two initial worst

years of the crisis (2008–2010, second quarter). The corresponding figures for women are 13.0 and 12.5 per cent.

14 Employment elasticity with respect to output takes the percentage variation in employment in ratio to the percentage variation in GDP.

15 Recall that the unadjusted gender wage gap declined in most countries implying that the cut in hourly wages was larger for men.

16 See Bettio *et al.* (2013: Box 2.2) and the related discussion.

17 The calculations refer to the wage gap that would have been observed in 2009 with 2009 wages by sector, had the sectoral composition of (male and female) employment remained the same as in 2008 (Croatia) or 2007 (Belgium). These calculations were undertaken by the Croatian and the Belgian experts (Mrnjavac 2011; Meulders and O'Dorchai 2011) on national data and EU-SILC data respectively. See Bettio *et al.* (2013: section 2.2).

18 Note that the 2009 figures are drawn from the EU-SILC 2010 survey. The values are weighted averages.

19 The acronym PIIGS, now entered in Wikipedia, stands for Portugal, Italy, Ireland, Greece and Spain, the five countries that raise the highest concern about fiscal sustainability.

References

Aldrich Finegan, T. and Margo, R.A. (1993) 'Added and Discouraged Workers in the Late 1930s: A Re-Examination', *NBER Historical Working Paper*, n. 45, National Bureau of Economic Research.

Bentolila, S. and Bertola, G. (1990) 'Firing Costs and Labour Demand: How Bad is the Eurosclerosis?', *Review of Economic Studies*, 57(3): 381–402.

Bettio, F. (1988) 'Women, the State and the Family in Italy: Problems of Female Participation in Historical Perspective' in J. Rubery (ed.) *Women and Recession*, London and New York: Routledge and Kegan Paul, pp. 191–217.

Bettio, F. (2008) 'Occupational Segregation and Gender Wage Disparities in Developed Economies: Should We Still Worry?' in F. Bettio and A. Verashchagina (eds) *Frontiers in the Economics of Gender*, Routledge, Siena Studies in Political Economy, pp. 267–85.

Bettio, F., Corsi, M., D'Ippoliti, C., Lyberaki, A., Samek Lodovici, M. and Verashchagina, A. (2013) 'The Impact of the Economic Crisis on the Situation of Women and Men and on Gender Equality Policies', External report commissioned by and presented to the EU Directorate-General for Justice, Unit D1 'Equality Between Women and Men', Available at: http://ec.europa.eu/justice/gender-equality/document/index_en.htm (accessed 03.04.2013).

Bettio, F., Simonazzi, A. and Villa, P. (2006) 'Change in Care Regimes and Female Migration', *Journal of European Social Policy*, 16(3): 271–86.

Bettio, F. and Verashchagina, A. (2009) *Gender Segregation in the Labour Market: Root Causes, Implications and Policy Responses in the EU*, Luxembourg: Publications Office of the European Union, 2009, Available at: http://ec.europa.eu/social/BlobServlet?docId=40 28&langId=en (accessed 03.12.2012).

Boeri, T. and Garibaldi, P. (2007) 'Two Tier Reforms of Employment Protection Legislation: A Honeymoon Effect', *Economic Journal*, 117: 357–85.

Doeringer, P. and Piore, M.J. (1971) *Internal Labor Markets and Manpower Analysis*, New York: Heath Lexington Books.

Edwards, R.C., Reich, M. and Gordon, D.M. (eds) (1975) *Labor Market Segmentation*, Lexington, Mass.: D.C. Heath.

Eurofound (2011) *Young People and NEETs in Europe: First Findings*. European Foundation for the Improvement of Living and Working Conditions, Dublin. Available at: www.eurofound.europa.eu/pubdocs/2011/72/en/1/EF1172EN.pdf (accessed 03.12.2012).

European Commission (2011a) *Progress on Equality Between Women and Men in 2011*, Commission Staff Working Document Accompanying the document "Report from the Commission to the European Parliament, the Council, the Economic and Social Committee and the Committee of the Regions 2011" and the "Report on the application of the EU Charter of Fundamental Rights", Brussels. Available at: http://ec.europa.eu/justice/gender-equality/files/swd2012-85-gendereq_en.pdf (accessed 03.12.2012).

European Commission (2011b) *Labour Market Developments in Europe*. Directorate-General for Employment, Social Affairs and Inclusion, Brussels. Available at: http://ec.europa.eu/economy_finance/publications/european_economy/2011/pdf/ee-2011-2_en.pdf (accessed 03.12.2012).

European Commission (2012a) *EU Employment and Social Situation*, Quarterly Review, March 2012, Directorate-General for Employment, Social Affairs and Inclusion, Brussels. Available at: http://ec.europa.eu/social/BlobServlet?docId=7548&langId=en (accessed 03.12.2012).

European Commission (2012b) *Employment and Social Developments in Europe 2011*, Directorate-General for Employment, Social Affairs and Inclusion, Luxembourg: Publications Office of the European Union. Available at: http://ec.europa.eu/social/BlobServlet?docId=7294&langId=en (accessed 03.12.2012).

Figari, F., Salvatori, A. and Sutherland, H. (2010) 'Economic Downturn and Stress Testing European Welfare Systems', *ISER Working Paper*, Series 2010–18, Institute for Social and Economic Research.

Gardiner, J. (1976) 'Women and Unemployment', *Red Rag*, 10: 12–15.

Ghignoni, E. and Verashchagina, A. (2012) 'Added Versus Discouraged Worker Effect During the Recent Crisis: Evidence from Italy', conference paper prepared for the IWPLMS and ESPANET conferences, September 2012, Rome. Available at: http://www.espanet-italia.net/images/conferenza2012/PAPER%202012/Sessione_C/C_3_VERASHCHAGINA_GHIGNONI.pdf (accessed 22.11.2012).

Humphries, J. (1988) 'Women's Employment in Restructuring America: The Changing Experience of Women in Three Recessions' in J. Rubery (ed.) *Women and Recession*. London and New York: Routledge and Kegal Paul, pp. 20–47.

Kofman, E. and Raghuram, P. (2007) 'The Implications of Migration for Gender and Care Regimes in the South', Paper prepared for UNRISD – IOM – IFS workshop on 'Social Policy and Migration in Developing Countries', 22-23 November 2007, Stockholm.

Meulders D. and O'Dorchai S. (2011) 'The Impact of the Economic Crisis on the Situation of Women and Men and on Gender Equality Policies': Belgium. National Report prepared for the 'European Network of Experts on Employment and Gender Equality Issues' (EGGE), European Commission, Brussels.

Milkman, R. (1976) 'Women's Work and Economic Crisis. Some Lessons of the Great Depression', *Review of Radical Political Economics*, 8(1): 71–97.

Morokvasic, M. (2003) 'Transnational Mobility and Gender: a View from Post-Wall Europe', in M. Morokvasic-Müller, U. Erel and K. Shinozaki (eds) *Crossing Borders and Shifting Boundaries*, Bd.1: Gender on the Move, Opladen: Leske+Budrich, pp. 101–31.

Mrnjavac Z. (2011) 'The Impact of the Economic Crisis on the Situation of Women and Men and on Gender Equality Policies': Croatia. National Report prepared for the 'European Network of Experts on Employment and Gender Equality Issues' (EGGE), European Commission, Brussels.

Piscová, M. and Bahna, M. (2011) 'The Impact of the Economic Crisis on the Situation of Women and Men and on Gender Equality Policies': the Slovak Republic. National Report prepared for the 'European Network of Experts on Employment and Gender Equality Issues' (EGGE), European Commission, Brussels.

Plantenga, J., Fagan, C., Maier, F. and Remery, C. (2012) *Rational for the Gender Quality Index for Europe*. European Institute for Gender Equality, Vilnius. Available at: http://www.eige. europa.eu/sites/default/files/Rationale-for-the-Gender-Equality-Index-for-Europe.pdf (accessed 03.12.3012).

Rubery, J. (1978) 'Structured Labour Markets, Worker Organization and Low Pay', *Cambridge Journal of Economics*, 2: 17–36.

Rubery, J. (ed.) (1988) *Women and Recession*. London and New York: Routledge and Kegal Paul.

Rubery, J. and Tarling, R. (1988) 'Women's Employment in Declining Britain' in J. Rubery (ed.) *Women and Recession,* London and New York: Routledge and Kegal Paul, pp. 100–34.

Wilkinson, F. (1981) *The Dynamics of Labour Market Segmentation*, London: Academic Press.

5

GENDER IMPACTS OF THE 'GREAT RECESSION' IN THE UNITED STATES

Randy Albelda[1]

Introduction

The 'Great Recession' in the United States officially began in December 2007. The National Bureau of Economic Research (NBER), the organization that dates US recessions, declared it over in June 2009. At 18 months, the Great Recession was the longest in the United States since the 1930s Great Depression. In many ways it was also the deepest with steep decreases in GDP, industrial production and housing prices (MacEwan and Miller 2011; NBER 2011), the slow recovery, and long average duration of unemployment spells (Allegretto and Lynch 2010; Goodman and Mance 2011). In addition, state and local revenues fell by 22 per cent ($587 billion) between July 2007 and July 2008, creating the largest state budget shortfalls on record (US Census Bureau 2011a; Table A-2). The Great Recession, part of a global economic downturn, has been accompanied by political upheaval reflected in a widely divided electorate over the role of government.[1]

While deeper than previous recessions, women's employment effects differed from men's in the Great Recession. Men's unemployment rose higher and faster than women's; after the recession there were more rapid employment gains for men than women; and young women, women of colour, and single mothers have been hit harder than other women. State and local government responses to this recession, as in all recessions, have been pro-cyclical (due to legally required balanced budget requirements), exacerbating problems.[2] Reductions in revenues have led to sustained budget cuts, which disproportionately affect women, especially low-income women. Countercyclical automatic stabilizers did operate, but in gendered ways and with somewhat less robustness than in the past. What truly distinguished the Great Recession from previous post-Second World War recessions was the large stimulus package passed in 2009, the American Recovery and Reinvestment Act (ARRA). The bill authorized close to $800 billion of new spending and tax reduction and while it likely affected women as much as men, there were uneven gendered effects. While gender differences matter over the recession, it should be understood within the context of steady growth in gender economic equality over the last 30 years which has taken place alongside heightened income inequality among households, including the large share of female-headed households that disproportionately fill the bottom ranks. The outcome is thus also increased inequality within each gender group. These short-term and long-term trends suggest promoting strategies that 'lift the bottom' as a key direction toward further and sustained gender equality.

Setting the context

The early 1980s recession and the Great Recession bookend a long-run economic cycle characterized by stagnating earnings, rising inequality, increased corporate influence and the rise of the neo-liberal state. The larger economic, demographic and political changes include steady declines in high-wage manufacturing employment accompanied by growth in both high-wage and low-wage service jobs, the shrinking share of married-couple households, stagnating male wages, increased women's employment, successful financial deregulation, extension of 'free' trade agreements, large tax cuts for the wealthy, employment-promotion policies for the poor and devolved federal government responsibilities.

Combined, these trends help account for a steady rise in income inequality despite solid economic growth before the financial and economic crisis of the late 2000s and a strained, if not fragile, fiscal situation at all levels of government. Between 1980 and 2008, on average, household incomes grew by just under $12,000, but the richest 10 per cent garnered 98 per cent of total income growth (Economic Policy Institute 2012).

Considered in the context of other industrialized nations, its weak collective bargaining structures and heavy reliance on competitive labour and product markets place the US firmly within the liberal market economies (LME) as discussed by varieties of capitalism (VoC) literature (e.g. Hall and Soskice 2001). LMEs are in part supported by social protection policies that place the risk of unemployment (or being in a non-earnings situation) on individuals rather than firms. These shallow employment protections, coupled with a host of means-tested policies to assure basic needs, place the US's decommodification structure squarely among liberal welfare states as discussed in the welfare state regime literature (Esping-Andersen 1990). The US, with no national paid leave policies and means-based child care and elder care supports, also lacks the sets of defamilialization policies that promote women's economic independence. Despite this, the levels of full-time employment among women are high compared to other countries with liberal welfare state regimes.[3]

Combined, these regimes create mixed conditions for promoting gender equality. While research on the ways in which employment and welfare state regimes affect gender equality is still developing and remains contested, there are some important points of agreement. First, it is clear that class matters. Women in the lower rungs of the employment ladder and low-income women, especially mothers, are impacted differently than women with high levels of skills and high income within any particular employment and welfare state regime. Second, countries with more generous decommodification policies will have less inter-class gender inequality and will reduce poverty among single-mother families. Third, policies that promote long leaves from the labour force increase gender wage inequality. Finally, women's over-representation in lower-skilled and lower-paying jobs increases overall gender earnings inequality, as does women's under-representation in highly skilled and higher-paying jobs.[4] While some of these impacts are confounding in terms of overall gender employment or wage equality in a LME and liberal welfare state, together they do suggest some gender convergence but in an income-polarizing way.

This seems to hold true of the United States. Men's and women's wage levels and labour market experiences are converging within the better-paying occupational echelons as well as in the lower ones, but there are larger inter-class disparities among women. LMEs' reliance on a system of education and training that promotes general over specific skills coupled with the liberal welfare state that provides little accommodation for long leaves, are consistent with college-educated women's strong foothold in high-paying occupations. Conversely, the lack of decommodification policies that characterize LMEs and liberal welfare states, coupled with aggressive labour activation policies for poor mothers, force women (and increasingly men) without college education or specific training to rely almost exclusively on earnings from a large low-wage labour market. The low levels of government support for paid care exacerbates the inequality among women through the privatization of care costs. Low-income women become the low-wage service and care 'solution' that enables higher earning women to work. All the while, low-income women cannot afford quality care or the sets of time-substituting services, resulting in a range of strategies that reduce investment in children and reproduce inter-class gender inequality.

Demographic changes since the 1980s heighten these polarizing trends. There has been a decline in the share of married-couple families and a rise in single-adult households. In 1980, 61 per cent of all households had a married couple and just over one-quarter had a single female adult not living with any family members. By 2011, 49 per cent had a married couple and 31 per cent had only single female adults. The US has the sixth lowest per cent of married-couple households compared to other OECD countries, but ranks in the middle for percentage of single-headed households, including single mothers. More married-couple families have two adult earners, distancing income levels from single females, with and without children.

Women's economic fortunes over the last 30 years have improved compared to men, with gaps in median earnings, labour force participation rates and poverty rates narrowing. Men's real median earnings have stagnated while women's have increased, raising the earnings wage ratio of women to men from 0.60 in

1980 to 0.77 in 2010 for year-round, full-time workers (US Census Bureau 2011b, Table P-38). The labour force participation rates of women aged 16 and older have risen from 51.5 per cent in 1980 to 58.6 per cent in 2010, while men's have fallen from 77.4 per cent to 71.2 per cent over the same period (US Census Bureau 2012: Table 588). Females are more likely to be poor than are males, but that gap has narrowed as well. In the late 1970s and early 1980s, female poverty rates were about 30 per cent higher than men's but by the late 2000s, they were about 20 per cent higher (US Census Bureau 2011c; People Table 7). However, there is more inequality among women. Women of colour and women in female-headed families have lost ground compared to white and married women. The black/white women's wage gap has grown over the last 30 years, with full-time, year-round working black women's median earnings at 95 per cent of those for white women in 1980 but only 86 per cent in 2010 (US Census Bureau 2011b, Table P-38). While the median family income of female-headed families was 45 per cent of that of married couples in 1980, it dropped to 40 per cent in 2010 (US Census Bureau 2011b, Table F-7); this, despite a dramatic increase in single mothers' employment rates in the 1990s. Poverty rates for single-mother families remained over five times that of married couple families with children over the period, as the share of single-mother families increased. The earnings gap between women at the 90th percentile of hourly earnings and those at the 10th percentile are wide and have increased since the early 1980s.[5]

The Great Recession has had a dramatic effect on the economy, but also on political responses. The election of President Obama and a Democrat-controlled legislative branch in 2008 at the onset of the recession was in response to economic fears and a repudiation of Bush-era policies. This allowed for the passages of ARRA as well as national health care reform early on in the Obama administration. But the backlash to these policies generated a large electoral swing toward fiscally and socially conservative Republicans in 2010. They have been attempting to implement a corporate-based neo-liberal agenda of debt reduction through austerity cuts, deregulation, tax cuts on unearned income, and further erosion of collective bargaining rights but they have also pursued a religious right agenda primarily geared toward restricting women's reproductive health choices. These emboldened Republicans have helped spur the Occupy movement, reignite parts of the labour movement, and generate a large gender gap in voting trends (but not a renewed women's movement or empowerment). President Obama's re-election in 2012 coupled with an historic increase in women's Congressional representation and the sound defeat of the most anti-choice candidates suggests a firm rejection, especially by women, of key parts of the conservative agenda. While the US economy has been more sound than many European ones since 2010, there is still considerable economic fragility as well as political volatility.

Gender and the great recession: employment effects

Women in the US still have different economic roles than men, so not surprisingly there are differential gendered impacts across the cycle. Women are over-represented in certain occupations and industries, while highly under-represented in others. Women still perform more unpaid work than do men (Bianchi 2011). Finally, women are more likely than men to earn a low wage and have low income (Albelda and Carr 2012).

Feminist economists have identified three possible reasons for differential employment effects of recessions on women (e.g. Milkman 1976; Humphries 1988; Rubery 1988). These include buffer effects in which women serve as a dispensable reserve army; substitution effects in which women's lower wages make them more attractive than higher-paid male workers; and job segregation effects in which female-dominated industries may be hit less hard than male-dominated ones or vice versa (see Rubery, this volume). The growing importance of government spending on employment, especially on female-dominated health, education and social service sectors, calls new attention to a potential fourth effect of fiscal austerity. In the US, the large and increased role of state and local governments in the provision of social infrastructure (care work) coupled with the concentration of women in those sectors, (Albelda *et al.* 2009), means that state responses to recessions have also played a role in gender employment patterns. What follows is an exploration of the employment flows over the Great Recession, with an eye toward these four potential gendered impacts.

Men's and women's unemployment rates

Since the early 1980s, there has been a consistent pattern of men's unemployment rates surpassing those of women during and immediately after the recession, but then improving quickly. Figure 5.1 depicts men's and women's seasonally adjusted monthly unemployed rates (ages 16 and older) and their differences from January

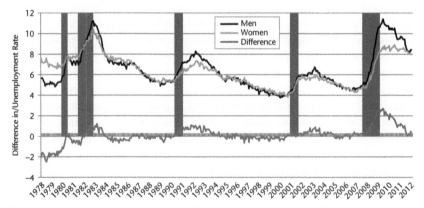

FIGURE 5.1 Men's and women's monthly unemployment rates and the gender gap in the US 1978–2012

Source: Current Population Survey.

Shaded areas correspond to recession months. Data are seasonally adjusted.

1978 through June 2012, which includes the last four officially declared recessions (the early 1980s was a double-dip recession), each seven to ten years apart. In the three previous recessions, men's and women's unemployment rates have converged several years following the recession and for short periods over the boom, women's unemployment rates have exceeded those of men.

The Great Recession was notable for the large gap between men's and women's unemployment rates of over two percentage points for 14 consecutive months (March 2009–April 2010). Also notable is the sharp fall in men's unemployment immediately following the recession but the lacklustre recovery for women. Men's unemployment rates have fallen from their peak of 11.4 per cent in October 2009 to a low of 8.3 per cent in March 2012.[6] Women's unemployment rates have hovered between 8.3 in June 2009 to their almost 30 year high of 8.9 per cent in November 2010. They were at 8.1 per cent in June 2012, three years following the official end of the recession. So what was initially labelled the 'He-cession' (e.g. Fortini 2009) became the 'He-covery' (e.g. Rampell 2011).

Employment changes by industry

Many analysts have argued the gender gap in unemployment rates since the 1980s is largely attributed to job segregation effects -- the uneven industrial distribution of male and female workers (Seeborg and DeBoer 1987; Goodman *et al.* 1993; Boushey and Cherry 2002; Şahin *et al.* 2010). Between December 2007 and June 2009, men lost 5.35 million jobs while women lost 2.14 million jobs. Figures 5.2 and 5.3 depict men's and women's change in employment by major industrial sector over the recession and three years since the official end of it. Over the recession, men's employment losses in construction, manufacturing and professional and business services were large and considerably higher than women's losses. This is not surprising since men held 87.5 per cent of construction jobs, 71.1 per cent of manufacturing jobs and 55.3 per cent of professional and business services jobs in December 2007. Men lost only a slightly higher percentage of jobs in two of these industries than their representation in them (90.8 per cent of construction jobs,

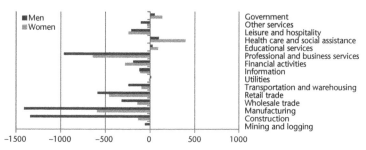

FIGURE 5.2   Change in employment (in 1000s) by gender and industry in the US 2007–2009

Source: Bureau of Labor Statistics, Current Employment Statistics Survey

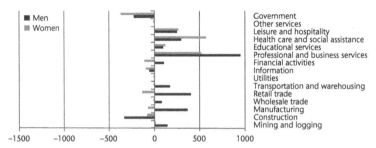

FIGURE 5.3 Change in employment (in 1000s) by gender and industry in the US 2009–2012

Source: Bureau of Labor Statistics, Current Employment Statistics Survey

70.2 per cent of manufacturing jobs and 59.8 per cent of professional services). Over the same period, men's and women's employment actually increased in government, educational, and health and social services, industries in which women are highly represented (57.0, 60.7 and 80.5 per cent respectively in December 2007). Women's gains, however, outpaced men's in government (78.4 per cent of new employment) and in education (76.9 per cent of job growth).

In the 36 months since the end of the recession, men's employment fortunes changed considerably. There was job growth for men in most industries, notably in manufacturing, retail trade, and especially professional and business services. Men continued to see job losses in construction, information industries and government. Women were no longer facing a net loss of jobs (which they had until August 2011), but gains were sluggish and uneven, with the largest losses in government (losing 62.7 per cent of all jobs in this industry). Unlike men, women continued to lose jobs in financial, retail and wholesale trade, and manufacturing industries.

These data, paired with the unemployment rates, are consistent with job segregation effects. But there may be additional or different factors at play. Part-time employment grew over the recession, suggesting employers were replacing full-time by part-time workers. At the start of the recession, 24 per cent of all employed women and 10 per cent of all employed men worked part-time (less than 35 hours a week), but men's part-time employment growth outpaced that of women's over the recession increasing by 20 per cent (1.7 million jobs) compared to 6 per cent growth for women (1.0 million jobs).

Fiscal austerity effects are consistent with the lacklustre rebound for women. Women are much more heavily concentrated in care sectors than are men. Measuring this sector in Massachusetts, Albelda *et al.* (2009) found that 22 per cent of all workers are in care jobs, with women holding 75 per cent of these jobs. Further, they estimated that state and local governments fund 49 per cent of the cost of paid care services, which include workers in the health, social services and a portion of education industries. The state fiscal impacts of the recession were felt most heavily in 2009–11, which is consistent with women's large losses in government employment depicted in Figure 5.3. At the end of the recession, government employees accounted for 16 per cent of all employed workers and 19 per cent of all employed women. In the United States, teachers are government employees, but most health care and social service providers and those in post-secondary education are not. Both women and men have seen job gains in health care and social assistance during and after the recession, suggesting that there is a continued demand in federally funded health care (including the large Medicare programme) as well as privately funded health care and social assistance.

Employment to population ratios and labour force participation rates

Figure 5.4 depicts the percentage of employed workers of the population for men and women 16 years and older from January 1978 to June 2012. Men's employment-to-population rates are much more sensitive to the business cycle than are women's, with men's rates taking steep dips in the 1980s and the late 2000s, with an overall trend toward convergence. After November 2011, men's rates began to increase slowly, while women's employment rates continued to fall. The steeper fall in men's rates is consistent with substitution and job segregation effects.

More men and women are exiting the labour force than in previous recessions. Figures 5.5 and 5.6 depict the cumulative change in men's and women's labour force participation for 36 months following the official end of each of the last four recessions. While men have exited the labour force in the extended period following a recession for each of the last four recessions, women have only recently done so, with a large decline following the Great Recession. Currently, women's labour force participation rates are at the lowest since March 1992. A closer look at which women are opting out of employment is merited.

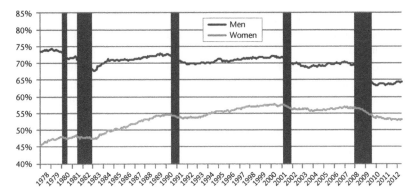

FIGURE 5.4   Men's and women's employment rates in the US 1978–2012
Source: Bureau of Labor Statistics, Current Population Survey. Shaded areas correspond to recession months. Data are seasonally adjusted.

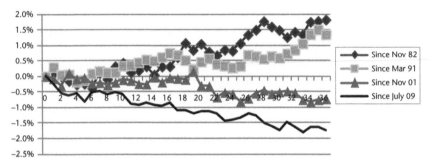

FIGURE 5.5 Cumulative monthly change in women's labour force participation rates in the last four recessions in the US

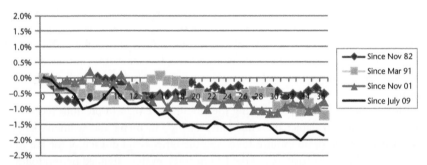

FIGURE 5.6 Cumulative monthly change in men's labour force participation rates in the last four recessions in the US

Differences among women: unemployment effects by race/ethnicity, marital status and age

There are some substantial differences among women when it comes to unemployment. Those with the most precarious economic status have considerably higher rates. Black women have much higher unemployment rates than do white women; unmarried women maintaining families have unemployment rates considerably higher than those of married women; and younger women have higher rates than other women.

Figure 5.7 depicts monthly unemployment rates for white and black men and women 20 years and older from January 1978 through June 2012. Black women's unemployment rate always exceed those of white women, although the gap has been closing over the last three decades. Unemployment rates for black and white women follow a similar trend over the business cycle, although white women recover longer and faster than black women. Black men's unemployment rate has diverged more sharply from those of black women over the Great Recession, reaching a peak of 17.7 per cent in January 2010 for men and 13.8 per cent in April 2010 for black women.

Figure 5.8 depicts monthly unemployment rates for married men and married women and for women who maintain families (mostly single-mother families) from

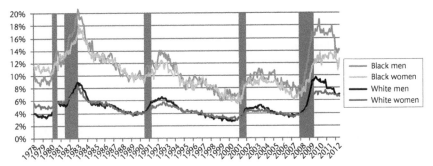

FIGURE 5.7 Black and white women's unemployment rates in the US 1978–2012
Source: Bureau of Labor Statistics. Shaded areas correspond to recession months. Data are seasonally adjusted.

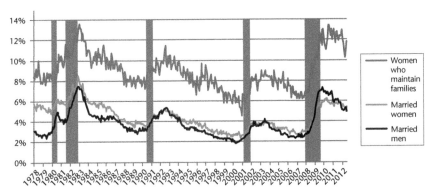

FIGURE 5.8 Unemployment rates by marital status in the US 1978–2012
Source: Bureau of Labor Statistics, Current Population Survey. Shaded areas correspond to recession months. Data for married men and women are seasonally adjusted; data for women who maintain families are unadjusted.

January 1978 to June 2012. (Note: data are seasonally unadjusted for women who maintain families.) Unemployment rates of married men and women track very closely over most of the period. The Great Recession is the first in which married men's rate far exceeds that of married women. Unmarried women heading a family (defined as two or more related people living together) have much higher unemployment rates than married women, and that gap has widened especially since the 1990s. Their unemployment rates have risen sharply over the Great Recession. Like married women's rates, they have not fallen much since the official end of the recession.

Younger women (ages 16–24) face unemployment rates two and three times higher than women aged 25–54 but the differences in unemployment rates over the late 2000s are very similar to those in the early 1980s. Young women's unemployment rates are less than those of young men, but have tracked closely since the recession of the early 1980s. In the Great Recession, young men's unemployment rates spiked more sharply, peaking at 22.3 per cent in April 2010 compared to young women's highest rate of 17.0 in October 2010.

Summary

To the degree that official employment statistics reveal the effects of recessions, the Great Recession has not had as severe an employment impact on women as it has on men. Unemployment rates for women remained considerably lower throughout the recession and employment rates did not fall as steeply as men's. The data are consistent with persistent gender job segregation, substitution of part-time for full-time work, and fiscal austerity effects. Still, this does not mean that women were not hit hard by the Great Recession (see also Hartmann *et al.* 2010). Three years following the recession, there were still just over 1 million fewer women employed than at the onset of the recession. Importantly, women of colour, women who head households and young women continue to face very high levels of unemployment.

Government responses to the recession

'Automatic stabilizers' – the sets of income-replacement programmes that kick into gear when incomes fall or jobs are lost – have counter-cyclical effects during recessions. However, countering those impacts are state and local governments' actions also triggered by recessions as balanced budget requirements push states and localities into deficit situations. They react with fiscal policies that make matters worse, namely raising taxes (or increasing fees) and also cutting spending. Another response is possible, but not assured. Depending on the size of the recession as well as the prevailing political will, the federal government can pursue expansionary fiscal or monetary policy to mitigate the impacts of the recession. Regardless of the response, there are distinct gendered impacts.

Automatic stabilizers? Increased demand for and gendered usage of government income supports

As discussed earlier, over the last 30 years the United States has witnessed an erosion of workers' strength relative to capital and a push to both devolve and unravel means-tested income supports for adults with no or very low earnings. As a result, the strength of automatic stabilizers has been firmly tested in the Great Recession. Data on usage or indicators of usage for three important programmes that should be sensitive to the business cycle in the United States are explored here. These are Unemployment insurance claims, the cash assistance programme for poor families with children called Temporary Assistance to Needy Families (TANF) and Supplemental Nutritional Assistance Program (SNAP – formerly Food Stamps) which is the main food assistance programme to low-income individuals and families.

Unemployment Insurance (UI) is a time-limited weekly benefit for eligible workers who have lost their jobs. Each state has its own eligibility rules, including minimum numbers of hours and minimum amounts of earnings over previous months. Employers contribute while states set benefit rates. Only 37 per cent of unemployed persons in 2008 received unemployment insurance (US Department of Labor, Employment and Training Administration 2012), about the same percentage as in 1981, the height of the last deep recession. The cash assistance programme for poor families with children was dramatically reformed in the mid-1990s by the creation of TANF, which introduced time-limits and stringent employment-promotion measures. States were given considerably more control over eligibility requirements and rules and continued to receive funding for part of the programme from the federal government. All states have very low income eligibility thresholds and stringent work requirements. It is clear that this programme has lost its effectiveness in covering poor families. Less than 1.5 per cent of the population and 4.4 per cent of all children received TANF in 2011, despite child poverty rates of 22.0 per cent. In 1992 child poverty rates were equally high, but 14.3 per cent of all children received this type of support (US Census Bureau 2011c: Family Table 4; US Department of Health and Human Services 2011). SNAP is the main food assistance programme in the United States. Eligible individuals are provided with a bank-type card that allows them to purchase food. This is a fully federally funded programme with mostly federally set eligibility requirements (states have some leeway). The most recent data indicate that 14.5 per cent of all persons in the US are receiving SNAP (US Department of Agriculture 2011) compared to 9.7 per cent of the population in 1981, the year Food Stamp usage peaked in the 1980s recession.

During a recession one would expect claims and usage of all of these programmes to increase and they did. Total UI claims were 46 per cent higher in 2011 than 2007, jumping 124 per cent between 2007 and 2009 at the height of the recession. The average number of persons receiving SNAP increased by 70 per cent from 2007 to 2011, with caseloads rising through 2012. TANF caseloads, however, only increased by 13 per cent over this same period despite high and rising levels of poverty among single-mother families.

There are important gender differences in the use of and claims for these programmes. Men are somewhat more likely to claim UI than women, even beyond the difference in unemployment rates. In 2009, 42 per cent of unemployed men claimed UI compared to 38 per cent of women (US Department of Labor, Employment and Training Administration 2012). Nationally, 90 per cent of adults receiving TANF are women and the vast majority of families receiving TANF are single-mother families (US Department of Health and Human Services 2009). The US Department of Agriculture does not collect data on receipt of SNAP by gender. But in an annual survey the Census Bureau asks if anyone in the household received SNAP. In 2010, 11.5 per cent of adult women and 8.9 per cent of adult men indicated they were in a household receiving SNAP (author's calculation using the March 2011 Supplement of the Current Population Survey). And while SNAP is a key anti-poverty programme (with eligibility rules that cover almost all poor adults) and widely used, many poor women do not participate in SNAP. In 2010, only 42 per cent of all adult women with family incomes below the official US poverty income threshold reported being in a household receiving SNAP (author's calculation).

Countervailing forces: gendered impact of state and local government spending

In the United States, state and local governments are the primary funders of health care and cash assistance for the poor, almost all public primary, secondary and higher education, public safety, police and fire protection, social services, transportation and prisons. And that role has increased over time. In 1978, just under 37 per cent of all non-defence government spending was financed by state and local governments. During the Reagan years, with an emphasis on federal tax cutting and devolution, that percentage rose to 40 per cent in the late 1980s, levelling out in the 1990s and increasing to 42 per cent for most of the 2000s. In 2009, with a large infusion of federal funds through ARRA, there was a sharp decline to 35 per cent (US Office of Management and Budget 2011; Table 15.4).

While states have considerable discretion around spending and do differ in per capita amounts spent on various items, all states spend on human and physical infrastructure. Looking only at the state of Massachusetts, Albelda et al. (2009) found that 57 per cent of state and local budgets goes to help assure the vitality of the state's human infrastructure, defined as expenditures on K-12 (primary and secondary) education, health care, and assistance to young children, troubled youth, disabled children and adults, and elders. In addition, most state expenditures go to private vendors (i.e. hospitals, nursing homes and child care providers) that provide the care. A large portion of state human infrastructure funding goes to low-income families and individuals through health care and social service expenditures. Many states also supplement locally financed educational costs in low-income municipalities.

During economic downturns, expected revenues decline as spending needs increase. All recessions create fiscal problems for state and local governments, but the depth of this recession created substantial needs and a large decline in revenues. In the fiscal year (FY) 2009 (July 2009–June 2010), states and localities took in $588 billion less revenue than they did in FY2008, a 22 per cent reduction even after an infusion of federal ARRA stimulus funds (US Census Bureau 2011a). The decrease in revenues and increased demand for services presented a formidable challenge, resulting in large budget shortfalls totalling $430 billion over FY09-FY11 (McNichol et al. 2011). States offset these revenue shortfalls in various ways. Thirty states increased taxes and fees (Johnson et al. 2011), but by far the most common response was to cut budgets. In FY09, overall states cut expenditure by 4.2 per cent and then cut an additional 6.8 per cent in the following fiscal year (National Association of State Budget Officers 2011).

From FY09 through FY11, 31 of the 50 states implemented cuts to health care services and/or restricted access to care and/or health insurance; 29 states cut funding to programmes that serve the elderly and disabled, mostly used by low-income individuals (and often provided by low-wage women workers); 34 states reduced funding for child care and for K-12 (primary and secondary) education; 43 reduced funding for higher education, typically resulting in higher fees and tuition; and 44 states imposed a range of cost-reductions on state employees, the majority of whom are women, including compulsory unpaid leave (furloughs), eliminating or not filling vacancies, and reduction in employee benefits (Johnson *et al.* 2011).

While there are no data on the gender composition of those receiving care through Medicaid and other types of state and local services to poor and low-income people and families, we do know that women are more likely to be poor than men and be the ones primarily taking care of children. Programme cuts directed toward low-income individuals and families disproportionately hurt women and children. This recession has led to significant funding decreases to services and programmes that are considered essential for the economic security of many women and families. It is also responsible for the reduction in government workers, disproportionately women, depicted earlier in Figure 5.3.

Impacts of government stimulus spending

The sudden and sharp increase in unemployment, rapid decrease in state and local spending, and the landslide victory of Democrats in 2008 federal elections, accounts for the federal government passing a substantial relief package in response to the recession. The American Recovery and Reinvestment Act (ARRA) was a $787 billion federal spending initiative signed in February 2009, equivalent to 5.5 per cent of GDP in 2008 (Executive Office of the President 2011: Table B-1). The bulk of the spending (70 per cent) took place in 2009 through 2010. In 2010, when it had its largest impact, the Congressional Budget Office (2011), calculating low and high estimates, found that ARRA improved GDP by between 0.7 and 4.1 per cent while reducing the unemployment rate by 0.4 and 1.8 percentage points, mitigating the effects of the Great Recession. Using publicly available data, I calculate the distribution of that spending, based on key categories in order to get a sense of the general distribution of the funds and possible impacts by gender. Given the nature of the spending and the way in which the data on spending are collected, it is hard to tease out the gendered effects of the spending, but it is possible to gauge the likely employment and family resource impacts.

Table 5.1 depicts the distribution of key ARRA funds (accounting for 98 per cent) spent through 2011 as well as the likely direct gendered impacts on employment or family resources.

Direct outlays through tax system (credits and tax reductions): at 37 per cent of total ARRA spending, this the largest single category. Of these funds, 25.5 per cent was distributed through broad-based tax cuts, an additional quarter (26 per cent) was targeted toward higher-income taxpayers by reducing the Alternative Minimum

TABLE 5.1 Key areas of spending under the American Recovery and Reinvestment Act and likely gendered impacts

Key areas of spending	Percentage of funds	Direct gendered employment and/or family resource impacts
Tax benefits/payments to individuals and families	37%	Neutral
Human infrastructure spending (deficit reduction)	20%	Mostly female: Women are 76 per cent of health and education workforce and intersect most in use of services
Support to unemployed workers/low-income people and families	19%	Neutral, but bifurcated. Men benefit more from unemployment extension, women from increase in supports for low-income families
Physical infrastructure	14%	Mostly male: women comprised 8.9% of all workers in the construction industry
Leading sector investment (Energy & Environment, Workforce training, Health technology)	8%	Slightly male: women under-represented energy sector; equal beneficiaries of workforce training and health technology

Source: Author's calculation from allocations at Recovery.gov (2011).

Tax (AMT) and 43.5 per cent was targeted toward low-income families as tax credits available only to low-income wage earners. The gender effects of both tax benefit changes are difficult to discern. While women comprise a larger percentage of the populations who are over 65 and are low income[7], the advantage is slight. Therefore, these provisions were probably gender neutral.

Human infrastructure through state budget deficit reduction: One out of every five dollars went to states to shore up their human infrastructure, with 60 per cent of that allocated to the health care programme Medicaid which serves low-income individuals. The rest was allocated to public education. ARRA spending is estimated to have allowed states to close almost 30 per cent of total state budget shortfalls over fiscal years 2009–2011 (Lav *et al.* 2010). These funds disproportionately benefit women through employment and family resource effects. Women comprise three-quarters of the workers in health care and education while women in families with children are the ones that disproportionately receive the provision of these services.

Direct payments to unemployed workers and low-income individuals and families: 19 per cent of ARRA funds were directed toward these purposes. Just under half of these funds were dedicated to serving the unemployed through emergency and extended UI benefits, some of which were contingent upon states modernizing their state-based UI systems to cover more low-wage and part-time workers as well as workers who leave employment because of compelling family reasons, of particular benefit to women. The other half of these funds were primarily allocated to programmes that assist poor and low-income individuals and families. These include food and nutrition programmes (such as SNAP), TANF, child care for poor and low-income children, and education and housing. Men benefit more from UI benefit extensions, while women benefit more from the other spending.

Physical infrastructure: Fourteen per cent of ARRA funds were allocated to the construction or repair of bridges, roads and buildings, and other public improvements. In 2010, women comprised 8.9 per cent of all workers in the construction industry and made up 2.3 per cent of all construction workers. Obviously, the bulk of these funds disproportionately benefited men.

Leading sector investments: Despite initial public claims by the Obama administration, designed to convince the public and legislators to support ARRA, that the funds would be used primarily to invest in future growth through workforce training, 'green environment' development, cutting edge research and upgraded health technologies, only a small percentage (8 per cent) were allocated to these. Gendered employment impacts are likely to be small. Men are currently more likely to be in jobs required in the clean energy sector than are women, but men and women are more equally represented in the other areas.

While there is no precise way to determine who benefited more or less from ARRA funds, this analysis points to a conclusion that overall impacts were probably in aggregate gender neutral, but still gendered by type of fund. Men were the main employment beneficiaries from funds directed toward physical infrastructure improvements (including the green economy), while women's employment clearly benefited from human infrastructure spending. Total ARRA funds allocated to tax benefits, support to unemployed workers and low-income individuals, families and communities, and for workforce development will probably benefit men and women equally – although the specific programmes have prominent gender distinctions. While subtle, the language used in promoting different aspects of ARRA also differed. Energy and physical infrastructure spending, disproportionately benefiting men's employment, were clearly labelled as important long-term investments. Education funding was portrayed as an investment as well, but much of the rationale for the funds allocated to the states was to help states from making more drastic cuts, not as an investment in our human infrastructure. Tax cuts were politically important for passage and the Obama administration was very adept at assuring a large portion of those went to low-income families. But these tax cuts as well as spending supplements to TANF and Food Stamps – the ones that benefit women more than men – were downplayed.

Reducing gender and income inequality

The data discussed in this chapter reveal important differential impacts of the Great Recession by gender. The most pronounced of these were differences in unemployment rates during and immediately following the recession. A cursory look at employment changes by industry and employment-to-population rates suggests that job segregation was a major contributor to a higher increase in male compared to female unemployment rates. There is, however, some evidence that fiscal austerity effects are contributing to women's sluggish recovery compared to men. But there are important differences among women. In particular, women of colour, single mothers and younger women were hit the hardest. These are the same groups of workers without the types of skills or experience that would provide them with an economic foothold in LMEs, making them the most vulnerable to economic fluctuations. While 'safety net' spending, a key element of the means-tested liberal state regime, should kick in with recessions, at least one key programme, TANF, has become considerably less responsive than it has been in the past, disproportionately affecting low-income women and their families.

The federal government in the United States responded to the recent recession with a large stimulus package that helped stem the economic tide at the time of deepest crisis. While expansionary overall, state and local governments' budget cuts have reduced spending on human infrastructure and downsized government employment, disproportionately affecting women, serving as a counterbalance to the federal government's response. While the recovery has been sluggish, unemployment rates have dropped and GDP has grown slowly. Despite the depth of the recession and the opportunity to make substantial changes to the financial sector, fundamental economic restructuring did not occur. And while the European experience provides clear evidence that austerity does not bring economic prosperity, there is a great deal of appetite for deficit reduction which will most likely result in deep federal budget cuts in the United States.

Larger economic and political trends over the last 30 years are resulting in a new gender convergence, with many of the precarious aspects of women's economic situation increasingly spreading to men, including stagnating male median wages, reduced men's labour force participation, a reduction in the percentage of men with employment-based benefits, a decline in male breadwinners, and growth in men's share in low-wage and part-time work. At the same time, the recession highlights the longer-term trend of inequality among women, with higher rates of unemployment for unmarried female heads and women of colour. These two trends conceivably could drive a political wedge among women along class lines. Ironically, the Republican party, driven by neo-liberal economic policies as well as conservative gender (and race) ideologies help to work against that or at least create a space for cross-class gender organizing. Certainly, an alternative economic narrative that promotes policies and economic structures that benefit the most economically precarious would include a large swath of women as well as men. The polices that would help the most include: lifting the wage floor; improving job quality (including employer-based and government-mandated policies, job progression through education and training, and worker flexibility); more universal quality provision of basic human infrastructure such as care of children and elders, education, and health care; and a modernized set of 'safety net' programmes that recognize the decline of the male breadwinner and patterns of female employment. Such changes would reduce income inequality and bolster a middle class, providing a better recipe for long-term economic growth and democratic participation than the current policies.

Notes

1   The author is grateful for the research assistance provided by Ryan Kling.
2   All states except Vermont have legislative or constitutional requirements to balance their budgets. These were instituted at various times starting from the mid-19th century.
3   Just under two-thirds (65 per cent) of all women in the US work 40 hours or more a week, compare to 46 per cent in New Zealand, 34 per cent in Canada, 30 per cent in Australia, and 20 per cent in the UK (OECD 2011; LMF2.1).
4   For a discussion of the possible gender equality impacts in VoC regimes, see Mandel and Shalev 2009a; Estévez-Abe 2005 and 2009; and Rubery 2009. For gender equality impacts of various welfare state regimes see Mandel and Shalev 2009b; Misra *et al.* 2007.
5   The 2009 ratio of hourly wage for women with positive earnings in the 10th percentile compared to the 90th percentile was 0.176 down from 0.229 in 1980 (author's calculations using the Current Population Survey, March Supplement).
6   All employment data reported in the text were downloaded from the US Department of Labor's Bureau of Labor Statistics (2012) that compiles employment and unemployment data using two major monthly surveys. One, the Current Employment Statistics (CES), surveys about 140,000 establishments (businesses and government agencies) and collects data on industry level employment, hours and earnings. The other is based on a monthly survey of households called the Current Population Survey (CPS). This is collected by the US Bureau of the Census and asks detailed questions about household members' labour force, employment and unemployment activity. The survey also has considerable data on demographic, earnings and work force characteristics of adult individuals in households.
7   Using 2010 CPS data, 57 per cent of all those 65 and older are women. Although 68 per cent of poor persons over age 65 are female. Of those with earnings and who are low income (i.e. have income less than 200 of the FPL) and likely to benefit from the low-income tax provisions, 52 per cent are female.

References

Albelda, R. and Carr, M. (2012) 'Low-wage and Low-income Workers in the US, 1979–2009', Working paper, UMass Boston Economics Department, Boston: University of Massachusetts Boston. Available at: http://www.umb.edu/csp/publications/papers (accessed 15.10.2012).

Albelda, R., Duffy, M. and Folbre, N. (2009) *Counting on Care: Human Infrastructure in Massachusetts,* Boston: University of Massachusetts. Available at: http://countingcare.org/, (accessed 15.10.2011).

Allegretto, S.A. and Lynch, D. (2010) 'The Composition Of The Unemployed And Long-Term Unemployed In Tough Labor Markets', *Monthly Labor Review,* 133(10): 3–18.

Bianchi, S.M. (2011) 'Family Change And Time Allocation In American Families', *The Annals of the American Academy of Political and Social Science,* 638: 21–44.

Boushey, H. and Cherry, R. (2002) 'The Severe Implications Of The Economic Downturn On Working Families', *Working USA,* 6(3): 35–54.

Congressional Budget Office (2011) 'Estimated Impact of the American Recovery and Reinvestment Act on Employment and Economic Output from July 2011 Through

September 2011', Washington DC: Congressional Budget Office. Available at: http://www.cbo.gov/ftpdocs/125xx/doc12564/11-22-ARRA.pdf (accessed 21.11.2011).

Economic Policy Institute (2012) The State of Working America: When income grows, who gains? Washington, DC: Economic Policy Institute. Available at: http://stateofworkingamerica.org/who-gains/#/?start=1980&end=2008 (accessed 30.04.2012).

Esping-Andersen, G. (1990) *The Three Worlds of Welfare Capitalism*, Cambridge: Polity Press.

Estévez-Abe, M. (2005) 'Gender Bias in Skills and Social Policies: The Varieties of Capitalism Perspective on Sex Segregation', *Social Politics,* 12(2): 180–215.

Estévez-Abe, M. (2009) 'Gender, Inequality, and Capitalism: The "Varieties of Capitalism" and Women', *Social Politics*, 16(2): 182–91.

Executive Office of the President, Counsel of Economic Advisors (2011) *Economic Report of the President 2010*, Washington DC: US Government Printing Office. Available at: http://www.gpoaccess.gov/eop/tables11.html November 2011 (accessed 08.05.2012).

Fortini, A. (2009) 'The Great He-cession,' *Salon,* June 26. Available at: http://www.salon.com/2009/06/26/death_macho/ (accessed 02.09.2011).

Goodman, C.J. and Mance, S.M. (2011) 'Employment Loss and the 2007-09 Recession: An overview', *Monthly Labor Review,* 134(4): 3–12.

Goodman, W., Antczak, S. and Freeman, L. (1993) 'Women and Jobs in Recessions: 1969–92', *Monthly Labor Review*, 116(7): 26–35.

Hall, P.A. and Soskice, D.W. (2001) *Varieties of Capitalism: The Institutional Foundations of Comparative Advantage*, Oxford: Oxford University Press.

Hartmann, H., English, A. and Hayes, J. (2010) 'Women and Men's Employment And Unemployment In The Great Recession', Washington, DC: Institute for Women's Policy Research. Available at: http://www.iwpr.org/publications/pubs/women-and-men2019s-employment-and-unemployment-in-the-great-recession/at_download/file (accessed 21.11.2011).

Humphries, J. (1988) 'Women's Employment in Restructuring America: The changing experience of women in three recessions', in J. Rubery (ed.) *Women and Recession* (pp. 15–47) London and New York: Routledge and Kegan Paul.

Lav, I., Johnson, N. and McNichol, E. (2010) *Additional Federal Fiscal Relief Needed To Help States Address Recession's Impact*, Washington DC: Center for Budget and Policy Priorities. Available at: http://www.cbpp.org/cms/index.cfm?fa=view&id=2988 (accessed 21.11.2011).

Johnson, N., Oliff, P. and Williams, E. (2011) *An Update on State Budget Cuts: At Least 46 States Have Imposed Cuts That Hurt Vulnerable Residents and the Economy*, Washington, DC: Center for Budget and Policy Priorities. Available at: http://www.cbpp.org/cms/index.cfm?fa=view&id=1214 (accessed 18.10.2011).

MacEwan, A. and Miller, J. (2011) *Economic Collapse, Economic Change: Getting to the Roots of the Crisis*, Armonk, NY: M.E. Sharpe.

Mandel, H. and Shalev, M. (2009a) 'Gender, Class and Varieties of Capitalism', *Social Politics*, 16(2): 161–81.

Mandel, H. and Shalev, M. (2009b) 'How Welfare States Shape the Gender Pay Gap: A Theoretical and Comparative Analysis', *Social Forces*, 87(4): 1873–911.

McNichol, E. Oliff, P. and Johnson, N. (2011) *States Continue to Feel Recession's Impact*, Washington DC: Center for Budget and Policy Priorities. Available at: http://www.cbpp.org/cms/index.cfm?fa=view&id=711 (accessed 21.11.2011).

Milkman, R. (1976) 'Women's Work and Economic Crisis: Some Lessons of the Great Depression', *Review of Radical Political Economics*, 8(1): 71–97.

Misra, J., Moller, S. and Budig, M.J. (2007) 'Work-Family Policies and Poverty for Partnered and Single Women in Europe and North America', *Gender & Society,* 21(6): 804–27.

National Association of State Budget Officers (2011) *Fiscal Survey of States,* Washington DC: National Association of State Budget Officers. Available at: http://nasbo.org/LinkClick. aspx?fileticket=yNV8Jv3X7Is%3d&tabid=65 (accessed 21.11.2011).

National Bureau of Economic Research (2011) *US Business Cycle Expansions and Eontractions,* Available at: http://www.nber.org/cycles.html (accessed 18.10.2011).

OECD (2011) *OECD Family Database,* Paris: OECD. Available www.oecd.org/social/family/database (accessed 28.08.2012).

Rampell, C. (2011) 'Mancession to He-covery', *New York Times,* July 6, 2011. Available at: http://economix.blogs.nytimes.com/2011/07/06/mancession-to-he-covery/ (accessed 18.10.2011).

Rubery, J. (1988) 'Women and Recession: Preface', in J. Rubery (ed.) *Women and Recession* (pp. ix– xii), London and New York: Routledge and Kegan Paul.

Rubery, J. (2009) 'How Gendering the Varieties of Capitalism Requires a Wider Lens', *Social Politics,* 16(2): 192–203.

Şahin, A., Song, J. and Hobijn, B. (2010) 'The Unemployment Gender Gap during the 2007 Recession', *Current Issues in Economics and Finance,* Federal Reserve Bank of New York, 16(2).

Seeborg, M. and DeBoer, L. (1987) 'The Narrowing Male-Female Unemployment Differential', *Growth and Change,* 18(2): 24–37.

US Census Bureau (2011a) *State and Local Government Finances Summary 2009.* Available at: http://www2.census.gov/govs/estimate/09_summary_report.pdf (accessed 21.11.2011).

US Census Bureau (2011b) *Income: Historical Tables.* Available at: http://www.census.gov/hhes/www/income/data/historical (accessed 08.04.2012).

US Census Bureau (2011c) *Poverty: Historical Tables.* Available at: http://www.census.gov/hhes/www/poverty/data/historical/index.html (accessed 08.04.2012).

US Census Bureau (2012) *The 2012 Statistic Abstract: The National Data Book.* Available at: http://www.census.gov/compendia/statab/cats/labor_force_employment_earnings/labor_force_status.html (accessed 08.04.2012).

US Department of Agriculture (2011) *Program Data.* 'Monthy data,' Available at: http://www.fns.usda.gov/pd/34SNAPmonthly.htm (accessed 21.11.2011).

US Department of Health and Human Services (2009) *TANF Eighth Annual Report to Congress 2009.* Available at: http://www.acf.hhs.gov/programs/ofa/data-reports/index.htm (accessed 11.01.2011).

US Department of Health and Human Services (2011) *Caseload Data. Administration for Families and Children.* Available at: http://www.acf.hhs.gov/programs/ofa/data-reports/caseload/caseload_current.htm (accessed 18.10.2011).

US Department of Labor, Bureau of Labor Statistics (2012) *Labor Force Statistics from the Current Population Survey.* Available at: http://www.bls.gov/cps/#data (accessed 08.04.2012).

US Department of Labor, Employment and Training Administration (2012) Characterisitcs of the Insured Unemployed. Available at:http://workforcesecurity.doleta.gov/unemploy/chariu.asp, (accessed 08.04.2012).

US Office of Management and Budget (2011) *Budget of the United States Government: Historical tables fiscal year 2011.* Available at: http://www.gpoaccess.gov/usbudget/fy11/hist.html (accessed 21.11.2011).

6

ICELAND IN CRISIS

Gender equality and social equity[1]

Thora Kristin Thorsdottir

Iceland was one of the first countries to be hit by the international financial crisis and the Icelandic story is rather dramatic, starting with a sudden collapse of the country's banking system in October 2008. The crisis that followed was simultaneously a banking crisis, a currency crisis, an economic recession and a crisis of societal and political trust (Ólafsson 2011a). Iceland shares with some other recession-hit countries, such as Ireland, the US and the UK, the problems of an overextended banking system that fuelled a debt-led growth bubble. What sets Iceland particularly apart from the other countries is the approach the government took, in collaboration with the IMF, to steer the country out of the crisis. In Paul Krugman's (2011) words it adopted 'very heterodox policies — debt repudiation, capital controls, and currency depreciation. It was as close as you can get to the polar opposite of the gold standard. And it has worked.'

One of the leading perspectives in welfare state research is that politics matters, that policy developments can be explained by which parties are in government (Korpi 1983; Esping-Andersen 1990). This theory certainly seems to apply to Iceland in the wake of the banking crisis. Iceland made a u-turn and elected a left-wing government in May 2009, after almost 18 years of continuous right-wing rule during which the conservative Independence Party presided over a far-ranging neo-liberalization of the Icelandic economy and society (Ólafsson 2011b). The current government, a coalition between the Social Democrats and the Left Greens, pledged from the beginning to be a Nordic Welfare government and to aim 'to protect low-income earners and those who are most vulnerable and to distribute the burden fairly, equitably and justly' (Government of Iceland 2009).[2] It has therefore used a mix of raising taxes and cutting expenditure to deal with the public deficit and has declared its long-term aim to move the country closer to the standard Nordic model. The cuts are thus to be considered a temporary measure (see e.g. Hannesson 2010).

Iceland has seen some improvements in gender equality since the collapse, especially in women's political representation. Indeed, in 2009, Iceland jumped to top place in the World Economic Forum's Global Gender Gap Index where it remains to this day (Hausmann *et al.* 2012). The current government was the first in Icelandic history to be led by a woman and to have an equal share of men and women in cabinet. It has emphasized gender equality more than any previous government and promised in its coalition agreement that 'women's influence in the country's recovery' would 'be ensured' and gender equality 'promoted at all levels of society, instituting specific measures to this end if necessary' (Government of Iceland 2009).

The aim of this chapter is to assess to what extent the government has kept its promises and whether this apparent rise in gender equality extends to the general public. The structure of the chapter is as follows. After a brief description of the economics of the recession, the focus moves first to the gender regime in Iceland and then to the labour market in recession and recovery. It then turns to the management of the crisis and the effects on women before reflecting on how the gender regime has changed in the wake of the crisis and on future prospects.[3]

The Iceland saga

The story of the Icelandic economy for the past decade is the familiar one of the creation of an asset growth bubble that burst, but what is unique about the Icelandic case is the size of the bubble. When the country's three largest banks were nation-alized in autumn 2008 the total asset side of their balance sheets had grown to almost ten times the Icelandic GDP (Sigurjónsson and Mixa 2011). Two of the banks were handed over to the foreign claimants in 2009 but one, Landsbanki, still remains in government hands.

The short history of the Icelandic banks as global financial institutions started in the late 1990s with the opening up of asset management subsidiaries in Luxembourg and Guernsey, primarily to offer financial services to wealthy Icelanders. While their operations expanded over the next years, mostly through acquisitions, growth was rather slow until the completion of the privatization of the state-owned banks in 2003 (Helgason 2010). The banks expanded rapidly during the 2000s, due to a combination of their managers' great appetite for risk, the strong Icelandic currency exchange rate, and the very favourable conditions in international financial markets providing an ample credit supply at low interest rates. Between 2003 and 2007 the banks' balance sheets grew by 60 per cent on average annually (Pétursson 2010). Much of this growth was through loans to Icelandic investment companies, mostly owned by individuals and firms with close connections to the banks. These loans were used to finance leveraged takeovers and corporate raids, frequently involving newly privatized state enterprises (Helgason 2010; Althingi Special Investigation Commission 2010). At the same time the banks entered the mortgage loan market (which previously was dominated by the state-owned Housing Financing Fund) and aggressively expanded their consumer loans. The result was a serious asset bubble, both in the stock market and housing market. Real house prices rose 128 per cent between 1997 and 2008 (Central Bank of Iceland 2008: 27) and the stock market index increased sevenfold between 2002 and 2007 (Ólafsson 2011b). National savings fell and private debt increased so that by the end of 2005 Iceland already enjoyed the dubious status of being the most debt ridden country in the world with net external debt (both public and private) of 160 per cent of GDP (Central Bank of Iceland 2007: 20).

Although to the general public the financial collapse seemed very sudden, it did not come as a surprise to everyone. Foreign analysts had started publishing negative reports on the Icelandic economy from early 2006, questioning for example the large role played by foreign exchange gains in the returns of the banks (Helgason 2010). An IMF report (2006) pointed to major macroeconomic imbalances in Iceland (a large current account deficit, high external debt and high inflation) that posed a risk to the banking sector and suggested that the banks' wholesale-funded asset growth, interconnected counterparties, and rapid foreign expansion were aggravating their vulnerability. Such warnings were not given due attention by the authorities (Althingi Special Investigation Commission 2010), resulting in the collapse of the banking sector in October 2008. The government then in power, a coalition between the Independence Party and the Social Democrats, started negotiations with the IMF immediately and on 24 October 2008 the IMF announced a $2.1 billion Stand-By Agreement with Iceland (IMF 2008), the key objectives of which were to: 1) restore early confidence in the currency by stemming its depreciation (done in part by the use of capital controls); 2) balance public finances through a multi-fiscal consolidation programme; and 3) re-build the banking system. The fund financing aimed at shoring up the low levels of international reserves, as well as strengthening investor confidence and the country's financing capacity (IMF 2012b). Total financing associated with this programme reached about $5 billion with about $3 billion provided by bilateral loans from the Nordic countries and Poland (Guðmundsson 2010).

Iceland completed the programme successfully, according to the IMF, with key objectives met (IMF 2011; 2012b). The country, however, still faces considerable challenges including when and how to lift the capital controls. Public debt remains high with the gross debt of the Treasury (excluding Icesave liabilities[4] as well as the aforementioned loans) estimated as 83.7 per cent of GDP in 2011 (Ministry of Finance and Economic Affairs 2012a). Iceland has now repaid about one-fifth of the loans received from the IMF and the Nordic countries by refinancing, ahead of schedule (IMF, 2012a).

The recession in Iceland was very steep and lasted from 2008 third quarter until the end of 2010. The cumulative contraction of GDP in 2009 and 2010 amounted to 10.6 per cent (see Table 6.1), the fifth largest contraction in Europe during this period, after Latvia, Estonia, Lithuania and Ireland (Ólafsson 2011a). Inflation was very high during the recession, in a large part due to the depreciation of the currency, peaking at 18.6 per cent in January 2009.

TABLE 6.1 Economic growth and inflation in Iceland 2007–2011

	GDP growth %	Inflation % (peak value – month)
2007	6.0	5.0 (7.4 – February)
2008	1.2	12.4 (18.1 – December)
2009	–6.6	12.0 (18.6 – January)
2010	–4.0	5.4 (8.5 – March)
2011	2.6	4.0 (5.7 – September)

Source: Statistics Iceland.

Growth in GDP returned at the end of 2010 and was 2.6 per cent in 2011. Similar growth rates are expected in 2012 and through to 2014 (Central Bank of Iceland 2012) but inflation remains rather high. After falling to a trough of 1.8 per cent in January 2011 it climbed slowly but surely to peak at 6.5 per cent in January 2012, declining gradually thereafter to stand at 4.2 per cent in December 2012.

The gender regime

Iceland has been one of the leaders in gender equality legislation since women were granted the same inheritance rights as men in 1850. Icelandic women also obtained equal right to grants, study and the civil service in 1911, the right to vote in 1915, and benefited from the first gender equality act in 1976 (Centre for Gender Equality 2012). In summer 2008, a new comprehensive gender equality law was passed, spearheaded by Jóhanna Sigurðardóttir, then the Minister of Social Affairs but now Prime Minister. The law[5] contains many improvements, including a minimum gender quota of 40 per cent on governmental committees and councils larger than three members and a ban on wage secrecy.[6]

Like the other Nordic countries the Icelandic gender regime belongs to the dual breadwinner model. Until the late 1990s, however, Iceland lagged behind its neighbours, retaining many of the features of a male breadwinner society with limited support for parents, including childcare (Ólafsson 1999). Employment rates for both sexes are very high, standing in 2007 at 89.1 per cent for men and 80.8 per cent for women aged 15–64 compared to EU averages of 72.5 per cent and 58.2 per cent respectively (Eurostat LFS). The duration of working life for both sexes is also longer in Iceland than in the other European countries,[7] partly due to the late retirement age (in general 67 years but retirement can be postponed until 70 in the public sector and 72 in the private sector). The employment rate of mothers is further exceptionally high in Iceland (OECD 2010), facilitated by high coverage of day-care in recent years. In 2007 42 per cent of children aged 0–2 years and 97 per cent of children aged 3–5 years were enrolled in pre-schools. One reason behind their high coverage is that the pre-schools are run by the municipalities and highly subsidized; so, for example, in 2010 fees paid by a lone parent for eight hours of care for a one year old would cover around 7 per cent of the total costs with married couples paying about 12 per cent (Eydal and Árnadóttir 2010).

Part-time work is quite common among women in Iceland, with 36 per cent of employed women (and 9 per cent of employed men) aged 15–64 working part-time (defined as below 35 hours a week) in 2007.[8] The working week for full-timers is comparatively long at around 49 hours a week on average for men and 42 for women in 2007. These long hours are the result of many factors but arguably the most important is the combination of relatively low pay and a high demand for labour (Ólafsson 1999), which encourages overtime work or double jobs. This is further accompanied by a relatively positive attitude towards work in Iceland (Ólafsson 1996).

Like elsewhere in Scandinavia, the Icelandic labour market is highly segregated by gender (Bettio and Verashchagina 2009), with women being over-represented in the service sector and men in the production sector. The service sector actually accounted for 89 per cent of employed women in 2007 against 61 per cent of employed men. Women are also over-represented in the public sector as 73 per cent of all workers in the public employment sectors of public administration, education and health were female in 2007. These sectors accounted for about 44 per cent of all employed women and 14 per cent of employed men in 2007. And partly due to the gender segregation of the labour market the gender pay gap remains considerable. The gap in median pay for full time workers was 15.2 per cent in Iceland in 2007, which is considerably larger than in Denmark (9.2 per cent) and Norway (9.8 per cent) but close to that of Sweden (16.4 per cent) (OECD Family Database).

What sets Iceland specifically apart from Scandinavia is the welfare state, due to its liberal characteristics (Ólafsson 1999). It is Scandinavian with regard to the system being largely individualized and universal, and education and health-care being primarily run by the state. The system is liberal in the sense that benefits are low and income-tested, with the exception of the parental leave, which was rather generous before the crisis.[9] Non-governmental organizations also play a relatively large role in welfare provision, especially in elderly care (Ólafsson 1999 and 2003). Regarding social expenditure in general, and expenditure on services and benefits to families in particular, Iceland has lagged behind the other Scandinavian countries (Ólafsson 1999 and 2003). Thus, although child poverty, defined as the proportion of children living in households with less than 50 per cent of the median income, is lower in Iceland than in most Western countries, it is higher than in Scandinavia, especially for single and couple households with only one breadwinner (OECD 2008). The share of children living in lone parent households is, however, slightly lower in Iceland than in the rest of Scandinavia (Eurostat: EU SILC).

All Nordic countries introduced some type of fathers' leave in the 1990s to encourage fathers to participate in the care of their children (Eydal and

Rostgaard 2011). The Icelandic scheme was implemented in stages but since 2003 (and until 2013) each parent has had three months of non-transferable parental leave with a further three months to apportion between them. Initially, parents could receive 80 per cent of their average income prior to the leave but a cap was introduced in 2004. Parental leave uptake by fathers has been above expectations, with 88.6 per cent of new fathers applying for leave in 2006 (Eydal and Gíslason 2008). In 2006 fathers accounted for about one-third of the days spent by couples on parental leave, the highest proportion among fathers in Scandinavia (ibid) and thus anywhere in the world.

Labour market trends in recession and recovery

Comparing 2011 to 2007, it is clear that the labour market has still far from made a full recovery, with unemployment more than triple the level before the crisis. And even though male workers have been more affected by the crisis than female workers, the impact is getting close to equal.

The net job loss between 2007 and 2011, measured by the decline in total number of employed persons is about 10,000 – 95 per cent of them men. Women's share of employment thus grew from 45.5 per cent in 2007 to 48 per cent in 2011 as did their share of labour force (the employed and the unemployed combined) from 45.5 per cent to 47.5 per cent. This change reflects not only men leaving the workforce but also a small added worker effect with the female workforce growing by 3.6 per cent during the period.

One practice Icelandic employers used to avoid redundancies was cutting working hours through overtime reductions and changing employment to part-time. As men work longer hours, their cut in working time was larger at 2.8 hours on average between 2007 and 2011 while women lost a negligable 0.2 hours (see Table 6.2).

TABLE 6.2 The Icelandic labour market by gender in 2007, 2009 and 2011

	2007		2009		2011	
	M	W	M	W	M	W
Employment rate % (15–64 years old)	89.1	80.8	80	76.5	80.3	76.6
Unemployment rate % (15–64 years old)	2.2	2.3	8.8	5.8	8	6.2
Average working hours (all ages)	46.9	35.6	43.8	34.9	44.1	35.4
Average working hours – full time (all ages)	49.4	42.1	46.8	41.6	47.4	41.3
Average working hours – part time (all ages)	22.5	24.5	22.3	23.2	21.5	24.4
Part-time employment rate % (15–64 year-olds)	8.7	36	11.6	35.5	9.9	31.7

Sources: European Labour Force Survey (Eurostat online database accessed on 21.01.2013). Data on working time provided by Statistics Iceland.

The number of men working part-time (defined as under 35 hours a week) has grown since the collapse, peaking in 2009, presumably mostly due to involuntary shifts to part-time work. At the same time the number of women working full-time has increased while the number working part-time decreased, so the share of employed women working part-time declined between 2007 and 2011.

Young people have been the most affected. At its peak point, in 2009, the unemployment rate for men aged 16–24 reached 19.9 per cent and that for women 12.0 per cent, more than twice the rates for the labour force as a whole. Workers of foreign origin (most of whom being migrant workers) have also been much more affected; thus at the peak of the recession in 2009 the registered unemployment rate of foreign citizens (all ages) was 11.2 per cent compared to the Icelandic citizens' rate of 8.1 per cent (The Directorate of Labour 2012). Long-term unemployment has risen extensively since the crisis, particularly among older cohorts and women. In December 2012, 51 per cent of the unemployed had been without work for more than six months and 35 per cent for more than a year (The Directorate of Labour 2013). Unemployment has further been increasingly concentrated among the low skilled and people with only elementary education have accounted for over half the unemployed since the beginning of the crisis. By Icelandic standards unemployment rates since the crisis have been unusually high, as before unemployment was close to non-existent. By international standards, however, these levels are unexceptional, as the unemployment rate for the 15–64-year-old population in Iceland has mostly stayed below the EU average over the crisis.[10]

As in other parts of Europe, the recession first hit male-dominated sectors, particularly construction and the financial sector. Consequently, unemployment rose more quickly for men than for women and almost doubled between the third and fourth quarter of 2008. From then on both sexes' unemployment rates rose steeply but men's more so than women's. It also reached a peak at 11 per cent for men in the second quarter of 2009, while that for women peaked one year later at 8.2 per cent. Between 2008 third quarter and 2010, the employment rate decreased by 7.3 percentage points for men and by 3.2 for women. So while both sexes were much affected by the recession, men were clearly much harder hit than women. With the recovery, the picture is not as simple.

The labour market showed no marked signs of recovery for either sex until 2011 when the unemployment rate for both sexes began to decrease. From the third quarter of 2011 onwards, men's recovery has surpassed that of women's with men's unemployment level over two percentage points below the previous year's while women's unemployment was only 0.6 and 0.7 percentage points lower in the last two quarters of 2011. Women's unemployment rose in the first part of 2012 but by the third quarter of 2012 it had declined by 1.3 percentage points compared to the previous year, but whether or not that indicates a reversal of the trend it is too early to tell.[11] In addition, women's registered unemployment rate has exceeded men's for most months from mid-year 2011 (latest data is for November 2012; Directorate of Labour). Similar trends are seen in employment, which has been

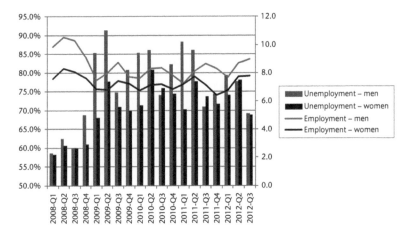

FIGURE 6.1   Employment and unemployment rates by gender in Iceland 2008–2012
Source: Eurostat.

rising for men but declining for women since the third quarter of 2011 (except for an upward turn in the third quarter of 2012, the latest data at the time of writing). It thus seems that women's situation in the labour market has been deteriorating lately while that of men has been getting better and that male and female workers are getting close to being equally affected by the collapse.

Changes in sectors and occupations

For the period as a whole (2007–2011) net job loss was concentrated in construction and wholesale, retail trade and repairs. At the same time, employment expanded in hotels and restaurants due in part to an increase in tourism by 30 per cent,[12] linked to the devaluation of the currency but also to the eruption of the Eyjafjallajökull volcano in 2010.

If we divide the period as before into recession and recovery, it appears that the trends during the two periods were somewhat opposite in nature. This explains the difference in gender impact because the Icelandic labour market is highly gender segregated as earlier noted. In the recession, 2008–2010, the employment contraction was almost exclusive to the private sector while the public services sectors of public administration, education, and health and social services were hardly affected. Due to the contraction in construction, men's job loss was primarily in manual occupations, among craft and related trades, plant and machine operators and elementary occupations, while among women it was clerks and service and sales workers who lost jobs. Although the employment decline in the private sector continued in the recovery, especially in construction and manufacturing, employment contracted more in the public sector (more specifically in education and public administration).[13] And contrary to developments in the recession, the employment reduction for men in the recovery was mainly in the highest-paid

TABLE 6.3 Employment by economic sector and gender in Iceland 2007, 2009 and 2011

	2007		2009		2011	
	Total	%W	Total	%W	Total	%W
Agriculture	6000	30	4300	35	4800	27
Fishing	4500	4	4700	6	5200	6
Fish processing	2900	38	3200	41	3800	42
Manufacturing	16400	28	16300	29	15400	26
Electricity and water supply	1700	24	1500	27	1600	25
Construction	15700	4	11700	8	10000	6
Wholesale, retail trade, repairs	25500	44	21100	41	21800	46
Hotels, restaurants	6200	60	7700	52	8800	61
Transport, communication	11200	34	12000	31	11300	33
Financial intermediation	8700	59	7900	61	8300	63
Retail, estate and business activities	17200	34	16400	40	18000	38
Public administration	9000	50	9100	53	7200	53
Education	13500*	66	20300*	77	18300	76
Health services, social work	26000*	85	19500*	81	20500	80
Other services and n.s.	12600	54	11800	54	12400	54
Total	177200	46	167700	47	167300	48

*Due to change from NACE 2008 to NACE 1995, data for employment in education and health/social work sectors are not comparable
W= women.
Source: Statistics Iceland.

occupations, among legislators and managers and professionals. For women the main employment reduction was felt by associate professionals, followed by clerks and workers in elementary occupations. For the labour market as a whole men lost more jobs than women so women's share of employment grew during both periods.

Icelandic and foreign migrant workers

Immigration to Iceland was rather limited until the 2000s boom when the need for migrant workers grew rapidly, leading to a spike in immigration flows, peaking in 2007. In these boom years about two men moved to the country for each woman, mirroring the construction boom. During the recession, however, the numbers of men and women immigrating to Iceland grew close to equal. The inflow of immigrants fell by almost half between 2008 and 2009 but has been mostly steady since. All recessions in Iceland have been followed by emigration by Icelandic nationals, looking for employment opportunities abroad or furthering their education, but the level of emigration has seldom if ever been as high as in 2009 (Agnarsson 2010). The Icelandic population lost over 4,800 individuals (all nationalities) during that year alone and over 8,300 people since the collapse (2008–2011), 73 per cent (6,100) of whom are men.

The gender pay gap

The gender pay gap has also been affected by the crisis, first falling in the recession but then starting to rise in the recovery. Figure 6.2 shows that the wage index for the private sector fell sharply in 2009 but rose in 2010 and 2011 while that of the public sector fell more slowly, reaching a trough in 2010 before starting to rise in 2011 – but at a rate well below that of the private sector. As about 42 per cent of employed women work in the public sector (in 2011), while about 85 per cent of employed men work within the private sector, these differences between the wage indices are likely to mean that the gender pay gap fell in 2009 as public sector wages rose more than private sector wages, but then expanded again when the opposite occurred in 2010 and 2011.

The gender pay gaps within the private and the public sectors have shown similar trends. According to the Union of Public Servants annual survey, the raw gender gap in public sector average total salaries fell from 27.0 percentage points in 2008 to 21.4 in 2009 before rising again to 23.7 and 24.0 in 2010 and 2011 (SFR 2012). A recent analysis of public sector pay has also revealed a gender bias in wage developments, for while most occupational groups have received a pay raise of above 10 per cent (in nominal terms) since the crisis, four occupations, all female dominated (nurses, occupational therapists, physiotherapists and development therapists; see RÚV 2012) have not. Turning to the private sector, Statistics Iceland's data show the gender gap at the median for full-timers' total salaries (including overtime and all irregular payments), fell between 2008 and 2009 from 25.1 percentage points to 18.2, rising to 19.4 in 2010 but falling again to 19.0 in 2011. So although the gender pay gap has not yet regained its 2008 level the data clearly show a slight upward trend during the recovery, both in the private and the public sector.

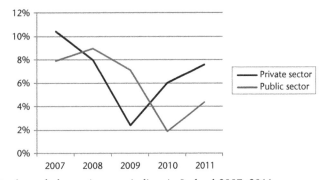

FIGURE 6.2 Annual change in wage indices in Iceland 2007–2011

The management of the crisis and its consequences for women

The current coalition government of Social Democrats and Left Greens came into power as an interim government in early 2009, as the previous one was toppled by massive protests. While it had a certain momentum in the beginning, it had a lot to prove as the first entirely left-wing government in the history of the Icelandic Republic and facing greater challenges than any previous Icelandic government. It pledged from the start to be a Nordic welfare government aiming at protecting the worst-off in the crisis as far as possible, with the long-term aim of moving the country closer to the standard Scandinavian model. But there was a constraint. When it took over, a stand-by agreement had already been signed between the previous government and the IMF, an organization hitherto not known for its support for welfare state expenditure (Chang 2012). The government was thus under considerable external pressures to introduce austerity measures. This pressure stemmed not only from the conditions of the IMF Agreement but also, as Irving (2012) points out, from international messages on the need to restore market confidence. Moreover, loans from the other lenders (Nordic countries and Poland) were conditional on the IMF programme and alternative lenders were not in sight. The government was thus in a far from ideal position to fulfil its goals but for some reason the IMF was 'surprisingly indulgent' (Irving 2012: 309) in response to the government's focus on welfare, approving its moderate and equitable cost-sharing approach of raising taxes and cutting expenditure, instead of pushing for a heavy and socially damaging austerity package.

Before we turn to changes in benefits and taxes, it is important to take a look at how the crisis affected standards of living. As earlier stated, Icelandic households are among the most debt ridden in the world and at its peak household debt amounted to 129 per cent of GDP (third quarter 2009; Central Bank of Iceland 2011: 12). The rise in household debt was partly due to the indexation of mortgage loans to inflation, which was very high in the recession (see Table 6.1), but debt levels had risen rapidly from 2003 to 2007. Real wages fell as a consequence by close to 3 per cent in 2008, about 7 per cent in 2009 and 4 per cent in 2010.[14] Private consumption fell as well by a total of 22 per cent between 2007 and 2010 (Ólafsson and Kristjánsson 2012). These cuts are very high by international standards and it has even been suggested that the real wage cut in Iceland was the largest experienced in Europe or the US in this recession (Ólafsson 2011a). Taking into account other factors, such as reduced work volumes, higher taxes and increased debt burden, the overall cut in per capita real disposable earnings amounted to about 27 per cent on average during the crisis, mostly due to the depreciation of the currency and associated inflation (Ólafsson and Kristjánsson 2012). Real wages started to increase in the latter part of 2010 and 2011, rising by 5.1 per cent in the beginning of 2012 so part of what was lost has already been regained, though as inflation is expected to rise this year (Central Bank of Iceland 2012), the annualised real wage rise may be lower.

Taxes were raised but the structure of the tax system was also modified so that between 2008 and 2010 the top 40 per cent of the income distribution experienced tax rises while tax fell for those on lower incomes (Ólafsson and Kristjánsson 2012). Nominal increases in the basic unemployment benefit, social assistance allowance, minimum pension as well as the minimum wage amounted to 31 to 41 per cent between 2007 and 2010 (Ólafsson 2011a), that is close to or above the rise in the consumer price index of 32.7 per cent. From a gender perspective, the rise in minimum pension is especially important, as women are the majority of disability pension claimants as well as the majority of those receiving only the minimum old age pension.

The changes in taxes along with the increase in benefits and specific measures to tackle household debt[15] thus worked to shelter the low-income groups to a certain extent. Estimates of changes in real disposable earnings of couples between 2008 and 2010 by income deciles (excluding capital gains as well as the effects of the increased debt burden) show that while on average real disposable earnings fell by a fifth, those of high-income earners fell by more with couples in the top income decile losing 38 per cent (Ólafsson and Kristjánsson 2012). Due to the inferior economic position of women, this policy has very likely sheltered women from the effects of the crisis to a greater extent than men. However, the fall in real disposable earnings was still 9 per cent for the couples in the two lowest income deciles, a group with the least flexibility to respond to such falls. The deterioration in quality of life and the increase in financial strain may thus be greater for the individuals in the lowest income groups than for the others, and thus on average for women rather than men.

Even if those on the lowest incomes have been partially protected, economic hardship has increased since the financial collapse, although it is similar to levels found in 2004, before the bubble. According to the EU-SILC data the proportion of Icelandic households experiencing difficulties making ends meet fell from 46 per cent in 2004 to 28 per cent in 2007 rising again to 52 per cent by 2011. Households with children experience more difficulties than those without; single parents were particularly affected with 78 per cent finding it difficult to make ends meet in 2011. This was a steep rise from 58 per cent in 2007 but about equal to the percentage in 2004. The vulnerability of single parents, the majority of whom are women, is evident in the data as in 2011 18 per cent had arrears on rent or mortgage payments and 28 per cent on other loans compared to 10 per cent and 12 per cent for all households respectively.

In addition to increases in basic unemployment benefits, the unemployment benefits system was modified to ease the pain for those losing their jobs or forced to go part-time. One temporary measure allowed part-timers to receive unemployment benefits in proportion to their working-time reduction no matter the salary, so some could receive benefits even if their wages exceeded the maximum benefit amount.[16] This measure, probably influenced by fear of a great rise in involuntary part-timers especially among men, was especially useful to women who were two-thirds of the claimants (Directorate of Labour 2012) when it was abolished in the beginning of 2012.

Unemployment has of course been a key concern for public policy since the collapse, both on the supply and the demand side. The budget for active labour market programmes has increased five-fold (OECD 2011), as the number and variety of labour market measures rose substantially. The new measures include subsidised 'trial hiring' for firms as well as public institutions, provisions to do volunteer work while on benefits and job retraining, but education has been a key strategy. One such important measure is that secondary schools have been opened to those under 25 who wish to complete their education.[17] The use of these measures as a whole is close to equal among the sexes (women were 42 per cent of users in 2010 and also 42 per cent of unemployment benefit claimants) but there are considerable gender differences in the choice of measure. Men are more likely to do the shorter courses and make use of the job-related measures while women are more likely to make use of the longer education options (Ministry of Finance and Economic Affairs 2011).

The government has also introduced a number of measures to assist businesses, including for example VAT rebates on maintenance work. It has also emphasized job creation but with a focus on boosting demand in sectors such as construction that are male-dominated. For example, the investment plan announced in 2012 by the Prime Minister's Office aimed at creating around 4,000 jobs (Prime Minister's Office 2012a), equivalent to two-fifths of the net job loss in the recession, made no mention of its gender impact but, as one-third of the investments are in property projects, men are the most likely beneficiaries.

A new reactivating initiative to tackle long-term unemployment will be implemented in 2013, aimed at offering a six-month temporary job to those who will have exceeded the four-year maximum claiming time for benefits in 2013.[18] The collaborative project across central government ministries, municipalities and trade unions provides subsidies to employers equal to unemployment benefits and provides participants with higher income than alternative municipality-based social benefits. Thus 2,200 temporary jobs should be created, split 60/40 between the private and the public sectors. Among those eligible women, older cohorts and immigrants are likely to be overrepresented but there are no details as to how gender issues will be taken into account so that the gender impact cannot be estimated. That in itself, however, raises concern over a potential male bias.

Although the government did seek to protect the lower paid and more vulnerable and to raise taxes rather than simply cutting expenditure, public spending cuts have still been substantial, with a total accumulated reduction estimated at 8 per cent of GDP between 2009 and 2012 (Ministry of Finance and Economic Affairs 2011). And although the cuts have decreased on an annual basis they are not over yet. As an example, it is expected that expenditures on general public services will be cut by 1.75 per cent in 2013 (Ministry of Finance and Economic Affairs 2012b).

Parents have been particularly affected by the cuts. While spending on benefits for the unemployed, the disabled and the elderly has increased, spending on benefits for families has decreased. Measured per capita, the cuts amount to 4 per cent between 2007 and 2010.[19] The main change is to child benefits; just before the crisis in the summer of 2008 these were increased by 5.7 per cent but below inflation of 12.4 per cent, and have been frozen throughout the crisis. They have also been made more subject to income testing, with a higher marginal deduction rate so that fewer parents now receive benefits and those still eligible often receive less. The government has, however, decided to raise expenditure on child benefits in 2013 by 30 per cent in nominal terms, by raising the ceilings for full benefits as well as the benefits themselves, with people at the upper end of those eligible likely to benefit more than those on lower income (Harðardóttir 2012).

Parental leave has also been cut three times since the collapse, twice under the current government. The cap has been lowered by 40 per cent and the replacement rate reduced from 80 per cent to 75 per cent for beneficiaries with income above 200,000 ISK a month, that is less than the lowest quartile earnings of female full-time workers in the private sector (252,000 ISK in 2008).[20] The cap has thus been below the average salary so a growing number of parents have experienced a loss of income while on leave. The share of parents on leave receiving the maximum amount thus rose quite extensively since the collapse: in 2008 8.3 per cent of fathers and 1.9 per cent of mothers received the maximum but in 2010, the year of the final cut, these figures had risen to 46 per cent and 19 per cent respectively (Childbirth Leave Fund 2010). These cuts have further had the effect that the uptake of parental leave among fathers, albeit still very high, has been declining.

The government in 2013 has announced plans to make good some of these losses (Ministry of Finance and Economic Affairs 2012b) by both increasing child benefits and immediately extending parental leave to a year in total, and each parent's entitlement from three to five months, leaving two months to apportion between them (instead of three).[21] The replacement rate has been raised to 80 per cent and the cap for full benefits raised back to 350,000 ISK, although in real terms the cap still remains lower than it was.

The current government has emphasized gender equality in its approach, as evident in the promises made in the coalition agreement (Government of Iceland 2009). One such example is the promise to give equal rights 'increased attention within public administration', which has been implemented by, for example, extensively increasing information gathering on gender equality issues, especially with the Well-being Watch, which is charged with analyzing and reporting to the government on the effects of the recession on Icelandic households as well as making policy suggestions. The government also promised to make gender budgeting 'a key concern in budget preparation and economic policy' and appointed a project manager on gender budgeting to work on its integration and implementation in 2009. The aim is to implement gender budgeting in stages over the period 2011–2014 according to the government's *Four year gender equality action programme* (Ministry of Welfare 2012a: 2).

Tackling wage inequality was one of the promises originally made and in 2012 the government resolved to implement a four-year action plan to close the gender pay gap (Ministry of Welfare 2012b). This plan includes the development and implementation of a special Equal Pay Standard, to help employers pay men and women equal wages for equal work, if they care to do so. Its development is in its final stages and its implementation is expected to start in 2013 (Prime Minister's Office 2012b).

The government also promised action to eliminate gender-based violence and made purchasing of prostitution illegal with changes to the general penal code[22] in 2009 so that perpetrators may now face prison for up to a year or two years if the victim is a minor. A full ban on strip clubs was enacted in 2010, with an amendment to the act on restaurants, accommodations and entertainment banning the profiting from nudity.[23] Finally, the Austrian model in domestic violence cases was legalized in 2011.[24] The laws authorize the removal of the party accused of domestic violence from the household and put in place a specific restraining order should there be a suspicion of domestic violence.

Other efforts towards gender equality not mentioned in the coalition agreement are also being made, for example efforts to increase education on matters of gender equality from pre-schools to the university level and to implement gender mainstreaming (Ministry of Welfare 2012b). Increasing women's access to power is another example and in that vein laws on gender quotas in corporate boards were passed in 2010. They state that in companies with 50 workers or more the board should comprise of at least three people and have members of both sexes. If more than three are on the board, each sex should have at least 40 per cent of the seats.[25]

Policy making following the crisis has thus addressed gender issues at the highest level, such as through policies to gather gender equality information, to implement gender budgeting, and develop the Equal Pay Standard. However, at a lower level, in individual policy areas and in specific policies, such as in efforts to boost employment, the gender perspective has not been as present. Due to the relatively high level of men's unemployment since the collapse and perhaps also due to the prevalence of traditional ideas about men as breadwinners and women as carers, unemployment has been construed as more of a men's problem in Iceland. The solutions have thus been biased towards men despite the government's initial promise to let gender perspectives guide efforts in job creation (Government of Iceland 2009). As we saw earlier, the approach taken, along with the economic recovery, has been successfully reducing men's unemployment but women's unemployment has been rising with the cuts in public expenditure. As men tend to work more in the private sector, which is more sensitive to economic fluctuations, one might expect men's unemployment to recover faster in the upturn than women's, particularly with depressed spending on public services. But with the emphasis on boosting male sectors, such as construction, in the government's job creation efforts, these developments are augmented. The prospects for women's employment in the near future are thus bleaker than men's, especially if there are further cuts in public spending.

Conclusion

When a government is faced with having to make huge cuts in public spending, and therefore with rethinking public policy, the gender regime is bound to be affected but the extent and form of the change depends on the political ideology of the respective government. In the Icelandic case the changes to the gender regime have not been excessive but the effects have been contradictory. On the one hand, gender equality has increased, especially in women's political representation. Public policy has particularly focused on reducing gender-based violence, with the ban on purchasing of prostitution, the ban on strip clubs, and the implementation of the Austrian approach to domestic violence cases, but gender awareness has also been raised in general by the focus on gender budgeting and the design of the Equal Pay Standard. At the same time, the main characteristic of the Icelandic gender regime, the dual earner-dual carer focus, has been undermined through cuts in family policy entitlements as well as by focusing more on men in labour market policy. The long-term effects remain to be seen.

The next governmental election (in 2013) is of critical importance for future development of the gender regime. Although the political parties more or less agree on the basics with regard to gender equality,[26] there are very big differences between the right and the left with regard to taxes and the appropriate size and functions of the welfare state. The government's emphasis has meant that the structure of the welfare state has been left more or less intact, as the policies previously implemented still prevail although cuts have been made. The government has also always made clear that the cuts were a temporary measure to be reversed as soon as possible. After having increased expenditure on benefits and services for other vulnerable groups, such as people with disabilities and the elderly, the government is now turning to making good some of the losses experienced by families and has raised child benefits and extended the parental leave, as well as partly reversed the former cuts. It thus seems likely that the cuts made, such as in family policy and welfare provision in general, will be rectified when possible if the current government is re-elected. That, however, is a very big *if* as the latest polls put government support at about 34 per cent of the electorate (Capacent 2012), while the parties in power before and during the boom, the Independence Party and the Progressive Party, have around 50 per cent support combined. It thus seems more likely than not that Iceland will take a neo-liberal turn in the next election, the consequences of which for both the welfare state and gender equality can be drastic, as demonstrated by numerous country cases explored elsewhere in this volume.

Notes

1 This study is a part of a research project supported by EDDA-Centre of Excellence and the Centre for Women's and Gender Studies, University of Iceland.
2 Official translation.
3 All data used in this chapter comes from Statistics Iceland, www.statice.is, unless otherwise stated.

4 The core issue in the Icesave dispute is whether Iceland is responsible for guarantee-ing the deposits in the Icesave accounts, which Landsbanki ran in its branches in the UK and the Netherlands between 2006 and 2008. The EFTA Surveillance Authority (ESA) has ruled that Iceland is responsible and has taken it to the EFTA Court over a breach of the Deposit Guarantee Directive (Directive 90/19/EC) (ESA 2011). The oral hearing was held on 18 September 2012 and the case is still on going when this is written (December 2012).

5 *Act No. 10/2008. Act on the Equal Status and Equal Rights of Men and Women.*

6 The custom in Iceland has been to keep salaries secret, not even mentioning them in job adverts and many employers demanded wage secrecy of their employees, allowing them to discriminate in wages and, in theory at least, against women.

7 According to Eurostat's duration of working life indicator, in 2007 the average Icelandic 15-year-old boy was expected to spend 47.8 years on the labour market and the average Icelandic girl 43 years. The second longest working life for boys was in Switzerland (44.1 years) and for girls in Sweden (38.5 years).

8 When defined as below 30 hours a week the incidence of part-time work is much lower, or 25 per cent among women and 8 per cent for men in 2007 (OECD family database).

9 This is reflected in the low share of public cash benefits in the disposable income of households of working age in Iceland at 12.4 per cent in the mid-2000s, much lower than in Scandinavia and even lower than the OECD average (15.8 per cent; OECD, 2008:103).

10 The unemployment rate of 15–64 year olds in Iceland once exceeded the EU average (9.4 per cent second quarter 2009, compared to the EU rate of 8.9 per cent) due to men's unemployment in Iceland rising above the EU average but that for women has remained below the EU average throughout the period (Eurostat ELFS).

11 It has to be noted that the Icelandic labour market is very small and there are rather great seasonal variations, as indicated in Figure 6.2.

12 The number of nights spent in Iceland by foreigners (all kinds of accommodation) increased from about 1,868,000 in 2007 to 2,435,000 in 2011.

13 Note that the combined trends in health and social services may be masking divergent tendencies; health services have suffered substantial budget cuts and as a consequence the National University Hospital lost close to 14 per cent of its staff between 2009 and 2012 (Zoega 2012) but staff may have been increased in some sectors of social services due to increased demand in the crisis.

14 The annual rate of the wage index, deflated by CPI, based on the change in the last 12 months. Reference month: April.

15 The authorities have implemented several measures to tackle private debt, some aimed at postponing or rescheduling debt service and some at reducing the stock of debt. See a summary and discussion of these in IMF 2012c (Box 3.2, p. 120).

16 *Act No. 54/2006. Unemployment Insurance Act*, with later amendments.

17 *Act No. 55/2006. Labour Market Measures Act*, with later amendments.

18 See the program's website, www.lidstyrkur.is.

19 Between 2007 and 2010 spending on cash benefits for families and children reduced from 74,300 ISK per capita (at 2010 prices) to 71,400 ISK; these corresponded to 1.40 per cent of GDP in 2007 but 1.48 per cent of the lower GDP in 2010.

20 *Act No. 95/2000. Maternity/Paternity Leave and Parental Leave Act*, with later amendments.

21 *Act no. 143/2012. Laws on amendments Maternity/Paternity Leave and Parental Leave Act.*

22 *Act no. 19/1940. The General Penal Code*, with later amendments.

23 *Act No. 85/2007. Laws on restaurants, accommodations and entertainment*, with later amend-ments.

24 *Act No. 85/2011. Laws on restraining order and removal from home.*

25 *Act No. 13/2010. Laws on amendment of laws on public limited companies and private limited companies.*

26 Progress along the stepping stones in equality legislation and policy over recent years have been made by different governments. Parental leave, for example, was implemented by the Independence Party and the Progressive Party, and the 2008 equality legislation was implemented by the Independence Party and the Social Democrats.

References

Agnarsson, S. (2010) *Labour Market Development and Policy in Iceland EEO Thematic Report*, The European Employment Observatory. Available at: http://www.eu-employment-observatory.net/resources/reports/Iceland-LabourMarketDevelopmentandPolicy.pdf (accessed 25.11.2010).

Althingi Special Investigation Commission (2010) *Report*, Reykjavik: Althingi Special Investigation Commission. Available at: http://sic.althingi.is/ (accessed 20.04.2011).

Bettio, F. and Verashchagina, A. (2009) *Gender Segregation in the Labour Market: Root Causes, Implications and Policy Responses in the EU*, Luxembourg: Publications Office of the European Union, European Commission. Available at: http://ec.europa.eu/justice/gender-equality/document/index_en.htm#h2-2 (accessed 30.05.2010).

Capacent (2012) 'Litlar breytingar á fylgi flokkanna', 6 September. Available at: http://www.capacent.is/frettir-og-frodleikur/frettir/frett/2012/09/06/Fylgi-flokka-ef-kosid-yrdi-til-Althingis-i-dag-og-studningur-vid-rikisstjornina/ (accessed 10.09.2012).

Central Bank of Iceland (2007) *Financial Stability Report 2007*, Reykjavík: Central Bank of Iceland. Available at: http://www.cb.is/publications-and-speeches/publications/financial-stability (accessed 18.08.2012).

— (2008) *Financial Stability Report 2008*, Reykjavik: Central Bank of Iceland. Available at: http://www.cb.is/publications-and-speeches/publications/financial-stability (accessed 17.09.2012).

— (2011) *Financial Stability Report 2011:2*, Reykjavik: Central Bank of Iceland. Available at: http://www.cb.is/publications-and-speeches/publications/financial-stability (accessed 03.03.2012).

— (2012) *Monetary Bulletin, 14* (2), Reykjavik: Central Bank of Iceland. Available at: http://www.cb.is/publications-and-speeches/publications/monetary-bulletin/(accessed 25.07.2012).

Centre for Gender Equality (2012) *Gender Equality in Iceland. Information on Gender Equality Issues in Iceland*, Akureyri: Centre for Gender Equality. Available at: http://www.jafnretti.is/D10/_Files/Gender_Equality_in_Iceland_2012.pdf (accessed 20.08.2012).

Chang, Ha-Joon (2012) 'The Root of Europe's Riots', *Guardian*, 28 September, p. 42. Available at: http://www.guardian.co.uk/commentisfree/2012/sep/28/europe-riots-root-imf-austerity?INTCMP=SRCH (accessed 10.10.2012).

Childbirth Leave Fund (2010) *Samantekt yfir tölulegar upplýsingar Fæðingarorlofssjóðs 2001–2009*, Reykjavik: Directorate of Labour. Available at: http://www.faedingarorlof.is/um-faedingarorlofssjod/utgefid-efni-og-talnaefni/tolulegar-upplysingar-faedingaror lofssjods-fra-2001-2009-pdf/ (accessed 10.01.2012).

Directorate of Labour (2012) *Directorate of Labour website*. http://www.vinnumalastofnun.is.

ESA (2011) *PR(11)79 Icesave: Iceland to be taken to Court for failing to pay minimum compensation*, Belgium: EFTA Surveillance Authority, 14 December. Available at: http://www.eftasurv.int/press--publications/press-releases/internal-market/nr/1560 (accessed 07.09.2012).

Esping-Andersen, G. (1990) *The Three Worlds of Capitalism*, Cambridge: Polity Press.

Eydal, G.B., and Árnadóttir, H.A. (2010) 'Family Policy in the Times of Crisis: The Case of Iceland', *Paper presented at XVII ISA Congress of Sociology*, Gothenburg, 28–30 July 2010.

Eydal, G.B., and Gíslason, I. (2008) *Equal Rights to Earn and Care. Parental Leave in Iceland*, Reykjavik: Social Science Institute, University of Iceland.

Eydal, G.B. and Rostgaard, T. (2011) 'Gender Equality Revisited – Changes in Nordic Childcare Policies in the 2000s', *Social Policy & Administration*, 45(2): 161–79.

Government of Iceland (2009) *Government Coalition Platform of the Social Democratic Alliance and Left-Green Movement.* Available at: http://www.government.is/government/coalition-platform/ (accessed 03.04.2012).

Guðmundsson, M. (2010) 'The Icelandic Economy Two Years after the Crash', Speech given by the Governor of the Central Bank of Iceland at a meeting of the Icelandic-American Chamber of Commerce, New York, 19 October. Available at: http://cb.is/lisalib/getfile.aspx?itemid=8159 (accessed 10.02.2010).

Hannesson, G. (2010) 'Ávarp Guðbjarts Hannessonar, félags- og tryggingamálaráðherra á ársfundi ASÍ, 21. október 2010'. Speech given by the Minister of Social Affairs at the annual meeting of the Confederation of Labour (ASÍ), 21 October. Available at: http://www.velferdarraduneyti.is/radherra/raedur-og greinar_GudbjHannesar/nr/5227 (accessed 08.09.2012).

Harðardóttir, O.G. (2012) 'Barnabætur. Bætt stuðningskerfi við barnafjölskyldur', Presentation given by the Minister of Finance at a press conference at the Ministry of Finance and Economic Affairs, 1 October. Slides are available at: http://www.fjarmalaraduneyti.is/media/frettir/barnabaetur.pdf (accessed 10.12.2012).

Hausmann, R., Tyson, L.D. and Zahidi, S. (2012) *The Global Gender Gap Report 2012*, Geneva: World Economic Forum. Available at: http://reports.weforum.org/global-gender-gap-2011/ (accessed 03.05.2012).

Helgason, M.S. (2010) 'Íslenskt viðskiptalíf - breytingar og samspil við fjármálakerfið' Appendix 5 of *Report*, Reykjavik: Althingi Special Investigation Commission. Available at: http://rna.althingi.is/eldri-nefndir/addragandi-og-orsakir-falls-islensku-bankanna-2008/skyrsla-nefndarinnar/vefutgafa/ (accessed 20.04.2012).

IMF (2006) *Iceland: Selected Issues. IMF Country Report No. 06/297.* Washington DC: International Monetary Fund. Available at: http://www.imf.org/external/pubs/ft/scr/2006/cr06297.pdf (accessed 10.08.2012).

— (2008) *IMF Announces Staff Level Agreement with Iceland on US $2.1 Billion Loan.* Press release no. 08/256, October 24. Available at: http://www.imf.org/external/np/sec/pr/2008/pr08256.htm (accessed 10.04.2012).

— (2011) *Statement at the Conclusion of an IMF Mission to Iceland.* Press release no. 11/39, February 11. Available at: http://www.imf.org/external/np/sec/pr/2011/pr1139.htm (accessed 15.03.2012).

— (2012a) *Iceland to Repay Early Some Outstanding Obligations to IMF.* Press release no. 12/84, March 15. Available at: http://www.imf.org/external/np/sec/pr/2012/pr1284.htm (accessed 15.03.2012).

— (2012b) *Iceland: Ex Post Evaluation of Exceptional Access Under the 2008 Stand-By Agreement. IMF Country Report 12/91.* Washington DC: International Monetary Fund. Available at: http://www.imf.org/external/pubs/cat/longres.aspx?sk=25855 (accessed 10.08.2012).

— (2012c) *World Economic Outlook. Growth resuming, dangers remain.* Washington DC: International Monetary Fund. Available at: http://www.imf.org/external/pubs/ft/weo/2012/01/ (accessed 05.01.2013).

Irving, Z. (2012) 'Refuge in the Nordic model: Social Policy in Iceland after 2008', in M. Kilkey, G. Ramia and K. Farnsworth (eds) *Social Policy Review 24.* Bristol: The Policy Press.

Korpi. W. (1983) *The Democratic Class Struggle*, London/New York: Routledge.

Krugman, P. (2011) '*Iceland Exits*'. *Conscience of a Liberal. NY Times blog*, September 1. http://krugman.blogs.nytimes.com/2011/09/01/iceland-exits/ (accessed 01.05.2012).

Ministry of Finance and Economic Affairs (2011) *2012 Fiscal Budget Proposal,* Reykjavik: Ministry of Finance and Economic Affairs. Available at: http://www.fjarlog.is (accessed 20.05.2012).

— (2012a) *2013 Fiscal Budget Information. Table 9. Central Government's Debt and Assets 2009– 2012.* Available at: http://eng.fjarmalaraduneyti.is/government-finance/fiscal-budget/ nr/15829 (accessed 14.09.2012).

— (2012b) *The Fiscal Budget Proposal for 2013. Consolidation Plan 2013–2016.* Reykjavik: Ministry of Finance and Economic Affairs, September 11. Available at: http://www. ministryoffinance.is/Frontpage-fjr/nr/15861 (accessed 22.09.2012).

Ministry of Welfare (2012a) *Parliamentary Resolution on a Four Year Gender Equality Action Programme 2011.* Reykjavik: Ministry of Welfare. Available at: http://eng.velferdarraduneyti.is/ newsinenglish/nr/33182 (accessed 03.05.2012).

— (2012b) *Aðgerðaáætlun um launajafnrétti kynjanna,* Reykjavik: Ministry of Welfare. Available at: http://www.velferdarraduneyti.is/media/rit-og skyrslur2012/ Adgerdaaaetlun_um_launajafnretti_kynjanna.pdf (accessed 30.10.2012).

OECD (2008) *Growing Unequal? Income Distribution and Poverty in OECD Countries,* Paris: OECD. Available at: http://www.oecd-ilibrary.org/social-issues-migration-health/ growing-unequal_9789264044197-en (accessed 14.10.2012).

— (2010) *Gender Brief,* Paris: OECD. Available at: http://www.oecd.org/dataoecd/ 23/31/44720649.pdf (accessed 15.06.2012).

— (2011) *Economic Surveys: Iceland June 2011 Overview,* Paris: OECD. Available at: http:// www.oecd.org/iceland/economicsurveyoficeland2011.htm (accessed 02.07.2012).

Ólafsson, S. (1996) *Hugarfar og hagvöxtur,* Reykjavik: Social Science Institute, University of Iceland.

— (1999) *Íslenska leiðin: Almannatryggingar og velferð í fjölþjóðlegum samanburði,* Reykjavík: University of Iceland Press and the Social Insurance Administration.

— (2003) 'Welfare Trends of the 1990s in Iceland', *Scandinavian Journal of Public Health,* 31, 401–04.

— (2011a) 'Iceland's Financial Crisis and Level of Living Consequences', *Working paper 3,* Reykjavik: Social Research Center, University of Iceland.

— (2011b) 'Icelandic Capitalism: From Statism to Neoliberalism and Financial Collapse', in L. Mjøset (ed.) *The Nordic Varieties of Capitalism, Comparative Social Research,* 28, Bingley: Emerald Group Publishing Limited, 1–51.

Ólafsson, S. and Kristjánsson, A.S. (2012) *Umfang kreppunnar og afkoma ólíkra tekjuhópa,* Reykjavik: Social Research Center, University of Iceland.

Pétursson, T. (2010) 'Iceland: From boom to bust and back again', a presentation for visitors from Lehigh University at the Central Bank of Iceland, Reykjavik, 14 May. Available at: http://www.cb.is/lisalib/getfile.aspx?itemid=7845 (accessed 26.03.2011).

Prime Minister's Office (2012a) *Investment Plan for Iceland 2013–2015 – new emphases on employment.* Available at: http://eng.forsaetisraduneyti.is/news-and-articles/nr/7180 (accessed 23.05.2012).

— (2012b) 'Jafnlaunastaðall', Prime Minister's speech at an introductory meeting on the Equal Pay Standard, Grand hotel, 19 June. Available at: http://www.forsaetisraduneyti.is/ radherra/raedur_greinar_JS/nr/7215 (accessed 01.09.2012).

RÚV (2012). *Heilbrigðisstéttir dragast aftur úr.* Evening news, The Icelandic National Broadcasting Service (RÚV), 8 December. Available at: http://www.ruv.is/sarpurinn/ frettir/08122012/heilbrigdisstettir-dragast-aftur-ur (accessed 20.12.2012).

SFR (2012) *Launakönnun SFR 2011.* Available at: http://www.sfr.is/kannanir-sfr/ launakonnun-sfr/launakonnun-2011/ (accessed 27.04.2012).

Sigurjónsson, T.O. and Mixa, M.W. (2011) 'Learning from the "Worst Behaved": Iceland's Financial Crisis and the Nordic Comparison', *Thunderbird International Business Review*, 53(2): 209–23.

Zoega, B. (2012). *Föstudagspistill 20.janúar*. Available at: http://www.landspitali.is/Um-LSH/Skipulag-og-stjornun/Stjornendur/Forstjori/Fostudagspistlar-forstjora/Frett/?NewsId=2fcc7d1b-d042-49f8-9500-0e1ee7bbb075 (accessed 05.01.2012).

7

GENDER, RECESSION AND AUSTERITY IN THE UK

Jill Rubery and Anthony Rafferty

Introduction

The UK entered the financial crisis comparatively early with the collapse of a major bank in summer 2007. The UK's reliance on financial services and its housing boom increased its vulnerability to the initial crisis, but being outside the Eurozone and having relatively long-dated government debt provided some protection from external pressures. There has, however, been no protection from political decisions by the coalition government formed after the May 2010 election between the Conservatives and Liberal Democrats to eliminate the so-called structural public deficit in one parliament by enacting a policy of intensified neo-liberalism based on a shrunken and privatized welfare state (Grimshaw and Rubery 2012). In this chapter we explore the experience of recession followed by austerity in the UK from a gender perspective. To contextualize the analysis we first describe the changes in the UK's gender regime in the period leading up to the crisis, focusing in particular on the contradictions in the UK's welfare and gender model. This is followed by an analysis of labour market developments from a gender perspective in the immediate recession and unfurling austerity phase. In the final two sections we first describe initial policy responses to the financial crisis and the turn towards severe austerity before developing the argument that the austerity policies are intensifying the underlying fault lines in the UK's high inequality economic model. Thus the current roll back on progress towards gender equality will have harmful impacts on women but will also close off options for low and medium income households seeking to adjust to tightening austerity.

Developments in the UK gender regime prior to the crisis

The financial crisis brought to an end a decade of above average growth (2.9 per cent per annum 1998–2007, see Corry *et al.* 2011) fuelled by a combination of growth in financial services, increased public expenditure and private household debt linked to a major housing boom and pressures to keep up with rising consumption norms in an increasingly unequal society. This New Labour decade witnessed both further increasing wealth and income inequality at the top end but also some development of the UK's social and gender model towards a more hybrid version, combining intensified privatization with some new supports for working families and new social floors, particularly aimed at reducing child poverty.

This hybridization is nothing new. The traditional classifications of the UK welfare regime as residual (Esping-Andersen 1990) and the gender regime as belonging to the strong male breadwinner variety (Lewis 1992) do not capture their essentially hybrid character derived both from legacies from the more collectivist pre-Thatcher period and from the grafting on of new elements in the decade preceding the financial crisis. The current austerity programme is aimed, in our view, at moving the UK model closer to a residual welfare model (Grimshaw and Rubery 2012) by undermining not only progressive policies added under New Labour but also those collectivist elements not even touched by Margaret Thatcher such as the National Health Service (NHS). While gender equality is likely to be a major casualty of the policy changes, the implementation of the austerity agenda will not be helped, as we discuss below, by women's now relatively well-established expectations of employment or by the lack of substitutes for state services due to traditionally weak family ties (Reher 1998). Here we focus first on characterizing developments in the gender regime over the past decades.

Once gender is brought into the analysis of social models some argue it becomes more difficult to characterize welfare states (Orloff 1993). This applies particularly to those welfare states classified as 'residual'; in some cases, for example the US, commodification of both male and female labour is high while in others women may be only contingent participants in employment and treated as primary carers and mothers to be supported by the family with limited access to the residual benefit system. Thus residual welfare states or liberal market economies have rather divergent gender regimes and patterns of gender equality that may also reflect contradictory characteristics within the specific welfare and labour market system. The UK can be said to have combined elements of the US model, with women's increased participation in employment an important part of the means by which low and middle income families have defended living standards in the face of wage stagnation for male workers. Yet this commodification has only been partial as most mothers work part-time in response to only residual welfare support for childcare.

The UK is characterized by contradictory policies, some supporting and reinforcing women's labour market participation and economic independence and others limiting their integration and confining them to low paid marginal part-time jobs, which underutilize their skills. These contradictions have been evident in the state's attitude to the family; for example, the UK state in both adopting independent taxation for women ahead of many countries and in channeling support for children through the primary carer had accepted that families do not always operate in the interests of all its members (Goode *et al.* 1998). However, these important policies indicating a rejection of a unitary and benevolent view of the family co-existed with the intensive use of household means-testing for determining levels and entitlements to benefits, often restricting in practice women's access to benefits and creating disincentives to female participation. These disincentives are significant because benefits are more widely claimed in the UK than for example in the US (Barbier 2006). These means-tested benefits also provide relatively generous support for those less likely to be receiving family economic support, such as lone parents in the absence of an employed partner, particularly because the means-tested Housing Benefit pays the high and rising housing costs.[1] These benefits, which unlike in the US are not time limited, are viewed in mainstream government policy circles as creating financial disincentives for employment, particularly for lone parents (Freud 2007: 8).

The labour market in the UK in the 1980s and 1990s provided both advantages and disadvantages for women; on the advantage side, female employment rates during these decades rose continuously alongside a low unemployment rate, relative to that for men. Furthermore, trade unions became highly committed to pursuing equal pay and gender equality issues particularly in the public sector. On the disadvantage side, the long hours expected from employees in full-time jobs in the increasingly deregulated labour market coupled with low childcare support resulted in mothers being integrated primarily into in low paid part-time work. Women tended to switch to a new employer when seeking reduced hours working and had limited opportunities to return to full-time work, at least compared to the US where mothers often decide against part-time work because they may be legally excluded from health benefits (Dex and Shaw 1986; Tomlinson 2007). In the UK health benefits are not tied to employment and EU law requires more equal treatment of part-time workers.

State support for care has also been uneven with childcare support less extensive than eldercare, where services in their own home or in care homes is organized through the state and largely funded by the state even though means tested (but with asset protection if the house is still occupied by a spouse). This relatively generous provision in the UK compared to some other European countries reflects the fragmentation and geographical dispersion of the family in the UK but also the lack of any legal responsibilities between family members after children reach age 18. However, childcare, at least up until New Labour, was regarded primarily as a private matter (Waldfogel 2011).

This contextual background is necessary to understand both the significance of changes under New Labour and the current austerity policy package. The New Labour policy objective was to reduce child poverty and to that end promote the neo-liberal recipe of paid work as the best way out of poverty, as well as serving to contain both welfare expenditure and wage inflation through increasing labour supply. These multiple aims led to a set of policies that tended to support women entering and staying in the labour market even though this was not their primary objective. There was a pragmatic acceptance of the need to adjust welfare systems to changed work and family patterns and in particular to the increased risk of child poverty associated with the rise in lone parent households (Rowlingson and McKay 2001). However, where gender equality issues were at odds with other aspects of the programme, the other objectives tended to take priority. Thus there was no coherent programme to address the contradictions in the gender regime and although some policies did ameliorate problems others even intensified them.

In line with this policy agenda the working tax credit system introduced by New Labour significantly increased incentives to enter paid work. This more generous in-work benefit programme, however, extended high disincentives to work to more second income earners due to benefit withdrawal rates of 60 per cent.[2] This was seen as a necessary price for moving breadwinners off benefits and into paid work and the gender equality consequences were not addressed. This policy was, however, complemented by extensive uprating of support for the costs of children, through improved child benefits, tax credits and through additional support for childcare costs and extended state-funded childcare provision. These supports for working families were framed as anti-child poverty measures and as ways of increasing economic activity rates, not as measures for gender equality. The extension of child tax credit eligibility up the income distribution, amongst other policies, was also seen as building political consensus around welfare expenditure, towards a more universal system which benefited most people, rather than residual support for the few which is more susceptible to political attack.

These 'enabling' policies were accompanied, even before the change of government, by increasingly coercive mandated activation for key 'economically inactive' groups of benefit claimants (Rafferty and Wiggan 2010). This applied to Incapacity Benefit claimants who were gradually moved to Employment Support Allowance and to those claiming benefits on grounds of lone parenthood. The age of youngest dependent child at which lone parents were required to seek paid work was progressively reduced so that by the election in 2010 it had already fallen to age seven. Under the preceding extended period of economic growth and expanding childcare support, lone parent employment rates increased from 44.6 per cent in June 1997 to 57.3 per cent by the end of 2009. However, by the crisis this more coercive approach, predicated on continuation of the preceding favourable conditions, collided with deteriorating labour market opportunities.

In the labour market two major developments assisted women. First, the introduction and subsequent uprating of the national minimum wage (Grimshaw 2009) improved women's wages, particularly those of part-timers. This uprating was aimed partly at ensuring that working tax credits did not subsidize employers paying low wages. In the absence of collective bargaining its implementation, however, led to compression of differentials around the minimum wage so that women's opportunities for pay advancement with experience reduced (Grimshaw 2009). The second favourable development was the growth in public sector jobs, accounting for 84 per cent of women's job growth over the past decade compared to 39 per cent for men (TUC 2011). However, outsourcing of public sector jobs accelerated under New Labour, for although more quality conditions were allowed into the competitive tendering process, no preference could be given to public sector providers in competitive tenders. Under New Labour the government also endorsed and promoted the so-called 'business case' for women's employment with a range of soft measures such as awards to companies to support work life balance policies. It further introduced a statutory right for parents of dependent children under six to request flexible working, later extended to 16 years and under. Although this right to request followed the neo-liberal non-interventionist approach, the policy did increase opportunities for women to return to the same job after childbirth instead of seeking a new and often low paid part-time job. Women made more use of this right than men, particularly in the public sector where both request rates and agreement by employers was higher than in the private sector (Hooker *et al.* 2007).

These flexible working opportunities were part of what Waldfogel (2011) describes as 'a sea change' in support for working parents involving extended parental and maternity leave (including paid leave but at a relatively low rate of pay), the introduction of paternity leave and a plan to allow fathers opportunities to take leave unused by mothers. Furthermore, in addition to financial support for childcare there was some development of facilities through the National Childcare Strategy and introduction of Surestart nurseries targeted, in principle, at the most needy children in line with the child poverty programme. After school and holiday provision for school-age children also expanded, albeit run by voluntary or for-profit organizations and paid for by families, partly from their childcare tax credits. Obligations were placed on public sector employers to promote and monitor progress towards gender equality and plans were laid to extend obligations to private sector employers to undertake gender pay audits. However, eldercare was increasingly outsourced to the private sector where the largely female workforce was paid little more than the minimum wage, a system reinforced by the low fees paid to the private providers (Rubery *et al.* 2011). In contrast, the health service enjoyed improved funding and protected pay rates for outsourced services (Grimshaw 2009).

Thus, by the end of the New Labour period, a number of significant changes had been introduced into the gender and welfare regime model with both positive and negative implications for gender equality. The focus on activation for all, combined with more support for employed parents and more requirements on employers to promote gender equality, could be seen as a step towards a Scandinavian adult worker model of welfare. However, these changes remained strongly influenced both by neo-liberalism and the notion of a residual welfare state. The in-work benefits extended means testing with negative implications for second income earners although lone parents were able, given the increased support for childcare costs, to consider entering employment and did so in increasing numbers. Childcare services also grew but remained expensive and fragmentary while leave opportunities were extended but still low paid. Opportunities for flexible working were increased but fell short of a right and were thus most applied in the public sector and there was no compensation for the reduced income of working shorter hours.

Perhaps most importantly, little was done to require private sector organizations to change behavior and promote gender equality. Thus the changes introduced were largely reliant on government policies and so were ripe for easy and ready reversal under austerity.

Recent labour market trends

The labour market impact of the economic downturn and government austerity so far can be depicted in a number of roughly defined periods, each with a distinct gender effect. The first covers the technical recession of negative GDP growth from early 2008 to late 2009 when job loss was higher for men than women. Sex segregation by industrial sector largely explains the differential gender impact as the initial recession was most strongly felt in the male-dominated sectors of manufacturing and construction as well as some more gender-mixed sectors such as wholesale, retail and hotels. In contrast, the main public sector employment areas of administration, education and health where women are more heavily represented continued to grow in this period adding 300,000 jobs (Rubery and Rafferty 2013). This growth was the result of counter cyclical public expenditure by the outgoing Labour government.

Although men's overall job loss exceeded women's during this initial period, female unemployment rates (Figure 7.1) and the proportion of job loss accounted for by women was gradually edging up (Rubery and Rafferty 2013). In the second period, identifiable from late 2009/early 2010 to early 2011, this trend intensified with growing female private sector job loss and added upward pressure on unemployment rates from public sector job cuts. During 2010 men, in contrast, benefited from a (very) modest post-recession jobs recovery. Taken together, the rise in the female and fall in the male unemployment rate narrowed the unemployment rate gender gap from 2.5 to around 1.5 percentage points (ONS 2011a, 2011b) by the beginning of 2011 onwards.

Women experienced a steady rise in unemployment during 2011 while men's unemployment rate stagnated before rising again. This may be in part attributable to women's higher representation in public sector work. In 2007 the public sector accounted for 43.8 per cent of all female employment compared to just 15.6 per cent for men, with women taking around 69.4 per cent of all public sector jobs.[3] The importance of the public sector for women's employment also comes from opportunities to work part-time but with a lower part-time wage penalty than in the private sector and more opportunities in higher skilled jobs (Rubery and Rafferty 2013). The government's public spending cuts were initially forecast to lead to a loss of around 490,000 jobs in the public sector by 2015 but revised estimates put the projected loss at over 900,000 jobs between 2011 and 2018, equivalent to 16 per cent of government employment in 2010 (Office for Budget Responsibility 2011; 2012) due to downward revisions of growth estimates. Public sector job losses began to manifest during 2010, eroding the previous protection offered by public sector employment in the earlier stages of the economic downturn, although it was

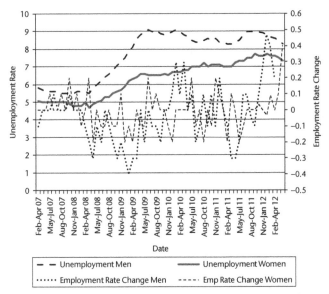

FIGURE 7.1   Unemployment rate and employment rate change by gender in the UK 2007–2012

Source: ONS, seasonally adjusted.

not until 2011 that public sector job losses began to gain momentum. Between March and June 2011 alone, 110,000 public sector jobs were cut (Figure 7.2). Given the size of the planned cuts to public sector employment and women's public sector representation, there is the possibility that by 2015 the female unemployment rate may surpass that for men. However, continued weak growth or the risk of a

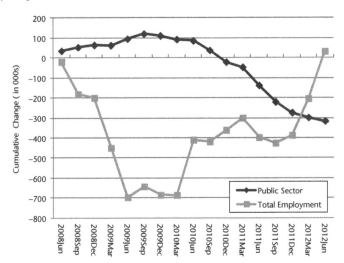

FIGURE 7.2   Cumulative change in public sector and total employment in the UK 2008–2012

Source: ONS, own calculations. Public sector excluding financial institutions.

third phase of recession in the broader economy make further male job losses also likely.

Figure 7.3 shows that most of the job losses in the public sector to date have occurred within Public Administration, where cuts were frontloaded, with over a quarter of a million jobs destroyed between December 2009 and June 2011, followed by education (c. 40,000). The female job loss in Public Administration was largely in line with their 2009 employment share prior to the cuts, although women's job losses in education are around 25,000 more than their 2009 share would predict.

The changing role of the public sector is evident if we compare women's share of job loss including and excluding the public sector areas of administration, education and health in 2007–9 to the situation in 2010 and 2011. In the 2007–9 period women's share of private sector job loss was 45.8 per cent, well above their 37.3 per cent share of overall net job loss.[4] During 2009–10 the protective role of the public sector had already begun to decline and women lost jobs in both the public and private sectors, whilst male employment recovered slightly. During the first half of 2011 men on aggregate began again to lose jobs but the female share of overall job loss was now not only higher than in 2007–9 (56.0 per cent compared to 37.3 per cent) but also higher than their share of private sector job loss which fell to 31.0 per cent compared to 45.8 per cent in 2007–9. Over the whole 2007–11 period the female share of job loss was fuelled in part by disproportionate loss of jobs for women in some private sectors. For example, in Banking and Finance, and Other Business Services, between 2007 and 2011, women lost around 112,000 more jobs than would be expected based upon their 2007 sector share (Figure 7.3).

To date, job loss has led to a slight increase in male inactivity rates (from 29.2 to 30.4 per cent between 2007Q1 and 2011Q3) but little change in women's inactivity rate.[5] Instead, women like men have continued their attachment to the labour market, being more likely to become unemployed or to take on involuntary part-time or temporary (see Table 7.1) work than move into economic inactivity. Compared to prior recessions, more women are likely to be eligible for contribution-based unemployment benefits for the first six months of unemployment due to more continuous and full-time work histories. These trends reflect women's rising labour market attachment over the last forty years accompanied by relative gains in educational attainment. However, it is also the increased importance of female earnings to household income, combined with high household debt, stagnating wages and rising costs of living that are maintaining pressures to maximize the labour supply of family members for reasons of financial necessity alone. In prior recessions there were also few incentives for women to stay in employment if their partner lost their job and claimed benefits but the more generous tax credit system appears to be supporting more families where there is a sole female earner, even if they remain very much in the minority (Rubery and Rafferty 2013).

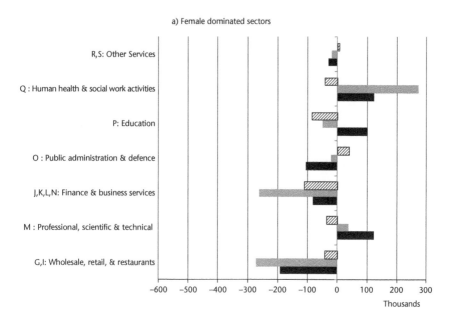

a) Female dominated sectors

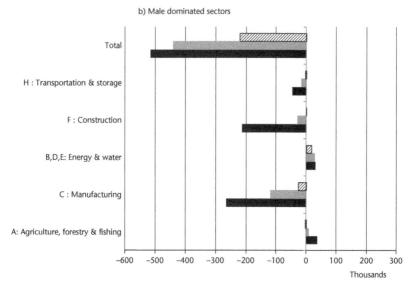

b) Male dominated sectors

☑ F Diff actual-predicted based on 07 sector share   ▨ Female actual change in jobs 07-11   ■ Male actual change in jobs 07-11

FIGURE 7.3   Change in employment by industry and gender and relative to gender share in the UK 2007–2011

* F Diff actual–predicted based on 07 sector share is the difference between actual female job loss and predicted job loss if proportionate to 2007 female sector share (actual minus predicted).

Source: ONS Workforce Jobs, own calculations, Dec 2007–June 2011.

TABLE 7.1 Involuntary part-time and temporary work in the UK 2007–2012

	Total part-time (000s)	Could not find full-time job (000s)	% that could not find full-time job	Total temporary (000s)	Could not find permanent job (000s)	% that could not find permanent job
Men						
2007	1716	290	16.9	699.1	201.2	28.7
2011	1895	553	29.2	734.6	306.2	41.6
2012	2055	632	30.7	750	327	43.6
Change 2007–12	+339	+342	+13.8	+50.9	+125.8	+14.9
Women						
2007	5608	435	7.8	791.4	178.6	22.6
2011	5754	709	12.3	775.7	276.2	35.6
2012	5891	778	13.2	870	322	36.9
Change 2007–12	+283	+343	+5.4	+78.6	+143.4	+14.3

Source: ONS Published tables, Oct–Dec 2007, July–Sept 2011, June–August 2012.

The impact of the recession on men's position in the labour market is also evident in the narrowing of the gender pay gap, particularly for full-timers, which in 2012 fell below 10 percentage points at the median level for the first time (at 9.6 percentage points). However, the gender gap for full- and part-time workers combined has also narrowed slightly but still stands at 19.7 percentage points. The main group with a higher than average pay rise was female full-timers but these are only just over half of the women employed in Britain. Much of the narrowing is explained by higher pay rises in the public than the private sector but the effects of austerity on public sector pay may soon change this position.

Public policy in the financial crisis and its aftermath

New Labour responded to the initial financial crisis with a policy of fiscal stimulus in which it also prioritized and protected the interests of families and children; child benefits were uprated more and earlier than planned and public expenditure on services continued to rise (Grimshaw and Rubery 2011). However, by the 2010 election New Labour was proposing stringent public expenditure cuts which, although slower and slightly less severe than the subsequent coalition government's programme, would have cut into the additional support for working families implemented over the previous decade. Post the 2010 election it fell to the Conservative and Liberal Democrats coalition to take the actual decision to cut public expenditure, with an 'Emergency Budget' in 2010. Concerns were raised that the equality impact of the proposed measures was not properly assessed (EHRC 2012). Furthermore, these cuts and associated reforms have been undertaken not only to satisfy financial markets but as part of a wider plan of permanent change in the role of the state within the economic and social model (Taylor-Gooby and Stoker 2011). The explicit intention is that the state should scale back its responsibilities and consequent gaps in the social fabric should be filled by not-for-profit organizations and volunteer labour as part of the 'big society'. This programme poses three specific challenges for women: first, women have been particularly reliant on the state both for the quantity and quality of their employment and for income support if lone parents; second, support for working parents has been one element in the recent increases in public expenditure, making this area potentially in line for cuts; third, the policy expects reduced public services to be in part made good by either domestic or volunteer labour for which women are the major supply source.

These vulnerabilities have proved to be far from theoretical threats and have influenced both policy choices and outcomes under the austerity programme. The decision to focus on areas of direct concern to women reflected in part a perspective that the initial recession had primarily hurt private sector and male workers. However, there is now explicit recognition that the coalition programme will disproportionately impact on women. A gender impact audit of the 2010 Emergency Budget, by the House of Commons Library, suggests that 74 per cent of the revenue generated from tax increases and benefit cuts would come from women and a similar audit in 2012 of new measures suggests that 81 per cent will come from women (Women's Budget Group 2012).

The changes either already introduced or planned are scheduled to have major gender impacts. Firstly there is a raft of measures reducing support for children, pregnancy and for childcare. One of the coalition's first acts was to freeze Child Benefits for all and remove them from any household where someone was paying the higher rate of tax, thereby further breaking with the principles of universalism introduced by Beveridge. Some revisions have already been introduced, providing for a stepped withdrawal as the 'unfairness' of the policy was widely recognized as it was not based on actual household income but on whether one person earning paid higher rate tax. At times the debate on this policy even led to the principle of independent taxation being criticized as the proximate cause of the implementation problems. Baby and pregnancy related grants are also being cut back: for example Surestart pregnancy grants are now restricted to the first child and the Health in Pregnancy Grant was abolished in January 2011. In addition, Child Tax Credits have been reduced particularly for middle-income households and the share of childcare costs that can be covered in tax credits cut from 80 to 70 per cent (Hirsch 2011).

Women generally receive a higher proportion of their income in benefits than men (Bellamy *et al.* 2006) so that general cuts to benefits, including the decision to uprate them by a lower index have gender effects. Women are also affected by the freeze on working tax credits. The medium-term plan is to replace all these benefits with a Universal Credit, ostensibly to simplify the system but only after the benefit budget has been severely cut, thereby moving the UK benefit system back towards a more residual form. The planned benefit reform will also switch resources from women to men within the household as now only one member of the household is to receive all the benefits, justified by the government on the grounds that it is not its role to intervene in intra-household distribution of resources. If enacted, this will reverse the successes over several decades in persuading governments of all kinds to pay benefits for children to the child's main carer (Goode *et al*. 1998). The Universal Credit also focuses explicitly on incentivizing primary breadwinners to move into employment and the resulting increasing tax disincentive to second income earners is dismissed by the government as unfortunate collateral damage but of insufficient concern to lead to policy modification (DWP 2011a). There are also policies to cap and cut housing benefits, one of the main areas of social support in Britain. Around three-fifths of those expected to be affected by the cap are single women (compared to 3 per cent single men), with the majority of these women being lone parents (DWP 2011b).

Pressures on benefit recipients to seek paid work have also increased even at a time of record rises in unemployment for women. Lone parents assessed as able to work now have to seek work to claim benefits unless they have a child under five. Reforms to the disability benefit system have introduced more stringent and controversial fitness-for-work tests. Even if someone is not deemed fit for work, incapacity benefits are now household-means tested after one year. This will affect more women as disabled women are more likely than disabled men to have a working spouse.

For those who enter employment there are also pressures. Public sector workers face a two year pay freeze followed by two years of capped one per cent increases and cuts and contribution increases to public sector pensions. This is having a disproportionate impact on women. The civil service, known for its good work–life balance policies, is also being asked to review working conditions including its flexible working policies to ensure they are more like the private sector (*Guardian* 2012c). The reforms under the guise of austerity are also promoting the provision of services from any qualified provider, now in health as well as other care services, likely to lead to further transfers of women's jobs to the private sector. This is being facilitated by the fragmentation of the NHS with commissioning now to be under control of local consortia, and the discontinuation of a requirement for subcontractors to observe the same minimum rate as in the NHS for all staff. The extent of the low pay problem is critically dependent on the level of the minimum wage. Since the crisis it has risen slightly as a proportion of median earnings and even rose in real terms in 2008–9 but has since fallen in real value, particularly steeply in 2011 despite a nominal increase each year (Manning 2012: Figures 1 and 2). Women also tend to have shorter job tenure and are thus more vulnerable to the extension from one to two years' service with an employer before unfair dismissal protection applies. There are further plans to remove employment rights from employees of small firms, again mainly women, although employers plans to transfer shares to employees in lieu of such rights have not been favourably received by employers.

Alongside the cuts in support for childcare costs, childcare facilities subsidized by Local Authorities can be expected to be scaled back as they deal with major budget cuts (minus 28 per cent on average by 2015) and focus on the most deprived areas (*Guardian* 2012a). A survey of Surestart nurseries in early 2012 found 7 per cent scheduled for closure and 86 per cent operating with reduced budgets (Daycare Trust 2012). The network of after school and school holiday facilities is also being shrunk. Social care provision, one of Local Authorities' main expenditures and already stretched prior to the austerity policies, is under major pressure. The current scale of cuts is threatening the availability of private sector supply as many care homes are closing due to freezing of care home fees (*Guardian* 2011). Cuts in care provision will not only reduce women's employment but also have indirect effects on women as the major providers of informal family-based care.[6] However, substitution of domestic for wage labour is restricted in the UK by the high share of elderly people living alone and at a distance from their children.

The outcome of this multifaceted change in policy will vary among groups of women and men as well as between men and women on average. The major impacts so far are on the young and on women with responsibilities for children, particularly lone parents, but followed by couple households (Browne 2011). Among young people, young women are faring better than men with an unemployment rate of 16.5 compared to 22.6 per cent (ONS July–September 2011) but the overall story is of relatively equally shared misery compared to prime age adults. In the prime age population, although the reduction in support for children in couple households affects both parents, it is mothers who will face most difficulties in managing with a reduced budget for the costs of raising children. Lone parents are the most exposed as they face not only benefit cuts but also increased pressure to enter paid work at a time of reduced opportunities to find stable jobs. Retired women have so far had their benefits protected and there is a commitment to raise the basic standard pension in 2016, which should eventually assist women in general. However, some pensioners are suffering from low interest rates on savings and some women are facing a particularly rapid increase in their retirement age as a consequence of a general increase in retirement ages for both men and women.

There are also differences in impact by sector, skill or educational group. The poor employment conditions in the private sector for women in the UK reflect the high level of wage inequality in general. Women in the private sector often have very limited access to occupational pensions as well as the limited opportunities for quality part-time work. These factors make the public sector particularly important for gender equality (Dex and Forth 2009; Rubery 2013) and the cutbacks are therefore of a particular concern for both low and high skilled women. The lower skilled or lower educated are most likely to be affected by the erosion of wage and employment protections, such as the national minimum wage and unfair dismissal regulations, by the outsourcing of public sector work, and the cuts in child tax credits, Surestart nurseries and support for childcare costs, and the freeze to Child Benefit. These women are also more reliant on Child Benefit to provide for basic necessities and will also be affected by the plan under Universal

Credit to channel benefits to one household member, which is likely to be the male partner. Low skilled women are less likely to be geographically mobile and therefore more likely to be living in proximity to elderly family members, making them thus more vulnerable to pressure to provide elderly care when state provision is cut. For higher skilled, higher paid women it is the pay freezes in the public sector and the scaling down of public sector work opportunities coupled with cuts to pension provision that may be having the most impact. Women in higher income households who are outside the labour market will also be affected by the removal of Child Benefit from this group, thereby perhaps inadvertently encouraging more dual earner households. In the future women with higher education will also face the problem of paying for both childcare and for student loans to cover high university fees. This may lead to an entrapment of graduate women in part-time work below £21,000 as to work more hours would incur both higher childcare costs and a 9 per cent additional marginal tax rate to repay loans. One estimate suggests that up to 80 per cent of female graduates will not earn sufficient to pay off their loans under the new systems before they are written off after thirty years (London Economics 2011).

To summarize, while the austerity programme involves clear elements of continuity with previous policy approaches, there is also evidence of ruptures with trends evident under New Labour and even with principles established by Beveridge and before. The continuity is found in the pursuit of neo-liberal welfare and labour market policies, including pressurizing benefit recipients, particularly lone parents and those claiming Incapacity Benefit, into work despite depressed demand, searching out cheaper and often private alternatives to public sector employment and providing only patchwork and voluntary support for working parents without impinging on employer rights to manage as they choose. The clear disjuncture or break with the past is evident in the rapid withdrawal of support for employed parents. This represents an ideological denial of the need for state support to meet new childcare and even eldercare requirements (Anxo *et al.* 2010). This redrawing of the boundaries of the state has involved the invoking of the family as a unitary and inviolate institution where the state has no business interfering. This is further followed through in the withdrawal of legal aid support in relation to domestic violence and family disputes over child custody and divorce. The fiction of family harmony, where family is largely equated with dual parent (heterosexual) households, despite over a quarter of households with dependent children being lone parent families, is used to reduce state costs and to reinforce the notion that women are not to be regarded as independent citizens but part of a joint and private unit where the distribution of power is not an issue for the state.

The austerity programme is thus drawing on traditional models of marriage and family to reverse support for dual earner households. Instead, employment decisions are regarded increasingly as a private matter, dependent on the ability of the family to fund and organize childcare. Benefit systems that disincentivize dual earning are regarded as fully acceptable, as activity among second income earners is not a priority. The risks of this policy approach are that many women will end up either choosing not to take on paid work, as the costs of unsupported childcare are often too high for families to fully fund, or choosing not to have children. This apparent endorsement of traditional gender role models is not extended to lone parents where the notion that women as well as men should aspire to paid work has been retained and reinforced. At the same time, cuts in welfare provision targeting lone parents may also be viewed as implicitly seeking to reinforce the traditional two parent family model by reducing the financial means for women to become lone parents such as through separation or divorce, even to escape troubled or violent relationships, and so further privatizing family matters. These developments indicate the risks for gender equality where an expectation of paid work is not matched by a right to care; the right to paid work is now selectively applied to reduce dependency on state benefits without regard to the impact on care or broader personal autonomy. While the state can regard childcare as a family or private responsibility, they have less scope to follow this approach for elderly care, both because of the long-standing geographical fragmentation of families and because there is no legal obligation on families to provide support for adults. Thus there is no direct way in which the state can call on domestic labour or funding to substitute for state-funded wage labour. Instead the policy is to appeal to the notion of the big society, involving primarily volunteer labour, to step in to fill the gaps in the social fabric. However, this notion of armies of available volunteers, traditionally primarily women or pensioners, is out of step with most women's aspirations for and need to be in paid employment and with the policy of keeping people in work to older ages.

Furthermore, in both shrinking the public sector workforce and reducing their relative pay the government is also taking private sector pay rates and conditions, particularly those for part-time workers, as a labour market norm against which all public sector employment and expenditure should be measured. Thus one group that has been most frequently identified as suffering from discrimination and below standard employment conditions is being treated as a benchmark for measuring whether employment is overpaid or overprotected.

Evidence that the austerity programme is not producing growth is leading to some minor adjustment policies but so far the stimulus measures have either tended to protect asset value for the better off, as in the case of quantitative easing, or are focused on physical infrastructure projects, to the benefit of male-dominated employment sectors, rather than social infrastructure (*Guardian* 2012d), providing further evidence that the withdrawal of state social support is intended to be permanent. The government is also scaling back support for the implementation of equality policy by reducing the budget of the Equality and Human Rights Commission by two-thirds, leading to a warning from the UN that the UK is no longer fulfilling its duties to promote human rights (*Guardian* 2012b). It is has also scrapped gender equality impact assessments and is reviewing the duty on public sector organizations to promote gender equality, which may lead to its repeal.

Discussion and conclusions

Understanding the likely impacts of the austerity programme requires some reflection on the causes of the economic crisis beyond the immediate events such as the crash in the housing and financial markets. In many developed economies, including the UK and US, the economic crisis was preceded by a sustained period of economic growth but also by longer-term growth in income inequality. Under these conditions the broad-based and sustained participation in the consumption norms promoted to maintain domestic economic growth under consumption-focused capitalism was not possible without increased reliance on personal debt and mortgages to finance household expenditure and home buying (Skidelsky 2012). Although the causes of growing inequality remain varied and complex (e.g. see Standing 1999), inequality in wage and wealth distribution nonetheless meant that, without the relaxation of credit, many groups such as the young (as new or 'late' market entrants) or single earner and low-income households would be unable to meet these consumption norms. Others developed aspirations for the life-styles of the super-rich, as sold through 'life-style' culture, with credit relaxation fuelling house price inflation[7] and equity from rising house prices being used to fuel consumption or secure greater debt in addition to lax unsecured lending. This divergence between consumption norms and the underlying economy was sustained through increases in labour supply within households, state redistribution and, in the lead up to the crisis, the increased supply and demand for cheap and under-regulated credit. It is in this culmination of long-term growing underlying economic inequality and consumer capitalism, especially although not exclusively in the liberal market economies of the US and UK, that the housing market and broader economic crisis require situating. That is they cannot be seen as solely caused by the deviance of financial sector actors or an aberration in an otherwise well-functioning and sustainable economic model.

Increasing female employment rates over the last few decades also partly require further contextualizing in this period of rising inequality. Although higher educational attainment and changing cultural attitudes have helped some women into higher skilled and better paid jobs, for many women the taking on of often menial, low paid and under-valued employment has been an act of economic necessity to maintain living standards and partially offset the stagnation in wages at the bottom end of the wage distribution for men rather than necessarily a route to financial or personal emancipation. This wage depression coupled with reduced demand for lower skilled manual work for men has been partly responsible for eroding the traditional male breadwinner dual parent model which current policy seeks to hark back to. Policy developments such as 'in-work benefits' and increases in childcare provision, although fitting with a more traditional redistributive role of governments or anti-child poverty strategies, can further be viewed as attempts to subsidize low wages and counter the failure of the labour market to provide a living wage for a sizeable proportion of households, thereby upholding a system of wage inequality in the absence of a political will to intervene in the wage distribution beyond measures such as minimum wage setting.

From this perspective, attempts through austerity measures to dismantle aspects of the social and employment infrastructure that essentially grew to support and maintain the prior economic order are implicitly conflicted. These measures will essentially lead to greater inequality in the long term and thereby intensify the economic conditions on which the crisis was predicated in the first place. This time, however, there will be a less relaxed approach to personal lending and debt, or state intervention, reducing the immediate scope to adjust to the financial squeeze in the immediate term.

Current trends taking into account planned austerity policies do indeed look set to intensify the labour market problems of both women and men. Women's prospects of both secure employment and reasonable pay and conditions are being eroded by the shrinkage and downgrading of public sector employment while labour market opportunities for lower skilled men are also converging towards those found in the female-dominated private services, with lower pay and more non-standard employment often taken up on an involuntary basis. The overall trend is likely to be towards more flexibility and more polarization, with fewer opportunities for reasonably paid and stable jobs for any but the more privileged higher educated in the private sector workforce.

If the poor conditions associated with female private sector employment spread to the jobs taken by less advantaged men, the trend towards dual earner households may intensify with both partners participating in less stable and lower paid jobs as breadwinner jobs decline further. This follows earlier developments in the US where real earnings decline for lower paid men in part explained an upward shift in female labour supply (Blau and Kahn 2006). Despite the increased withdrawal of the state from active support for working parents, there is little evidence that either recession or the second phase of the austerity programme in the UK will lead to women voluntarily withdrawing from the labour market; some may not be able to continue to work because of withdrawal of public services but the long term trend may be towards poorer care of children or even a downturn in fertility.

The actual future will still depend on whether the current government is able to carry through its goal of both reducing the state's role in supporting citizens and families and in transforming the public sector into mainly a commissioner of services from the private sector. The expectations of state responsibility for citizens' welfare is still stronger in the UK than the prime neo-liberal example of the US and it is the central government which is still held ultimately to account for short-falls in minimum acceptable public services even when it tries to devolve decision making to lower levels of government (for example for failings in social care).

The outcome of current policies towards the family and gender roles is also far from clear. Sections of the Conservative party may take a socially conservative, 'traditional,' or religiously inspired approach to gender roles in the family and this may underpin some of the policies to remove state support from lone parents. However, the austerity programme is primarily concerned to reduce costs to the state and it is the opportunity to reduce benefit costs which primarily explains the intensified coercive approach to lone parents' involvement in wage work while policy towards mothers working in general is now ambivalent, regarded primarily as a private issue rather than one for public policy. Nevertheless, as evidence that the childcare issue will not go away, the government set up a childcare commission to look into issues of affordability and availability of childcare and is proposing a new childcare voucher system which will mainly help middle or higher income households while reducing regulation on staffing levels to reduce costs through downgrading of quality standards. The last forty years have witnessed an overall growth in levels of female attachment to the labour market and rising importance of female earnings to household income. In a period of intensified insecurity and squeeze on living standards, women's attachment to work can be expected to be further reinforced even in the absence of support structures for care. The important role women's employment plays at both the micro family level and the more macro level in sustaining living standards, contributing to economic growth and maximizing society's productive potential provides a further reason why the current retreat from gender equality policies under austerity cannot necessarily be sustained into the longer term. The immediate and medium-term prospects for promoting gender equality are indeed bleak but there is also little evidence that there will be any sustained attempt to reestablish a traditional gender order or that such efforts would be successful. The conundrum of how to sustain a dual earning society in the presence of a small state still remains.

Notes

1 The OECD social expenditure database shows expenditure on housing in the UK as over 1.4 percentage points of GDP in 2007, some 0.5 of a percentage point higher than the nearest other EU country, Hungary.
2 The marginal rate was reduced from 70 per cent but more families were in the net.
3 Based on percentage employed in public sector dominated sectors (SIC codes O, P and Q). However, based on an alternative self-report definition using the UKLFS micro-data 34 per cent of female employment is in the public sector compared to 15 per cent of male employment, with women accounting for 63.4 per cent of total public sector employment (October–December 2007). The differences between these two sets of figures largely reflect the inclusion of private sector health and education workers in the industry-based definition and that a larger proportion of male self-reported public sector employees work outside sectors O, P and Q.
4 ONS Workforce Jobs, own calculations – private sector defined as excluding public administration, education and health.
5 ONS, seasonally adjusted.
6 Around 60 per cent of unpaid carers for people on grounds of ill health, disability or old age are women (NHS Information Centre, 2011).
7 The dismantling of private sector pensions and absence of sufficient alternative public provision led to many seeing the housing market as an alternative place to invest pension funds.

References

Anxo, D., Bosch, G. and Rubery, J. (2010) 'Shaping the Life Course', in D. Anxo, G. Bosch and J. Rubery (eds) *Welfare State and Life Stage Transitions: a European Perspective*, Cheltenham: Edward Elgar.

Barbier, J-C. (2006) 'Has the European Social Model a Distinctive Activation Touch?' in M. Jepsen and A. Serrano Pascual (eds) *Unwrapping the European Social Model*, Bristol: Policy Press.

Bellamy, K., Bennet, F. and Millar, J. (2006) *Who Benefits? A Gender Analysis of the UK Benefits and Tax Credits System*, London: Fawcett Society. Available at: http://www.fawcettsociety.org.uk/documents/Benefits%20final%20copy.pdf (accessed 09.11.2012).

Blau, F. And Kahn, L. (2006) 'Changes in the Labor Supply Behavior of Married Women: 1980–2000', *IZA Working Paper 2180*. Available at: http://www.econstor.eu/dspace/bitstream/10419/33907/1/514361352.pdf (accessed 18.10.2012).

Browne, J. (2011) 'The Impact of Tax and Benefit Reforms by Sex: Some Simple Analysis', *IFS Briefing Note 118*, London: Institute For Fiscal Studies. Available at: http://www.ifs.org.uk/publications/5610 (accessed 08.09.2012).

Corry, D., Valero, A. and Van Reenen, J. (2011) 'UK Economic Performance Since 1997', Centre for Economic Performance, November 2011, London: London School of Economics. Available at http://cep.lse.ac.uk/conference_papers/15b_11_2011/151111_UK_Business_slides_final.pdf (accessed 04.01.2013).

Daycare Trust (2012) 'Children's Centre Managers Survey'. Available at: http://www.daycaretrust.org.uk/pages/-research-336.html (accessed 31.12.2012).

Dex, S. and Forth, J. (2009) 'Equality and Diversity', in W. Brown, A. Bryson, J. Forth and K. Whitfield (eds) *The Evolution of the Modern Workplace*, Cambridge: Cambridge University Press.

Dex, S. and Shaw L. (1986) *British and American Women at Work*, New York: St Martin's Press.

DWP (Department for Work and Pensions) (2011a) 'Universal Credit Policy briefing note 5: Second earners'. Available at: http://www.dwp.gov.uk/docs/ucpbn-5-second-earners.pdf (accessed 10.10.2012).

— (2011b) *Household Benefit Cap Equality Impact Assessment*, July 2012. Available at: http://www.dwp.gov.uk/docs/eia-benefit-cap-wr2011.pdf (accessed 10.12.2012).

EHRC (Equality and Human Rights Commission) (2012) 'Making Fair Financial Decisions: An Assessment of the HR Treasury's 2010 Spending Review conducted under Section 31 of the 2006 Equality Act', Manchester: EHRC. Available at: http://www.equalityhumanrights.com/uploaded_files/Inquiries/s31exec_summary_final.pdf (accessed 30.12.2012).

Esping-Andersen, G. (1990) *The Three Worlds of Welfare Capitalism*, Cambridge: Polity Press.

Freud, D. (2007) *Reducing Dependency, Increasing Opportunity: Options for the Future of Welfare to Work*, Independent report to the Department of Work and Pensions. Available at: http://www.dwp.gov.uk/docs/welfarereview.pdf (accessed 02.12.2012).

Goode, J., Callender, C., Lister, R. and Institute, P.S. (1998). *Purse or Wallet?: Gender Inequalities and Income Distribution Within Families on Benefits*, London: Policy Studies Institute.

Grimshaw, D. (2009) 'The UK: Developing a Progressive Minimum Wage in a Liberal Market Economy', in D. Vaughan-Whitehead (ed.) *The Minimum Wage Revisited in the Enlarged EU*, Geneva: ILO.

Grimshaw, D. and Rubery, J. (2012) 'The End of the UK's Liberal Collectivist Social Model? The Implications of the Coalition Government's Policy During the Austerity Crisis', *Cambridge Journal of Economics*, 36(1): 105–26.

Guardian (2011) 'Care for elderly in "absolute crisis", charity warns', *Guardian*, 28 December. Available at: http://www.guardian.co.uk/society/2011/dec/28/care-elderly-crisis-charity-warns (accessed 14.09.2012).

— (2012a) 'Council cuts "targeted towards deprived areas"', *Guardian*, 14 November. Available at: http://www.guardian.co.uk/society/2012/nov/14/council-cuts-targeted-deprived-areas (accessed 31.12.2012).

— (2012b) 'Budget cuts could downgrade UK rights watchdog's UN status', *Guardian*, 26 October. Available at: http://www.guardian.co.uk/society/2012/oct/26/budget-cuts-rights-watchdog-un-status (accessed 31.12.2012).

— (2012c) 'Leaked documents reveal plan to lengthen public sector working hours', *Guardian*, 10 October. http://www.guardian.co.uk/politics/2012/oct/10/leaked-documents-public-sector-hours (accessed 31.12.2012).

— (2012d) 'Equality: coalition is missing the point about women', *Guardian*, 12 February. Available at: http://www.guardian.co.uk/commentisfree/2012/feb/12/observer-editorial-women-equality-benefits (accessed 31.12.2012).

Hirsch, D. (2011) *Childcare Support and the Hours Trap: the Universal Credit* Resolution Foundation and Gingerbread. Available at: http://www.resolutionfoundation.org/media/media/downloads/Childcare_and_the_hours_trap_under_Univeral_Credit.pdf (accessed 19.10.2012).

Hooker, H., Neathey, F., Caseborne, J. and Munro, M. (2007) *The Third Work – Life Balance Employee Survey: Main Findings*, Institute for Employment Studies for the Department for Business, Enterprise and Regulatory Reform Employment Relations Research Series No. 58. Available at: https://www.gov.uk/government/uploads/system/uploads/attachment_data/file/32187/07-714x-third-work-life-balance-employee-survey-findings-revised.pdf (accessed 12.03.2012).

Lewis J. (1992) 'Gender and the Development of Welfare Regimes', *Journal of European Social Policy*, 2: 159–73.

London Economics (2011) 'Written Submission on the Future of Higher Education to Select Committee Business, Skills and Innovation'. Available at: http://www.publications.parliament.uk/pa/cm201011/cmselect/cmbis/writev/885/m16.htm (accessed 10.11.2012).

Manning, A. (2012) *Minimum Wage: Maximum Impact*, Resolution Foundation. Available at: http://www.resolutionfoundation.org/media/media/downloads/MinimumWage MaximumImpact.pdf (accessed 20.12.2012).

NHS Information Centre (2011) 'Survey of Carers in Households 2009/10', NHS Information Centre. Available at: http://www.ic.nhs.uk/webfiles/publications/009_Social_Care/carersurvey0910/Survey_of_Carers_in_Households_2009_10_England_NS_Status_v1_0a.pdf. (accessed 10.12.2012).

Office for Budget Responsibility (OBR) (2011) *Economic and Fiscal Outlook*, November. Available at: http://budgetresponsibility.independent.gov.uk/pubs/Autumn2011EFO_web_version138469072346.pdf (accessed 30.12.2012).

— (2012) *Economic and Fiscal Outlook*, December. Available at: http://cdn.budgetresponsibility.independent.gov.uk/December-2012-Economic-and-fiscal-outlook23423423.pdf (accessed 30.12.2012).

ONS (2011a) *Labour Market Statistics, November 2011 Release*, Office for National Statistics. Available at: http://www.ons.gov.uk/ons/rel/lms/labour-market-statistics/november-2011/index.html (accessed 18.10.2012).

— (2011b) *Labour Market Statistics, October 2011 Release*, Office for National Statistics. Available at: http://www.ons.gov.uk/ons/rel/lms/labour-market-statistics/october-2011/index.html (accessed 10.10.2012).

Orloff, A. (1993) 'Gender and the Social Rights of Citizenship: The Comparative Analysis of Gender Relations and Welfare States', *American Sociological Review*, 58(3): 303–28.

Rafferty, A. and Wiggan, J. (2010) 'Choice and Welfare Reform: Lone Parents' Decision Making Around Paid Work and Family Life', *Journal of Social Policy*, 40(2): 275–93.

Reher, D.S. (1998) 'Family Ties in Western Europe: Persistent Contrasts', *Population and Development Review*, 24: 203–34.

Rowlingson, K. and McKay, S. (2001) *Lone Parents, Employment and Social Policy: Cross National Comparisons*, Essex: Pearson Education Ltd.

Rubery, J. (2013) 'Public Sector Adjustment and the Threat to Gender Equality', in D. Vaughan-Whitehead (ed.) *Public Sector Shock*, ILO and Edward Elgar, forthcoming.

Rubery, J. and Rafferty, A. (2013) 'Women and recession revisited,' *Work, Employment and Society* forthcoming.

Rubery, J., Hebson, G., Grimshaw, D., Carroll, M., Marchington, L., Smith, L. and Ugarte, S. (2011) *The Recruitment and Retention of a Care Workforce for Older People*, EWERC Manchester Business School and Department of Health. Available at: http://www.kcl.ac.uk/sspp/kpi/scwru/dhinitiative/projects/ruberyetal2011recruitmentfinal.pdf (accessed 20.10.2012).

Skidelsky, R. (2012) *Skidelsky on the Crisis 2008–2011*, London: Lightening Source UK.

Standing, G. (1999) *Global Labour Market Flexibility: Seek Redistributive Justice*, Basingstoke: Macmillan.

Taylor-Gooby, P. and Stoker, G. (2011) 'The Coalition Programme: A New Vision for Britain or Politics as Usual?', *The Political Quarterly*, 82(1): 4–15.

Tomlinson, J. (2007) 'Employment Regulation, Welfare and Gender Regimes: A Comparative Analysis of Women's Working-time Patterns and Work-life Balance in the UK and the US', *International Journal of Human Resource Management*, 18(3): 401–15.

TUC (2011) 'Women's Unemployment Will Rise as Public Sector Job Cuts Kick in September', TUC Press Release. Available at: http://www.tuc.org.uk/economy/tuc-19982-f0.cfm (accessed 31.12.2012).

Waldfogel, J. (2011) 'Family-friendly Policies', in P. Gregg and J. Wadsworth (eds) *The Labour Market in Winter: The State of Working Britain*, Oxford: Oxford University Press.

Women's Budget Group (2012) 'The Impact on Women of Autumn Financial Statement 2012 and Welfare Benefits Up-rating Bill 2013' WBG response. Available at: http://wbg.org.uk/pdfs/WBG-AFS-2012-FINAL-[2](1).pdf (accessed 11.01.2013).

8

THE LABOUR MARKET IMPACT OF THE ECONOMIC CRISIS IN HUNGARY THROUGH THE LENS OF GENDER EQUALITY

Mária Frey

Introduction

Hungary was engaged in fiscal consolidation even before the 2008 crisis. Measures launched in 2006 to improve the economy's external and internal balances reduced the general government sector deficit from 9.3 per cent of GDP in 2006 to 3.4 per cent in 2008, with complementary reductions in both the current account deficit and the net external financing requirement. These factors were expected to reduce the vulnerability of the Hungarian economy but the financial turbulences stemming from the US mortgage markets escalated to a global turmoil, reducing the net inflows of foreign capital into emerging markets. Thus, in autumn 2008, Hungary faced the risk of substantially reduced foreign capital inflows alongside still high levels of internal and external debt and slow economic growth. Hungary was forced to seek external finance from the IMF and the EU. The economic crisis compelled Hungary to adopt an early and front-loaded consolidation but the government resigned shortly afterwards. An interim Social-Liberal government under Bajnai provided short-term crisis management until the general election in May 2010 when the Conservative Orbán government took office.

Although the Bajnai government introduced strong austerity measures including changes to pensions and public sector wages, even harder measures were adopted by the Orbán government, among others extraordinary levies and taxes on particular sectors, the nationalization of private pension contributions to reduce the deficit, the adoption of flat rate income taxes (from 2011) and structural reforms in key areas such as labour market policy, the welfare system, public transport and education. These measures affected women and men differently. In addition, the new government enacted a policy programme aimed at addressing the demographic crisis and low fertility rate. This programme is considered to be family-friendly, a concept that has replaced and is also seen as in potential conflict with gender equality in the policy discourse.

This chapter investigates the labour market impact of the economic crisis though the lens of gender equality. To provide a starting point for understanding the gendered effects of the current crisis, developments in the gender regime prior to the crisis are first assessed. The labour market effects of the recent global crisis on men and women are then described. This is followed by an analysis of the characteristics of the crisis and the policy responses to it, evaluated from a gender aspect. The chapter closes with a concluding summary.

Developments in the gender regime prior to the crisis

To understand the most important trends and processes in Hungarian labour market inequalities, its roots in the socialist period need to be considered. Under socialism, women and men achieved a high level of workforce participation. This reflected the social policy of full employment which also resulted in an excessive utilization of labour resources. This was the outcome of two self-reinforcing factors. First, it was in the basic interest of every member of the working age population to get and keep a job. This was the prerequisite for obtaining income, both wages and social benefits, and for avoiding the disadvantages and punishment of 'work-shirkers'. Second, employers were interested in over-employment, being both indifferent to production costs and tolerant of low work intensity and productivity (Frey 1997a). As a result, the employment rate of women well exceeded that of the highly developed market economies. Paid activity meant everybody working full-time under inflexible time arrangements, supported by a broad network of services to ease reconciliation of paid work and family life.

Today there is a dispute about what role gender equality played in the communist ideology. Was the two breadwinner model introduced to meet the huge labour demand of industrialization or the political objectives of controlling as many citizens as possible and keeping wages as low as possible? Furthermore, there are also debates over the extent to which women themselves wanted to be involved in employment or were simply responding to pressure from 'above'. Full employment of women undoubtedly had certain negative consequences, such as the overloading of women and the weakening of family functions. Moreover, despite legislation providing for equal rights for women, discrimination against women still prevailed on the labour market. Yet, the increasing labour market participation of women did bring improvements in their actual situation. Their employment outside the household contributed to the family's financial well-being, enriched their own lives, mitigated their poverty and decreased their exposure to the family and to men (Frey 1997b).

In the transformation from centrally planned to market economy Hungary lost around 1.1 million jobs, more than one-fifth of total employment. Men and women absorbed these losses relatively equally. Women's labour market and economic situation was influenced by several factors: the economic re-structuring; the demographic trends and policies; the eradication of political quotas adopted under the socialist regime; but mostly by the upsurge of conservative values which offered women completely different roles than the ones defined within the social-ist emancipator project. The weakening of women's labour market status was paralleled by a strengthening of traditional value orientations.

The social and economic transformations brought about by de-industrialization, as well as the massive reduction of the former state and local administrative appara-tuses – an important employer of the female labour force – resulted in a sudden increase in unemployment for both genders, with the rate peaking in 1993. The female unemployment rate was consistently lower than men's during the 1990s, in part because male-dominated industries, such as coal mining, metal processing industries and construction were hardest hit by economic re-structuring. In addi-tion, however, the lower unemployment rate for women masked a withdrawal of women from the labour market. Some of them were able to choose child care leave, early retirement or disability pension, the rules for which were relatively generous. By the year 2000, pensioners of working age actually outnumbered the registered unemployed and the rate of increase was higher among women in both these categories.

Women's activity rates remained well below the EU-average even in the 2000s, which caused problems for a number of obvious reasons.

> While both men and women seem to give preference to providing jobs for men when these are scarce and are overall more amenable to women's withdrawing from the labour force, in practice very few families can afford the resulting loss of income, and women's lack of gainful employment often exposes a family to poverty.
>
> *(Fodor 2005: 9)*

In addition, high divorce rates and unstable social policy measures place women who are outside the labour force in a particularly vulnerable position.

Gender segregation of occupations, already significant in Hungary, continued and even increased in some fields during the 1990s (Frey and Lukács 2003). The transformation brought a reallocation of labour through downsizing, mergers and liquidations of state-owned enterprises, while jobs were being created in the newly established private enterprises. This reallocation also caused labour to shift out of agriculture and into industry and services. The regrouping into the service sector was modestly higher for women than for men and there was also a slight decline in the number of women holding industrial jobs. The occupations in which women dominate are mostly focused on the provision of services, education, health and care, while men are more typically found in production jobs. The majority of professional and semi-professional occupations in the public sector including public administration, education and health are filled by women. These jobs acknowledge women's education and allow them to combine family and work responsibilities to the best effect. The price for that is the low pay which has tended to characterize the whole public sector in Hungary. Moreover, while women are well represented in the professional ranks, the 'glass ceiling' prevents

TABLE 8.1 The distribution of employees according to their employment status in Hungary 1992 and 2007 (%)

Status	Women		Men		Female share (%)	
	1992	2007	1992	2007	1992	2007
Wage and salary earners	83.7	90.8	76.1	84.9	48.7	47.1
Members of co-operatives	3.8	0.1	7.1	0.1	31.6	31.8
Members of partnerships/corporations*	5.3	2.1	5.3	4.0	38.3	30.9
Self-employed	5.4	6.3	8.8	10.7	35.0	32.7
Assisting family members	1.8	0.7	0.6	0.3	68.6	68.7

*Working members/owners of Ltd-s, joint stock companies.
Source: CSO, Labour Force Survey.

them reaching the level of senior officials and managers. Men are significantly more likely to supervise a large number of people at work (Nagy 2012). Women also dominate many lower level occupations; almost all clerks are women, and they are overrepresented in jobs requiring little or no training, as well as in the lower technical and professional categories. There has been a continuous long run shift towards working as a wage and salary earner particularly for women, with this form of employment accounting for nine out of ten women but only 84.9 per cent of men in 2007.

After the change of political system, members of co-operatives almost disappeared along with the collapse of the old agricultural co-operatives. Expectations at the beginning of the transition that women would significantly increase their representation among the self-employed have not been realized. Between 1992–2007, the proportion of employed women in self-employment grew from 5.4 per cent only to 6.3 per cent, while for men, the share increased from 8.8 per cent to 10.7 per cent. Assisting family members – more than two thirds of them are women – play a negligible role in the labour market.

Women's inferior position in the labour market is indicated by a noticeable gender wage gap despite women having on average a higher level of education than men. This was explained in the past by a lower tendency for women to learn a trade or skill which guaranteed higher income than a purely academic qualification, particularly in the public sector. In the first years after the political regime change, differences between male and female earnings declined significantly. Research indicates that men's income advantage decreased from 35 per cent to 20 per cent between 1986 and 1994 as non-manual work, where women had obvious dominance, became relatively more valued. A second reason is that the wages of men in certain declining industries that were important for unskilled male workers fell relative to the wages of women (Kertesi and Köllő 1995). While average gender wage inequalities in comparable jobs did not change much in the competitive sector during the 1990s, they increased in the public sector to the detriment of women, as Table 8.2 indicates.

TABLE 8.2 Male and female earnings in comparable jobs in budgetary and non-budgetary sectors in Hungary 1997–2000 (indices)

Sector	1997			1999			2000		
	Total	Male	Female	Total	Male	Female	Total	Male	Female
Budgetary	65.8	72.0	63.5	62.5	68.9	60.2	65.0	73.5	61.9
Competitive	100.0	104.9	92.2	100.0	105.0	92.1	100.0	105.1	92.2

*The source of information is the representative annual survey of individual earnings with the reference month of May in each year. Data refer to earnings in comparable jobs.
Budgetary sector: state administration, public services (e.g. education, health) and armed forces.
Competitive (non-budgetary) sector: private and public enterprises.
Source: National Labour Centre Wage Survey.

However, the growing public–private sector wage gap[1] was even more unfavourable for women, as the majority of them work as public employees. Hámori and Köllő (2012) showed that the increasing private–public wage gap of the 1990s was caused by the stabilization programme of 1995–6, so that the public sector relative wage was 25 per cent below the private sector level. In order to narrow the pay gap, a series of rises were introduced from 2000. The minimum wage was almost doubled and the pay of civil servants and public employees increased. As a result, the public sector wage penalty (-6 per cent in 2002) changed into a substantial premium of 11 per cent in 2003, and 15 per cent in 2004. Women were strongly affected by the wage rise, which reduced the overall gender wage gap to a level of 7 to 11 per cent although this benefit was quickly eroded (Hámori and Köllő 2012). Public sector wages have fallen significantly since 2006 and lag substantially behind private sector earnings. Wage losses affected mainly women as Hungary has a very high share of female graduates in the public sector.

Historically Hungary has had a rather well-developed social protection system; child care benefits were introduced gradually from the end of the 1960s and subsequently became an integral part of the system. However, in the communist era, social protection was linked almost entirely to employment and open unemployment did not exist. The system therefore needed to be re-structured to deal with a market economy in which unemployment was an overt problem. As a result, the following social protection sub-systems were established (Frey and Lukács 2003):

- a compulsory social insurance system, including health, pension and unemployment insurance;
- family support schemes, which provided a mix of universal benefits, needs-related benefits and earnings-related benefits;
- a social assistance system funded by the central budget and to some extent by the local governments;
- social and child care facilities run by local governments.

Hungary has generous parental leave policies; some would argue they are generous to the point of acting as a deterrent to women's labour force participation. New mothers in paid employment before the birth of their child are entitled to 24 weeks maternity leave and receive 70 per cent of their full salary. After this period, they (or the child's father) are entitled to child care benefit (GYED) up until the child is two, during which they receive 70 per cent of their salary (with a salary ceiling of twice the minimum wage). With children aged two to three either parent is entitled to child care allowance (GYES), which is a leave paid at the level of the minimum pension. This benefit is also available for parents not eligible for the higher benefits due to not working in an insured job for 180 days in the two years prior to the birth of the child. Yet another type of child care provision, the child raising aid (GYET), may be utilized by women who have at least three children up until the youngest is eight years of age. Any parent can take the leaves and these third and fourth types of leave may be used by grandparents as well. The leave counts as service towards old-age pensions and also health insurance if social insurance contributions are paid. Parents also are allowed to work part-time while keeping benefits but very few of them do, mostly because of the dearth of nursery places and the unavailability of part-time work. Most young mothers take the leave and many do so for the full three-year period or even longer but less than one per cent of those on parental leave are fathers. As a result, about 10 per cent of women in working age are inactive at any point in time because of being on child care leave. However, better educated and professional women tend to take the shorter, better paid leave which, in fact, was designed to increase the birth rate within this group in the mid-1980s.

As women tend to take their full paid leave entitlements, very few nursery places are available in Hungary. Cause and effect are unclear for even if women do want to return to work, high quality nursery places are hard to find, especially outside large cities. Overall, about 10 per cent of children between ages one to three are in nurseries but almost none under the age of one. These are far from the Barcelona targets. Currently it is ideologically almost unacceptable for Hungarian parents to send children under three to public day care: psychologists and fellow mothers extol the virtue in the public media of family-based care for small children. It is difficult to go against cultural norms, even for young professional women who could afford private care for their children and who may lose the most when giving up their jobs. As a result, women often drop out of the labour force for three to even six or more years. However, use of kindergarten from age three onwards is the norm with over 80 per cent of children between ages three and six being in day care and kindergarten from age three set to be compulsory from 2014.

These parental leave options obviously provide incentives for women to take a long break from employment, which may make it difficult for them to gain high quality positions. On the other hand, they serve as unemployment and poverty relief for women living in impoverished areas, where they have no chance of being employed anyway: at least they are paid for their work of raising children, however meagre these benefits may be. For this reason, and because of the widely shared conviction that it is best for children under three to stay at home, it is a real challenge for any government to reform the management of this complex problem.

As a consequence, there are large gender differences in the balance between paid and unpaid work. Time use surveys show that women in all categories devoted more time to housework and child care than did men. Overall, less time was spent in waged productive activity by women in the transition period (1986/87–2000) but those women in employment were working longer hours. Gender differences in time devoted to housework declined over this period but women still spent 2.6 times longer on housework than men. Child care activities also remained mostly the responsibility of women. The involvement of women on child care leave in waged productive activity decreased substantially (by 88 minutes a day, to one-quarter of the previous level), similar to the reported additional time spent on child care activities (+76 minutes a day). This reflects the strengthening of traditional patterns fostered by a declining labour market and the lack of support for combining employment and child care (CSO 2000). The 2010 survey reports little change (CSO 2012).

In sum, although gender equality was part of the communist ideology, the social benefits were not aimed at achieving equal treatment of women and men. Rather, in an environment of substantial gender inequality, the benefits rewarded women for motherhood and eased their dual role of worker and principal family care giver. At the beginning of the 1990s, gender equality was eclipsed by other concerns that were seen as more pressing, namely, the need for new benefits to protect workers and families against high inflation, job loss and poverty.

Labour market impact of the recent global crisis, with respect to gender

The transitional recession of the early 1990s and a brief austerity package in 1996 were followed by steady and relatively high growth in output, but very little increase in employment. Moreover, the economic crisis resulted in a significant deterioration of the already low employment rates in Hungary. Before the global crisis in late 2008 the female employment rate stood at 50.6 per cent, 8.5 percentage points lower than the EU27 average, and that of males was 63 per cent, lagging almost 10 percentage points behind the EU average. The low employment rates for men as well as women kept the gender employment gap at 12.4 percentage points, lower than the average for the EU27 (13.7 percentage points).

Employment began to decline in the second half of 2008, falling by a maximum of 4 percentage points for men and 1.8 for women before starting to increase in the third quarter of 2010. At the end of 2010, the female employment rate had already regained its pre-crisis level (Table 8.3), but that of males remained significantly below its pre-crisis level.

The greater impact on men is also evident in the faster rise in unemployment rates from 7.6 per cent in 2008 to a peak of 11.6 per cent in 2010 before falling

TABLE 8.3 Employment and unemployment rates by sex and age groups in Hungary 2008–2011(%)

Years and age groups	Employment rates		Unemployment rates	
	Males	Females	Males	Females
15–24				
2008	23.2	16.8	19.1	20.9
2009	19.9	16.3	28.2	24.2
2010	20.0	16.6	27.9	24.9
2011	19.9	16.7	27.3	22.1
25–54				
2008	81.0	67.9	6.9	7.4
2009	78.9	66.9	9.2	9.0
2010	77.9	67.1	10.6	10.1
2011	79.6	66.6	9.8	10.4
55–64				
2008	38.5	25.7	5.0	5.1
2009	39.9	27.0	6.4	6.2
2010	39.6	30.1	8.2	7.3
2011	39.8	32.4	9.5	7.8
15–64				
2008	63.0	50.6	7.6	8.1
2009	61.1	49.9	10.3	9.7
2010	60.4	50.6	11.6	10.7
2011	61.2	50.6	11.0	11.0

Source: CSO, Labour Force Survey.

slightly to 11.0 by 2011. Women's unemployment rate started off higher than men's at 8.1 per cent in 2008 but by 2010 it had reached 10.7 per cent, almost one percentage point below men's. However, women's unemployment rate has continued to rise, leading to an equalization of rates at 11 per cent in 2011. It was almost exclusively men who were affected by the immediate layoffs due to the crisis as the drop in foreign and domestic demand was concentrated on male-dominated industries such as the car-industry, manufacturing and construction. It was mostly the skilled male workers that lost their jobs, mainly in the more developed west and north-west regions. The decrease in female employment can be explained by the budget cuts in the public sector, where numbers employed had been continuously declining from 2004. The dismissed male employees immediately appeared among the unemployed while the rise in the female unemployed and discouraged workers reflected principally the activation of the inactive (Table 8.4).

The decline in employment has been concentrated in the private sector. Public sector employment also declined initially but in 2009 it started to increase, the year when the 'Path to Work' programme[2] was introduced, whereby the long-term unemployed are required to engage in large-scale public work schemes.

TABLE 8.4 Changes in the number of employed, unemployed and discouraged workers due to the crisis in Hungary 2008–2010

Years	Men			Women		
	Employed	Unemployed	Discouraged	Employed	Unemployed	Discouraged
Q2–2008	2114,7	169,3	44,0	1753,8	149,9	39,8
Q3–2008	2140,0	172,1	42,8	1784,3	155,6	39,9
Q4–2008	2096,1	182,5	50,9	1784,6	154,6	42,4
Q1–2009	2033,3	224,3	60,6	1730,8	178,5	48,0
Q2–2009	2058,3	225,5	55,4	1738,8	176,2	45,1
Q3–2009	2048,9	241,4	53,2	1734,6	194,8	48,7
Q4–2009	2038,9	243,2	62,0	1743,9	198,9	52,4
Q1–2010	1979,5	283,8	63,9	1739,8	214,0	58,5
Q2–2010	2008,5	271,4	59,2	1747,9	211,8	54,8
Q3–2010	2050,0	252,7	56,7	1772,5	213,0	52,3
Q4–2010	2043,0	253,6	61,9	1761,3	208,5	57,1
Q2–2008/09	−56,4	+56,2	+11,4	−15,0	+26,1	+5,3
Q2–2009/10	−49,8	+45,9	+3,8	+9,1	+35,6	+9,7
Q2–2008/10	−106,2	+102,1	+15,2	−5,9	+61,7	+15,0
Q2–2008– Q4–2010	−71,7	+84,3	+17,9	+7,5	+58,6	+17,3

Source: LFS CSO Hungary.

This scheme has noticeably increased the size of the public sector (Bálint *et al.* 2011).

Enterprises adapted to the decreasing demand by limiting hiring, thereby hitting particularly hard those who were hoping to start their careers, especially young men whose employment rate fell by more than three percentage points. Young women's employment rate remained significantly below that of young men but the gender gap narrowed from 6.4 to 3.2 percentage points in 2011. The employment rate of men aged 25–54 also deteriorated until the end of 2010 but started to increase in 2011 while that of women stagnated. The employment rate of 55–64 year olds, however, improved, especially for women, probably related to the rise in the mandatory retirement age, which in the period of the crisis affected mainly women.

Unemployment rates became particularly high among the youth. Even in the pre-crisis period three quarters of the 15–24 population were inactive, with early school-leavers without work experience who have difficulties finding jobs dominating the labour market entrants. The gender gap in youth unemployment rates is widening, with young women's unemployment rate now 5.2 percentage points below young men's. The increasing volume of dismissals hit the prime age population most, whose unemployment rates deteriorated similarly, but by 2011 this process seemed to have come to an end. The unemployment rate of the 55–64 year olds also worsened, in part because the conditions for obtaining entitlement to old-age pension were tightened although some women may have benefited after 2011 from a special provision allowing early retirement for women with at least 40 years' employment (Table 8.3).

While total employment was stagnating and unemployment continued to increase, the inactive population decreased by nearly 40,000. This affected mainly women, whose inactivity rate reduced from 45 per cent to 43.3 per cent between 2008 and 2011, suggesting an added worker effect. Male inactivity stagnated at the level of 31.7 per cent.

Hungary's index of occupational gender segregation slightly decreased (from 28.2 in 2008 to 27.8 in 2010) during the crisis but remained some 1.4 percentage points higher than the EU average. The decline is probably due to the reduction in the well-paid manual industrial jobs where skilled men were concentrated. Calculations based on Hungarian LFS data show that, between 2007 and 2010, the number of craft and related workers fell by 12.2 per cent and that of plant and machinery operators by 8.6 per cent. These occupational groups with a female share below 15 per cent contributed over nine-tenths of the overall employment drop. On the other hand, only two main occupations had employment growth: professionals (+7.3 per cent) where women's share within employed persons was 54.8 per cent before the growth and elementary occupations (+31.1 per cent) in which women were represented at 56.1 per cent. The latter may reflect the substantial expansion of public works.

The sector gender segregation index increased from 19.4 in 2008 to 20.9 in 2010, slightly exceeding the 2010 EU average (20.3). Between 2007 and 2010, employment in male-dominated sectors declined most (-9.7 per cent). In mixed-sex sectors the number of workers fell by 2.7 per cent but increased in female-dominated sectors by 0.8 per cent. The male-dominated sectors account for 58.8 per cent of the overall shrinkage of employment during the crisis. Men, especially in construction, agriculture and transportation, were hit by job losses that were disproportionate to their employment share. Although women's overall share of job decline in the mixed-sex sectors was much lower than their employment share, in the hardest hit sector, manufacturing, job losses by gender were largely proportional to their overall employment shares. In wholesale and retail trades men suffered particularly from employment contraction while in accommodation and food services it was women who suffered disproportionately. In contrast, the number of employees increased by 11.4 per cent in public administration/social security and by 30 per cent in other services, including communication and arts and recreation activities. Both sexes increased their employment, but in the former women captured 60 per cent compared to an overall female sector share of around 50 per cent while in the latter women only accounted for 34.5 per cent of the increase, despite an overall employment share of 54.5 per cent. Women also benefited to some extent from the employment growth in female-dominated sectors. Although this was positive overall it only offset around 4 per cent of the net overall employment decline. Women benefited disproportionately from growth in the financial sector at over 90 per cent of the employment increase but in the public sector industries of education and health, women's share of the employment change was lower than their sector shares. This applied in both sectors even though education expanded and health contracted (Table 8.5).

Companies tried to adapt to the new conditions through several methods: wage freezes, working hour cuts, and some immediate termination of temporary contracts. In addition, part-time employment was introduced, including the four-day working week as well as cutbacks on bonuses. This was possible because there are few legal constraints on employment and wage setting in Hungary with the most important one being the minimum wage. Hiring and firing is relatively easy and inexpensive too. Hungary's employment protection (EPL) index has been one of the lowest in the EU (Cazes and Nesporova 2007), although public sector employment has been protected with cuts mainly made in wages (Köllő 2011). The first and foremost form of labour adjustment after the initial downturn was the expansion of fixed-term contracts, whose incidence among male employees increased from 7.7 per cent in 2007 to 10.1 per cent in 2010 and from 6.8 to 9.2 per cent for female employees (Table 8.6).

The proportion of self-employed remained stable for both sexes in the period investigated and the negative gap below the EU average widened. A more subtle form of labour capacity reduction was work sharing through the spread of part-time employment. Although a mildly rising trend was evident before, the share of part-time among all employees perceptibly increased at the time of the crisis. Among male employees the part-time share grew from 2.8 per cent in 2007 to 4.7 per cent in 2011 and among women from 5.8 to 9.2 per cent. During this period the proportion of involuntary part-timers rose from 27.7 to 39.2 per cent for men and from 30.2 to 36 per cent for women. This strengthens the suggestion that the extension of part-time work was partly an adjustment strategy by employers. The mild increase in both part-time work and fixed-term contracts might also reflect the extension of public work schemes.[3]

Research indicates that most part-time workers are uneducated women and/ or social transfer recipients such as women on child care leave, pensioners or people receiving social allowance. For these groups part-time employment is less expensive for employers, particularly if it is unregistered (Budapest Intézet 2012). As there is limited availability of part-time work for the prime age population and other forms of flexible working-time arrangements are also missing, young parents are usually forced to 'choose' between full-time employment or inactivity. The employers have no interest in offering part-time work to their regular workforce as unit costs are higher than for full-time work because fixed costs in the form of contributions to travel costs and meals apply. Furthermore, the working process may not be suitable for or has not been adjusted to accommodate part-time work. To reduce these higher part-time employment costs, the government in 2011 reduced employers' payroll taxes for new hires of parents returning to work after parental leave. In addition, public sector employers are now obliged to provide part-time jobs upon request from employees with a child below age three.

TABLE 8.5 Sector segregation and impact of recession on employment in Hungary 2007–2010

	Change in employment 2007–2010 (%)	Sector contribution to employment 2007 (%)	Sector contribution to change in employment 2007 (%)	Female share 2007 (%)	Women's contribution (%) to change in employment
All sectors	-3.7	100.0	100.0	45.4	17.2
Male-dominated sectors*	-9.7	22.6	-58.9	17.9	14.3
Construction	-16.0	8.4	-36.5	6.7	0.9
Mining and quarrying	-26.2	0.4	-3.0	10.4	9.3
Agriculture	-6.4	4.6	-8.0	22.8	10.3
Electricity and water supply	+36.7	1.6	+15.7	25.7	16.7
Transportation and storage	-13.2	7.6	-27.1	26.0	35.4
Mixed-sex sectors***	-2.7	60.4	-45.0	47.0	29.4
Manufacturing	-10.1	22.2	-61.1	38.6	39.8
Real estate (+ professional and administrative) activities	-3.7	7.3	-7.4	45.9	-15.0
Public administration and social security	+11.4	6.7	+21.6	50.0	60.4
Wholesale, retail trade and repair	-8.2	15.1	-33.5	53.0	44.0
Other services (+ info-communication and arts)	+30.0	4.7	+37.9	54.5	35.6
Accommodation and food service	-2.3	4.4	-2.5	57.0	70.3
Female-dominated sectors**	+0.8	7.0	+3.9	76.3	117.5
Activities of households as employers	+16.7	0.1	+0.3	63.8	133.3
Financial and insurance activities	+7.3	2.2	+4.3	67.0	91.9
Education	+2.0	8.0	+4.3	77.4	45.2
Health	-2.8	6.7	-5.0	78.0	35.6

*Men>70%; **Women>60%; ***70%≤men>40% and 60%≤women>30%.

Source: Data elaboration from Labour Force Survey (Hungarian Statistical Office).

Note: In 2008, a new sector classification system was introduced and it was further modified in 2009. Some branches had to be combined to make the data before and after the change comparable.

TABLE 8.6 The spread of part-time working, fixed-term contracts and self-employment in Hungary 2007–2011

Share of all employed (%)	2007		2008		2009		2010		2011	
	Men	Women	Men	Women	Men	Women	Men	Women	Men	Women
Part-timers	2.8	5.8	3.3	6.2	3.6	7.1	3.9	8.0	4.7	9.2
Fixed-term contracts	7.7	6.8	8.7	7.0	9.0	7.8	10.1	9.2	9.4	8.4
Self-employed	14.2	8.6	14.2	8.0	14.8	8.4	14.8	8.2	n.a.	n.a.

Source: Eurostat LFS; Employment in Europe Report 2010.

Because part-time employment is infrequent, women's full-time equivalent employment rate (49.3 per cent in 2010) is very close to the headcount female employment rate (50.6 per cent in 2010 and 2011) and also almost equal to the average full-time equivalent employment rate of EU member states (49.9 per cent in 2010). This means that fewer women have paid work in Hungary but those who are employed work more than their Western European peers.

The gender pay gap in Hungary is in the middle range of EU countries. As mentioned earlier, the pay gap decreased between 2002 and 2006 because public sector pay rose significantly in 2002 and 2003. Due to these pay-corrections, a lot of female-dominated jobs were upgraded. However, their positive influence started to disappear by 2008, when the gender pay gap started to increase again. One recent analyses of the gender wage gap, based on the TÁMOP 2010 survey found the gender pay gap narrowed between 2009 and 2010 by 1.1 percentage points to 16.2. This decrease may reflect the decline of occupational gender segregation mentioned earlier. Another study based on the Wage Survey Data base highlighted the emergence of a persistent gender pay gap after age 30 and a sharp increase in the pay gap with the level of education. One explanation may be the low pay for professionals in the public sector. Thus in Hungary the higher the labour market status, the larger is the pay gap (Equal Treatment Authority 2011).

The current crisis and the policy response

Hungary was severely hit by the crisis in autumn 2008, when the country lost access to market-based financing. To overcome these difficulties, Hungary implemented an adjustment programme in 2009 which focused on fiscal consolidation and financial sector supervision and was supported by financial assistance from the EU, the IMF and the World Bank, amounting to a credit facility of €20 billion. Against this background, the country regained market access and the economy emerged from recession: after a contraction of 6.7 per cent in 2009, GDP grew by 1.2 per cent in 2010, supported by increasing exports. In the second half of 2010, the new government announced significant tax cuts to be implemented over 2010–2013. To limit the fiscal deterioration, it introduced, in parallel, extraordinary levies on several sectors and abolished the mandatory private pension pillar, thereby nationalizing the private savings to reduce public debt. Although this made it possible to limit the slippage in 2010 to 0.4 per cent of GDP above the deficit target of 3.8 per cent of GDP and resulted in a surplus in 2011, the country's reliability in the eyes of investors deteriorated significantly. Against this background, the government announced a structural reform programme in March 2011 and adopted further consolidating measures.

With respect to the social effects of the economic crisis, its different phases need to be distinguished (Tóth and Medgyesi 2011). In the second half of 2008, the crisis was primarily of a financial nature and affected mainly those with substantial savings. Some managed to avoid realizing the loss but those who for some reason had no choice but to sell their investments, suffered an actual rather than only a virtual drop in their assets. The next crisis phase essentially reached households through two channels. One was the fluctuations and effective devaluation of the Hungarian Forint which initially most affected those with foreign currency denominated (housing or car) loans for whom both interest rates and repayments rose. This significantly affected the living standards and consumption potential of affected households, although these effects were not captured in income distribution statistics. The second channel by which households were affected was the plunge in employment and the rise in unemployment.

In the third phase, the effects brought on by the crisis were intensified by the crisis package announced in spring 2009. The main elements of this package are as follows.

- In the public sector, the gross wage bill was frozen for two years and the 13th month salary was abolished.
- The 13th month pension benefit was eliminated and the minimum pension benefit left unchanged for two years.
- Family allowances and social benefits related to the retirement minimum pension have been unchanged since 2009.
- The general rate of sick pay was reduced from 70 to 60 per cent.
- Housing and heating subsidies were restricted.
- Cuts were made in health expenditure.

At the same time, the Banjai government took measures by budget allocations to ease the adverse impact of the global crisis on unemployment. These included the large-scale public work scheme, the so-called 'Path to work' programme, for social allowance recipients, and the Labour Market Fund which compensated firms applying reduced working time instead of dismissals by four-fifths of one day's wage costs (up to twice the minimum wage) or provided subsidies for training programmes held in the period of time reduction.

In addition, structural reforms aimed at long-run increases in labour market participation for older generations and young mothers were introduced. With respect to older generations' activity rates, increased participation was to be achieved by pension reforms. These included replacing the so-called Swiss indexation by a simple inflation only adjustment if economic growth was below three per cent. The retirement age was also increased from 62 to 65 years. With respect to young mothers, the duration of cash support for child care leave was shortened, ending when the child reached age two rather than three. The minimum duration of employment to be eligible for salary-related child care benefit was lengthened from half a year to one year.

A fourth phase was entered in mid-2010 when the newly elected Conservative government continued the consolidation of the budget by introducing a range of even more severe measures. In addition to freezing ministries' budgets, eliminating early retirement and establishing a ceiling to public sector top salaries, this new government made major reforms to unemployment support, both passive and active. First of all, the job-search allowance was eliminated and the eligibility period for job-search benefit shortened from 270 days to 90 days[4]. Research shows that shortening the benefit period has only slightly increased labour supply but the financial situation of claimants became significantly worse (Bush and Cseres-Gergely 2012). Total social benefits were also capped at below the public work wage.

The public work programme was also reformed to involve a higher number of unemployed people but on more part-time hours or short duration contracts of two to three months, so that the 220,000 people engaged in this programme in 2011 corresponded to only 100,000 full-time equivalents. While more people were involved the budget was halved, although future expansion of the budget is planned. The scheme is said to be aimed at creating strong financial incentives to resume work but, although it provides a higher income than the social allowance, this is still considerably below the minimum wage. In 2011, unskilled workers could earn 73 per cent of the minimum wage for full-time work and this ratio increased to 77 per cent in 2012 (Kierzenkowski 2012). Up until 2011 public work schemes successfully reduced poverty. The most vulnerable groups, the low educated and long-term unemployed persons, usually spent 3–12 months in the programmes where they worked full time and earned the minimum wage. Under the 2011 new rules working conditions deteriorated, especially wages which have become only a little higher than the means-tested social allowance in the case of part-time working.

In addition to consolidation measures, structural reforms were also implemented to underpin fiscal sustainability. They focused on the context of both demographic and economic crisis. The reason for the focus on demography is that Hungary has the third lowest fertility rate across the OECD, at 1.33 children per women. The government strongly believes that the demographic issue is now a matter of survival for the country and it has implemented a series of measures which it expects to promote fertility. These include some of the measures already discussed, such as reductions in the costs of part-time work for returning parents and the right to a part-time job if a child is under three. The early retirement for women with forty years of work also allows for up to eight years of child care to be counted towards the forty years. At the end of 2010, the new government also re-established the three year child care leave with the original forms of compensation (GYED, GYES) and parents taking GYES are now allowed to work after the child is one year old, provided working time is under 30 hours a week, although paid employment at home has no time limitation. In line with the shift in objectives, the development of children's day care facilities returned to the government agenda: the maintenance requirements imposed on local governments have been tightened, the funding rate per child has been increased for nursery schools, regulations on starting and running alternative day care facilities for children under three (family day care, integrated kindergarten) have been simplified and more resources have been allocated for institutional investments. Attempts at expanding the capacity of nursery schools have remained at a modest level, however.

Another measure considered to promote fertility is the introduction of the flat rate tax combined with relatively generous allowances for children. In 2011, alongside the flat rate tax of 16 per cent, the previous family credit system, which only provided tax credits for families with three or more children, was replaced by a wider and more generous tax relief for families with children, which is a deduction from the tax base that can be shared among spouses. The monthly reduction in the tax base is HUF 62,500 per child for one or two children, but goes up to HUF 206,250 per child for three or more children. As a result, persons with one, two or three children and gross monthly incomes up to approximately HUF 109,000, HUF 158,000 and HUF 487,000, respectively, are exempted from personal income tax (Ministry of National Economy 2010). The Financial Council estimated the take-up rate of family credit before the introduction of the new tax system. It came to the conclusion that only 70 and 40 per cent of taxpayers with one or two children could take advantage of the full amount of the benefit, while the vast majority of persons with three or more children would be able to use only part of it due to low incomes (Fiscal Council 2010). Unfortunately, there are no detailed empirical analyses and no demonstrable signs of short-term effects of the new tax system available to assess the accuracy of this estimation.

As we can see, although the authorities took a host of measures, with potentially profound effects, several of the policies contradict each other by either favouring participation or non-participation. While the low labour supply of mothers is a real challenge in Hungary, there has been a reversal of cuts to parental leave which does not seem to be encouraging work among mothers, and the improvements to child care provision are only limited. The reduced retirement age for women with at least 40 years of employment history, regardless of their age, has been popular among eligible women and is presented as an acknowledgement of the 'double burden' of women. However, it not only runs counter to the policy of ending early retirement but may be more designed to allow for 'grandmother babysitters' as alternatives to nurseries (Juhász 2012). The new tax system can also be criticized not only for being regressive, which affects women most, but because the take-up of family credit is lower at low income levels than the maximum available amount of the credit. For prime age women, part-time work arrangements may appear to provide a relatively quick response to Hungary's low employment and fertility rates but there is also a need to consider different alternatives including: more flexible or negotiable work schedules for all full-time workers, more rights for those engaged in care and more encouragement to men contributing to household and child care work. Above all, the policy package currently developed is regarded as promoting family policy and family friendliness, an objective which has replaced gender equality as a government priority, although gender equality was never a core objective.

Gender equality and women's employment will also be negatively affected by other policies, not explicitly aimed at gender issues or even the family. Thus women's employment will be influenced by the further fiscal and structural adjustment policies focusing on the public sector. Here, the main form of adjustment to the crisis so far has been wage cuts rather than job cuts as employment has even increased. The cuts to salary-augmentation and bonus payments resulted in a decrease in gross average wages in the public sector of 8.2 per cent between 2008 and 2010, which was the price of higher job safety (CSO 2012). Public/private wage differentials significantly increased, in favour of the latter. The general problem of low pay in the public sector is most acute for health and education professionals, the majority of whom are women (Hámori and Köllő 2012).

Furthermore, policies to centralize schools and take away most of the responsibilities of local self-government will result in the closing down of hundreds of small elementary schools in the rural regions, forcing the pupils to commute by bus to central schools. All these changes will influence mostly women's lives, as most teachers are women, and it is usually the mother who has to organize children's travel to and from school (Juhász 2012). Women are also disproportionately reliant on welfare benefits which are being cut. Among households with a child younger than eight, only 35 per cent of women were employed and in dual earning households. Single earner households, primarily with a male breadwinner, accounted for a further 47 per cent with most of the women receiving child care benefits. Nearly one-fifth lived, however, in a family where neither she nor her husband/cohabiting partner had a job and received only income from social security or other social income (CSO 2011). Hungarian governments are concerned that these benefits reduce incentives to work and have implemented gradual changes over recent years and these reforms are set to continue. This process will affect more women than men, as the inactivity is higher among them.

Conclusions

Hungarian employment rates remained well below EU average for both men and women but the gender gap in employment rates is also below the EU average due to particularly low employment rates for men. Moreover, women's employment rate in full-time equivalents is relatively high by EU standards due to low part-time rates. Against this background this chapter assessed the labour market impact of the downturn and early recovery from a gender perspective. It was found that in Hungary, one of the Eastern European countries most affected by the crisis, women's employment suffered less damage than men's even though it still remained below that of men's throughout the crisis. The price for that protection was the decline in wages as the main form of adjustment to the public spending cuts in the public sector, where the majority of employees have always been women.

Prospects for employment growth and reduced unemployment are poor even if growth returns. First, labour hoarding increased in the crisis as companies sought to minimize the headcount adjustment but this may reduce new hiring in the future. Second, many of the unemployed may have become long-term job seekers by the time of the economic upswing, which may cause cyclical unemployment to transform into structural unemployment. Thus unemployment rates may remain high in the forthcoming years, especially for men.

Gender and women's issues have never been in the forefront of public debates and on the table of policymakers, which might reflect the rather conservative public mentality regarding gender mainstreaming in Hungary. Recent decades, especially the years following the EU accession, opened up and enriched thinking about the content of the male and female roles. However, the current government, which took office in May 2010, has taken a very traditional approach to gender issues, rolling back past progress. The Fidesz-KDNP-led conservative government considers the family as a basic unit of the economy and as a target unit for social policy instead of individual women and men. This is not a new phenomenon; this was the situation between 1990–4 and 1998–2002, when conservative governments came into power in Hungary. The speciality of the present government is the combination of the fight against the dual economic and demographic crises, in which gender equality policies have been replaced by family policies focusing on demographic growth. Consequently, gender mainstreaming has not been taken into consideration in policy design and policy implementation over the crisis. These policies deal with women only as actual or potential mothers, without addressing fathers. Moreover, several of the policies contradict each other by either favouring participation or non-participation of women. The decrease of public spending on social benefits negatively influences women – as inactivity is higher among them than among men – and increases their care-giving burden. Overall, the majority of the measures can be considered likely to risk putting women's full integration into the labour market into reverse.

Notes

1   Hungarian law distinguishes employees into those covered by the Labour Code and those – civil servants and public employees – who are subject to the Acts on Civil Servants and Public Employees. Wages are set in both the public and private sectors, according to wage grids determined by aforementioned laws and updated by the government. The grids define wage brackets for civil servants and minimum salaries for employees, taking into account educational attainment, skill requirements and tenure in employment. Employers are allowed to pay more than the base wage depending on their financial capacity and the worker's merits.

2   Under the 'Path to Work' programme (introduced April 2009 but new scheme in 2011) persons in active age and disadvantaged in the labour market could obtain a benefit

entitlement instead of the means-tested social allowance. Persons capable of performing work and being able to participate in public work schemes (mainly communal activities) were eligible for standby allowance, but only in that case if working possibility was not available. For young people under 35 years who had not completed primary school the key activation was attending training. Persons incapable of working remained eligible for means-tested social allowance. Due to this initiative, recipients of regular social allowance declined from an average of 180,000 in 2008 to 33,000 in 2009 and the participants involved in public work increased from 31,000 in 2008 to 61,000 in 2009 and 87,000 in 2010 (CSO 2012). The share of public work schemes participants among public sector employees increased from 4.3 per cent in 2008 to 11.3 per cent in 2010. Unfortunately, gender disaggregated data are not available.

3   The share of part-time workers among all participants of public work schemes was 35 per cent in 2007 and 66 per cent in 2011 (CSO 2012).

4   Previously there were two types of unemployment support schemes: the insurance-based unemployment benefit (job-search benefit) and the unemployment allowance (job-search allowance) which was paid (1) for unemployed who either failed to satisfy criteria for membership in unemployment insurance scheme or (2) who exhausted their insurance-based benefits. The third type of unemployment allowance is for those unemployed within five years of old age pension age provided they have received unemployment benefit for at least 140 days and exhausted their benefit entitlements. From September 2011 the higher benefit was reduced and the maximum payment period shortened from 270 to 90 days. Unemployment allowance was phased out, except for the unemployed within five years of old age pension age.

References

Bálint, M. and Cseres-Gergely, Zs. and Scharle, Á. (2011) 'The Hungarian Labour Market in 2009–2010', in K. Fazekas and Gy. Molnár (eds) *The Hungarian Labour Market 2011*, Budapest: Institute of Economics, HAS; National Employment Foundation, 17–36. Available at: http://econ.core.hu/file/download/HLM2011/TheHungarianLabour Market_2011_Labour_Market2009-2010.pdf (accessed 10.01.2012).

Bush, I. and Cseres-Gergely, Zs. (2012) 'Institutional Environment of the Labour Market between September 2010 and September 2011', in K. Fazekas and G. Kézdi (eds) *The Hungarian Labour Market 2012*, Budapest: Institute of Economics, HAS, National Employment Foundation, 179–221. Available at: http://econ.core.hu/file/download/HLM2012/TheHungarianLabourMarket_2012_Environment.pdf (accessed 10.07.2012).

Cazes, S. and Nesporova, A. (2007) *Flexicurity – A Relevant Approach in Central and Eastern Europe*, Geneva: International Labour Office.

Central Statistical Office (CSO) (2000) '*1986–87 and 1999–2000 Survey of Lifestyle-time-utilization of Population*', Budapest: CSO.

—— (2011) *Reconciliation Between Work and Family Life 2010*, Budapest: CSO, March. Available at: http://www.ksh.hu/docs/eng/xftp/idoszaki/emunkavegzescsalad.pdf (accessed 05.02.2012).

—— (2012) 'Magyarország, 2011', Budapest: CSO. Available at: http://www.ksh.hu/docs/hun/wftp/idoszaki/mo/hungary2011.pdf (accessed 08.08.2012).

Equal Treatment Authority (2011) *Gender Wage Gap and Segregation in Contemporary Hungary*, The research was co-financed by the ESF. Budapest: Equal Treatment Authority, April. Available at: http://www.egyenlobanasmod.hu/tamop/data/TAMOP_EBH_1_english.pdf (accessed 03.08.2012).

Fazekas, K. and Scharle, Á. (2012) '*Nyugdíj, segély, közmunka – A foglalkoztatáspolitika két évtizede 1990–2010*', Budapest: Budapest Institute for Policy Analysis LTD and Institute of Economics, HAS. Available at: http://econ.core.hu/file/download/20evfoglpol/kotet.pdf (accessed at 29.11.2012).

Fiscal Council, Republic of Hungary (2010) 'Assessment of the Fiscal Council of the Republic of Hungary of the Fiscal Impacts of Bill No. T/1376 on the Amendment of Tax and Social Contribution Legislation, the Accounting Act and the Act on the Chamber of auditors as well as Tax and Customs Related Acts for Harmonization with European Union Laws', 21 October, Budapest: Fiscal Council of Hungary.

Fodor, E. (2005) 'Women at Work. The Status of Women in the Labour Markets of the Czech Republic, Hungary and Poland', United Nations Research Institute for Social Development, Occasional Paper, No. 3. Available at: http://www.unrisd.org/80256B3C0 05C2802/(ViewPDF)?OpenAgent&parentunid=655D60DC55B78527C125701100386 6BA&parentdb=80256B3C005BCCF9&parentdoctype=paper&netitpath=80256B3C0 05BCCF9/(httpAuxPages)/655D60DC55B78527C1257011003866BA/$file/OPGP3.pdf (accessed 20.04.2011).

Frey, M. (1997a) 'Employment Policies and Programmes in Hungary', in M. Godfrey and P. Richards (eds) *Employment Policies and Programmes in Central and Eastern Europe*, Geneva: International Labour Organization, 77–114.

Frey, M. (1997b) 'Women in the Labour Market', in K. Lévai and I. G. Tóth (eds) *The Changing Role of Women. Report on the Situation of Women in Hungary 1997*, Budapest: Social Research Informatics Centre, Ministry of Social and Family Affairs and UNDP, 15–36.

Frey, M. and Lukács, E. (2003) 'The Gender Dimensions of Social Security Reform in Hungary', in E. Fultz (ed.) *The Gender Dimensions of Social Security Reform in Central and Eastern Europe: Case Studies of the Czech Republic, Hungary and Poland*, Budapest: International Labour Office, Subregional Office for Central and Eastern Europe, 43–108. Available at: http://www.ilo.org/public/libdoc/ilo/2003/103B09_160_engl.pdf (accessed 20.06.2012).

Hámory, Sz. and Köllő, J. (2012) 'Public Sector Labour Market from Crisis to Crisis', in Vaughan-Whitehead (ed.) *Public Sector Adjustments in Europe: Scope, Effects and Policy Issues*, Geneva: International Labour Office.

Juhász, B. (2012) 'Orbán's Politics – A Gender Perspective', a working paper prepared for the Friedrich Ebert Stiftung Büro, Budapest. Available at: http://www.fesbp.hu/common/pdf/Nachrichten_aus_Ungarn_1_2012.pdf (accessed 02.10.2012).

Kertesi, G. and Köllő, J. (1995) 'Wages and Unemployment in Hungary Between 1986 and 1994', Manuscript. ILO/Japanese project on Employment policy of the transition period in Hungary, Budapest: Ministry of Labour.

Kierzenkowski, R. (2012) 'Towards a More Inclusive Labour Market in Hungary', OECD Economics Department Working Papers No. 960. Online. Available at: http://www.oecd-ilibrary.org/economics/towards-a-more-inclusive-labour-market-in-hungary_5k98rwqw3v8q-en (accessed 01.11.2012).

Köllő, J. (2011) 'Employment, Unemployment and Wages in the First Year of the Crisis', in K. Fazekas and Gy. Molnár (eds) *The Hungarian Labour Market 2011*, Budapest: Institute of Economics, HAS and National Employment Foundation, 43–63. Available at: http://econ.core.hu/kiadvany/mt.html (accessed 16.06.2012).

Ministry of National Economy (2010) 'Hungary's Flat-rate Personal Income Tax', Budapest: Ministry of National Economy. Available at: http://www.kormany.hu/download/3/11/10000/Hungary%20s%20flat%20rate%20personal%20income%20tax.pdf (accessed 04.02.2012).

Nagy, B. (2012) 'Women in Management: The Hungarian Case', in C. Fagan, M. González Menéndez and S. Gómez Ansón (eds) *Women on Corporate Boards and in Top Management: European Trends and Policy*, Palgrave Book Series: Work and Welfare in Europe, London: Palgrave, 221–244.

Tóth, I. Gy. and Medgyesi, M. (2011) 'Income Distribution and Living Difficulties in the Midst of Consolidation Programmes and Crises in Hungary', in K. Fazekas and Gy. Molnár (eds) *The Hungarian Labour Market 2011*, Budapest: Institute of Economics, HAS and National Employment Foundation, 171–186. Available at: http://econ.core. hu/kiadvany/mt.html (accessed 23.01.2012).

9

STRUCTURAL CRISIS AND ADJUSTMENT IN GREECE

Social regression and the challenge to gender equality

Maria Karamessini

Introduction

The Greek economy has been in continuous recession since 2008. GDP decreased by 20.4 per cent between 2007 and 2012 and employment fell by 18.5 per cent between December 2008 and December 2012. Greece was one of the EU Member States least hit by the global financial crisis in 2008–9, but is currently undergoing the most severe structural crisis of her recent history, triggered by a sovereign debt crisis that erupted at the end of 2009. Since the beginning of 2010, a series of austerity packages have been implemented while in May 2010 the country was granted financial aid by the other Eurozone countries and the IMF, conditional on the strict implementation of an Economic Adjustment Programme (EAP) for the years 2010–14, accompanied by a memorandum of understanding between the Greek government and its creditors (European Commission 2010). EAP is built around two main objectives: fiscal consolidation and internal devaluation, linked to two quantified targets (a) bringing government deficit below 3 per cent in accordance with the European Growth and Stability Pact requirement and (b) curbing nominal labour costs in the business sector by 15 per cent in order to recoup losses in price competitiveness during 2001–9.

The fiscal consolidation programme was of the 'shock therapy' type, i.e. front-loaded and entailing a large-scale adjustment in a short time span. It has so far brought sharp cuts in public spending; considerable erosion of the welfare state; great reductions in public sector wages and employment; successive cuts in pensions; and huge rises in taxes. It has caused the depression of economic activity, raised unemployment to historically unprecedented levels (26 per cent in December 2012), fuelled a vicious circle of austerity-recession-more-austerity and created a debt trap. The cost of debt servicing as a proportion of GDP rose sharply – interest payable amounted to 7.6 per cent of GDP in 2011 – and led to a restructuring of the sovereign debt held by private investors in March 2012 and a second financing package by Eurozone countries and the IMF, accompanied by a second Economic Adjustment Programme (European Commission 2012a). The two parliamentary elections in May and June 2012 slowed the implementation of the EAP, but in early November 2012 the parliament passed a very large number of fiscal and structural measures and reforms, some already agreed but falling due, and also some new measures. These were all included in the Omnibus Law, the Medium Term Fiscal Strategy 2013–16 and the 2013 budget. At the same time, the fiscal adjustment period was prolonged until 2016.

Between 2009 and 2012, the deficit of the primary balance of general government was reduced by 9 percentage points of GDP. However, the underlying fiscal effort is significantly larger if one takes into account that GDP contracted by 16.5 per cent over the same period (European Commission 2012b). In spite of this tremendous effort and the recent substantial restructuring of the share of sovereign debt held by private investors, the current level of debt is still unsustainable.

As in other European countries, the current crisis in Greece has interrupted women's progress towards equality with men through better integration in paid work and led to a narrowing of gender gaps in employment, unemployment and job quality since men's employment and working conditions deteriorated more than women's. However, as the crisis evolves, its labour market implications are equally impairing women. At the same time, radical institutional reforms in the employment model and welfare state during the crisis are expected to have major implications for the gender regime.

The literature on gender and economic crisis distinguishes between first-round effects of recession on employment and second-round effects resulting from participation strategies used by households to cope with declining income; both effects vary by gender (Sabarwal *et al.* 2010). As regards first-round effects, several authors have pointed to the fact that the higher concentration of women relative to men in industries and occupations with low cyclical variation protects them more than men from the negative impact of the crisis on employment, while their overrepresentation among flexible workers makes them more vulnerable than men to this impact (Milkman 1976; Bettio 1988; Humphries 1988; Rubery 1988). With respect to labour supply strategies, the added and discouraged worker effects (Mincer 1962, 1966) operate simultaneously during the crisis, leading respectively to an increase or a decrease of female activity rates. Policy responses to the crisis and changes in the character of policies matter since their labour market effects differ by gender. Economic policies can be counter-cyclical or aim at fiscal consolidation while employment and social policies may be used to maintain employment or facilitate withdrawal from the labour force (Smith and Villa 2010).

The aim of the chapter is to explore the labour market effects of the crisis from a gender perspective as well as changes in the gendered division of paid work in Greece by taking into account the decisive change in the character of economic, employment and social policies in 2010. Two phases are distinguished: the initial one, during which crisis-management policies were counter-cyclical, the public sector was sheltered by changes in the rest of the economy and existing labour market institutions were not yet challenged; the subsequent phase, during which crisis-management policies became pro-cyclical, the public sector and welfare state subject to thorough restructuring and downsizing and industrial relations undermined. Following the societal approach (Rubery 1988 and this volume) which emphasizes the role of the institutional context in explaining the gendered effects of the crisis in concrete country cases, the starting point for our analysis is the specificities of the gender regime in Greece prior to the crisis and its links with the particular features of the employment system and the welfare state.

The structure of the chapter is the following. We first briefly outline women's labour market position, gender gaps and trends in Greece before the crisis, with reference to the organization of the family and the welfare state, and perceptions about gender roles and gender equality. We then turn to the labour market impact of the crisis and describe gender differences and within-gender differences and go on to discuss the immediate and long-term effects of policies and reforms under the fiscal and structural adjustment programme. Finally we take stock of changes in the gendered division of paid work at both the macro and societal level and the micro and household level before pulling all our conclusions together in the last section.

Women's labour market position and gender regime before the crisis

Women's massive involvement in paid work is a recent phenomenon in Greece, although their contribution to production through unpaid work in family farms and businesses and informal work for wages in towns and cities was very important throughout the first eighty years of the twentieth century (Karamessini 2012a). The take-off occurred in the early 1980s. In 1981 the employment rate of the female population aged 15–64 years was 27.4 per cent while 30 per cent of all employed women were unpaid family workers. In 2008, the female employment rate had reached 48.7 per cent while the rate of unpaid family workers had fallen to 9.7 per cent. Progress was constant until the eruption of the current crisis, with the exception of a downward swing during the recession of the early 1990s.

Increasing female involvement in paid work went hand in hand with the erosion of the male-breadwinner family model and the expansion of wage employment, in an economy where self-employment and family businesses were extensive even outside agriculture. These developments were a result of converging processes, i.e. changes in the aspirations of women owing to the spectacular rise in their educational attainment and to the ideological influence of the feminist movement; changes in the consumption patterns and standards and in parental investments in children's education, making a second income in the family necessary for the middle classes and beyond; the rapid tertiarization of the economy fuelled by the expansion of both private services, state activity and the welfare state; the growth of female-dominated manufacturing industries (e.g. apparel);

the introduction in the 1975 Constitution of the principle of equal pay for work of equal value; the adoption of equal treatment and anti-discrimination legislation for pay, employment and social security, and the establishment of leaves for workers with family responsibilities. The aforementioned processes pushed and pulled women into the labour market, offering them access to both low-paid and/or atypical jobs in tourism, apparel, retail or personal services and well-paid stable white-collar jobs in the public sector and banking. In so doing, they also led to the feminization of professional and technical alongside clerical, sales and service occupations.

It should be noted that the role of the family remained critical for life stage transitions in Greece throughout the 1990s and 2000s, especially for the transition of young people from education to work (Karamessini 2010). The rapidly increasing enrolment rates in higher education and post-graduate studies and the high unemployment rates of young people until the end of their twenties, made a second income necessary in thousands of Greek families willing to financially support their offspring in their preparation for access to higher education, during their studies and in their effort to find suitable jobs once the studies were over. This pushed ever growing numbers of women to join paid work and remain employed for longer periods than before.

Growing female activity and employment rates greatly influenced labour market flows. A recent study of these flows has found that the contribution of inflows from unemployment to the increase of employment over the period 1988–2009 was somewhat smaller than the contribution of inflows from inactivity (Kanellopoulos 2011). Women have constituted the main bulk of flows from inactivity to employment since the early 1980s. Another interesting finding of the same study was that transition from inactivity to employment was counter-cyclical over the period 1988–2009. That is, during recession inactive persons were more likely to enter employment.

In spite of the rapid growth of women's employment in the 1980s, 1990s and 2000s, demand for female labour remained short of labour supply leading to the expansion of female unemployment. This hit more medium- and low-educated women of all ages and young women of all education levels. Moreover, notwithstanding successive reforms since the early 1990s, the pension system maintained a lower legal age of retirement for women insured before 1.1.1993 and early retirement schemes for mothers, thus keeping the activity and employment rates of women aged 45–54 years low and those of women aged 55–64 very low. Finally, coverage of children up to school age by public childcare services grew very slowly in the 1980s and 1990s, constantly remaining in short supply relative to social needs, while the opening hours of nurseries were limited and incompatible with work schedules. Inadequacy of social care impaired the involvement of women from low income families in paid work (Karamessini 2010). The massive inflow of women migrants from the early 1990s onwards removed child and elderly care constraints from middle-class families and allowed the acceleration of the increase in the activity rate of mothers, a permanent trend since the early 1980s (Lyberaki 2011a).

Being uneven and constrained by a number of institutional factors, women's progress in paid work since the early 1980s had created in the 1990s and 2000s significant inequalities among women with respect to adherence to the male-breadwinner model for longer or shorter periods in the lifetime and access to good jobs. The male-breadwinner model was prevalent in couple families with children where the woman was low or medium educated while the dual full-time-earner model was prevalent in couple families with children where the woman was high educated. As for inequalities based on national origin, although the employment rates of female migrants were the same as those of Greek nationals, their employment and working conditions differed substantially since the former were concentrated in low-skill and low-paid and – to a great extent – informal jobs and suffered from extensive de-skilling.

Although progress in the involvement of women in paid work had been important over the three decades preceding the crisis, at the advent of the crisis the Greek female activity and employment rates were still among the lowest in EU27, especially among low- and medium-educated and older women, while the female unemployment rate was among the highest in EU27. Greece had also the largest unemployment gender gap and the second largest employment gender gap in the EU-27. In 2008, female activity and employment rates were increasing but were still low (55.1 per cent and 48.7 per cent respectively) while the female unemployment rate was decreasing but still high (11.4 per cent). In the same year, the incidence of fixed-term contracts was higher among female than male employees (13.7 per cent against 9.9 per cent), although these contracts were mainly concentrated among young people and migrants. Women were also overrepresented among part-timers and unpaid workers in family businesses and farms. It should also be noted that Greece had the highest share of unpaid family workers in total female employment in EU-27 and was among the EU countries with the lowest female part-time employment rates (9.9 per cent in 2008). Finally, the incidence of uninsured work was the same among native men and women but was much higher for female than male migrants (Kanellopoulos *et al.* 2009).

Women were overrepresented among the flexible workforce before the crisis. But, on the other hand, native women had made important inroads into permanent employment, the protected segments of the labour market and the most prestigious occupations. In 2008, 81.5 per cent of all women employees were permanent full-time workers and 33.1 per cent were permanent employees in the public sector. Moreover, 49.2 per cent of all professionals and 50.2 per cent of all technicians and associate professionals were women – pointing to their overrepresentation in these occupations – but only 28 per cent of managers were women.

The gender pay gap was relatively stable in the pre-crisis period. The female-to-male earnings gap ranged from 14.7 percentage points to 16.6 percentage points on average between 2004 and 2007 and was higher at the top and lowest end of the earnings distribution than in the middle of it (Papapetrou 2010). Male-female differentials in pensions were much higher. In 2004, the average female work-related old-age pension[1] was 59 per cent of the average male pension although the within-fund relative female pensions were much higher, ranging from 70.5 per cent in the case of peasants and the self-employed to 73.2 per cent in the case of private and public sector employees (Lyberaki and Tinios 2010). It follows that a substantial part of the gap is due to women's disproportionate concentration in the funds with the lowest pensions.

Labour market effects of the crisis: gender and within-gender differences

Since the 1970s and until the current crisis, Greece had experienced three recessions in 1974, 1980–3 and 1990–3. In all of them, the tertiary sector had played a protective, compensating and enhancing role for women's employment (Karamessini 2012c). This is not the case in the current crisis and this is due to its structural nature, long duration and the severity of the austerity policy implemented as a response to it.

The effects of the current crisis on both male and female employment are devastating. They appeared from its very beginning in the case of men and one year later in the case of women. Over four years, male employment fell by 19.1 per cent and female by 14.3 per cent, while the number of unemployed men increased by 3.3 times and that of unemployed women by 1.6 (Table 9.1). As a result, the male unemployment rate climbed from 4.7 per cent to 21 per cent and the female rate from 11.1 to 27.5 per cent between the second quarter of 2008 and the second quarter of 2012. Youth unemployment reached vertiginous heights, impelling young people to emigrate. In the second quarter of 2012, the unemployment rate

TABLE 9.1 Labour force, employment and unemployment by sex in Greece 2008–2012

	Year-to-year and across the period changes (%)		
Years – 2nd quarter	Labour force	Employment	Unemployment
	Men		
2008–09	−0.4	−2.1	35.2
2009–10	0.1	−3.1	47.7
2010–11	−1.3	−6.0	44.2
2011–12	−1.1	−9.2	50.3
2008–2012	−2.7	−19.1	333.3
	Women		
2008–09	2.2	0.4	16.9
2009–10	2.1	−1.1	24.6
2010–11	−0.7	−6.2	29.9
2011–12	1.2	−8.0	38.3
2008–2012	5.0	−14.3	161.6

Source: ELSTAT, Labour Force Survey.

TABLE 9.2 Male and female unemployment rates in Greece 2008–2012

per cent rates (%) and changes across the period in p.p.*			
	2008q2	2012q2	2008q2–2012q2
	%	%	p.p.
Men	4.7	21	16.3
15–19	18.8	55.2	36.4
20–24	14.5	45.4	30.9
25–29	9.6	35.0	25.4
30–44	3.5	19.3	15.8
45–64	2.5	14.8	12.3
Women	11.1	27.5	16.4
15–19	36.1	75.3	39.2
20–24	26.4	60	33.6
25–29	17	38.9	21.9
30–44	10.3	26.1	15.8
45–64	5.6	17.9	12.3

*p.p. = percentage point difference of rates between the start and end years.
Source: ELSTAT, Labour Force Survey.

was 60 per cent among young women aged 20–24 and 45.4 per cent among their male counterparts (Table 9.2).

The sources of the rise in unemployment and their relative importance vary by gender. Given that the male labour force has been constantly contracting during the crisis, the upsurge in male unemployment is mainly accounted for by huge job losses. An upward push was also exerted by the fall in the male transition rate from unemployment to inactivity until mid-2010. Conversely, the rise in female unemployment has been equally driven by the very large inflows of women in the labour force. The activity rate of the female population aged 15 to 64 years climbed from 55.1 per cent in the 2008q2 to 57.6 per cent in 2010q2 and 58.2 per cent in 2012q2, pointing to the dominance of the added-worker over the discouraged-worker effect. The rise in the activity rate of migrant women, defined here as non-EU nationals, was more spectacular than that of Greek women (Figure 9.1).

As for employment rate trends by sex, the male rate started falling in the last quarter of 2008 among both Greeks and migrants, compared to the same quarter of the previous year, while Greek women's employment rate started declining from the last quarter of 2009. The respective rate of migrant women increased during the first two years of the crisis and then collapsed: it plunged from 50.9 per cent in the third quarter of 2010 to 38.6 per cent in the second quarter of 2012 (Figure 9.2). The initial increase and subsequent reversal of the trend were driven by the rise and

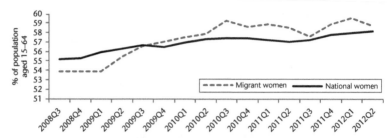

FIGURE 9.1 Female activity rates by nationality in Greece 2008–2012
Source: Eurostat, ELFS data online (extracted on 21.11.2012).

fall in demand for domestic services by households where about 80 per cent of migrant women are employed. The fall in demand resulted from the huge income losses suffered by middle-class households. These were the outcome of both wage and pension cuts and tax increases that took place in 2010 and 2011 and a significant reduction in the income of the self-employed either because their activity and profits shrank or their business closed down.

It is also noteworthy that, to date, the negative effects of the crisis on male employment are higher, the lower their educational attainment. Between the second quarter of 2008 and the second quarter of 2012, the employment rate of low-educated men dropped by 17.4 percentage points while those of medium- and high-educated men fell by 14.4 and 11.5 respectively. Exactly the opposite occurred in the case of women. The employment rate of high-educated women declined by 12 percentage points, while those of medium- and low-educated women fell by 9.6 and 5.2 respectively. It could be thus argued that the employment crisis is mostly one of low-educated men and high-educated women.

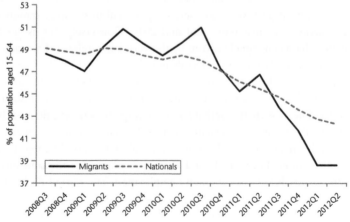

FIGURE 9.2 Employment rates of national and migrant women in Greece 2008–2012
Source: Eurostat, ELFS data online (extracted on 21.11.2012).

The greater overall contraction of male employment up to now is due to the earlier and more severe impact of the crisis on male-dominated sectors. These were the sectors through which the global crisis was transmitted to the Greek economy and then to employment. The employment crisis started from construction and manufacturing in the third quarter of 2008; it passed to business services (professional, scientific, technical, administrative and support activities) in the third quarter of 2009, arrived at retail and transport in the first and second quarters of 2010 respectively and ended up in the public sector, education and domestic services to households in the last quarter of 2010. Between the second quarter of 2008 and the second quarter of 2012, employment in male-dominated sectors decreased by 34.3 per cent against 12.2 per cent and 5.3 per cent in mixed-sex and female-dominated sectors respectively (Table 9.3). The male-dominated sectors account for 53.8 per cent of the overall contraction in employment since the beginning of the crisis; while mixed-sex and female-dominated sectors for 42 per cent and 4.2 per cent respectively. Besides, men in male-dominated sectors were hit from net job losses more than their share in employment. This occurred for women in mixed-sex and female-dominated sectors. Until mid-2012, only the financial and insurance sector was spared by the employment crisis!

Women's employment started falling from the last quarter of 2009 onwards. The fall became dramatic after mid-2010 and reversed women's continuous progress in paid work over recent decades. The female employment rate for those aged 15 to 64 years fell from 49.3 per cent in the third quarter of 2009 (the highest rate ever recorded) to 42.1 per cent in the second quarter 2012. As previously mentioned, this development was determined by the transmission of the crisis from construction and manufacturing to private services and, after the sovereign debt crisis had burst out, to the public sector where a substantial proportion of women is employed in female-dominated activities (education, health, social care). Since the structural adjustment programme adopted as a response to the sovereign debt crisis is ongoing, it is still premature to anticipate its full impact on employment by gender. It is though certain that it is responsible for the dramatic contraction of women's employment since mid-2010, at a speed rivalling that of men.

Temporary workers are considered in the literature as a 'flexible buffer' at the firm-level, ensuring numerical flexibility during the business cycle while part-time work can also serve to adjust a firm's payroll to the fall in activity by allowing a reduction in working-time. Hereafter we use empirical evidence to test the hypothesis, stated in the introduction, that women's overrepresentation among flexible workers makes them more vulnerable than men to the negative impact of the crisis on employment.

To start with, male temporary workers have proved more vulnerable than their female counterparts to the downward adjustment of employment. Indeed, the number of male temporary employees declined by 34.6 per cent between the second quarter of 2008 and the second quarter of 2012 whereas the number of female temporary employees declined by 26.8 per cent over the same period. Additionally, although women represented 49.6 per cent of temporary wage

TABLE 9.3 Sector segregation by sex and impact of recession on employment in Greece 2008–2012

Sectors of economic activity	Change in employment 2008q2– 2012q2 (%)	Sector contribution to change in employment	Female share 2008q2	Female share 2012q2
All sectors	17.2	100.0	39.1	40.5
Construction	46.5	23.5	2.1	5.2
Mining and quarrying	42.8	1.0	12.3	12.4
Transportation and storage	15.2	4.1	15.5	15.6
Water supply; sewerage, waste management	32.5	1.2	18.1	18.0
Activities of extraterritorial organisations	26.5	0.1	21.3	44.8
Electricity, gas, steam and air conditioning	28.0	1.3	24.7	31.9
Manufacturing	33.3	22.7	26.4	24.8
Male dominated sectors★	34.3	53.8	16.2	17.6
Information and communication	2.2	0.2	34.5	42.0
Public administration, defence, social security	15.2	7.4	36.9	32.6
Arts, entertainment and recreation	29.1	2.2	37.7	36.4
Agriculture, forestry and fishing	4.8	3.1	41.1	40.2
Real estate activities	29.0	0.3	41.1	48.9
Wholesale and retail trade; repair of motor	18.4	19.4	42.7	42.2
Professional, scientific and technical activities	0.5	0.1	45.0	43.5
Accommodation and food service activities	15.5	6.4	45.9	44.2
Administrative and support service activities	7.1	0.7	48.8	47.8
Financial and insurance activities	1.2	0.2	51.4	50.0
Other service activities	19.2	2.3	57.4	59.7
Mixed sex sectors★★	12.2	42.0	42.9	41.9
Education	5.4	2.2	63.5	64.0
Human health and social work activities	0.5	0.1	66.1	63.5
Activities of households as employers	20.4	1.9	96.1	92.6
Female dominated sectors★★★	5.3	4.2	68.2	66.6

★Men>70%; ★★70%≤men>40% and 60%≤women>30%; ★★★Women>60% .
Source: Data elaboration from Labour Force Survey (ELSTAT).

earners just before the crisis, their share of the overall reduction of temporary workers has been 43.3 per cent. It follows that, up to now, women's role as a flexible buffer of disposable workers has been less important than men's in the current crisis in Greece.

As for part-time work, the number of male and female part-timers increased by 37.5 per cent and 0.2 per cent respectively between the second quarter of 2008 and the second quarter of 2012. There are different hypotheses about this large discrepancy. In the case of men, the increase in part-time contracts is to a large extent due to the conversion of full-time contracts, in firms willing to reduce labour costs but also to prevent dismissals. In the case of women, the slight increase may imply that new hires – probably also fixed-term – have slightly outnumbered dismissals in industries making frequent use of part-time work, such as retail. Testing the above hypotheses requires empirical research. It is though evident that the higher pace of involvement of men in part-time work during the crisis leads to a 'feminization' of their employment conditions and a 'masculinization' of part-time work.

Last but not least, the number of women unpaid family workers declined by 31 per cent compared to 29.3 per cent for their male counterparts between the second quarter of 2008 and the second quarter of 2012. Women's contribution to the overall reduction was 66 per cent, which is roughly the same as their share of such workers before the crisis (64.8 per cent). Although, in times of growth, unpaid family workers provide to small family firms labour flexibility and cost savings, allowing them to face competition, the great reduction of such workers in times of recession indicates that this form of flexibility is unable to keep small family firms alive if these face a falling demand for their product for a long time.

Austerity and structural adjustment: gender dimensions and effects

The crisis management by the Greek government was strongly counter-cyclical in 2009. The adverse impact of the crisis on GDP and employment was attenuated but the public deficit rose steeply along with sovereign debt. The sovereign debt crisis that followed led to a series of austerity packages whose measures proliferated after the Economic Adjustment Programme 2010–14 was adopted in May 2010, in exchange for the financial aid provided by Eurozone countries and the IMF (European Commission 2010). The change in the nature of economic policy marks a turning point in the labour market effects of the crisis. Austerity did not only produce a deep and prolonged recession and a steep rise in unemployment but also a critical fall in women's employment.

The EAP has two main objectives: a) fiscal consolidation, to be achieved through sharp cuts in public spending, rises in taxes and wide-ranging privatizations; (b) promotion of an export-led growth pattern by enhancing price-competitiveness through drastic reduction in labour costs in the business sector of the economy. Economic transformation through the reduction in labour costs is called 'internal devaluation', as opposed to external (national currency) devaluation which is impossible with Greece in the Eurozone.

The policies and measures so far implemented to achieve these two objectives have imposed significant cuts in public sector pay and the level of private and public pensions and also brought radical changes in the employment model, wage determination system and welfare state, the effects of which are different for men and women, as analysed below.

Cuts in public sector wages and pensions

Cuts in the public sector wage bill and in public and private pensions are an important component of the fiscal consolidation programme. Between May 2010 and May 2011, nominal pay in the civil service decreased by 15 per cent and those in public utilities, agencies and undertakings by 25 per cent. In November 2011, a comprehensive reform of the public sector salary grid further reduced overall public sector pay by almost 20 per cent. The wage package adopted in November 2012 completes this process through imposing this new grid on the employees of all state-owned public law entreprises and modifying the special wage regimes of some public sector workers, notably the higher paid ones. Cuts in salaries were applied on the permanent employees of the public sector out of which 45.2 per cent were female in mid-2010. With respect to public and private retirement pensions – main, supplementary and lump-sum – these have also incurred a substantial cumulative reduction in ten successive rounds. Women represented 42.8 per cent of all pensioners at the onset of the crisis.

There is no study on the gender impact of cuts in public sector salaries and bonuses and in nominal pensions. However, the rate of reduction has in all cases varied with the level of pay and pension, with the lowest rates being applied to the bottom end of the pay and pension scales and the highest rates being applied to the top end of the same scales. Given the gender pay and pension gaps (discussed above) and the higher male than female share of public sector employees and pensioners, we can assume that men have been more negatively affected than women by the aforementioned cuts.

Employment model and wage determination system

The main changes in the employment model and wage determination system consist of a drastic reduction in public sector employment and self-employment; limiting the protection of permanent employees against dismissals; undermining collective bargaining and union power at the national level; and making flexible forms of work less costly for employers (Karamessini 2012b).

The drastic reduction of public sector employment is an important component of the spending-reducing strategy of the fiscal consolidation programme. In 2010 the contracts of the temporary personnel were not renewed and a hiring freeze was imposed for the permanent personnel. Next the government committed itself to reduce public sector employment by at least 150,000 by the end of 2015. This would be achieved by applying the rule of one hiring for ten exits in 2011 and one hiring for five exits from 2012 onwards; by substantially reducing contractual employment and by transferring redundant permanent staff to a labour reserve scheme for one year prior to their dismissal.[2]

Many of the above measures are ongoing, but the provisional outcome is a very significant reduction of public sector employment (-16.1 per cent) between the second quarter of 2010, when the EAP was adopted, and the second quarter of 2012, for which the latest data are available. It should be taken into account that the net reduction in public sector jobs is not only accounted for by the sharp reduction in contractual employment and natural exits to retirement but also by the great increase in the number of voluntary retirements ahead of or after the pension reform, the cuts in lump-sum pensions and the establishment of the labour reserve scheme in order to avoid loss of rights.

Since the adoption of the EAP, women's employment in the public sector has decreased more than men's (-14.8 per cent against -12 per cent) and this is due to the greater reduction of female than male permanent employees (Table 9.4). A possible explanation is the higher female than male rate of voluntary retirement among this category of employees. As regards temporary employees, the reduction in their numbers was slightly higher for men than for women (−41.5 per cent against -39 per cent). It should be mentioned though that if we look at the contraction of public sector employment since the beginning of the crisis, this has been more important for men than for women because, in the first phase of the crisis and until the adoption of the EAP, permanent female employment in the public sector kept increasing, probably due to hires in female-dominated sectors, while permanent male employment was declining, probably due to non-replacement of exits to retirement.

An important structural measure of the EAP is the removal of restrictions to competition in regulated professions and services. Although this is promoted in the name of freedom of market entry and lowering fees, prices and remuneration, the real expected outcome is a reduction in the number of self-employed and micro-businesses, and the entry of larger firms leading to capital concentration in the respective activities. If the removal of restrictions to competition is combined with the other problems that all small- and medium-sized enterprises (SMEs) are facing in Greece because of the great fall in demand and the credit crunch, the

TABLE 9.4 Change in public sector employment in Greece 2008–2012

	Final-to-initial year change (%)		
	2008q2–2010q2	*2010q2–2012q2*	*2008q2–2012q2*
Both sexes (total)	-3.2	-13.3	-16.1
Permanent	-3.7	-10.4	-13.7
Temporary	1.2	-40.1	-39.3
Men (total)	-6.2	-12.0	-17.5
Permanent	-7.3	-9.5	-16.1
Temporary	8.9	-41.5	-36.2
Women (total)	0.5	-14.8	-14.3
Permanent	1.1	-11.4	-10.5
Temporary	-3.7	-39.0	-41.3

Source: Data elaboration from the Labour Force Survey (ELSTAT).

prospects of the self-employed and micro-businesses in the regulated professions or outside are gloomy. Up until now the number of male employers has decreased by 31.2 per cent and that of female employers by 14.4 per cent, pointing to the closure of thousands of small and medium firms since the beginning of the crisis (Table 9.5). Own-account workers (self-employed without employees) have better resisted the crisis, but just staying in activity by keeping books and accounts does not mean they are not surviving on very low income. Moreover, a large proportion of own-account workers are dependent workers working for one employer. Women have suffered proportionally more than men from the reduction of own-account workers.

As regards the employment regime, the following measures have been adopted after successive reforms: a reduction in the notice period for individual dismissals to a maximum of four months and a capping of the level of severance pay at 12 months of pay for those in employment and six months for new hires; an increase in the minimum threshold for collective dismissals; extension of probation period for new hires from three months to one year; extension of the cumulative maximum duration of fixed-term contracts to three years and easing of conditions for derogations; extension of maximum duration of spells of employment for temporary agency workers from 18 to 36 months; extension of maximum duration of rotating work at a given firm in case of financial difficulties from six to nine months per year; permission for part-time work in public utilities; abolition of the 10 per cent wage premium for short part-time working; reduction of overtime pay by 20 per cent; increase in weekly working time in public administration from 37.5 to 40 hours; easing of flexible working time arrangements.

With respect to the wage determination system, this has been completely reshaped. Collective bargaining on wages in state-owned public law enterprises was abolished; collective agreements on remuneration are now binding only to signatories and not extended by the Minister of Labour has been abolished; derogations to all provisions of sector/occupational agreements by company-level agreements are now allowed; the scope of arbitration is limited to basic wages and recourse to it now requires employers' consent; collectively agreed national minimum wage in February 2012 was reduced by law by 22 per cent (and 32 per cent for youth aged less than 25 years) and frozen until 2016; from April 2013 onwards the minimum wage will no longer be agreed by social partners but set by the government.

TABLE 9.5 Impact of the crisis on employees and self-employed in Greece 2008–2012

	Change (%) between 2008q2 and 2012q2			
	Employers	Own account workers	Employees	Family workers
Men	-31.2	-2.3	-22.8	-29.3
Women	-14.4	-3.5	-14.6	-31

Source: Data elaboration from the Labour Force Survey (ELSTAT).

The above changes entail a net downgrading of workers' rights and pay, sweeping away 'male privilege' along with the gains made by women in the primary sector of the labour market. At the same time, cuts in minimum wages and premiums for short part-time work in the private sector disproportionately hit women and youth who are more concentrated than men and older workers at the lower end of the pay scale.

Welfare state retrenchment

Recent years have seen great cuts in social spending and radical welfare state reforms. Some have a greater gender effect than others. For instance, state budget allocations to municipalities have been reduced, temporary staff in public services have been severely limited, and employees that have exited to retirement have not been replaced. These developments have caused understaffing in public childcare services and the closing down of a number of municipal crèches and nurseries. Moreover, due to cuts in public spending in education, children with at least one inactive parent have been excluded from all-day schools and the optional afternoon band of daylong schools (16:15–17:00) has been abolished. Finally, co-payments by patients for medical and pharmaceutical expenses have been increased while the cost for diagnostic tests is partly or not covered any more by social security. These developments have negatively affected breast cancer and prenatal diagnostics and microbiological tests for sexual health problems.

From all welfare state reforms of the last years, that of main pensions in July 2010 is the one with the greatest gender effect. This replaced the former one-pillar system by a two-pillar one (basic and contributory pension); equalized the legal retirement ages for men and women at 65 years by December 2013 also for women insured before 1993, who were until then entitled to retire at age 60; equalized the minimum early retirement age of women and men by increasing the minimum early retirement age of women from 55 years to 60 by 2015; raised the minimum contribution period for retirement on a full pension from 33.33 years (women) and 35 years (men) to 40 years (both sexes) by 2015; cut pension levels by 6 percentage points a year for people retiring between the ages of 60 and 65 with less than 40 years of contributions; reduced the average annual accrual rate from 2 per cent to 1.2 per cent; and extended the calculation of pensionable earnings from the current last five years to the entire lifetime earnings.

As for mothers of minor children who could retire on a full pension at the age of 55 or on a reduced pension at the age of 50 if they had an insurance record of 18.33 years, the pension reform raised their pensionable age to 65 years (full pension) and 60 years (reduced pension) by 2013. However, it also granted to mothers born before 1977 a new entitlement to early retirement at the age which applies/applied when they fulfill(ed) 18.33 years of insurance and provided that their child is/was still a minor at that time. Only for women born after 1977 onwards will there be no difference in pensionable age on grounds of maternity (Koukoulis-Spiliotopoulos and Petroglou 2010: 162).

As a result of the pension reform, the actual age of retirement will increase and the level of pensions will decrease for both women and men. Women's actual retirement age will rise more than men's, since they used to retire much earlier than men on average due to a lower legal retirement age and more frequent use of early retirement. Additionally, women's level of pensions will be more negatively affected than men's, since they rely on average on lower contribution records. To attenuate female poverty in old age because of very low pension levels, the law allows women to 'buy contribution time' at retirement for reasons related to bearing and caring for children. Namely, they can pay ex post contributions for time spent on pregnancy and confinement (up to 17 weeks for each child) if they were not on maternity leave (which is fully insured) and for time spent on raising children and not on insured childcare/parental leave (one, three and five years for one, two and three or more children respectively). At the same time, the law allows men to pay ex post contributions for the time spent on compulsory military service. However, only the better-off workers can make use of these provisions.

A gender impact assessment study of the pension reform mentioned that 'the new system for calculating the pension amount on the basis of one's whole working life penalizes women, who often have shorter and/or irregular working patterns... Moreover, the equalization of the pensionable ages and length of service requirements for men and women was made in an abrupt and inflexible way with very short transition periods' (Koukoulis-Spiliotopoulos and Petroglou 2010: 157).

However, the short-term impact of the reform was that exits to retirement enormously increased among employees with established rights under the previous pension regime or those that could/can benefit from the transitional provisions of the reform. This is still an ongoing process, particularly evident in the case of women. It is not only women in their late fifties and early sixties that want to benefit from lower pensionable ages still in effect. An unknown number of women in their late forties and early fifties have already made or are expected to make use of their new entitlement to early retirement as mothers of minor children (Lyberaki 2011b).

Finally, the Omnibus Law, voted in November 2012, raised the legal retirement age of both sexes from 65 to 67 years and their minimum age for early retirement from 60 to 62 years from 1.1.2013 onwards. The new law has thus shortened the transition periods of the July 2010 reform but has not abolished the entitlement to early retirement granted by this reform to mothers born before 1977.

Gender equality policy in times of austerity

It is ironic that the sovereign debt crisis and the definitive turn to austerity in 2010 coincided with the launch of the ambitious National Programme for Substantive Gender Equality 2010–2013 (General Secretariat for Gender Equality 2010). This includes all the prerequisites for the implementation of a fully-fledged and all-embracing gender mainstreaming strategy at all levels of government (central, regional and municipal) for the first time in Greece, entirely co-financed by the European Social Fund. It also provides for the creation of a wide network of counselling centres for women and shelters for victims of domestic violence over the whole national territory.

The programme also encompasses measures to facilitate women's participation in employment and advancement at work (vouchers to employed/unemployed mothers for access to childcare services free of charge and to unemployed women for home help services free of charge to the elderly and non-self-sufficient dependants), to encourage female entrepreneurship (positive action schemes) and promote the social integration of vulnerable groups of women (victims of trafficking and domestic violence, heads of single-parent households, women working under precarious forms of employment, etc.). It has, however, proved totally inadequate to compensate for the massive destruction of jobs, the unrestrained rise of unemployment, the loss of income and spread of poverty, and their disruptive effects on women's lives and those of their families, caused by 'one of the biggest fiscal consolidation that any EU country has done over the past 30 years' (European Commission 2012b, p. 2).

Gendered division of paid work: equality through social regression

The effects of the crisis and the policy responses to it described above on the gendered division of paid work can be studied at two complementary levels: the macro/social and the family/household level. In the second quarter of 2012 women were 40.5 per cent of all employed, 49.3 per cent of all unemployed and 38.9 per cent of the long-term unemployed against 39.1 per cent, 61.7 per cent and 66.3 per cent respectively in the second quarter of 2008. Besides, they had improved their share of employers and employees, while their share of own-account workers, part-timers, temporary and unpaid family workers had decreased. Finally, the gender pay gap fell from 16.5 percentage points to 13 over the same period.[3]

It follows that, at the macro level, the crisis has so far reduced gender inequalities in employment, unemployment and pay at the expense of men and to the benefit of women, though in a socially regressive way, i.e. by deterioration in employment conditions of both men and women and by interrupting women's progress in paid work.

The crisis is also having major implications for the family model and the division of paid work in heterosexual couple households in particular. In three years it has reduced the share of both two-earner and male-breadwinner households among couples aged 20–49 years with children. This has occurred in parallel with the spectacular rise of jobless households from 1.7 per cent to 14.1 per cent and the increase in the share of female breadwinner families from 1.9 per cent to 5.7 per cent of all households of couples aged 20–49 years with children between the last quarter of 2008 and the last quarter of 2011.

TABLE 9.6 Impact of the crisis on the gendered division of paid work in Greece 2008, 2012

	2008q2	2012q2
Female shares (%) of the:		
Employed	39.1	40.5
Employers	20.2	23.9
Own-account workers	31.7	31.4
Unpaid family workers	64.8	64.2
Permanent employees	42.1	43.2
Temporary employees	50	52.4
Part-timers	69.9	62.9
Unemployed	61.7	49.3
Long-term unemployed	66.3	38.9

Source: Data elaboration from Labour Force Survey (ELSTAT).

TABLE 9.7 Crisis effects on the family model and the gendered division in paid work in Greece 2008, 2012

Couples aged 20–49 years with children under 18 years – distribution (%)		
	2008q2	2012q2
Man and woman working (two earners)	55.1	46.0
Man and woman working full-time	48.6	40.3
Man working full-time and woman part-time	5.7	4.5
Man working part-time and woman full/part-time	0.9	1.2
Man working – woman not working (male breadwinner)	40.3	37.3
Man working full-time – woman inactive	34.4	24.0
Man working full-time – woman unemployed	5.7	11.8
Man working part-time and woman not working	0.2	1.5
Woman working – man not working (female breadwinner)	2.1	6.7
Woman working full-time – man not working	2.0	5.5
Woman working part-time – man not working	0.1	1.2
Man and woman not working (jobless parents)	2.5	10.1
All couples aged 20–49 years with children under 18 years	100	100

Source: Data elaboration from Labour Force Survey (ELSTAT).

Conclusions

Until now the economic crisis has had more damaging labour market effects on men than on women. However, women and men are almost equally hit since mid-2010. As the Greek economy is still in the middle of the crisis and the latter's impact on public sector employment is in progress, the final outcome by gender remains to be seen. Moreover, a full assessment of the impact of the crisis on the gender division of labour and men's and women's lives should also consider the effects on unpaid work and its gender distribution. Unfortunately, there are no available data on this issue.

Fiscal and structural adjustment policies are about removing the 'privileges' of the most protected male-dominated segments of the workforce and 'feminization' of working conditions, by spreading part-time work among male workers. The downsizing and restructuring of the welfare state have also major gender implications both immediate and longer term. At the same time, changes in the employment model, wage determination system and the welfare state have created critical conditions for the most vulnerable groups (low income and jobless households, migrants, lone mothers, etc.) and led to the impoverishment of very large social strata, especially the middle classes (well-paid employees, owners of small businesses, own-account workers).

The crisis has accelerated the pre-crisis trend of erosion of the male-breadwinner model but has also hit dual-earner households with children and increased the proportion of female-breadwinner and, most importantly, jobless households. These developments have major implications for gender relations and identities as well as for strategies to cope with the crisis that vary by gender.

In the first place, however, the crisis has interrupted women's progress towards gender equality in paid work through their better integration in employment and gender equality policy proved incapable of containing the damage caused by the recessionary impact of fiscal consolidation. Gender gaps in employment, unemployment and pay have narrowed since the beginning of the crisis. Ironically, gender equality is now achieved through the deterioration of employment and social conditions of both women and men.

Since the Enlightenment and the French Revolution, all movements for freedom and equality have inscribed their goals within the conceptual framework of 'social progress', although the meanings and approaches of social progress have differed and still do. The movement for women's liberation from male oppression and societal discrimination and for gender equality is no exception. Today, we need to rethink the link between gender equality and social progress in order to reconsider political priorities and the wider socio-economic reforms that are needed to overcome the structural crisis in Greece and elsewhere and to re-launch the process towards a gender equal society while improving the living and working conditions of both men and women.

Notes

1 Excluding survivor pensions.
2 Staff in the labour reserve are paid at 60 per cent of their basic wage (excluding overtime and other extra payments) for up to 12 months and such payments are considered part of severance payments. If the employees are not reassigned to other public sector posts during this period, they are dismissed.
3 Own calculations based on Labour Force Survey data published by ELSTAT.

References

Bettio, F. (1988) 'Sex Typing of Occupations, the Cycle and Restructuring in Italy', in J. Rubery (ed.) *Women and Recession*, London and New York: Routledge and Kegan Paul, 74–99.

European Commission (2010) 'The Economic Adjustment Programme for Greece', *European Economy Occasional Papers* No. 61, Brussels: Directorate-General for Economic and Financial Affairs Publications. Available at: http://ec.europa.eu/economy_finance/publications/occasional_paper/2010/pdf/ocp61_en.pdf (accessed 10.05.2013)

— (2012a) 'The Second Economic Adjustment Programme for Greece', *European Economy Occasional Papers* No. 94, Brussels: Directorate-General for Economic and Financial Affairs Publications. Available at: http://ec.europa.eu/economy_finance/publications/occasional_paper/2012/pdf/ocp94_en.pdf (accessed 10.05.2013)

— (2012b) 'The Second Economic Adjustment Programme for Greece – First Review – December 2012', *European Economy Occasional Papers* No. 123, Brussels: Directorate-General for Economic and Financial Affairs Publications. Available at: http://ec.europa.eu/economy_finance/publications/occasional_paper/2012/pdf/ocp123_en.pdf (accessed 10.05.2013)

General Secretariat for Gender Equality (2010) *Our Goal: Substantive Gender Equality. National Programme for Substantive Gender Equality 2010-2013*, Athens. Available at: http://www.isotita.gr/en/var/uploads/HOME%20PAGE/NATIONAL_PROGRAMME_GENDER_EQUALITY_2010_2013.pdf (accessed 10.05.2013)

Humphries, J. (1988) 'Women's Employment in Restructuring America: The Changing Experience of Women in Three Recessions', in J. Rubery (ed.) *Women and Recession*, London and New York: Routledge and Kegan Paul, 20–47.

Kanellopoulos, C., Gregou, M. and Petralias, A. (2009) *Size Profile and Labour Market Analysis of Immigration in Greece*, Reports 59, Athens: Centre of Planning and Economic Research.

Kanellopoulos, C. (2011) 'Size and Cyclicality of Worker Flows in Greece', in S. Balfoussias, P. Hatzipanayotou and C. Kanellopoulos (eds) *Essays in Economics. Applied Studies on the Greek Economy*, Athens: Centre of Planning and Economic Research, 259–83.

Karamessini, M. (2010) 'Life Stage Transitions and the Still-critical Role of the Family in Greece', in D. Anxo, G. Bosch and J. Rubery (eds) *The Welfare State and Life Transitions. A European Perspective*, Cheltenham: Edward Elgar, 257–83.

— (2012a) 'Female Activity and Employment Trends and Patterns in Greece: Women's Difficult Road to Economic Independence', in A. Buğra and Y. Özkan (eds), *Trajectories of Female Employment in the Mediterranean*, Houndmills, Basingstoke: Palgrave MacMillan, 65–90.

— (2012b) 'Sovereign Debt Crisis: An Opportunity to Complete the Neoliberal Project and Dismantle the Greek Employment Model', in S. Lehndorff (ed.) *A Triumph of Failed Ideas. European Models of Capitalism in the Crisis*, Brussels: ETUI, 155–82.

— (2012c) 'Labour Market Impact of Four Recessions on Women and Men in Greece: Comparative Analysis in a Long-term Perspective', *Social Cohesion and Development*, 7(2): 93–104.

Koukoulis-Spiliotopoulos, S. and Petroglou, A. (2010) 'Greece', in S. Regna, D. Molnar-Hiddasy and G. Tisheva (eds) *Direct and Indirect Gender Discrimination in Old-Age Pensions in 33 European Countries*, European Network of Legal Experts in the Field of Gender Equality, European Commission. Available at: http://ec.europa.eu/justice/gender-equality/files/conference_sept_2011/dgjustice_oldagepensionspublication3march2011_en.pdf (accessed 14.12.2012).

Lyberaki, A. (2011a) 'Migrant Women, Care Work, and Women's Employment in Greece', *Feminist Economics*, 17(3): 103–31.

— (2011b) 'Greece Caught Between Labour Market and Macroeconomic Imperatives', in European Parliament, Directorate General for Internal Policies, *Gender Aspects of the Economic Downturn and Financial Crisis*, Note PE 453.208, Brussels: European Parliament, 139–59. Available at: http://www.europarl.europa.eu/RegData/etudes/etudes/femm/2011/453208/IPOL-FEMM_ET(2011)453208_EN.pdf (accessed 14.12.2012).

Lyberaki, A. and Tinios, P. (2010) 'Women and Employment: Review and Prospects', in *The Greek Labour Market: Features, Developments and Challenges*, conference proceedings, Athens: Bank of Greece, 135–55 (in Greek).

Milkman, R. (1976) 'Women's Work and Economic Crisis: Some Lessons of the Great Depression', *Review of Radical Political Economics*, 8(1): 71–97.

Mincer, J. (1962) 'Labour Force Participation of Married Women', in H.G. Lewis (ed.) *Aspects of Labor Economics*, Princeton N.J.: Princeton University Press, 63–106.

—. (1966) 'Labour Force Participation and Unemployment', in R.A. Gordon and M.S. Gordon (eds) *Prosperity and Unemployment*, New York: Wiley, 73–112.

Papapetrou, E. (2010) 'The Trend in Wage Differentials Between Men and Women in Greece', in *The Greek Labour Market: Features, Developments and Challenges*, conference proceedings, Athens: Bank of Greece, 135–55 (in Greek).

Rubery, J. (1988) 'Women and Recession: A Comparative Perspective', in J. Rubery (ed.) *Women and Recession*, London and New York: Routledge and Kegan Paul, 253–86.

Sabarwal, S., Sinha, N. and Buvinic, M. (2010) 'How Do Women Weather Economic Shocks? A Review of the Evidence', *Policy Research Working Paper* 5496, The World Bank Poverty Reduction and Economic Management Network. Gender and Development Unit. Available at: http://www-wds.worldbank.org/external/default/WDSContentServer/IW3P/IB/2010/12/07/000158349_20101207080622/Rendered/PDF/WPS5496.pdf (accessed 14.12.2012)

Smith, M. and P. Villa (2010) 'Gender Equality, Employment Policies and the Crisis in EU Member States', Synthesis Report 2009, EU Expert Group on Gender and Employment. Available at: http://ec.europa.eu/justice/gender-equality/document/index_en.htm (accessed 14.12.2012).

10

IRELAND IN CRISIS

Women, austerity and inequality

Ursula Barry and Pauline Conroy

Introduction

Ireland was the first EU country to declare itself officially in recession in August 2008 and the second Eurozone country to have a structural adjustment programme imposed by the International Monetary Fund/European Central Bank/European Commission (IMF/ECB/EC), which became known as the 'troika'. The turn-around of the Irish economy in just a few short years has been dramatic – from one with the highest levels of GDP and employment growth to among those with the highest unemployment, emigration and debt levels across the EU. Ireland's economic policy throughout the 'boom decade' from 1998–2008 was based on a neo-liberal low tax strategy and the consequences of this have shaped the particular way in which the recession has unfolded and its enormous negative impact on Irish public finances: firstly, through the overreliance on taxation income from an overblown property and construction sector and secondly, the high level of public subsidy that has been made available to a crisis-ridden Irish banking sector.

Successive governments have committed a huge level of state financial resources to the banking sector through nationalization, capital injections and taking over of 'bad loans'. The Irish government has guaranteed since 2008, not just depositors but also all bondholders, secured and unsecured, in Irish banks and credit institutions, even those who had already failed. Private corporate debt has been transformed into sovereign debt placing a huge burden across the economy and with particularly serious consequences for low- and middle-income households.

In this context, the troika became involved in high level loans to the Irish government, known as the 'bailout' in November 2010. In reality it is made up of credit at initially controversially high rates of interest. The terms of the agreement with the troika mean that severe restrictions on Irish public expenditure have been imposed under the European Financial Stability Fund (EFSF) and a limited period fixed until 2015, to reduce the current deficit from 12 per cent in 2010 to 3 per cent of GDP by 2015. It means that Irish economic policy has become subject to a detailed Memorandum of Agreement signed with the troika covering all areas of public expenditure and taxation policies – subject to quarterly review – including a commitment to repay all debt.

The consequences were a sudden drop in public expenditure, a fall in income levels across the economy, a severe contraction in demand with a particular negative impact on those with low to middle level incomes. An estimated 20 per cent of households fell into significant debt. The depth of the economic crisis over the 2008–12 period has had complex effects on the structure and the internal workings of the Irish labour market. Almost every sector of the Irish economy has been deeply affected by the crisis, with the exception of the export sector, largely driven by US multi-national companies. Women account for less than 30 per cent of manufacturing employment and that percentage has remained relatively stable over the crisis. There is no available evidence as to the effect on female employ- ment of foreign direct investment in industry and services in Ireland. The sector that initially was the worst hit was construction, resulting in a dramatic rise in unemployment among men, including many thousands of migrant workers. As the crisis intensified it spread into the services sector, impacting on women both as employees in public and private services and in households and communities as primary users of services subjected to severe cutbacks.

Policy decisions that have been implemented since the onset of the crisis have prioritized the stated aim of reducing the public deficit but their consequences in practice for gender and equality are analysed below over two distinct phases. Rising levels of poverty, unemployment and indebtedness have created a widening inequality across Irish society. The decline in public sector pay and employment has been mirrored (and even exceeded) by falling wage rates and employment levels across the private sector. The consequent reduction in demand has affected most sectors of the economy, some worse than others. From a gender and equality perspective many of these policy measures clearly have an unacknowledged yet significant negative impact.

Gender, welfare regime and employment

Ireland's welfare regime is a mixed hybrid model combining strong elements of market organized and delivered services with women in the family expected to deliver care and support across a range of social needs. Not surprisingly this has generated considerable ambiguity in public policy in terms of whether women should be on the labour market earning individual wages or staying at home and working occasionally or part-time while caring for children and persons who are long-term frail or with disabilities. This dilemma has been described ironically by Kennedy (2002: 227) as a choice between 'a patriarchal employment market, patri- archal health care and the patriarchal social welfare system.'

In the years prior to the onset of the economic crisis in 2008, women dramatically increased their proportion of paid employment from 34 per cent in 1991 to 41 per cent in 2001, despite the structural obstacles placed in their way (Russell 2002). Their ever-increasing presence at work did not generate a corresponding lifting of the ideological construct of the family as headed by a male breadwinner. Among the barriers women faced then and now is the absence of decent and affordable childcare, after-school care and elder care, the discriminatory barriers to careers in the workplace, the poor provisions for maternity leave, unpaid parental leave, no paternity leave and the expansion of low-paid atypical employment in service sectors such as shops, hotels and restaurants. Inside the social security system women are frequently designated as dependants of their husbands or partners – becoming beneficiaries only as dependants of the principal claimant. An OECD Report (2010) revealed that households with young children spend as much as 41 per cent of their income on childcare.

Women's labour force participation has been consistently under-estimated in Ireland due largely to the conceptual weakness of statistical tools in capturing women at work in family enterprises. Women's activity on farms, or supporting the management of private bars, cafes, doctors' surgeries and pharmacies have tended to render them invisible in official statistics. The self-employed were outside of the social security system until 1988. The EU Directive on Equal Treatment in Social Security took 16 years and several visits to the European Court of Justice to implement in Ireland (Cousins 1995).

An additional factor in the Irish State and party system's attachment to the male breadwinner regime in the face of a reality that declared it otherwise, is the Poor Law. The Poor Law system was introduced into Ireland in 1838 and became 'one of the strongest roots of Irish social policy from which many of the statutory social services subsequently developed' (Burke 1987: 1). Poor Law notions of entitlement to public support, eligibility for services and the proper place of everyone in the family still prevail in today's public administration. For example, with the passage of the UK Abortion Act in 1967, the then Government of Ireland introduced a weekly stay-at-home payment for unmarried mothers of children as an incentive to stop them going to England for abortions. Lone parents still receive the allowance today and about 230,000 women have had to go to the UK to access abortions on the private marketplace (Conroy 1993; Conroy 2012). Ireland currently has the highest share of children living with one parent in the EU (joint place with Latvia). Figures for 2011 show that 23 per cent of young people aged under 18 in Ireland live with a single parent (second only to the US according to OECD at 26 per cent). At the other end of the spectrum is Greece where 5 per cent of children live with one parent – the EU average is just under 14 per cent (OECD 2011).

Changing employment structure pre- and during crisis

Following the dramatic increase in women's share of paid employment through the 1990s, women's employment rate showed a systematic rise in the pre-crisis years from 55 per cent in 2001 to 61 per cent in 2007. This increase was driven primarily by significantly rising employment rates among women in the middle and older age groups. Irish employment rates among both men and women were above the EU average before the recession, meeting and even surpassing the EU Lisbon employment targets of 60 per cent by 2007. Rates of employment fell across the Irish economy during the crisis years of 2008 to 2010 and continued to fall through to 2012. Both men and women have been significantly negatively affected by this fall (Table 10.1).

The employment crisis can be analysed under two phases: *Phase 1* shows a dramatic fall in employment rates across the economy, particularly among men, linked to the collapse in the construction sector. *Phase 2* reveals a gradual slowing down of employment decline but impacting differently across age and gender. Women's employment rates continue to be lower than men's rates, particularly in the middle age groups, but gender gaps in employment narrowed considerably during both phases of the crisis. This is less a result of more equal access to the labour market for women, and rather more the depth of the deteriorating employment situation among men, mainly young men (Table 10.1).

TABLE 10.1 Employment rates by sex and age in Ireland 2001 to 2012

Employment rates (ILO) %	Age group	2001	2004	2007	2008	2009	2010	2011	2012*
Females	15-19	23.0	18.8	22.9	20.7	14.1	9.8	10.6	9.8
	20-24	64.3	62.7	66.9	66.1	59.8	54.2	50.8	49.0
	25-34	73.7	72.6	75.7	74.4	71.6	70.1	69.6	68.1
	35-44	63.2	63.9	66.2	66.5	64.5	63.0	62.1	63.2
	45-54	53.3	59.3	64.8	65.1	63.7	63.9	63.4	60.9
	55-59	35.4	42.2	47.7	48.9	50.0	52.9	53.3	53.0
	60-64	20.4	23.4	30.7	32.8	31.6	31.9	33.1	30.3
All females	15-64	54.6	56.1	60.7	60.4	57.8	56.4	56.0	54.9
Males	15-19	30.8	25.1	25.4	21.6	13.9	10.6	8.7	8.9
	20-24	74.5	72.5	75.0	70.1	53.3	47.8	45.1	40.2
	25-34	90.1	87.3	87.7	85.8	75.1	73.5	70.0	70.6
	35-44	91.4	89.5	89.8	88.2	81.1	78.3	78.3	77.4
	45-54	84.7	85.4	85.7	85.2	78.5	75.3	75.2	75.0
	55-59	73.9	73.4	75.2	73.1	70.7	66.4	65.4	62.9
	60-64	53.7	53.8	59.6	58.7	52.6	49.5	49.7	47.5
All males	15-64	76.7	75.7	77.6	75.7	67.3	64.5	63.3	62.4
Combined male and female rate	15-64	65.7	65.9	69.2	68.1	62.5	60.4	59.6	58.6
Gender gap		22.1	19.6	16.9	15.2	9.5	8.1	7.3	7.5

Note: *2012 data is for 1st quarter.
Source: CSO 2001-2012 QNHS Table 9a.

When the impact of falling employment rates on different age groups is examined some key points emerge (see Table 10.1). Young women and particularly young men have been very badly hit. Men aged 20–24 years saw their employment rate fall dramatically from 70 per cent in 2008 to 48 per cent in 2010 during the Phase 1 – mainly due to the collapse of construction sector – and to 40 per cent in the first quarter of 2012. Young women saw their employment rate drop from 66 per cent in 2008 to 54 per cent in 2010 and to 49 per cent in the first quarter of 2012. The crisis years have brought about a situation in which for the first time employment rates of young women are higher than those of young men, mainly due to different rates of contraction in sex-segregated economic sectors. Older women aged 45–59 have bucked the trend – their employment rates have increased over both phases from a relatively low base of 49 per cent in 2008 but stabilizing at 53 per cent in 2010. Phase 2 has also seen a stabilization of the relatively low employment rate among women aged 35–44 that has traditionally been linked to care responsibilities.

The combined impact of these contrasting trends is a sharp narrowing of the gender gap in employment rates from a level of 15 percentage points in 2008 to 8 in 2010 during Phase 1 of the crisis and to 7 during Phase 2 compared to an EU average gender gap in 2011 of 12 percentage points (ENEGE 2012). Effectively the gender gap in the younger age groups has been reversed over Phase 2 as young men suffer the consequences of the economy's over-reliance on a construction industry that has effectively collapsed.

Analyzing unemployment data from the perspectives of both gender and age reveals some contrasting trends between women and men and over the two phases of the crisis (see Table 10.2). The dramatic impact of the crisis in Phase 1 (2008–10) is evident in the increase in the unemployment rate among men from 6 per cent to 14 per cent and among women from 4 per cent to 10 per cent. The overall unemployment rate currently stands at 15 per cent and at 29 per cent for those under 25 years. Young men, many of whom left school early in the height of the 'boom' to take up job opportunities in construction, now find themselves unemployed and, for some, without even basic second level qualifications.

The majority of those registered as unemployed are now long term. While unemployment rates continued to rise during Phase 2 to an overall 15 per cent (2012), the rate of increase has been lower, although noticeably higher among women than men as women's unemployment rate continued to increase from 10 per cent in 2010 to 11 per cent in 2012 while men's remained stable at around 18 per cent. This reflects the way the recession has moved from construction into services affecting key important sectors of women's employment, such as the retail and hospitality sectors.

It is important to analyse Table 10.2 in the context of two key characteristics of the Irish economy. Firstly, through the crisis years emigration has become a very significant factor in that unemployment rates would have been substantially higher if there had not been a dramatic rise in emigration levels particularly among young women and men. Secondly, women's unemployment rates need to be

TABLE 10.2 Unemployment rates by sex and age in Ireland 2001 to 2012

Unemployment rates (ILO) %	Age group	2001	2004	2007	2008	2009	2010	2011	2012*
Females	15–19	12.6	15.2	16.2	17.1	32.3	38.7	33.7	33.3
	20–24	5.7	7.3	7.5	7.6	15.7	18.7	21.8	20.0
	25–34	3.2	3.2	3.8	4.2	8.1	9.8	11.0	12.1
	35–44	2.6	3.0	3.8	3.2	6.5	8.6	9.1	10.7
	45–54	2.7	2.6	3.1	3.0	4.5	6.5	7.0	7.6
	55–59	2.5	1.7	2.4	2.8	3.9	5.6	5.7	5.7
	60–64	–	–	–	–	–	4.1	5.1	7.1
All females	15–64	3.8	3.9	4.4	4.4	8.1	9.8	10.4	11.1
Males	15–19	11.9	14.2	17.7	21.7	40.0	42.1	46.1	40.5
	20–24	5.8	8.0	8.1	12.8	30.2	32.9	33.7	35.8
	25–34	3.7	5.0	4.9	7.2	18.0	18.9	21.5	20.7
	35–44	2.7	3.8	3.6	5.1	12.3	14.6	14.8	15.2
	45–54	3.4	4.3	3.8	4.5	10.4	13.4	13.3	14.7
	55–59	3.1	3.1	2.9	4.2	7.7	10.5	11.8	14.6
	60–64	–	2.9	1.8	2.8	8.0	10.3	11.0	11.2
All males	15–64	3.9	5.0	4.8	6.6	15.1	16.7	17.5	17.7
Combined male and female rate	15–64	3.8	4.5	4.6	5.7	12.0	13.6	14.3	14.7

Note: *2012 data is for 1st quarter.
Source: CSO 2001–2012 QNHS Table 9a.

understood in the context of the traditionally high level of women recorded as 'engaged on home duties' in the Irish economy and the likely under-registration and under-declaration of unemployment status linked in part to the eligibility rules for unemployment registration which only allow registration of those seeking full-time employment, thus discriminating against many thousands of women. Those who have been self-employed or 'engaged on home duties' are strongly discouraged from registering as unemployed.

During the period of the so-called 'celtic tiger' Ireland was a country of high levels of net in-migration. The last two years have seen a reverse of this trend and a return to the historical colonial pattern of a highly mobile workforce. Emigration showed a dramatic increase, including a particularly steep rise among men in Phase 1 and among women over Phase 2 of the crisis. Estimated migration levels doubled during the crisis to a level of 87,100 in 2012 – a significant figure in a small economy and substantially above the figure for the full age cohort of graduates from the second-level school system that same year (CSO 2012a). Emigration is predominantly of younger people – 50 per cent of those emigrating are under 25 and their numbers have increased sharply as the economic crisis deepened. While most were young men over the early crisis years, 2012 estimates show 44 per cent of the increasing numbers of emigrants were women. Irish nationals accounted for 52 per cent of emigrants during 2012, 55 per cent of them male and 45 per cent female (Barry 2011; CSO 2012a).

The characteristics of those deemed as 'engaged on home duties' reveals the depth of historical gender differences in Irish society. Some 98 per cent of working age people in this category in 2012 are women, accounting for nearly 30 per cent of all women – and this percentage has remained unchanged over the crisis despite expectations that their share might rise. There is little evidence of this other than a slight increase among older women. What this demonstrates is the resilience of younger and middle-aged Irish women's attachment to the labour force despite significant discouragement.

This is not the only way in which prevailing gender norms are reflected on the labour market. Flexibility, for example, means different experiences for women and men workers; women have tended to predominate among short-hours jobs and men among long hours. Men worked an average of 39 hours a week in 2012 compared with 31 for women. Recession has disrupted this gender pattern to a certain extent with an increase of part-time employment particularly among men and also among women but from a significantly higher base. The proportion of men working part-time has almost doubled from 7 per cent to 12 per cent between 2008 and late 2012, while the proportion of women working part-time has increased from a much higher base of 32 per cent to 35 per cent over the same period (CS0 2012).

Women who are concentrated in part-time employment are most often those with children or with a combination of caring responsibilities. However, maybe even because of the crisis, overtime continues to be prevalent among mainly male workers (around 25 per cent of men work overtime). Research by Russell and McGinnity (2011) compares data between 2003 and 2009 and shows the extent to which part-time work is also low-paid work, particularly when it is women's work. Women part-timers earn 6 per cent less per hour than full-timers in contrast to men part-timers who do not seem to experience a 'pay penalty'. An important feature of the economic crisis has been not just the increase in part-time employment, but the rise in involuntary part-time employment or

TABLE 10.3 Trends in female and male part-time employment in Ireland 2008–2012

	2008		2010		2012	
	Female	*Male*	*Female*	*Male*	*Female*	*Male*
Part-time employment as % of total employment	32.5%	7.4%	35.2%	11.7%	34.6%	12.2%
Involuntary part-time as % of all part-time	17.1%	34.6%	21.2%	43.9%	26.1%	52.0%

Source: CSO Labour Force Survey. Population 15-64 years. Special calculations requested for 2008, 2010, 2012.

underemployment which has shown a sharp increase among women but even more particularly among men. This rise in involuntary part-time employment is a reflection of the overall crisis in employment in the Irish economy and is likely to continue, at least in the short term. This phenomenon is exacerbated by the sub-contracting and outsourcing of public services to privatized agencies employing a casualized workforce (CSO 2012c).

Employment data for 2012 show that women's overall share of paid employment rose from 43 per cent to 47 per cent during Phase 1 of the crisis but has been stable during Phase 2. Wide variations in the percentage of women and men are evident across different occupational and sectoral groups, revealing a highly segregated Irish labour market. Women account for over 60 per cent of those employed in personal service and sales and only just over 5 per cent of those employed as craft and related trade workers, a little over 16 per cent of those employed as plant and machine operatives and only around a third of those employed as managers and administrators. Broad occupational groups that reveal a more equal distribution between women and men are professional and technical occupations. What is clear is that the numbers employed have fallen from a peak in 2007, particularly steeply in certain occupations (craft and related trades and plant and machinery operatives), whereas they have risen in others (professional and technical workers and personal service workers). Some occupations that employ a large proportion of women have contracted at a slower rate or, in some cases, expanded during the period of the recession. Other important employers of women, such as sales occupations, rose rapidly until 2007 and then fell sharply due to contracting demand to 2012 (CSO 2012c).

The public sector is a very significant employer of women in Ireland, partly because there are better conditions of work, including greater flexibility, for example, in leave arrangements. In contrast to other sectors, education (76 per cent female) and health care (81 per cent female) have increased employment through the recession although both sectors have begun to show vulnerability to employment decline over 2011–12. Some 44 per cent of those employed in public administration and defence were women in 2010 – down from 51 per cent in 2007 (CSO 2012d). Latest data show that 9 per cent of public sector employment has been lost between 2009 and 2012, including a 6 per cent reduction between the second quarter 2011 and 2012 (Barry and Conroy 2012).

Regulation and deregulation

Ireland has had a strong system of centralized collective bargaining dating back to the 1980s which sets pay levels and rates of increase across both private and public sector employment over a three-year period. During the late 1990s and 2000s the national agreements were expanded to include many areas of economic and social policy including equality, and to broaden the range of negotiators to include many civil society organizations as well as the traditional social partners.

Following the end of the social partnership agreement in 2009 and after a period of conflict and unrest, a limited agreement was signed applying to the public sector. The 'Croke Park Agreement' includes a pay freeze across the public sector, no increase in core tax rates, no reduction in core social welfare rates until the end of 2013, increased flexibility and a public sector early retirement scheme to achieve significant reductions in the numbers employed. Civil society organizations were no longer included as negotiators and equality policy was not on the agenda.

Apart from a statutory National Minimum Wage (NMW) established in 2000 and a maximum hourly week, Ireland can be viewed as a country with a relatively low level of labour market regulation. Despite significant pressure to abolish it, Ireland continues to have a statutory NMW which has been frozen at a pre-crisis level of €8.65. There is a series of ministerial orders that covers, for example, night-time working, short-term working, zero-hours contracts, breaks and sick leave. Regulation generally encompasses entitlements to specific conditions of employment as well as compensation when those conditions are not met. However, the regulation of the Irish labour market has come under threat as the crisis has persisted and it is the collective bargaining system that has protected pay rates of (mainly) low-paid workers that has been the first to come under fire.

Joint Labour Committees (JLCs) operating at regional level were founded in 1946 to establish minimum wage rates and conditions in a range of sub-sectors of the economy occupied by low-paid and weakly unionized workforces. Decisions of JLCs are called Employment Regulation Orders (EROs). They cover employment in such areas as hairdressing, industrial cleaning and security work. The Dublin regional JLC applies to 65,000 workers in hotels and catering. They are a form of sectoral collective bargaining. In a case taken by a group of fast food outlets, the Supreme Court ruled in May 2013 that the Joint Labour Committee system of setting wages for lower paid workers was unconstitutional because, in their view, the system gave too much power without adequate guidance and supervision by the Oireachtas (parliament).

The Minister for Jobs, Enterprise and Innovation subsequently announced a series of changes diminishing the rights and conditions of employees covered by EROs, such as pay rates and Sunday premium payments. Pay rates for the many tens of thousands of workers in catering, hotels, retailing and hairdressing, mainly women, have been reduced. Women are more than twice as likely as men to be working for pay rates determined by JLCs according to a recent paper (Turner and Sullivan 2012). A Report by Mandate Trade Union analysing the impact of the recession on low-paid workers reveals that 40 per cent had experienced a drop in pay during 2011–12 and also highlights 'the extraordinary level of working time flexibility demanded by retail employers' (Mandate 2012: 21). The most important change taking place allows companies to derogate from the terms of the EROs in cases of 'financial difficulty'. These changes have been strongly criticized as an attack on 'an essential mechanism for protecting the incomes of the lowest paid and most vulnerable workers' (EAPN 2011: 4).

Recession and changes in public policy

A wide range of policy measures have been implemented over the two phases of the crisis with the stated aim of reducing the gap between government revenue and expenditure. Phase 1 focused on reducing the public sector pay bill primarily through cutting welfare payments, reducing public sector pay and pensions and freezing recruitment. Phase 2 continued these policies but with an additional focus on new and increased taxation, lowered levels of social transfers and the implementation of an untargeted early retirement scheme in the public sector. From a gender equality perspective most of these measures clearly have an unacknowledged yet significant negative impact.

Phase 1: 2008–2010

A series of measures was introduced at the on-set of the crisis with the stated objective of reducing the public deficit by €6 billion through direct pay cuts in the public sector and a reduction in public sector pension entitlements into the future. These changes have involved creating a new single lower level set of working conditions for all entrants to the public service from 2010, providing significantly lower pension entitlements and lower pay rates for specific categories of new entrants. This is a new two-tier public sector structure – a hierarchical and gendered inter-generational structure – within which women account for the majority of the lower strata. Student nurses are no longer paid while working, for example, and new and younger entrants to teaching will work alongside slightly older colleagues who have significantly higher pay levels and pension entitlements – recent estimates put the differential as high as 30 per cent (*Irish Times* 2012a).

Reductions in all public service salaries have taken place as follows:

- 5 per cent on the first €30,000 of salary;
- 7.5 per cent on the next €40,000 of salary;
- 10 per cent on the next €55,000.

Reductions in public service pension entitlements have taken place as follows:

- Public service pension age raised from 65 to 66 years;
- Maximum retirement age increased from 65 years to 70 years;
- Pensions to be calculated on 'career average' earnings rather than final salary level;
- Non-targeted early retirement scheme introduced.

As these changes have been implemented they have impacted differently on women and men. Relatively high levels of pay cuts were introduced at relatively low levels of pay, with the severest cut of 10 per cent imposed from €55,000 per annum upwards, still more a middle level of income. The public sector is critical to women – wage rates are higher and the gender pay gap is generally lower in the public sector. Some 47 per cent of those employed in public administration and defence and around 75 per cent of those employed in the education and health sectors are women. Consequently, the reduction in pay levels is having a negative impact on large numbers of women employees. The introduction of a freeze on recruitment until at least 2013, followed by an indiscriminate non-strategic early retirement scheme between 2010–12, are having major consequences, especially in health. It means higher job losses and fewer job opportunities for women. Reductions in social expenditure have resulted in the contraction of a range of services, for example, home help and public nursing home places, special needs assistants and language assistants in the educational sector. These cutbacks put pressure back onto communities and families where women continue to be the primary carers, effectively displacing paid work with unpaid work.

A vast range of welfare cuts were also introduced over Phase 1 and not even the smallest allowance or benefit was untouchable: unemployment and welfare payments were cut generally by circa 10 per cent; child benefit (paid directly to women) was reduced with a further reduction for a third or more child; carers' allowance claimed mainly by middle to older aged women looking after elderly or disabled relatives was reduced; jobseekers' benefit and jobseekers' allowance paid to those aged 18 to 21 years was capped; disability payments, rent subsidies, pensions for the blind, traveller supports, and emergency payments were cut.

When these diverse cuts are looked at closely it is evident that while old age pensions have been frozen but not cut in nominal terms, payments to young unemployed and large families have been hit hardest. Child benefit has traditionally been a source of direct income to women and this reduction will have a negative impact, particularly among women in low-income and one-parent households. Some 79 per cent of carers are women in Ireland. Women – particularly lone parents – experience the highest risk of poverty and are disproportionately affected by these changes. Pressure on government towards the end of Phase 1 has led to a commitment, under the current limited social partnership agreement (the Croke Park Agreement), that headline or basic social welfare rates would be maintained, income tax rates would not be raised, public sector pay rates would not be reduced and there would be no compulsory redundancies, at least until the end of 2013. It has not, however, prevented a whole series of welfare allowances and benefits being reduced or removed, such as fuel vouchers, double Christmas payments and back-to-school allowances.

Phase 2: 2011–2012

The most significant change during the second phase of the crisis affecting those on middle and lower incomes – predominantly women – has been the introduction in January 2011 of a new charge on gross incomes which has badly hit disposable income. The Universal Social Charge (USC) is paid on all gross incomes and is a new and highly regressive tax/levy. Despite its appearance as a progressive tax, and arguments to this effect (Callan *et al.* 2012), its impacts, even at very low income levels, have been severe. There are only a few steps up the payment ladder and the highest rate of payment comes into force at a rate barely above the minimum wage. It represents a new historical negative shift in Irish taxation policy transforming the welfare system based, at least in part on the concept of universal provision, into a new ideology of 'universal payment'. This cynical rediscovery of the principle of universality (associated as it is with the most progressive aspects of systems of social protection) and applied to this most regressive charge/tax, represents a new low in Irish economic policy.

This charge, which came into effect in January 2011 and in 2012, is paid as follows:

- 2 per cent on those with income of €10,037;
- 4 per cent on additional income between €10,037 to €16,016;
- 7 per cent on additional income above €16,017.

It is only when these figures are closely examined that the truly regressive nature of this charge is clearly evident. There is an exemption level – which was raised in the 2012 budget after some pressure – however, once a person's income goes *even one euro* over the exemption level of €10,036 per annum they pay 2 per cent on all their income and graded amounts of 4 per cent and 7 per cent after that. The USC is paid on gross income, including pension contributions. Medical card holders (free health services) who were normally exempt from such levies and taxes are now obliged to pay the USC. Only those that are fully dependent on welfare payments are exempt. In practice the highest rate of 7 per cent is paid on those earnings that are barely above minimum wage. Government policy is pushing people further down under the poverty threshold. The exemption threshold is less

TABLE 10.4 The poverty threshold, the minimum wage and the Universal Social Charge in Ireland in 2012

Universal Social Charge	Universal Social Charge	Minimum wage	At risk of poverty threshold	Average adult welfare payment
Exempt from payment	Only when total income < 10,036			
Liable for payment at 2 per cent on ALL income	10,037	17,092	10,831	11,440
Liable for payment of 4 per cent on additional income above €10,036	10,037 to 16,016	17,092	10,831	11,440
Maximum payment rate of 7 per cent on rest of income	16,017 and above	17,092	10,831	11,440

Source: Based on author's own calculations and CSO SILC data published in 2012.

than the 'at risk of poverty' threshold and is generating poverty traps around the payment percentage bands of just above €10,000 and again at around €16,000. The government makes much of the exemption levels but the picture is very grim.

Lone parents on welfare in Ireland have traditionally had a specific amount of income that could be earned before their welfare payments were cut. In another hugely significant measure this critical 'earnings disregard' that enabled many to reattach to paid employment has been drastically cut, creating new and deeper poverty for lone parents, the vast majority of whom are women. New government stated policy is to transfer lone parents from One Parent Family Payment (OPFP) onto Jobseekers' Allowance once their youngest child reaches seven years of age (the current age is 14 years) thus moving to a system of compulsory attachment to the labour market by 2015. Due to this reduced level of the earnings disregard, lone parents who had been in a position to take-up subsidized employment schemes and retain their OPFP, are no longer able to do so. The effect of this change will mean many single parents will not be able to afford to work and will be trapped in welfare dependency. Currently 59 per cent of OPFA recipients participate in part-time employment, but this is now expected to decrease (SPARK 2012). Evidence has been revealed that this has brought about a significant reduction in applications for subsidised Community Employment (CE) places. It is estimated that 70 per cent of CE participants are lone parents and the result is a 'staffing crisis' in, for example, childcare services in disadvantaged areas, which have been heavily reliant on the continuation of such programmes (*Irish Times* 2012b).

A new €100 per annum universal household charge was introduced at a flat rate (with a waiver scheme for those on particularly low incomes). Without carrying out the necessary water metering or site/property valuation, these taxes/charges are seen as regressive, negatively impacting on low-income households, in which women are the majority. Huge controversy greeted the introduction of the flat-rate charge and over 30 per cent of households have refused to pay and are facing court appearances and penalties. A new and even contentious property tax is due to come into force in July 2013.

Commenting critically on the negative impact of these cutbacks, together with loss of funding to significant community-based programmes, the Report by the UN High Commissioner on Extreme Poverty on her visit to Ireland stated:

> The impact of these measures will be exacerbated by funding reductions for a number of social services which are essential for the same vulnerable people, including disability, community and voluntary services, Travellers' supports, drug outreach initiatives, rural development schemes, the Revitalizing Areas by Planning, Investment and Development (RAPID) programme and Youthreach. By adopting these measures, Ireland runs a high risk of excluding those most in need of support and ignoring the needs of the most vulnerable. In particular, due to multiple forms of entrenched discrimination, women are especially vulnerable to the detrimental effects of reductions in social services and benefits.
>
> *(UN 2011: 9)*

The new Coalition Government (Christian Democrat majority/Social Democratic minority) elected in March 2011 promised to introduce a stimulus package to generate employment by the end of its first 100 days in office. A number of specific initiatives were announced in May 2011 with the stated aim of stimulating employment, the main one was the Jobs Initiative. The Jobs Initiative was planned to be 'fiscally neutral' – i.e. will not create additional demands on the budget deficit. The stated aim of government for the overall jobs initiative is to target young unemployed people and is targeted at construction. An internship programme was announced as well as a 'Pathways to Work' programme – there is no reference to gender in the planning of this initiative.

Undermining the equality agenda

Ireland was recognized across the EU as a country with strong and comprehensive equality legislation covering a broad range of grounds in relation to both employment and services backed up with an Equality Authority and enforced by an Equality Tribunal. That was up until 2007. This situation has changed radically since the onset of the recession in 2008. An entire architecture of public and statutory bodies established or supported to promote equality, monitor progress, enhance awareness and innovative practice has been restructured, closed down, endured drastic budget cuts or been part absorbed into departments of Government. The greater part of these changes occurred in the period 2008–10. Table 10.5 illustrates the scope and scale of closures which dismantled the structures, most of which had been built up between 1996 and 2008.

The budgets of the Equality Authority and the National Women's Council were cut, prompting the resignation of both directors and considerable public disquiet (Equality and Rights Alliance 2011). A proposed merger of the equality and human rights agencies will likely see a further erosion of its powers and resources for investigation and support of individual cases and less emphasis on development and implementation of equality policy. An interim group to bring the merger into effect decided to stand back from the process in 2012 in the face of criticisms. On a parallel track the independence of important statutory agencies has been undermined where government departments have absorbed the work of key bodies such as the Combat Poverty Agency, National Consultative Committee on Racism and Interculturalism, the Women's Health Council and the Crisis Pregnancy Agency.

Resources were also reduced to gender-specific policies. This is reflected in the reduced budget for the Equality for Women Measure (EWM) – first announced in 2008. In April 2009 a budget of €5 million was provided for equal opportunities measures, positive actions and structures to promote gender equality. Almost €4 million was subsequently diverted to non-gender related areas. The National Women's Council of Ireland described the appropriation of gender funds as a 'ransack' of the equality budget (NWCI 2009). The outcome of this process has been that the strength of equality related infrastructure has been very substantially and disproportionally weakened (ERA 2011).

TABLE 10.5 Disappearing equality institutions in Ireland 2008–2012

Name of institution	Fate of institution and its budget 2008–2010	Fate of institution and its budget 2011–2012
Equality Authority	Budget cut by 43 per cent in 2009 Director resigned	At risk of disappearing – to be merged with the Human Rights Commission 2012
Women's Health Council	Closed down in October 2009, some functions taken over by the Department of Health and Children.	–
Crisis Pregnancy Agency	Closed down 2009, functions taken over by the Health Service Executive under the Department of Health and Children	–
Irish Human Rights Commission	Budget cut of 32 per cent 2009	In process of being merged with Equality Authority 2012
Equality for Women Measure co-funded by EU Operational Programme	Budget partly transferred elsewhere and residue transferred to the Department of Enterprise from where it is managed by a state company – Pobal	–
National Consultative Committee on Racism and Interculturalism (NCCRI)	Closed down in December 2008. Its functions, but not its staff, were subsumed into the Office of the Minister for Integration at the Department of Justice	–
Gender Equality desk at the then Department (Ministry) of Justice, Equality and Law Reform	Budget reduced	–
National Women's Council of Ireland with 158 member organisations	Budget cuts of 15 per cent 2008–2011	Budget cut of 38 per cent for 2012 Director resigned 2012
National Office for the Prevention of Domestic, Sexual and Gender-based Violence, COSC, at Department of Justice, Equality and Defence	Established 2007	Budget rose in 2012

TABLE 10.5 (*Cont'd*)

Name of institution	Fate of institution and its budget 2008–2010	Fate of institution and its budget 2011–2012
Rape Crisis Network Ireland	Core Funding by the Health Authority removed 2011. Cuts of up to 15 per cent for some refuges and 2–10 per cent for others	Some funding restored 2012. Additional budget cuts to some centres capped at 5 per cent in 2012
SAFE Ireland Network of Women's Refuges and Support Services	Core Funding for Network by the Health Authority removed 2011 as well as cuts to Refuge budgets	Some funding restored 2012. Newly built refuge cannot open due to budget cuts. Some cuts 2011–12 capped at 5 per cent
Combat Poverty Agency	Closure announced in 2008. Subsumed with some staff into Department of Social Protection on 1.7. 2009	–

Addressing the UN, the Irish Human Rights Commission stated:

> Ireland has undergone a severe economic crisis since late 2008. This should not be used as an excuse to reduce the promotion and protection of human rights … Disproportionate cuts to the human rights and equality infrastructure that have taken place since 2008 will have long-term negative impact on human rights and equality in Ireland.
>
> *(IHRC 2011: 3)*

Following a Mission to Ireland undertaken by the UN Independent Expert on Human Rights and Extreme Poverty, Magdelena Sepulveda Carmona's report argues that 'these cuts have substantially reduced Ireland's capacity to protect the most disempowered segments of Irish society' (UN 2011: 4). Clearly, dismantling of the equality infrastructure has eroded resources devoted to gender equality and distanced Ireland from the European Gender Equality Pact.

The critical importance of organizations to protect against discrimination and promote equality was highlighted in a recent report commissioned by the Equality Authority and the Health Service Executive Crisis Pregnancy Programme, on discrimination in the workplace, focusing specifically on the treatment of women in paid employment during pregnancy. Their research revealed that '…unfair treatment, financial penalties, denial of promotion and even dismissal, caused 30 per cent of working women to experience severe stress and "crisis pregnancies"' (Russell *et al.* 2011a: 11). Those most at risk of unfair treatment were found to be young women expecting their second child and working in the retail or wholesale sectors. The study found that in companies in which equality policies were in place pregnant women were far less likely to experience discrimination.

Consequences of austerity

The consequences of austerity in Ireland have been felt predominantly among three sectors of the population: low-income households, lone parents and low-paid strata of the public sector. Women make up the majority of each of these sectors and are experiencing disproportionately the negative effects of austerity, mainly as low paid workers but also of those experiencing poverty and material deprivation. The risk of poverty and social inclusion has a definite gender dimension in Ireland, although the gender gap has narrowed significantly. Between 2008–10 the risk of poverty and social inclusion for men rose from 22.7 to 29.3 per cent while the rise for women was from 24.7 to 30.5 per cent (ENEGE 2012). Nearly 16 per cent of the Irish population are at risk of poverty, including nearly one in five children. Lone parents, large families, households with no adults in paid employment or with persons in low-paid employment and people with disabilities are particularly at risk. The overall risk of poverty rose from 14.1 per cent to 15.8 per cent over just one year (from 2009 to 2010). Those experiencing 'severe material deprivation' increased for women from 5.8 to 8.0 per cent and for men from 5.3 to 7.1 per cent (ENEGE 2012). The reduction in child benefit by 15 per cent in 2011 (on top of a 10 per cent cut in 2010) means a further increase in child poverty rates. Nearly 20 per cent of those in households classified as at-risk of poverty have a 'head of household' in paid employment. Clearly paid employment is no guarantee of exiting from poverty.

With the recession and accompanying austerity measures, the indebtedness of poor and lower middle-class households increased. Tens of thousands are unable to repay the loans they have taken out to buy their houses and the interest payment on those loans. The crisis has resulted in a sharp increase among those at risk of poverty who are in arrears with household bill payments from 20 per cent to 34 per cent between 2008 and 2010. Their problem is not one of over-consumption of goods and services, their problems are survival on low incomes. Some 20 per cent of Irish households did not have a bank account in 2008 – one of the main indicators of financial exclusion (Russell *et al.* 2011a). Financial exclusion compounds social exclusion. Bank-less or unbanked people have no cheque book or credit card, cannot effect electronic transfers, have no access to mainstream credit such as a bank overdraft, cannot earn interest on any savings and cannot pay for services using a direct debit facility. Their unmet banking needs were met in some instances by moneylenders – legal and illegal. Among those seeking help with their debts, lone parents, most of whom are women, are the largest group (Conroy and O'Leary 2006). In an interesting analysis of Budget 2011 from a gender perspective, TASC carried out an audit which revealed that households of lone parents and children experienced the most adverse effects – their gross average income fell by 5 per cent as a result of this one budget in 2011 (TASC 2011).

Ireland is a country with high rates of poverty but it is also a highly unequal society – a point that has been highlighted by various national and international organizations including the OECD and the UN. When the actual distribution of income is analysed the picture of a highly unequal society emerges (Social Justice Ireland 2011). The difference between those on the lowest incomes and those on the highest incomes is wider than in any other EU country. In fact, there was an increase in income inequality between 2009 and 2010 as shown by the quintile share ratio. The ratio showed that the average income of those in the highest income quintile was 5.5 times that of those in the lowest income quintile compared to a ratio of 4.3 just one year earlier (CSO 2012b).

Conclusions

Successive Irish governments have been guilty of mismanaging the economic crisis. Low-income households, lone parents and low-earning public sector workers have been key targets and, among those, women are affected disproportionately. Economic policy has been dominated by the single priority of reducing public expenditure with little evidence of a gender-informed strategy to combat unemployment, tackle poverty or address inequality. Employment policy has shifted from a pre-recession emphasis on increasing the supply of labour (through increasing women's employment rate and net in-migration) to a focus on registered long-term unemployment leading to a definite gender displacement effect and penalizing a specific category of women: lone parents in receipt of welfare payments.

Over the two phases of the crisis unemployment spread across the economy from construction (affecting mainly men) to private and public services affecting mainly women as both employees and primary users of public services. Gender gaps in employment rates have narrowed, primarily as a result of the scale of deterioration in men's employment rates. While the persistence of an almost ten point differential between women's and men's employment rates is the result of historical disadvantage and cultural differences, there is evidence that despite the severity of the crisis in employment, women are maintaining a strong attachment to the labour market.

To raise the employment rate of women to the government's stated aim of 69–71 per cent between 2011 and 2020 would require the attainment of around a 15 percentage point increase over a nine-year period. There is no evidence of gender-specific policy measures, action plans or supports required to achieve this aim, notwithstanding plans to compulsorily 'activate' lone mothers off welfare and onto the labour market (over half of whom are already working part-time). As a consequence the employment rate targets set by government for women must be regarded as, at the very least, highly unlikely to be achieved both in the short and medium term.

Policy changes through both phases have had negative impacts on those on low incomes and experiencing difficulties accessing paid employment. Poverty has increased and more than half of those who are registered unemployed are now long-term unemployed. Through the imposition of a new highly regressive tax, the USC, across the economy, the introduction of pay cuts and a pension levy on the public sector as well as a series severe of cutbacks in welfare entitlements and in service provision, the government has attempted to regain control over a debt-ridden public financial system. The USC represents a new departure in Irish taxation policy and a fundamental change to the Irish social contribution system – one that is clearly regressive – a payment system that deepens an already highly unequal society and a system that increases gender inequality by targeting those on the lowest incomes. Low-paid workers, mainly women, lone parents on welfare and those living in poverty have been badly affected.

Changes to the public sector, a critical employer of women, have created a new two-tier public sector – a hierarchical inter-generational structure. Reduction in the 'earnings disregard' of lone parents pushes them further into poverty traps. Child benefit has been cut year-on-year, in an economy in which parents are forced to rely on the private market for childcare consuming large portions of reducing incomes. A non-targeted early retirement scheme across the public sector leaves women in households and communities picking up the pieces left after the withdrawal of important services. Health services have been cut, community and local area programmes have lost resources and budgets for important equality agencies and equality initiatives have been disproportionately cut. Out-sourcing of community and household-based services has seen a growth in private agencies employing casualized mainly women workers under precarious contracts of employment.

The absence of gender equality as part of the policy-making framework, or even to inform the current policy process, is an indication of the extent to which equality, anti-discrimination and gender issues have been, and are likely to continue to be, completely marginalized within the crisis mis-management approach to this economy. Many of the policies pursued since the onset of the crisis have had definite negative consequences – some severe – from a gender, equality and social inclusion perspective.

There are a variety of factors that might account for the sudden collapse of the equality infrastructure in Ireland. Among these are the weakness of the social-democratic project, the continued dominance of centre-right political parties, the failure to embed equality policies and practices at grass-roots level in workplaces, the lack of independent status of key agencies, the scale and immediacy of the economic crisis provoking both a high level of fear as well as anger among the population as a whole. No social movement has been able to effectively galvinize and represent these diffuse sentiments.

The economic crisis in Ireland is persistent and has brought with it new levels of poverty and inequality as incomes fall, public services are reduced, household debt levels rise and unemployment and emigration reach new highs. Forecasts for the Irish economy indicate an economy in a continuing state of crisis. Ireland belongs to the group of countries that are experiencing sustained recession affecting men and women. Austerity policies and the contraction of demand extinguish the few signs of recovery. Gender equality policy has clearly become a victim of the recession and crisis mismanagement of the Irish economy.

References

Barry, U. (2011) *Gender Perspective in the National Reform Programme for Employment: Ireland.* University College Dublin, School of Social Justice. Available at: http://hdl.handle.net/10197/3663 (accessed 10.05.2012).

Barry, U. and Conroy, P. (2012) '*Ireland: Untold Story of the Crisis – Gender Equality and New Inequalities*', TASC Think Series. Dublin, May 2012. Available at: http://www.tascnet.ie/upload/file/BarryConroyMay12.pdf (accessed 10.10.2012).

Burke, H. (1987) *The People and the Poor Law in 19th Century Ireland*, Dublin: Argus Press.

Callan, T., Keane, C., Savage, M. and Walsh, J.R. (2012) 'Distributional Impact of Tax, Welfare and Public Sector Pay Policies 2009-2012', *Quarterly Economic Commentary*, Winter 2011/Spring 2012, Dublin: Economic and Social Research Institute.

Conroy, P. (1993) 'Managing the Mothers: The Case of Ireland', in J. Lewis (ed) *Women and Social Policies in Europe*, Aldershot: Edward Elgar Publishing Limited.

— (2012) 'Ireland – Rape and Incest not Grounds for Abortion', Washington: Center for Women Policy Studies. Available at: http://www.centerwomenpolicy.org/programs/health/statepolicy/REPRO_IrelandRapeandIncestNotGroundsforAbortion_Pauline Conroy.pdf.pdf (accessed 10.09.2012).

Conroy, P. and O'Leary H. (2006) *Do the Poor Pay More?* Dublin: OPEN, MABS and St. Vincent de Paul. Available at: http:// www.mabs.ie/fileadmin/user_upload/documents/Reports_Submissions/MABS_Reports_Documentation/Do_the_Poor_Pay_More_OPEN_May2005_1_.pdf (accessed 10.08.2012).

Cousins, M. (1995) *The Irish Social Welfare System*, Dublin: The Round Hall Press.

CSO (2001) *Quarterly National Household Survey*. Cork: CSO.

— (2006) *Quarterly National Household Survey*. Cork: CSO.

— (2008) *Quarterly National Household Survey*. Cork: CSO.

— (2009) *Quarterly National Household Survey*. Cork: CSO.

— (2010) *Quarterly National Household Survey*. Cork: CSO.

— (2011) *Quarterly National Household Survey*. Cork: CSO.

— (2012) *Quarterly National Household Survey*. Cork: CSO.

— (2012a) *Population and Migration Estimates*, Dublin: Stationary Office.

— (2012b) *Survey on Income and Living Conditions 2009, 2010*, Dublin: Stationary Office.

— (2012c) *Quarterly National Household Survey*, Cork: CSO.

— (2012d) *National Employment Survey 2009-2010 Supplementary Analysis*, Cork: CSO.

EAPN (European Anti-Poverty Network Ireland) (2011) *Pre-Budget Submission to Government*, Dublin: EAPN.

ENEGE (2012) *The Impact of the Economic Crisis on the Situation of Women and Men and on Gender Equality Policies*, Brussels: ENEGE.

ERA (Equality and Rights Alliance) (2011) *Response on Merger of the Equality Authority and the Irish Human Rights Commission*, Dublin: ERA.

IHRC (Irish Human Rights Commission) (2011) *Submission for the Twelfth Session of the Working Group on the Universal Periodic Review: Ireland*, Dublin: IHRC. Available at: http://www.ihrc.ie/download/pdf/ihrc_report_to_un_universal_periodic_review_march_2011.pdf (accessed 10.03.2012).

Irish Times (2012a) Sean Flynn 'Pay for new teachers down 30% since 2010', 28 August, Dublin. Available at: http://www.irishtimes.com/newspaper/ireland/2012/0828/1224323097262.html (accessed 03.09.2012).

— (2012b) Kitty Holland, 'Childcare services face "staffing crisis,"' 8 May, Dublin. Available at: http://www.irishtimes.com/newspaper/ireland/2012/0508/1224315744458.html (accessed 10.05.2012).

Kennedy, P. (2002) *Maternity in Ireland*, Dublin: The Liffey Press.

Mandate (2012) *Decent Work? The Impact of the Recession on Low Paid Workers, Dublin:* Mandate Trade Union. Available at: http://issuu.com/mandate/docs/mandate_decent_work_report_2012 (accessed 10.11.2012).

NWCI (2009) *Press Release: Women's Organizations are Facing Closure as Government Ransacks Equality Budget, According to the National Women's Council of Ireland*, Dublin. 29.07.2009. Available at: http://www.nwci.ie/news/prarchive/2009/07/29/womens-organizations-are-facing-closure-as-government-ransacks-equality-budget-according-to-the-national-womens-council-of-ireland/ (accessed 03.01.2012).

OECD (2010) *Payment for Childcare*, Paris: OECD.

— (2011) *Doing Better for Families* Paris: OECD.

Russell, H. (2002) 'Gender Gaps in Participation and Employment Rates', in *Impact Evaluation of the European Employment Strategy in Ireland*, Dublin: ESRI. Available at: http://www.esri.ie/UserFiles/publications/20070327115344/BKMNEXT018.pdf (accessed 10.02.2012).

Russell, H. and McGinnity, F. (2011) *Workplace Equality in the Recession? The Incidence and Impact of Equality Policies and Flexible Working*, Dublin: The Equality Authority and the Economic and Social Research Institute. Available at: http://www.esri.ie/UserFiles/publications/20091113090533/BKMNEXT200.pdf (accessed 14.02.2012).

Russell, H., Maître, B. and Donnelly, N. (2011a) *Financial Exclusion and Over-indebtedness in Irish Households*, Dublin: Department of Community, Equality and Gaeltacht Affairs. Available at: http://www.esri.ie/UserFiles/publications/bkmnext184.pdf (accessed 11.02. 2012).

Social Justice Ireland (2011) *Budget 2012 – Analysis and Critique*, Dublin: Social Justice Ireland. Available at: http://www.socialjustice.ie/sites/default/files/file/Budget/2012/2011-12-07%20-%20Budget%202012%20Analysis%20and%20Critique.pdf (accessed 01.01.2012).

SPARK (Single Parents Acting for the Rights of Our Kids) (2012) *Seven is Too Young*. Pre-budget submission, Dublin: SPARK.

TASC (2011) *Winners and Losers? Equality Lessons for Budget 2012*, Dublin: TASC. Available at: http://www.tascnet.ie/upload/file/Winners%20and%20Losers%20141111%20final.pdf (accessed 20.01.2012).

Turner, T. and O'Sullivan, M. (2012) *Economic Crisis and the Restructuring of Wage Setting Mechanisms for Vulnerable Workers in Ireland*. Dublin: TASC and University of Limerick.

UN (2011) *General Assembly, Human Rights Council, Seventeenth Session Agenda Item 3, Report of the independent expert on the question of human rights and extreme poverty*, Magdalena Sepúlveda Carmona, Mission to Ireland in January 2011, 17 May 2011. Available at: http://www.ohchr.org/Documents/Issues/EPoverty/A.HRC.17.34.Add.2_Ireland.pdf (accessed 20.11.2011).

11

EMPLOYMENT AND AUSTERITY

Changing welfare and gender regimes in Portugal

Virgínia Ferreira

Introduction

The Portuguese economy is in crisis. Since mid-2011 Portuguese policies have been supervised by a troika of international institutions (the European Commission, the European Central Bank and the International Monetary Fund). Defining the nature of the crisis affecting the country is, in itself, a complex exercise. Very different results may emerge depending on the time scale chosen to analyse the beginning of the crisis. According to Santos, we are experiencing a

> ... short-term financial crisis, a medium-term economic crisis and a long-term cultural-political crisis. In financial terms, it is the crisis in state funding. In economic terms, it is the Portuguese economy's lack of international competitiveness due to its level of expertise (selling shoes is not the same thing as selling aircraft) and the fact that it is part of an economic block with an excessively strong currency that favours more developed economies. In politico-cultural terms, it is a historic deficit in the form of political, economic and social elites created by an excessively long colonial cycle that, for far too long, licensed easy solutions to difficult problems and illusionary ways out for actual sieges.
>
> *(Santos 2011: 11)*

From a citizen's perspective, the most obvious signs of the crisis in Portugal are rising unemployment, higher taxes, higher prices for consumer goods and credit, both for individuals and enterprises, and a reduction in the amount and the extent of social support provided to those in need. In short, the disposable income of families has fallen while prices are rising and the welfare state is shrinking. The international bailout and austerity measures have plunged the country into recession, leading to the breakdown of private investment, drastic cuts in public investment, declining gross domestic product and a general impoverishment of both individuals and the country as a whole.

This chapter aims to analyse how the crisis is changing the labour market, welfare and gender regimes in Portugal, in the context of developments in these areas over the last four decades. The analysis is predominantly concerned with ascertaining the extent to which policies designed to fight the crisis will have the effect of reversing the process of constructing the sex/gender, citizenship and welfare schemes initiated over recent decades and thereby eroding the gains in autonomy that women have been making.

Developments in the gender regime prior to the crisis

Women in the labour market

The position of women in Portugal has been defined by a context of legal equality, weak individualization of lifestyles and pronounced social and economic elitism (Ferreira 1994; 1998; Portugal 2008). Women's involvement in the labour market began to intensify in the 1960s in an ideological context marked by the social doctrine of the Church or, in other words, the more traditional, family-based values based on male-dominated social relations. The official discourse of the authoritarian regime of the Estado Novo on the separation and complementarity of the sexes inexorably promoted a domestic focus for women's lives. However, a combination of various factors directly affected the availability of labour during the 1960s (in particular, the colonial war and emigration) and coincided with the growth of the labour-intensive export industries for finished consumer goods. Industrialization took place mainly in the more traditional textile, clothing, machinery and transport equipment sectors, following a strategy of containment of production costs not infrequently controlled by foreign capital. The coastal urban centres that supplied the internal market grew, thereby leading to the expansion of the service industries as a whole. Consequently, during this decade the feminization of the labour force increased from 18 to 26 per cent.

Employment in the 1970s was characterized by the rapid growth of the tertiary and public administrative sectors, particularly after the April 1974 revolution, when the tertiary sector accounted for 36 per cent of employment and rose to 56 per cent by 1991, also reinforcing the feminization of the labour force. By 1991, the rate of feminization of the working population had reached 40 per cent, rising to 47 per cent in 2008 (Eurostat 1994; 2009).

During the economic crisis of the 1970s there was no decline in employment in Portugal. The huge public sector investments made in the wake of the 1975 nationalizations and the expanding public sector consumption contributed significantly to this development. The economic policies of the 1970s were essentially based on a redistributive logic which gave priority to raising wages: the establishment of a minimum wage, employment subsidies, maternity leave and other pregnancy, maternity and family rights had a direct impact on levels of female employment. Pregnant women were allowed to take time off work to visit the doctor without losing benefits or pay, and rights to 90 days of maternity leave were established without a concomitant loss of service time, remuneration or benefits. Women could also take two hours off per day for breastfeeding until children reached one year old. They could miss up to 30 working days per year to care for sick children and take up to two years unpaid leave in special cases (Rodrigues 1988; Ferreira 1998). These measures undoubtedly encouraged mothers of small children to become full-time workers. In 1999 the employment rate for Portuguese mothers in couples with a child aged under six was 74.5 per cent, one of the highest in EU. The pattern was the same for mothers in single-parent families (75.7 per cent) (OECD 2001: 134–5).

The Portuguese economy's capacity to absorb these changes was, however, limited. Thus the female-dominated informal economy and the more precarious forms of employment both expanded. A study on atypical employment in Portugal at the end of the 1980s showed that it was mostly women who suffered from the late payment of salaries, clandestine work and casual labour (Grupo de Peritas/os 1988). This meant they were the workers most affected by practices such as part-time hours, short-term contracts, subcontracting, unpaid family work, paid domestic work, underemployment and even atypical employment in the public sector. The net effect of government policies, the growth of public services and the informalization of the economy resulted in a significant expansion of female employment. The relaxation of labour market regulations in the 1980s to allow more flexible contracts reinforced the incorporation of women into the labour market through an increased demand for workers who were not unionized, whose labour was cheaper and whose relationship with the labour market was less stable. The need to multiply sources of family income also contributed to this feminization, as increased consumption came under attack from high inflation rates that were not brought under control until the 1990s.

On the other hand, throughout this period the expansion of employment in the public sector facilitated women's access to well-paid and skilled employment, which offered job security and a friendly environment from the point of view of reconciling work/family commitments. The education and health sectors, together with justice and social security, created more opportunities, contributing towards the feminization of the scientific and technical professions in Portugal (around 50 per cent by the end of the 1980s). In the private sector, financial services also helped to provide higher skilled employment opportunities for the higher educated.

In fact, since the 1990s, there has been a real explosion in higher education with the number of students in public and private universities and colleges more than doubling between 1990/1 and 2000/1, from 184,764 to 381,078. Women reinforced their position, increasing the rate of feminization from 55.5 to 56.9 per cent (INE 1991; 2001). This investment in education has, until recently, been rewarded by better labour market opportunities (OECD 2011).

From the mid-1990s onwards the opening up of world trade and the arrival of extremely cheap products from Asian countries forced many companies in the footwear, textile and other sectors to close down.[1] Unemployment began to rise as a consequence of the many difficulties the Portuguese economy was beginning to experience. In addition to losing competitiveness in the industrial sector, multinationals operating in traditional sectors began to relocate to countries with cheaper labour forces and corporate restructuring in some sectors such as the banking sector also added to restrictions on the volume of employment (Gonçalves 2003).

In fact, the economy has failed to match the EU average growth levels since 2000, mostly due to the limited modernization of the economic fabric which still consists mainly of small and micro enterprises and firms with low innovation rates and weak sustainability, often led by poorly qualified managers who are reluctant to hire highly qualified staff or invest in vocational training. It is in this context that the increasing share of low-skilled jobs for female employees should be understood. Within 20 years the share rose from 11.6 in 1992 to 17.7 per cent in 2010 (in comparison with the slight change registered in male employment – up from 7.6 to 7.8 per cent) (INE 2011), indicating the intensive exploitation and marginalization experienced by women.

Many factors therefore converged in the dynamics of a labour market that facilitated women's participation in economic activity and access to employment, providing the basis for the high rates of female employment, but also for the predominantly poorly qualified, badly paid full-time profiles of female employment.

Developments in the gender and welfare regimes

The Portuguese welfare system has a hybrid profile which scarcely fits the typology produced by Esping-Andersen, or even the modified alternatives proposed by, for example, Andreotti *et al.* (2001) to include southern European countries, in relation to which Portugal presents significant differences. As shown elsewhere (Ferreira 1994), until the late 1990s the specific profile of the welfare system in Portugal included three central features: the large number of women (including married women with children) in full-time (formal and informal) employment; the shortage of social care services for the family; and the lack of male involvement in housework and care. It shares a low level of part-time employment and a high level of self-employment with other southern European countries. Finally, the country was unique in terms of the high employment rates for certain groups of women, in particular mothers with small children, low-educated and older women, and the high rate of employment in agriculture and industry (primarily textiles).

With regard to measures designed to reconcile work and family life, during the 2000s, the country differed from other southern European countries in the extension of maternity leave, the percentage of average wage paid and social care services for children aged under three (which were higher than the figures for the south but far below those of the Nordic countries) (OECD 2001: 144).

Between 1994 and 2007, the percentages for the full-time double income model in families with at least one child under six increased from 54.3 to 66.5 per cent, one of the highest in the EU. The high rate of working Portuguese women brought into being a dual earner family model but one which took the ideology of a separation between the male productive role and the female reproductive role as its main reference. Both members of the couple work and have access to social rights and benefits, which they can enjoy on almost equal terms as workers with family responsibilities. The state, for its part, treats men and women equally as producers and caregivers (with a few exceptions) but does not create the essential means to enable them to play both roles adequately. The market is still imbued with the ideology of the male breadwinner, discriminating against women in general and against women with family responsibilities in particular, as well as against men who seek to share family responsibilities. Intrinsically, as pointed out by Portugal (2008), the familialist ideology, in which the family prevails as the main provider, endures in the country.

This is evident in the results of opinion studies on work and family attitudes, such as the European Social Survey. As summarized by Wall, Portugal occupies a complex position: '– *neither too conservative nor too modern* regarding attitudes to women's participation in the labour market; – *very modern* in affirming the need for men to increase their involvement in family life; – *extremely conservative* in evaluating the impact of women's employment on the care of infants and on family life' (Wall 2007: 247). The idea that women are better equipped to care for the family and children and that they are the ones who must sacrifice their career for the family still prevails (Matias *et al.* 2011). The social practices directed towards reconciling work and family life reflect this complex attitude, but it may be said that they are governed by necessity (Lopes and Ferreira 2009). That is, ideology is tempered by a certain degree of pragmatism.

Over recent decades the average size of Portuguese families has fallen from 3.1 people per household in 1991 to 2.6 people in 2011. Since 1993 net migration has been the factor responsible for population growth, although its relative contribution has fallen since 2003. In the 1990s Portugal became an immigration country, receiving people from Brazil and other Portuguese ex-colonies (especially Cape Verde, Guinea and Angola), but also from eastern European countries (in particular Ukraine, Romania and Moldavia). Many female immigrants found work in domestic and care services, either in private households or firms, as part of the international employment networks responding to care needs not covered by middle-class female workers.

During the 2000s, and particularly in the latter half of that decade, the introduction of policies to encourage men to become more involved in childcare and to reinforce social investment were recognized by the government to be necessary measures to promote gender equality and pursue the Lisbon Agenda, which proposed mixed responsibility by the state as well as families for welfare in recognition of the so-called new social risks that called for improved parental leave, childcare and other forms of social support for family life.

Stepping back a bit, we should also note that in 1984 employed fathers acquired the legal right to all or part of the maternity leave in the event of the death or illness of the mother, the right to unpaid annual leave of 30 working days to care for sick children aged under 10, and the possibility of interrupting work for six months up to a maximum of two years to provide care, the same as for mothers (Law n° 4/84, of 5 of April). Since 1995, the public policies of Socialist Party governments have extended working fathers' rights as a means of increasing gender equality and sharing responsibility for family care.

The investment in social care services launched by the Portuguese government from 2006 onwards was crucial to expanding support for the family. When the crisis began, this policy was discontinued, although the projects already being implemented (mainly crèches, homes for the elderly, domiciliary services and long-term care units) were not affected. In 2009, the decision to give continuity to these investments was justified as a means of combating unemployment and attenuating the effects of the crisis. On the other hand, other important policies adopted since 2006 clearly counter the familialist ideology. In addition to the policies already mentioned, the new measures include: legalization of abortion on demand (2007); full-time schooling for children in primary school (2006); new cash benefits including for infants the prenatal allowance (2007); the allocation of structural funds to implement gender equality schemes in businesses and municipalities (2007); reinforcing policies to prevent and combat domestic violence (2007); legalization of same sex marriages (2009).

There are, however, fears that these still fragile political measures to transfer welfare responsibilities away from the family and towards a stronger role for the state may be undermined by the crisis and the return to power of the political right.

This brief summary shows that it is only in recent years that public policies have been significantly oriented towards building a welfare scheme that does not focus primarily on the family and, even among recent reforms, somewhat contradictory trends can be identified. For example, family means-testing has become more widespread which limits women's individual access to social rights, such as, to the 'social old-age pension', 'solidarity supplement for the elderly', 'social disability pension', 'family allowance' and 'prenatal family allowance'. In general, familialism continues to be one of the characteristics of the Portuguese benefits system. Social protection is increasingly family based, restricting the decommodification of the individual wage earner.

The effect of the crisis and the austerity measures on the labour market

In this section we analyse the effect of the current crisis and the austerity measures the government has chosen to impose on the labour market from the dual perspective of the demand and supply sides of employment. Firstly, the changes in the employment figures are examined. As already emphasized, Portuguese employment structures are highly feminized, but also highly sex segregated. This has a great influence on how these structures change under the impact of the economic crisis, with the initial impact of the crisis falling on the dominant workforce within the affected sectors and only later are other sectors equally or even more severely affected as a consequence of the capillary effect from the shrinkage of these sectors and the austerity measures adopted to combat the crisis.

As already stated, Portugal has high employment rates, particularly for women, in almost all age groups. The gaps between male and female employment rates are closing, in general, but increasing slightly in the 15–24 age group (from 4.4 percentage points to 4.8 in 2011), precisely the age group which is registering an extraordinary rise in unemployment (over 35 per cent in the second quarter of 2012, for both sexes). Portugal started losing jobs in the first quarter of 2009. Since then until the end of December 2011, men have lost 222,600 jobs and women a little more than half of this amount (138,200), amounting to reductions of 8 and 5.8 per cent, respectively.

Male employment was hit first by the crisis, from January 2009 onwards, as manufacturing (the automobile sector) and construction were the first sectors to register significant job losses, whereas female employment began to be affected one year later. Table 11.1 shows that in the period between 2008 and 2011, two out of every three jobs lost were held by men. These losses did not occur uniformly. Whereas men lost more jobs as salaried employees (ten times more jobs lost), women lost more jobs as self-employed, unpaid family workers and as employers (twice as much as men).

Female self-employed workers without employees have been hit particularly badly by the crisis, and their weighting within total female employment has significantly declined from 17.9 per cent to 13.2 per cent, in 2011, falling by almost

TABLE 11.1 Net job losses and gains by employment status and sex in Portugal 2008–2010, 2011

		Change 2010/2008 (%)	Change Q4 2011/Q1 2011 (%)
Employees	Men	−5.1	−2.8
	Women	0.1	−0.7
Self-employed	Men	−5.4	−2.2
	Women	−13.1	−12.8
Employers	Men	−9.4	−4.9
	Women	−14.1	5
Unpaid family workers	Men	−6.2	−16.3
	Women	−3.4	−14.1

* In the first quarter of 2011 the definition of categories and the methodology changed in the Labour Force Survey.
Source: Own calculations. Based on Statistics Portugal. Labour Force Survey 2008; 2011 (Inquérito ao Emprego 2008; 2011).

5 percentage points in comparison with 0.1 for men. This shows how rapidly self-employment adjusts to downturns in demand. However, behind the self-employed category in the Portuguese labour market there are often many dependent workers using the so-called 'false green receipts' to be treated as false independent workers. These false independent workers are in a very precarious situation in which employers reap all the benefits: they do not pay the 23.75 per cent social security contributions on top of wages and can 'dismiss' workers whenever they want. Workers, in turn, have to pay contributions that are much higher than salaried employees and since they often avoid paying their contributions, they lack any kind of protection if they lose their jobs.

The fiscal changes introduced in January 2011 offer some explanation for this decrease in self-employment. Employers now have to pay 5 per cent for each 'independent worker' they engage and independent workers saw their contributions increase from 25.4 to 29.6 per cent. This measure was introduced as a means of combating fraud, although to a certain extent by imposing taxes it has 'legalised' previously illegal practice. Some self-employed workers have become individual entrepreneurs, a status that has fiscal advantages for them and for the companies that contract their services. However, as the statistical category in which they are classified remains the same, there is no trace of this change, which cannot account for the registered reduction of self-employment.

Male and female job losses were not uniform throughout the period (see Table 11.2) with 2009 the worst year for men and 2011 for women while 2010 was the best (or rather the least bad) year for both sexes. Moreover, in 2011, women and men lost virtually the same number of jobs. Construction was responsible for

TABLE 11.2 Sectors with greatest net job losses by sex in Portugal 2009, 2010, 2011

	2009	*2010*	*2011*
Men	1. Construction	1. Construction	1. Construction
	2. Manufacturing	2. Manufacturing	2. Wholesale and retail trade
	3. Public administration, defence, social security	3. Public administration, defence, social security	3. Agriculture
	All sectors = −109,500	*All sectors = −43,100*	*All sectors = −70,000*
Women	1. Private households	1. Agriculture	1. Agriculture
	2. Manufacturing	2. Wholesale and retail trade	
	3. Hotels and restaurants	3. Manufacturing	
	All sectors = −34,200	*All sectors = −32,900*	*All sectors = −71,100*

Source: Own calculations. Based on Statistics Portugal, Labour Force Survey, 2009, 2010 and 2011 (*Inquérito ao Emprego* 2009; 2010; 2011).

the greatest male losses, which were most marked in 2009, followed by the trade sector, particularly in 2011.

Women's job losses over 2009–11 period were concentrated in agriculture (89,000), and to a lesser extent in manufacturing (40,500) and in private households (28,600). Losses in agriculture were particularly severe in 2011 (52,000 out of 71,100 lost jobs). However, manufacturing and private households with employees accounted for one-third of all female job losses over the period, with the greatest job losses in 2009 for both these sectors. The drop in employment in private households may, as discussed below, reflect the strategies used by middle-class women to confront cuts in salaries and rising taxes and consumer prices. With respect to manufacturing and taking 2005 as a reference point, the production index has decreased systematically since then, falling to 84.4 per cent in 2012. The textile industries, for instance, lost more than 30,000 jobs between 2007 and 2009 (see also endnote 1).

In addition, there are job losses caused by shrinking consumption, which include restaurants and hotels and wholesale and retail trade. In this latter case men are the worst affected, because they constitute the majority of the workforce involved in these activities (55.5 per cent). Like most of the southern countries, and in contrast with the Nordic ones, in Portugal the share of young workers in retail aged 15–24 and the feminization rate are below the EU average. This may be associated with a higher incidence of self-employment, full-time jobs and fixed-term contracts in southern countries (Eurofound 2012). This sector, including all the branches, registered one of the highest increases of the rate of feminization during the period analysed (2 percentage points). This is all the more important as the sector as a whole accounts for nearly 15 per cent of male and female employment. The sectors registering the highest growth in the feminization rate were recreational, cultural and sporting activities (plus 8.46 percentage points), and fishing, mining and quarrying (plus 5.3 percentage points). The weight of these employment sectors is, however, quite smaller (around 1 per cent).

It is, however, worth noting the net gains in employment in certain sectors, particularly education and health, where full-time staff, dominated by women, increased throughout this three-year period, at a time when public employment in general was contracting. The explanation for this change in these two sectors of public sector employment, where there have been no redundancies and the new recruits are frozen, can be found in the fact that some employees have seen their situation legalized and acquired the full status of civil servants, after many years working under illegal fixed-term contracts or false green receipts in public institutions.

Amongst the sectors with the greatest employment shares (more than 10 per cent for males, females or for both sexes), the health sector is the only one in which the changes have reduced the sex segregation of the labour market (a decline of 2.7 percentage points in women's share of the employment). In all the other more important sectors, the changes have tended to reinforce segregation – either increasing already high rates of feminization or decreasing already low ones.

TABLE 11.3 Changes in employment by sector, professional status and sex in Portugal 2008–2011

Main activity	Sex	Employment change (000s)			Female share of employment (%)	Change in female share percentage points
		Employees	Other Status	Total	2008	2008–2011
Total employment	Men	-150.1	-72.5	-222.6		
	Women	15.6	-153.8	-138.2	46.2	0.6
Agriculture, hunting and forestry	Men	-4.1	-7.6	-11.7		
	Women	-1.6	-89.5	-91.1	50.4	-8.6
Fishing, mining and quarrying	Men	1.3	-1.8	-0.5		
	Women	2.4	-0.3	2.1	6.7	5.3
Manufacturing	Men	-38.3	-1.9	-40.2		
	Women	-34.3	-6.2	-40.5	41.2	-0.9
Electricity, gas etc.	Men	-3.1	0.1	-3		
	Women	-2	0.2	-1.8	19.4	-4.8
Water	Men	-2.8	1.2	-1.6		
	Women	-1.8	-0.3	-2.1	19.3	-4.4
Construction	Men	-85	-31.9	-116.9		
	Women	5.6	-3.4	2.2	4.3	1.6
Wholesale, retail trade, repair of motor vehicles	Men	-30.1	-15.9	-46		
	Women	2.9	-13.7	-10.8	44.4	2
Transport, storage	Men	6.1	-10.7	-4.6		
	Women	-0.9	0.8	-0.1	16.9	0.4
Hotels and restaurants	Men	-1.2	-12.3	-13.5		
	Women	-2.1	-13.5	-15.6	59.9	0.6

Post and tele-communications	Men	1	-3.2	-2.2		
	Women	-7.8	-0.2	-8	37.5	-5
Financial intermediation	Men	4.5	1.3	5.8		
	Women	3.8	-0.9	2.9	45.4	-1
Real estate activities	Men	0.5	-1.8	-1.3		
	Women	-0.5	0.3	-0.2	46.1	1.6
Business activities	Men	-1.1	4.5	3.4		
	Women	-4.3	0.8	-3.5	53.5	-1.9
Administrative and support activities	Men	4.1	-0.3	3.8		
	Women	5.2	-1.6	3.6	52.3	0.2
Public administration, defence and social security	Men	-24.2	0	-24.2		
	Women	-5.3	-0.4	-5.7	35.4	1.6
Education	Men	4.8	0.4	5.2		
	Women	16.6	1.8	18.4	76.6	0.1
Health and social work	Men	16.7	3.8	20.5		
	Women	46.3	-2.6	43.7	83.4	-2.7
Recreational, cultural and sporting activities	Men	-2	1	-1		
	Women	5.3	1.5	6.8	40.9	8.5
Other service activities	Men	3.6	2.3	5.9		
	Women	-0.9	2.1	1.2	71.8	-3.9
Private households with employees	Men	-0.7	0.5	-0.2		
	Women	-11	-28.6	-39.6	98.8	-0.1

Source: Own calculations. Based on Statistics Portugal, Labour Force Survey, 2008; 2011 (Inquérito ao Emprego 2008; 2011).

Table 11.4 shows the rate of change over the past two years, highlighting the segments of the workforce that are gaining jobs and those that are losing them. It is obvious that part-time jobs have increased, in particular for men, since they tend to have a positive, although not very high, rate of change. In addition, some growth can be seen in other flexible types of employment, although the greatest change is found mainly in the category of visible underemployment[2]. It is evident that many men and women would like to work more hours.

The specialization pattern of the Portuguese economy is marked by the growth of the less skilled, low-paid employment sectors, with a particular emphasis on construction and tourism (including accommodation and catering). This explains why female (and immigrant) employment benefited and also explains the high levels of temporary work (only surpassed in Europe by Spain). In recent years, fixed-term contracts cover almost one in every four employees. The crisis has affected the trends for male and female employees with regard to the share of temporary work. The proportion of employees on fixed-term contracts at the end of 2009 was 16.9 per cent for men, and 19.2 per cent for women but this had changed to 18.2 and 18.9 per cent by the end of 2011. Effectively, in this type of fixed-term work there has been a convergence between the male and the female workforces.

TABLE 11.4 Net job losses and gains by work regime, contract and sex in Portugal 2009–2012

		Q1 2012/Q4 2009
Total employment	Men	−7.6
	Women	−6.7
Full-time	Men	−11.6
	Women	−7.5
Part-time	Men	37.6
	Women	−3.0
Employees		
Part-time	Men	61.4
	Women	24.4
Permanent work contracts	Men	5.5
	Women	3.3
Fixed-term work contracts	Men	−10.3
	Women	−19.3
Another type of contracts	Men	−30.7
	Women	−5.3
Visible underemployment	Men	220.9
	Women	189.6

Source: Own calculations. Based on Statistics Portugal, Labour Force Survey, 2009; 2012. (*Inquérito ao Emprego* 2009; 2012).

With regard to the categories of people most affected by unemployment, it can be seen that unemployment increased throughout the decade for all age groups. Graduates are among the least affected by the current crisis, although their rate of unemployment is also rising.

In short, this analysis identifies the following groups and economic sectors as being the worst affected by the crisis:

- Younger male and female workers – the hardest hit – with an unemployment rate of over 35 per cent in the first quarter of 2012;
- Male employees;
- Female self-employed workers, civil servants, domestic employees and unpaid family workers and fixed-term contract workers;
- Construction, manufacturing, agriculture, trade and household services.

There is a clear trend towards a reduction in working hours, with the masculinization of part-time work and the rise and masculinization of visible under-employment. An analysis of job losses by type of employment contract highlights the role of fixed-term contract staff as buffers during the crisis. Portuguese employers have placed the burden of the crisis on the most vulnerable segments of the labour force – workers with fixed-term contracts – and restricted the entry of newcomers into the labour market.

With regard to trends in inactivity, it is important to note that the male inactive population has increased in all age groups with the sole exception of the youngest. The situation is slightly different for the female population, for whom inactivity starts to increase from the age of 35 upwards. The reduction in the inactive population in younger age groups may be the result of suspending or giving up studies to find work in response to the difficulties faced by families in supporting students and the rising unemployment amongst female graduates. There is no data available, but student organizations have revealed the critical situation of many of their members who have lost the right to grants due to changes in eligibility requirements. Finally it is known that many young people are emigrating (especially to Switzerland, France, Angola and Brazil), although we do not have reliable numbers.

Women are still more numerous amongst inactive discouraged workers, but discouragement is growing faster among men – in 2011 male discouraged workers registered an increase of 56.5 per cent (from 22.3 to 34.9 thousand), compared to 26.3 per cent for women (from 38 to 48 thousand).

The current crisis and the policy response

When the crisis began, the country was already very indebted due to a decade of slow growth. The public debt, which amounted to around 60 per cent of the GDP in the middle of the last decade, quickly rose with the outbreak of the crisis, due to the increased interest that the state had to start paying to finance itself.

In 2010, it totalled 93 per cent, and the Portuguese government finally succumbed to pressure from the financial markets regarding the national debt (when the interest rate topped 7 per cent at the beginning of 2011) and requested a bailout from European institutions. International institutions, whose priority was to avoid a bankruptcy within the Eurozone, approved the bailout in May 2011, to the sum of €76 billion.

It is possible to identify two distinct but linked phases. During the first half of 2009, the Portuguese government launched measures to help enterprises and individuals to deal with the damage caused by a lack of orders, difficulties in accessing credit and loss of income. The overall national strategy in response to the employment crisis included measures directed towards enterprises, to promote employment, and individuals, to deal with unemployment. In general, they complied with EC guidelines: maintaining individuals in employment, upgrading skills, and increasing access to employment. In brief, they can be presented as follows:

1.   *Income support measures*: purchases of goods and services; corporate tax cuts; personal income tax cuts; indirect tax cuts; cuts to social security contributions.
2.   *Measures to stimulate the economy*: investment in infrastructures; government purchase of goods; transfers to households.

Taking everything into account, the packages of measures that were launched led to an enormous increase in state spending, raising the public deficit to 10.1 per cent of the GDP and accelerating the public debt crisis. When Portugal requested international financial assistance from the European Financial Stabilization Mechanism and the IMF, the negotiations were concluded with a memorandum of agreement for a fiscal consolidation strategy, deep, frontloaded structural reforms to the labour market, the judicial system, network industries and the housing and services sectors, and safeguards for the financial sector (European Commission 2011).

From 2011 onwards, the following main measures for combating the public deficit can be identified:

•   Reductions in what is generally termed 'the privileges of the public service workers' (tenure, pay, pensions) – salary cuts, recruitment and career freezes, changes in retirement policies;
•   Restructuring of the public administration, merging or eliminating agencies, intermediary management positions and other jobs;
•   Raising direct and indirect taxation and the price of transport, gas and electricity;
•   Partial or total privatization of state-owned enterprises – electricity and water, television, airline and others;
•   Deregulation of labour relations – easing of dismissals and flexibility of working hours and labour mobility.

The current government strategy for tackling the crisis includes increasing exports of internationally tradable goods by strengthening competitiveness through reducing wages. The pattern of specialization underpinning this strategy is a continuation of the traditionally dominant model in the Portuguese economy – low wages for low-skilled workers who produce goods for final consumption with low added value. Female employment is particularly desirable in almost all the exporting sectors but offers no benefits for workers in terms of quality of employment and standards of living. Since the mid-2000s, policies have been launched to support and encourage the development of industry and services with a higher technological profile but the emphasis on technology, energy and green jobs does not take the masculinization of these sectors into account. This omission is all the more worrying at higher education level, since the feminization of sciences and technologies, as well as engineering, has been systematically declining. In 2000/01, 58.8 per cent of science, technology and computer science graduates, in addition to 35.3 per cent of engineering graduates, were female. By the end of the decade, in 2009/10, this had fallen to 54.2 and 26.2 per cent, respectively (GPEARI 2011). The female flight from engineering is particularly worrying, since this has involved a drop of more than 9 percentage points. Another sign of this trend is the 5 percentage point fall in the feminization of employment in the post and telecommunications sector, which was already well below the average of the overall employment (37.5 per cent in 2008 compared to 46.2 per cent) (see Table 11.3).

All these trends converge to reinforce segregation in the labour market. An increase in sector-based segregation is therefore evident (the dissimilarity index – ID – was 30.1 per cent, in 2007, and rose to 31.3 per cent, in 2011), in addition to the unadjusted wage gap of average gross hourly earnings of male and female paid employees, which rose from 8.3 in 2007, to 12.8 percentage points in 2010) (Eurostat 2012).

It can therefore be said that men are becoming more like women in terms of work regimes and modalities, as seen in the last section, but not in terms of job and pay status. This converges in the 'feminization of the labour force', but only in the sense that the male workforce is becoming as flexible and disposable as the female workforce has been. The strategy is to level down employment standards, feminizing the labour market, not in numerical figures, but in material and regulation terms. Portugal has shifted the cost of adjustment onto the most precarious segments of its labour market – temporary workers and the self-employed – who are used as leverage for adjustment.

Planned net job losses up until 2015 will particularly affect the highly feminized public administration sector, traditionally at the forefront of policies to reconcile work and family life in addition to the transport sector, which is highly masculinized. The importance of the public sector in female employment justifies a special focus on the changes it is experiencing. Given the diverse nature of their activities, policies directed towards state-owned companies (transport, manufacturing, media, airlines, etc.) are more difficult to analyse.

The first of these adjustments will mainly affect women in a sector that has so far been a source of better quality employment, particularly for women with lower qualifications.

Drastic changes to public administration

Fiscal austerity measures have had a drastic effect on civil servants, whose prospects include wage cuts, reduced employment, career stagnation, rising taxes and the loss or reduction of welfare provisions. It is expected that by the end of 2012, the loss of income in two years will amount to 25 per cent (5 per cent in wage cuts, on average, in 2011, plus 3.8 per cent from the extraordinary tax levy, equivalent to 50 per cent of the fourteenth monthly wage, plus more than 14 per cent in 2012, by planned cuts to the thirteenth and fourteenth monthly wages). This last measure has generated the most opposition, as no equivalent measure was envisaged for the private sector. In fact, to counterbalance this, the government proposed a half hour extension of working time in the private sector, but this proposal has been rejected by social partners, including both trade unions and employers, who have preferred to negotiate more flexible terms for dismissals.

It is commonly observed that the wages in the public sector are excessive in comparison with other countries. In 2005, 13.2 per cent of the workforce worked for the state (Central and Local Administration), a lower proportion than the average for the Eurozone, but whereas the Eurozone countries spent 11 per cent of their GDP on payrolls, Portugal spent 13.9 per cent (Observatório do Emprego Público 2011: 1). Analysts then concluded that the problem was not with public employment, but with salaries. Studies show that, on average, individuals with similar profiles (education, experience, etc.) earn more in the public sector, particularly the lower educated. This 'premium', which was 9 per cent in 1996, increased to 16 per cent in 2005 (Campos and Pereira 2009). In addition to higher salaries, most public employees have job security, which those working in the private sector lack in practice, even if formal employment protection is regarded as high.

In addition, several studies show that women in the public sector benefit even more from this imbalance than men. Adjusting for all the recorded differences in individual characteristics, women's wages in the public sector were, by the end of the 1990s, 26.5 per cent higher than in the private sector, in comparison to a differential for men of 12.9 per cent (Portugal and Centeno 2001, in Coelho 2010: 11), reflecting, of course, men's higher pay in the private sector.

Here we find the explanation for two issues:

1. The reason why women will be hit hardest by the loss of public sector jobs;
2. Why women with lower qualifications will be specially affected by the restructuring of the public administration, together with the elimination of intermediary management positions, which will also have a dramatic impact on women.

In general, career freezes, wage cuts, and the almost total halt to new recruitment will affect women's employment and prospects severely. This is evident in all job profiles, whether they require low, medium or high qualifications. In fact, different analyses have shown the positive effect of the public sector on women's employment (Estévez-Abe 2010), and it is not by chance that in countries with higher standards of living and greater equality, public sector employment ranges from one quarter to one third of the employment overall. The lack of recruitment also has another consequence – the downgrading of the quality of both services and working conditions in the public sector.

As it is an employment sector with fewer discriminatory practices, the shrinking of public employment may mean a downgrading of the overall gender inequality index. This also threatens women's emancipation and autonomy, since it reduces their average contribution to the household income. A recent study based on the European Community Household Panel showed that the income autonomy of women in dual earner households increases in line with levels of education and is highest amongst female public sector employees. While women's overall share of household income was 25 per cent in 2000, it amounted to 43 per cent for female graduates. Furthermore, whereas the share for privately employed women was 33 per cent, it amounted to 43 per cent for public employees (Coelho 2010), confirming the existence of this premium. In addition to downgrading the overall gender inequality index, the changes in public employment also affect the general inequality index because, as can be seen in the next section, they also have an impact on prospects for disadvantaged women.

Changing patterns of paid and unpaid work

As described above, women with higher education qualifications are one of the groups that have fared better in terms of employment opportunities and living standards in Portugal. This has been one outcome of the high returns to education in the labour market (OECD 2011).

The higher purchasing power of these graduate women working in the public sector creates a demand for domestic services, which generates job opportunities for women with few qualifications and provides a possibility for the uneducated, long-term unemployed and migrant women with poor employability to enter the labour market, albeit in dead-end jobs in insecure and frequently informal employment.

While acknowledging that this benefits high income groups the most, and is a class-based phenomenon, we agree with Coelho's argument that it is also an income distribution mechanism amongst women that helps reduce social inequalities. Thus, wage cuts lower the demand for domestic help, thus reducing job opportunities for less qualified women (Coelho 2010). In 2008, 7.2 per cent of all female jobs were in 'private households with employed persons', while a similar figure were in 'hotels and restaurants' (8 per cent). By 2011, however, the share of 'private households with employed persons' in female employment had dropped by 3.1 percentage points, the highest among the main sectors, corresponding to an elimination of 39,600 job positions (INE 2008; 2011). In our view, the shrinking of private households' demand for employees leads to increased income inequality between different groups of women.

Moreover, given that middle-class women are doing more of their own domestic work, and there is an uneven distribution of power and resources between women and men in the household, it is probably correct to surmise that this means an added workload for women. The expansion of women's unpaid domestic work may imply a relative disinvestment in professional careers, thus threatening their professional status. The alternative is to extend the sharing of domestic chores and care to all members of the family. One way or another, the changes identified in employment will have repercussions on the gender contract.

The media has discussed many of the strategies that people have adopted to tackle the economic recession and loss of income, including: reducing fertility; cutting consumption; dispensing with domestic help; intensifying domestic work; choosing informal care for children and the elderly (in general low-quality arrangements); leaving children unsupervised or taking them to the workplace; leaving dependent elderly people unaccompanied at home without support; taking on a second shift or job. No studies have been produced yet, but media reports frequently feature or quote interviewees who state a preference for women returning to the home, concluding that their salary scarcely pays for childcare, transport and taxes and that they have opted to save money and stay at home. This is, of course, the case with women in low-paid jobs with short-term perspectives. Even so, as many studies have already shown, the commitment to employment is very high among low-qualified women in Portugal, and goes beyond economic need. It is not therefore expected that this option will be widely preferred. As stated by one of the interviewees in Távora's study, they can thus 'avoid men bossing them all along their lives' (2010: 109).

Where do we go from here?

As previously stated, we are experiencing increasing unemployment, a reduction in family incomes and the shrinking of formal social protection. We may therefore ask where all these changes are leading and who is paying for the crisis. The more vulnerable segments of the labour market are facing major difficulties. Younger workers face great difficulty in entering the labour market. Education is no longer a safeguard, pushing many graduates to look for work abroad. Long-term unemployment has also increased. The self-employed have lost work due to the crisis and new fiscal obligations that have made the 'false green receipt' employment status less attractive to employers. Another factor that has lead to the deterioration of women's labour market situation is the loss of job opportunities in the public sector, whose share in the employment market has been declining since 2005.

The poor are paying for the crisis in Portugal. A recent study (Callan *et al.* 2011) on austerity measures in six EU countries (Greece, Portugal, Spain, the UK, Ireland and Estonia) between 2009 and the middle of 2011 shows Portugal is the only country where these measures demand more from the poor – 20 per cent of the poorest lost between 4.5 and 6 per cent of their income, with the situation proving worse for those with children (in which case, losses can amount to 9 per cent), whereas the richest 20 per cent lost only 3 per cent. Retired people, pensioners and civil servants are among the worst affected, most of whom are women and many of whom are poor. The study's conclusion is that, of the six countries considered, the burden of austerity as measured by disposable income is most regressively distributed in Portugal.

It is, then, time to assess the hypothesis put forward in the beginning of this chapter that, in Portugal, due to the 'crisis', we are experiencing a backlash against the attempt to abandon the traditional southern European welfare regime enacted in government policies over the last decade. The empirical evidence collected in support of this hypothesis is multiple.

Measures designed to combat the crisis have had an important impact on the welfare system, namely:

- The changing philosophy of social protection involving cuts in cash transfers, increased charges, reduced coverage and income replacement rates, restrictions on criteria for eligibility for benefits and increased household means-testing;
- Cuts to family allowances and other social benefits;
- The changes to pension schemes involving: cuts to income replacement rates; increased contributions for public sector pensioners to equalize with the private sector; reductions in tax allowances.

The principle of universalism of social protection has been abandoned in favour of selectivism. The intensified means-testing of social protection reinforces family subsidiarity and reduces women's autonomy in the key areas of citizenship: the individual, the social and the political. Women are once again thrust back into the black box of the family, reducing them to their past status of dependants. The retrenchment of the formal welfare state leads to a reinforcement of the informal welfare society, whose main pillar is the family or, in other words, the unpaid work of women. Half of the unemployed (48 per cent in 2011) are not eligible for unemployment benefit. Half of these are supported by their families, which is the case with young people who face a labour market that will either not admit them or only offer them insecure jobs, and are thus forced to remain in the family home. It is the family that is supporting the cost of unemployment and offering protection from the worst consequences of the crisis.

As Bauman (2010) stresses, the welfare state fits in a society of producers but is useless in a society of consumers. There is no need to support the reproduction of a disposable workforce and, in addition, there are no jobs available to occupy this workforce. Within this framework, the poor are put under surveillance so that they cannot claim benefits they do not deserve. Workers and rights are being de-nationalized and dealt with as a variable of market adjustments (Ferreira 2012). Social investment is not being seen as necessary to the economic success of society. This is why the current government only accepts social investment within a framework of impoverishment and the lowering of quality standards (evident in the recent measure to enlarge the number of places per room in nurseries and kindergartens, for instance).

It may therefore be stressed, in very general terms that, during the crisis, gender gaps have closed slightly with regard to employment in Portugal, mainly because unemployment did not hit women as badly as men during the first two years of the crisis. Some 'feminization' of the male situation and conditions in the labour market may be occurring but gender-based discrimination in the labour market still remains.

What kind of welfare mix will emerge from the current policies? The current challenge must be to determine how we can influence the building of new sex/gender, citizenship and welfare regimes that do not represent a loss of autonomy for women in terms of the triple dimensions of the individual, the social and the political. To rely on the family to provide social protection to individuals is to revive the old model of welfare of southern Europe that had begun to fade away in Portugal.

Notes

1 Employment in the textile sector has been decreasing. It employed 243,264 workers in 2002, but over eight years more than one-third of jobs have been lost (ATP 2011).
2 The category of visible underemployment was defined differently in the new series of the Labour Force Survey. It includes the individuals aged at least 15 years that, in the reference period, had a job with less than the normal duration of the job and that want to work more hours – hours worked in both the main and the secondary activities now fall under this category. These changes explain the increase in this category from 71,000 to 173,900 between the last quarter of 2010 and the first quarter of 2011.

References

Andreotti, A., Garcia, S.M., Gomez, A., Hespanha, P., Kazepov, Y. and Mingione, E. (2001) 'Does a Southern European Model Exist?' *Journal of European Area Studies*, 9(1): 43–62.
ATP (Associação Têxteis e Vestuário de Portugal) (2011) 'The Portuguese Textile and Clothing Industry in Numbers, in 2010'. Online. Available at: http://www.pofc.qren.pt/ResourcesUser/2011_Documentos/Noticias/20110919_boletim_da_itv.pdf (accessed 06.06.2012).
Bauman, Z. (2010) *Living on Borrowed Time – Conversation with Citlali Rovirosa-Madrazo*, Cambridge: Polity Press.
Callan, T., Leventi, C., Levy, H., Matsaganis, M., Paulus, A. and Sutherland, H. (2011) 'The Distributional Effects of Austerity Measures: A Comparison of Six EU Countries', *EUROMOD Working Paper*, EM6/11.
Campos, M.M. and Pereira, M.C. (2009) 'Salários e Incentivos na Administração Pública em Portugal', *Boletim Económico do Banco de Portugal*, Verão: 61–83.
Coelho, L. (2010) 'Women, Economy and the State in Portugal: Where are They Going Together?', paper presented to the International Colloquium *The Revival of Political Economy*, University of Coimbra, 21–23 October 2010.

Estévez-Abe, M. and Hethey, T. (2010) 'Women's Work, Family Income and Public Policy', paper presented to the conference 'Inequality and the Status of the Middle Class', University of Luxembourg, June 2010.

Eurofound (European Foundation for the Improvement of Living and Working Conditions) (2012) *Working Conditions in the Retail Sector*. Online. Available at: http://www.eurofound.europa.eu/ewco/studies/tn1109058s/tn1109058s_1.htm (accessed 18.08.2012).

European Commission (2011) The Economic Adjustment Programme for Portugal, *European Economy Occasional Papers* No. 79, Brussels: Directorate-General for Economic and Financial Affairs Publications. Available at: http://ec.europa.eu/economy_finance/eu/forecasts/2011_spring/pt_en.pdf (accessed 17.11.2011).

Eurostat (1994; 2009; 2012) *Labour Force Survey*, Online. Available at: http://epp.eurostat.ec.europa.eu/ (accessed 12.11.2011).

Ferreira, A.C. (2012) *Sociedade da Austeridade e Direito do Trabalho de Exceção*, Porto: VidaEconómica.

Ferreira, V. (1994) 'Women's Employment in the European Semi-peripheral Countries: Analysis of the Portuguese Case', *Women's Studies International Forum*, 17, 2/3: 141–55.

—— (1998) 'Engendering Portugal: Social Change, State Politics and Women's Mobilization', in A. C. Pinto (ed.) *Modern Portugal*, Palo Alto, CA: Sposs — The Society for the Promotion of Science and Scholarship, 162–88.

Gonçalves, C.M. (2003) 'Evoluções recentes do desemprego em Portugal', *Sociologia*, 15: 125–64.

GPEARI (2011) 'Diplomados do Ensino Superior [2000–2001 a 2009–2010]'. Online. Available at: http://www.gpeari.mctes.pt/es> (accessed 05.03.2012).

Grupo de Peritas/os (1988) 'As mulheres e o emprego', in *As Mulheres em Empregos Atípicos*, Lisboa: CISEP/CCE: 37–48.

INE (1991; 2001) *Estatísticas da Educação*. Online. Available at: http://www.ine.pt/ (accessed 17.07.2012).

—— (2008; 2011) *Estísticas do Emprego*. Online. Available at: http://www.ine.pt/xportal/xmain?xpid=INE&xpgid=ine_publicacoes (accessed 17.07.2012).

Lopes, M. and Ferreira, V. (2009) *Os Custos da Maternidade e Paternidade na Perspectiva dos Indivíduos, das Organizaçõ|es e do Estado,* Coimbra: CES.

Matias, M., Silva, A. and Fontaine, A.M. (2011) 'Conciliação de papéis e parentalidade: efeitos de género e estatuto parental', *Exedra*, 5: 57–76.

Observatório do Emprego Público (2011) 'Dados Estatísticos', *Boletim boep*, 4: Maio. Online. Available at: http://www.dgaep.gov.pt/upload/OBSEP/BOEP_04/DGAEP-OBSEP_BOEP_04.pdf (accessed 27.08.2012).

OECD (2001) 'Balancing Work and Family Life: Helping Parents into Paid Employment', *Employment Outlook*, chapter 4: 129–66.

OECD (2011) *Education at a Glance* Online. Available at: http://www.oecd.org/dataoecd/61/61/48630790.pdf (accessed 20.05.2012).

Portugal, S. (2008) 'As mulheres e a produção de bem-estar em Portugal', Oficina do CES, 319.

Rodrigues, M.J. (1988) *O Sistema de Emprego em Portugal: Crises e Mutações,* Lisboa: Dom Quixote.

Santos, B.S. (2011) *Portugal: Ensaio Contra a Autoflagelação*, Coimbra: Almedina.

Távora, I. (2010) 'Understanding the High Rates of Employment Among Low Educated Women in Portugal: A Comparatively Oriented Case Study', *Gender, Work and Organization*, 19(2): 93–118.

Wall, K. (2007) 'Atitudes face à divisão familiar do trabalho em Portugal e na Europa', in K. Wall and L. Amâncio (eds), *Família e Género em Portugal e na Europa*, Lisboa: ICS: 211–57.

12

WOMEN, GENDER EQUALITY AND THE ECONOMIC CRISIS IN SPAIN

Elvira González Gago and Marcelo Segales Kirzner

Introduction

The effects of the international financial crisis that started in the US in 2007 have added to and multiplied the problems stemming from Spain's already existing specific economic imbalances, among them the construction bubble which had underpinned Spain's previous strong economic growth. The international crisis accelerated the bursting of the bubble with devastating effects in destroying jobs and increasing unemployment and the risk of poverty. Moreover, even if many people's problems started with the initial crisis, the austerity policies adopted to address the financial imbalances are adding to rather than resolving these difficulties.

This chapter explores the effects that the crisis and the policy responses are having on women and on gender equality, with a main focus on the labour market. After initial expansive and expensive measures to limit the destruction of mainly male employment, the subsequent pressure and rapid actions to achieve quick fiscal consolidation have seriously damaged the possibilities of recovery. In this context, the economic approach adopted has been accompanied by a notable drop of political commitment to equality policies and institutions. This is a clear message that gender equality is a luxury good we can no longer afford; and that women's perspective is not crucial for the economic recovery.

Two rounds of recessionary effects on employment can be observed and a third one is still to come, each with different predicted gender impacts. While men's employment suffered most in the initial round, some female-dominated sectors soon became affected even though the worst period of job destruction had ended. The sectoral segregation of women, particularly their participation in public services, protected them during the first phase of the crisis and to a lesser extent during the second but in the most recent phase policy responses are concentrated precisely on the sector, public employment – particularly education, health and social services – which had protected women's employment in the earlier phases. Not only is women's participation in public employment higher but they also benefit from better reconciliation policies in the public sector and from public services such as childcare and long-term care. Moreover, women constitute a higher share of pensioners and receive lower pensions and are thus more vulnerable to pension reforms.

The structure of this chapter is the following: the first section explores how women increased their involvement in paid work in the pre-crisis period and highlights the resulting evolving tensions in the Spanish social model; the second analyses the effects of the crisis on employment and unemployment from a gender perspective, as well as exploring the family and individual strategies adopted to cope with the problems; the third section concentrates on the policies adopted since 2010, when the first set of expansionary measures came to an end and austerity became both the strategy and the goal. The final section presents the main conclusions and messages.

The gender regime prior to the crisis

The consequences of the crisis for women and men depend not only on its impact on economic performance but also on the institutions and societal arrangements prevailing in Spain prior to the crisis. Ever since the political transition at the end of the 1970s, Spanish society and institutions have been evolving, resulting in significant changes in the specifics of the Spanish welfare model. Nevertheless it is still a Mediterranean model where the family network still provides core welfare support. During the period of uninterrupted economic growth after the early 1990s crisis, the Spanish economy and society modernized irreversibly. Europeanization, globalization, openness, enrichment, decentralization and migration have changed habits, traditions, expectations and institutions. This modernization included significant progress in integrating women into paid work and ongoing changes in the family model as it evolved from the prevailing sole breadwinner towards a dual earner model. However, men continue to spend much less time than women in childcare and housework and more time in paid work and leisure activities. Moreover, the current social protection system, though changing slowly, is based on the previous breadwinner family model and on the standard employment relationship such that full social security requires permanent contracts and full-time work. People – both women and men – on atypical contracts are not equally insured with respect to unemployment benefits, contributory pensions, parental leaves (paid and unpaid), working-time reductions, or other significant measures related to life-work balance, since all them depend on the time spent previously in employment (Gonzalez and Castellanos 2011a).

The development of the Spanish economy from the second half of the 1990s until 2007 is manifest in the increasingly higher levels of employment, wealth and welfare state development, which indicate a convergence towards conditions prevailing in our more developed neighbouring countries. In a context of growth, gender differences were reduced, although not sufficiently: the gender employment rate gap (aged 20–64) declined from 33.8 percentage points in 1995 to a still unacceptable level of 22.7 percentage points in 2007 (Table 12.1). In only 12 years the number of women in a paid job doubled, increasing from 4.1 to 8.2 million. The employment rate gap between Spanish women and the average in EU countries also diminished sharply, falling from 18 percentage points (for 20–64 population) in 2000 to only 4.1 in 2007. Still, Spain in 2007 was the EU country with the fifth lowest female employment rate.

The pathway women had to follow to achieve greater involvement in paid work was, however, characterized, among other factors, by high unemployment, very high rates of temporary contracts, high rotation between employment and unemployment, confinement to low-skilled jobs and take-up of most of the part-time jobs. This occurred in spite of the share of higher educated women exceeding that for men by 9 percentage points in 2007 (for individuals aged between 15 and 64). The archetypical form of segmentation in the Spanish labour market remains that between fixed-term (around one-third of workers) and permanent-based workers, and research has shown the particularly low rate of transformation of temporary into permanent jobs for women even during the 'best years' of the expansion period (Caparrós and Navarro 2006) due to horizontal segregation and gender discrimination (Toharia and Cebrian 2008). Even highly educated women had less stable jobs than men (Acosta and Osorno 2009; Caparrós and Navarro 2006). As a result, temporary work became a trap rather than a stage towards regular employment and this affected more women due to their working conditions and vertical and horizontal segregation.

TABLE 12.1 Main indicators of a gendered labour market in Spain in 1995, 2001 and 2007

	1995		2001		2007	
	Men	Women	Men	Women	Men	Women
Employment rates (20–64)	68.6%	34.8%	77.9%	46.1%	80.7%	58.0%
Unemployment rates (20–64)	17.0%	29.5%	6.9%	14.4%	5.9%	10.3%
Temporary work rates (15–64)	33.3%	38.3%	30.5%	34.5%	30.6%	33.1%
Part-time work rate (15–64)	2.5%	16.3%	2.7%	17.2%	3.9%	22.7%
Self-employment rates (20–64)	24.0%	16.6%	21.0%	13.3%	19.9%	11.8%

Source: Eurostat (2012).

The increased employment of women did not occur within sectors and occupations traditionally dominated by men and with better labour conditions. On the contrary, the Duncan dissimilarity index increased during the period (Hidalgo Vega 2007). Already feminized sectors absorbed the bulk of new female employment, so that, for instance three out of four workers in health and social work activities were women in 2007. The majority of the new jobs taken by women between 1995 and 2007 were in real estate (16 per cent of total new jobs for women), retail (another 16 per cent), health and social work (12 per cent) and hotels and restaurants (11 per cent), while increases in sectors where women were under-represented such as industry and transport were insufficient to make major inroads into gendered employment patterns (Figure 12.1). During the same period, 82 per cent of the total new public sector jobs were held by women (representing 52 per cent of the total public employment in 2007, 9 percentage points more than in 1995).

Vertical segregation increased also during this period according to the Duncan dissimilarity index (Cebrián and Lopez 2008; Hidalgo Vega 2007). In a context where the female share of total employment grew by seven percentage points we find women increasing their presence by between 10 and 12 percentage points in female-dominated occupations, such as clerical work, services and sale workers and elementary occupations but by only one percentage point for managers where the female share rose only to 32 per cent. According to Hidalgo Vega (2007), while men are now found across all occupations, even in professions where women were overrepresented, women continue to have a low or almost non-existent presence in better-paid higher quality male-dominated occupations.

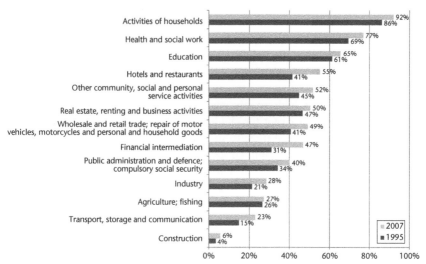

FIGURE 12.1   Women's percentage share of total employment by sector in Spain in 1995 and 2007
Source: Eurostat (2012).

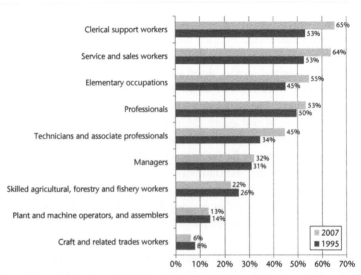

FIGURE 12.2 Women's percentage share of total employment by occupation in Spain in 1995 and 2007
Source: Eurostat (2012).

Moreover, the increase in Spanish women's employment was mostly due to the incorporation of those aged 25–49, who represented three out of four newly employed women. As a result, inactivity rates reduced sharply. However, women aged 30–39 still had to interrupt their careers due to their gender-imposed roles, reinforced by the continuing inadequacy of policies to support reconciliation and men's lack of involvement in family responsibilities. Indeed, in 2007, women with children under six registered employment rates 17.5 percentage points lower than women without children; the proportion of inactive women not seeking employment due to care burdens and family related responsibilities was 18 per cent. In both cases these represent larger impacts of children on employment than in the rest of EU countries. Childcare coverage did increase between 1998 and 2007, from 1 per cent to 20 per cent for children under three and from 75 per cent to 98 per cent for children aged three to six (Ministry of Education 2008), reflecting the policy of fully integrating children aged three to six in public education. Elderly care services started to emerge and improve following the Dependency Law (39/2006) which allowed for elderly care services to be provided to those living with their families or alone (but see below for impact of austerity on this development). These developments had a positive influence on the transformation of the previous employment model: indeed, female employment rates (aged 25–49) with children under six increased 3.4 percentage points between 2005 and 2007, 1.1 percentage points more than the EU average increase. However, the employment rates gap between women with and without children did not start to narrow until 2008.

In this context, the combination of women's traditional low involvement in paid work and the gendered employment model configured during the expansion period, resulted in a social protection system that did not cover men and women equally and an employment market that did not pay equally for women and men. Since severance pay, unemployment benefits and pensions are related to the time worked and the wage previously received, women more often receive non-contributory benefits, which are significantly lower. Moreover, they also receive 19 per cent lower contributory benefits, which reflects the gender pay gap within the Spanish labour market. Finally, the coverage and amount of pensions for women and men have been far from equitable. The gender pay gap perpetuated women's vulnerability throughout generations as female pensioners receive pensions 25 per cent lower than male pensioners (Ministry of Employment 2012).

Impact of the crisis

This massive employment growth and declining unemployment was too reliant on an enormous housing bubble fuelled by too low interest rates and an increasing trade deficit after Spain's entry into the EMU. The financial and economic crisis in 2008 started to reveal the construction bubble. Thus, GDP grew by a low 0.9 per cent in 2008 before falling -3.7 per cent during 2009. Over the next two years GDP stagnated, falling -0.1 per cent in 2010 before rising 0.7 per cent during 2011 but the prospects for 2012 point to a new recession equal to -1.7 per cent of GDP. Spain is consequently experiencing excessive instability in employment and the highest unemployment rate of the EU, fuelled by its traditionally strong segmentation of the labour market (González Gago and Castellanos Serrano 2010b), which leads to dramatic adjustment of employment to cyclical economic conditions (Conde-Ruiz et al. 2010).

As a result, public finances deteriorated. The much praised fiscal surplus of 1.9 per cent GDP in 2007 turned sharply negative and reached in 2009 an unsustainable fiscal deficit of 11.1 per cent of GDP followed by deficits of 9.2 per cent in 2010 and 8.9 per cent in 2011 (data 18/05/2012). In July 2012, the European Commission approved an easing of the requirement to diminish the debt ratio with a new target of 6.3 per cent in 2012 and 4.5 per cent in 2013.

At the same time, the Spanish public debt reached its highest peak in the second quarter of 2012, amounting to 75.9 per cent of GDP, having doubled since the beginning of the crisis. However, private debt is three times the public debt level and represents over 220 per cent of GDP. The high-risk activities engaged in by banks during the economic boom lie behind these developments and the failure of several financial market reforms led the Spanish government to apply in June 2012 for financial aid to its European Union's partners to support the recapitalization of the financial system.[1] The markets have already anticipated the conversion into public debt, increasing the country risk premium and the financing cost of the public sector, so that severe public spending cuts are said to be 'unavoidable' by the Economy and Competitiveness and Public Administration Ministers. In fact, a new and heavier austerity package was launched in July 2012; subsequent reforms and a 2013 restrictive budget are expected to be announced at the end of September.

Employment gender impacts

In this context, the labour market has responded with its traditional high elasticity to GDP growth and total employment (20–64) has decreased by 14.5 per cent, that is by 3 million workers, between the first quarter 2008 and the first quarter 2012[2]. Employment is expected to decrease by a further 650,000 jobs (-3 to -3.8 per cent) in 2013 (FUNCAS, 2012). Two rounds of effects of the recession on employment can be observed and a third one anticipated, with different observed and anticipated gender impacts. During the first two years of the crisis (2008–10), the concentration of net employment losses in construction and manufacturing activities (85 per cent of the jobs destroyed) affected mainly men (85 per cent of the workers affected); later (2010–12), the effects on employment softened but spread also to other activities, so that 26 per cent of the total net job losses between 2010Q1 and 2012Q1 affected women. For them, the impact was felt more heavily in activities such as: accommodation and food services; professional, scientific and technical activities; administrative or support service activities; or arts, entertainment and recreation, where the major part of the job losses were borne by women.

As in other countries, the sectoral segregation of women (particularly their concentration in public services, defined as education, health and social work) protected female employment during the first phase and to a lesser extent during the second. In light of the most recent evolution of the crisis and of the policy response analysed below, the third round of anticipated effects on employment are likely to concentrate precisely on public employment (mainly education, health and social services), with a higher share of women (62 per cent on average) and which constitutes today 31 per cent of total female employment.

Moreover, one out of four temporary jobs have disappeared (1.4 million) which means that more than half of all job losses have affected temporary workers, the easiest and cheapest to dismiss according to the Spanish law. As a consequence, the temporary rate has decreased from 29 per cent to 24 per cent. Although the most feminized sectors suffer from high rates of temporary employment, the concentration of job losses in construction and manufacturing has resulted in many more men on fixed-term contracts being affected and thus in a convergence of temporary employment rates, which used to be around 3 to 5 percentage points higher among women.

Without doubt, young workers have been the most affected by the crisis with massive job losses (Figure 12.3). Particularly worrying is the situation of young men and women under 25, with unemployment rates over 50 per cent, which could offset the former positive evolution in closing gender gaps of the younger cohorts. The opportunities for young men in construction, which encouraged many to quit formal school early, has made them into a more vulnerable group than young

TABLE 12.2 Sector segregation by sex and employment change in Spain 2008–2010, 2010–2012

| | | | Employment change (%) | | | | |
| | | | Women | | Men | | |
		Share of women (2008Q1)	2008Q1-2010Q1	2010Q1-2012Q1	2008Q1-2010Q1	2010Q1-2012Q1	Share of women (2012Q1)
Female-dominated sectors (>60%)*	Activities of households as employers	92.9	−1.7	−13.0	25.8	−8.1	92.7
	Human health and social work activities	76.6	11.6	6.0	10.5	4.5	77.6
	Other service activities	68.1	−9.2	0.0	−8.0	8.5	69.5
	Education	65.0	7.5	−0.2	−0.6	−1.3	63.2
Mixed activities	Administrative and support service activities	58.9	−8.2	−2.8	1.8	−3.1	59.2
	Accommodation and food service activities	55.7	−7.6	−8.7	−1.2	−1.7	56.7
	Real estate activities	49.8	−34.3	22.1	−27.6	9.7	48.3
	Wholesale and retail trade	49.3	−9.1	−1.6	−9.6	−2.3	49.2
	Professional, scientific and technical activities	47.9	0.8	−4.8	−7.4	0.0	47.5
	Financial and insurance activities	45.8	−8.3	−0.6	−8.5	−9.8	46.2
	Arts, entertainment and recreation	43.5	13.7	−12.6	11.1	−6.0	43.3
	Public administration and defence	41.2	13.0	2.3	13.2	−4.2	40.6
	Information and communication	34.0	−8.7	2.8	−3.5	2.6	34.4
Male-dominated sectors (>70%)#	Agriculture, forestry and fishing	28.2	−3.4	−13.5	−2.9	−4.1	25.5
	Manufacturing	26.1	−23.7	−6.1	−23.0	−6.9	25.0
	Electricity, gas, etc.	20.8	17.3	0.6	7.0	6.1	21.3
	Transportation and storage	17.6	−9.0	7.7	−7.4	−7.3	18.2
	Water supply, sewerage, waste management	16.9	−22.7	52.7	4.8	10.9	16.3
	Mining and quarrying	10.2	−31.5	67.6	−13.1	−23.0	8.0
	Construction	6.7	−16.3	−38.6	−39.3	−27.8	7.1
	Total – all NACE activities	41.6	−4.0	3.1	−14.1	−7.0	42.2

Source: Eurostat (2012) * >60% women in total employment; # >70% men in total employment.

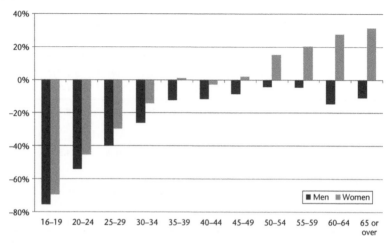

FIGURE 12.3 Accumulated employment change by age and sex in Spain, 2012 employment as percentage of 2008 level
Source: Eurostat (2012).

women. It is notable that men in all age groups have experienced employment losses, whereas women over 45 have even seen small employment gains[3]. Low-educated workers are also bearing the major burden of the crisis with 75 per cent of net job losses among the low qualified while high-educated employment has increased by 1.8 per cent during the crisis. Almost three out of every four women who have lost their job are low educated but for every low-educated woman who has lost their job more than three low-qualified men have lost theirs.

In contrast to the general employment trends, part-time employment has increased slightly (2.3 per cent) during the crisis, constituting a kind of refuge or a forced option for many. In fact, in 2008 and 2009 working time reduction was promoted as an alternative to dismissals in collective redundancy procedures. The result is that the increase in part-time has been concentrated exclusively on men, with a 20 per cent increase, in contrast to a slight reduction among women (2 per cent compared to 7 per cent total female employment drop). However, since it constitutes a minor share of men's jobs (6 per cent in 2012), women are still the vast majority of total part-timers (76 per cent). In light of expected further job destruction in 2012, the question is whether these trends in male and female part-time work will continue and whether part-time work will constitute a refuge or a source of further employment precariousness.

The household and individual strategies adopted to cope with the economic downturn reveal some interesting patterns worthy of further analysis. Whereas men have reacted to their massive job losses in part by retiring from the labour market (300,000 men became inactive during the four years), some 800,000 women have in contrast entered the labour market to counteract family income losses from higher male unemployment. While a higher education level has deterred men from leaving the labour market (the high educated recording only -0.4 percentage points activity rate drop compared to -1.3 among the low qualified), exactly the opposite has occurred among women, who have become more active the lower their education level (7 percentage point increase among the low qualified and only 1.6. among the higher educated), confirming the household compensating strategy. On the other hand, women aged 35–59, with traditionally lower activity, have increased their activity more than others, thus equalizing, to some extent, activity rates across age brackets.

Also the impact of parenthood on female employment rates (Table 12.3) has decreased over the period, although it is still negative (and still positive among men). Hence, having children below six reduces the probability of women entering or remaining in the labour market by 21.9 percentage points more than that of men. Low education levels make participation of these women even more difficult,

TABLE 12.3 Employment rates by sex and type of household in Spain 2008–2010

Age of the youngest child	Men (aged 20–49)(%)		Women (aged 20–49)(%)		Gender gap	Gender gap evolution
	2008	2010	2008	2010	2010	2008–2010
Total						
With no children	81	70.1	76.2	70.3	0.2	−5
Children less than 6	87.7	79.7	59.5	57.8	−21.9	−6.3
Children 6–11	87.3	78.9	64.8	62.9	−16	−6.5
Children 12 or over	84.9	74.8	66.4	62.1	−12.7	−5.8
Low educated						
With no children	74.4	59.9	64.2	57.1	−2.8	−7.4
Children less than 6	82.6	70.7	42.5	41.1	−29.6	−10.5
Children 6–11	82.1	71.9	54.2	49	−22.9	−5
Children 12 or over	83.6	72.1	57.9	53.1	−19	−6.7
Medium educated						
With no children	82.3	73.2	76.4	71.3	−1.9	−4
Children less than 6	87.8	81.5	60.6	58.4	−23.1	−4.1
Children 6–11	90.2	79.8	68.6	65.5	−14.3	−7.3
Children 12 or over	85.1	76.3	69.1	65.3	−11	−5
High educated						
With no children	90.1	80.8	84.5	78.4	−2.4	−3.2
Children less than 6	95	90.9	75.6	73.6	−17.3	−2.1
Children 6–11	94.1	89.9	78.7	78.6	−11.3	−4.1
Children 12 or over	87.1	78.8	78.6	73.9	−4.9	−3.6

Source: Eurostat (2012).

so that their employment rate only reached 41.1 per cent in 2010 and the gender gap was close to 30 percentage points. However, in line with the findings described above, it is precisely among this group of men and women that the gap has closed most since the beginning of the crisis (10.5 percentage points less than in 2008), meaning that low-educated women with children under six are not leaving the labour market as before.

In a context of negative employment trends, the most vulnerable groups of women seem to be carrying the heaviest burden of the crisis. The crisis has affected their social roles and thereby changed the relationships between women and men. Some of them bring the only income into their household as they have kept their jobs or found new ones while their partners were dismissed. Female and male employment rates have converged and the impact of parenthood is reduced, although largely due to a worsening position for men. Moreover, as household responsibilities are not equally shared, this 'progress' involves an additional heavy burden which many women have to add to their family responsibilities, almost suffocating them in a context of low incomes and economic pressures. As a conse-quence of the crisis and the austerity packages described later in this chapter, women, particularly the lowest qualified, may have to choose between the devil and the deep blue sea: looking for increasingly precarious and scarce jobs or exiting the labour market and returning to their gender-imposed home-based roles.

The worst effect of the crisis is the dramatic rise in unemployment. Up to the first quarter of 2012, the number of unemployed had grown in four years by two-thirds from 3.3 million workers to 5.3 million workers. If young workers aged 15–19 are also included, the total unemployed rises to 5.6 million workers, pushing up the unemployment rate to 24.4 per cent (24.1 for men and 24.9 for women). The increased participation of women has resulted in their higher unemployment rate, particularly among the low educated.

Since unemployment grew faster among men, male and female rates have con-verged. This reduction of the gender gap is thanks, however, to a deterioration of both female and male unemployment rates, especially for the low-educated. In this case, 'equality' has implied that everyone is worse off. Moreover, unemployed women are still less likely to exit unemployment and find a job in the coming months and years, since many have only recently entered the labour market after prolonged periods of inactivity. A likely outcome is that the unemployment gender gap will rise again when the economy eventually recovers.

The policy responses

The initial policy response was counter-cyclical, with expansive and expensive measures adopted to cushion the negative effects of the economic downturn, par-ticularly in the male-dominated construction, financial and automotive sectors. After a while, however, the Spanish government faced pressure from the EU institutions and the financial markets to implement orthodox fiscal consolidation packages and structural reforms and a first wave of standard reforms (labour market, collective bargaining, pension system) were initiated in May 2010.

Economic policies have been addressed through a 'gender-blind' approach, particularly since this date. After a timid economic recovery at the end of 2010 and the first half of 2011, the sovereign debt crisis in the second half of 2011 led to further deterioration in the situation. After the general election in November 2011, the new conservative government, under much pressure from EU institutions and the increasing risk premiums for Spanish debt[4], begun passing a package of tougher policy measures aimed at regaining the confidence of the markets and the EU. These include large public spending cuts, more and/or tougher structural reforms, such as new labour market reforms and the never-ending financial reforms. After several financial reforms since the beginning of the crisis, the Spanish government has had to seek aid for recapitalizing its financial system, which still has enormous amounts of 'toxic' assets due to the bursting of the real estate bubble. In turn, the austerity measures announced in July 2012 can be interpreted as the counterpart to the Eurozone bailout.

The first wave of austerity measures (May 2010–November 2011)

In May 2010 a first set of policy measures was passed, aimed at showing foreign investors and the EU that the effects of the crisis were being addressed and controlled. In this context, equality policies suffered severe shocks, which are symbolized by the short life of the Equality Ministry, established only in 2008 and closed on 20 October 2010 for – ridiculous – savings reasons. This has been part of a broader process in which gender institutions in some regional administrations have been withdrawn, again in theory for cost reasons. However, given the relatively small savings, these developments are more an 'austerity' message, showing that it is important to save and that the gender equality objective is a kind of waste we can no longer afford. The gender equality policy has been integrated in the Health and Social Services *and Equality* Ministry. This downgrading has relevant consequences for equality policies, both practical and symbolical. It decreases the consideration of gender problems in public policies (identified as a sort of capricious luxury issue no longer affordable) and hampers the coordination of multi-ministerial, multi-level and territorial equality policies among the diverse public administrations (González and Castellanos 2011c, 2011f; González et al. 2011). Certainly, the capacity of a minister to influence policies is considerably higher than that of, for example, a director general.

Another disappointing initiative from a gender perspective is the delay in the extension of paternity leave. The extension from 13 days to 28 should have been adopted in January 2011 but was postponed to 2012, again on savings grounds. The new government has postponed it again until 2013. The discriminatory situation between maternity and paternity leaves and the lack of action in this regard does not contribute to achieving an equality model. Besides, since it is a decision by the mother whether or not to transfer part of the maternity leave to the father, the model does not foster co-responsibility, thereby reinforcing gender stereotypes.

A medium-term element especially damaging for women's economic and social situation is the pension system reform. The most controversial measure in the public debate has been the raising of the retirement age from 65 to 67 but substantial and far-reaching debates concerning its gender effects have been almost absent. The entitlement to receive the full pension will require paying contributions for 38.5 years and not the current 35 years, regardless of the pensioner's age which, given women's labour market participation, will affect a larger number of women than men (González and Castellanos 2011d). Moreover, the pension calculation basis will also be tightened and will take into account the last 25 years of working life, 10 more than the current 15 years. The minimum contributory period required for having a right to a contributory pension is 15 years, too many for many women and it has not been changed by the reform.

The purchasing power of the minimum wage has been reduced as it was not raised fully in line with the cost of living in 2010 and 2011. This negative trend has two important consequences: firstly, it produces a negative effect on the rest of the wage system, especially for the lowest paid; secondly, the minimum wage is used as a reference for calculating other benefits. Women's economic situation is expected to be affected since they have lower-paid jobs and they heavily depend on those benefits related to non-contributory schemes that are calculated based on minimum wage levels.

In May 2010, public servants' wages were cut by 5 per cent on average, with higher wages reduced more than lower ones. Although these cuts could have slightly improved the gender pay gap within the public administration as women's average salaries are lower than men's, they also constitute a significantly regressive measure from a gender perspective, since women are more affected due to their higher participation in public employment (7 percentage points above men in 2010, while their private sector share is 11 percentage points lower than men's). However, the freezing of public pensions from 2011 onwards may have acted more to the detriment of men as those who receive the minimum and non-contributory pensions were excluded from the freeze, the majorty of whom are women.

The further development of long-term care benefits was suspended. The so-called Dependency Law (*Ley de Dependencia*) was passed in 2006 and together with the creation of the Ministry for Equality, constituted one of the most important policy measures adopted in the field of equal opportunities. According to the Law, the target population is classified in three groups according to their dependency level (moderate, severe and great). In case that local and regional administration does not provide the elderly care services (domiciliary care, home help services, day care centres, etc.) foreseen in the Law, seriously dependent people can ask for monetary benefits that can be used to pay somebody (including a member of the family) to care for them. This pathway came to a stop in 2010 and the assigned budget was cut which was in practice at the expense of women, either as beneficiaries or as workers.

Furthermore, a €2,500 subsidy for new parents irrespective of their income (called 'baby-check') was removed in 2011. It had been set up in 2007 and was aimed at increasing a low birth rate. Though controversial, it was a relevant help for low-income families.

The VAT rise, from 16 per cent to 18 per cent in 2010, has a more severe impact on those with less purchasing power and saving capacities. While Spain has both the scope and the need to raise taxes to finance the needs of the welfare state, as the tax burden in Spain is amongst the lowest in the EU, nevertheless raising VAT as an indirect tax affects more those with lower incomes, such as the unemployed, poor workers, retired people and pensioners. Women are, in all four cases, the most vulnerable group. It is notable that the scope to charge, for instance, capital gains and/or CO_2 emissions, has not been used.

Moreover, all these initiatives aimed at reducing public spending were complemented by further cutbacks in public spending by regional and local governments, responsible for the biggest spending areas related to public education, health and social services. However, as the limited reduction of fiscal deficit achieved in 2010 and 2011 shows, the reduction in public spending was not enough to offset diminishing public revenues, giving momentum for a new wave of cuts in 2012.

In regard to the much touted 'structural reforms', a labour market reform was passed in June 2010 aimed at fighting segmentation in the labour market through a gradual *downwards* equalization of firing costs of temporary and permanent contracts. Additionally, a collective bargaining reform was approved in June 2011; here the most important point was the decentralization of collective bargaining, thereby increasing the importance of company level agreements and individual bargaining between workers and employers, to the detriment of sectoral and regional bargaining. While collective bargaining in Spain is far from gender sensitive, the employers' sensitivity towards gender issues is even lower, so that a direct negotiation procedure between women and employers is most likely to lead to a deterioration in women's position.

The second wave of austerity measures (December 2011–)

All these policy measures and reforms implemented during 2010 and 2011 have not been able to stabilize the Spanish economy. The conclusions reached by the European institutions and the Spanish government have not been that the recipes are not effective for solving the most severe current problems[5] and that the approach is obviously not working. On the contrary, the lesson learned is that more of the same is needed. Thus, an invigorated wave of austerity measures has been deemed necessary after the change to a conservative government. In the face of a further deteriorating economy, an even more drastic strategy has been adopted with the objective of calming the financial markets and the EU, both still concerned by the disappointing trends in public deficit. The strategy adopted is, however, exactly the same and will very likely deliver the same disappointing results. It consists of the same two key elements as in the previous period, but reinforced: brutal fiscal consolidation on the one hand; and new and/or new versions of the former structural reforms on the other.

Accordingly, a new Budget Stability Organic Law (*Ley Orgánica de Estabilidad Presupuestaria*) has been passed to enforce all administrative levels (especially the regional and local governments) to meet a balanced budget. Some taxes have been increased (VAT to 23 per cent, income, corporate and property taxes) and public spending cuts amounting to some €22 billion have been approved. This has been accompanied by an anti-fraud plan against undeclared work and people receiving unemployment benefits unlawfully; and a so-called temporary 'fiscal amnesty' aimed at repatriating capital from tax havens.

In this context, public enterprises and, in general, civil servants have become one of the targets of the austerity measures in what could be understood as a broader strategy to downgrade their working conditions, their public image and reputation, and, even more importantly, the very image of the welfare state. Public enterprises that 'do not pass an objective utility test'[6] and public services that do not prove to be 'profitable' are to be cut, as if public services had to be subject to private business criteria. Accordingly, some measures have been announced to downsize areas of public administration and reduce the provision of public services. A brief summary of the most important austerity measures follows.

The public health system has been the object of a significant reform to reduce public spending. A new national catalogue of basic services will exclude some important services (non-urgent ambulance transport, for instance) and/or introduce new co-payment for some services, such as diagnostic tests. In this context, primary care for illegal immigrants has been cancelled (except for emergencies, children and pregnancies). Additionally, pensioners, who used to be entitled to free medicines, are now subject to a co-payment of 10 per cent of their costs of medicines, up to a monthly maximum of €8 (for those with annual pensions below €18,000). However, among these pensioners 59 per cent of women and 28 per cent of men receive less than the minimum wage (641.4 euros/month in 2012); that is far below the income limit, so that the chronically ill elderly will bear a high cost. The co-payment rate increases also for active workers (from the current 40 per cent to 50 or 60 per cent depending on income).

The dismantling of the public long-term care system (dependency system) is in progress as the whole strategy is being revised. Funding of regional retirement homes and social services centres has been drastically decreased; public assistance to moderately dependent people has been temporarily cancelled; the assistance to 176,916 people in their homes is expected to be eliminated; the payments to family carers (mainly women) has been cut by 15 per cent and their social security contributions have been eliminated.

Public education is also at stake. The 'Educa3 Plan' for supporting under three year olds pre-primary school infrastructures, a response to Country Specific Recommendations made by the European Union to Spain several times in the past, has been cancelled. In order to reduce the number of teachers needed, their weekly working hours have been extended and regional governments are allowed to increase the ratio of students per classroom by 20 per cent. University fees have been increased (especially for immigrants) and access conditions to scholarships tightened. Moreover, new regular vocational training courses that should provide young people with new competences demanded by companies have been postponed until 2014.

Female employment is expected to be hit hard as public employment recruitment came to a stop at the end of 2011 and public job losses are expected in 2012. Moreover, civil servants' working time has been increased to 37.5 weekly hours and sick leaves will be penalized. According to the Labour Force Survey (2012), in 2012Q1 women represented 55 per cent of civil servants and were overrepresented in the areas most affected (67 per cent in education, 73 per cent in health and 87 per cent in long-term care). The real wages of female and male public servants have diminished. Besides, women benefit more from these services, particularly from pre-primary education and long-term care. The cancellation of the pre-primary school 'Educa3 Plan' and the elder care cuts will hamper the incorporation of women into the labour market. The savings made are likely to be paid for by less and worse employment for women and less equality.

A new comprehensive labour market reform has been passed in February 2012. After several attempts in recent years, this one intends again to reduce the segmentation of the labour market by: *once and for all* easing and making cheaper the firing of permanent workers; increasing internal flexibility mainly through the changes in the collective bargaining; promoting more precarious open-ended contracts with the aim of creating employment; and enhancing individuals' employability through training. It is a comprehensive and profound reform that can change the functioning of the Spanish labour market substantially. The results are yet to be seen, but some can be advanced. The reduction of segmentation in the labour market could in principle lead to a convergence in labour conditions between fixed-term and permanent workers. Although this could potentially reduce the gender gap in employment contracts, it might be achieved through a downward equalization with no reduction in precariousness for women. Additionally, a lesser but still important difference remains between fixed-term and permanent contracts[7], so that segmentation and precariousness will not disappear.

Moreover, the changes in the collective bargaining system can be seen as one of the most serious attempts to transform the most powerful institutions within the labour market. Changes affect three main features: employers' management decisions can effectively suspend collective agreements on economic grounds (defined as current or expected losses during two consecutive quarters); the collective agreements at firm level are given priority over other levels (provincial, sectoral, national, etc.); the so-called ultra-activity is no longer valid which specifically means that in case a collective agreement is denounced or social partners do not reach a new agreement, the prevailing agreement can no longer hold for more than one year. These changes are supposed to contribute to improving firms' competitiveness as they seek to introduce internal flexibility rather than resorting to individual and collective dismissals in recessionary contexts. However, the reform entails an unbalanced transformation of labour relations in favour of the employers, as workers are given little room for manoeuvre. Employers are now entitled to substantially modify working conditions without any significant possibility of reply by workers. This will eventually lead to specific groups of persons, particularly mothers or fathers with reconciliation needs, lacking protection. More specifically, a lack of gender perspective in the labour market regulation may impact negatively on female participation. For instance, some of the current labour rights associated with childbearing might be affected by the prevalence of firm or individual bargaining. Accordingly, reconciling working and family life and sharing responsibilities between women and men may become more difficult as, for instance, breastfeeding leave can no longer be simultaneously taken by mothers and fathers. Furthermore, the conditions through which internal flexibility has been introduced can be a restrictive factor as women may no longer be able to choose the time schedule to make effective this right, due to the fact that collective agreements can be modified for economic, technical and organizational reasons by the employer. The possibility of extending part-time working hours without modifying the labour contract can also be interpreted as another element that could eventually make reconciliation difficult.

Conclusions

The economic crisis in Spain began a bit later than in the rest of the EU but after numerous reforms and fiscal consolidation packages, the economy faces in 2012 a renewed recession and little prospect of overcoming its problems. Although obvious evidence exists that the measures and reforms have not worked and indeed that the most important problems (that is the situation of the financial sector in Spain and of the euro in the Eurozone) have not been adequately addressed, the approach currently adopted is to call for more of the same and with more intensity. Consequently, the expected results are also more of the same. The €100 billion bailout may partially help in recapitalizing banks' portfolios but the restoration of normal lending to the Spanish economy is yet to be seen. Thus, the European institutions and economic governance in the Eurozone have not been able to manage the crisis with the consequence not only that the situation in the bailout countries continues to deteriorate after the reforms imposed but also that the whole Eurozone remains at risk. The financial crisis is posing a serious challenge to the European institutional capacity-building with uncertain consequences for its credibility among citizens.

Four years of crisis *and* of gender blind and or damaging political responses have led to certain downwards convergence in gender gaps in employment and unemployment but not because of better conditions for women but to a worse situation for men. Still women continue to be worse off as regards the main indicators of the labour market.

Although the crisis initially hit men harder than women, its effects in terms of employment losses and unemployment have already spread to women and in the expected third phase women may experience harsher employment losses. The elimination of the gender equality infrastructure, such as the Ministry for Equality, has worsened the position and visibility of women. Furthermore, women are clearly more affected by the reduction in public sector wages, the real term reduction in the minimum wage, the pension reforms and the general public spending cuts in health, education, family and well-being policies. The delay in the extension of paternity leave is also a step backward, away from a more equal family model. The strengthened austerity package recently adopted and the associated downsizing of the welfare state will affect women both as workers and as carers and thus as beneficiaries of primary school facilities, long-term care systems and other social services.

Whereas women have reacted by entering the labour market to offset the family income losses from their partners' redundancy, the awareness of the importance of women's contribution for families and the economy in emerging from the crisis is almost non-existent. Women, particularly the lower educated, are bearing a heavy cost in the form of a double or triple workload, in a context of family responsibilities not shared by men and of low incomes and economic constraints. The new austerity package will increase their precariousness and there is even a risk that they may leave the labour market due to lack of support. The savings made in early education and long-term care will have to be paid for by reduced female employment.

Additionally, only some institutions and NGOs specifically devoted to gender have analysed and highlighted the gender impact of the measures adopted, and these assessments have had limited resonance in national debates[8]. In general, the message is that the situation is difficult enough without having to attend to such minor issues. It is now evident that all actors, including all levels of government, trade unions or employers' associations, have proved incapable of introducing a serious gender perspective into reform negotiations whether on the labour market, pensions or other topics. The position of the EU has not helped as gender mainstreaming principles have not been used in its policies and strategies, especially in those related to economic policy. The crisis is unfortunately changing the perception of the urgency and importance of addressing gender imbalances in the Spanish society.

The impact of the economic crisis and the policy response in relation to women is depressing so far and for the foreseeable future. Even if one imagines an eventual economic recovery, whenever it will occur, the likely outcome is far from heartening. The basis for an unbalanced future growth has been laid and women risk seeing their social role and autonomy eroded in a context of renewed economic pressures and austerity packages, but also in a context of eventual growth. The gender mainstreaming infrastructures, the sensitivity to gender issues and the role of the welfare state in promoting equality have all been seriously damaged, These developments could lead to a reversal of the progress that the Spanish gender agenda has made during the last 20 years.

Notes

1 Approved at the Euro Area Summit on 29 June 2012 and followed by agreement of an up to €100 billion aid after the signature of the Memorandum of Understanding. At the time of writing, the aid has not yet been delivered and the country risk premium is around 450 basis points (November 2012).
2 The source for the employment data is Eurostat (Labour Force Survey) or the National Statistics Institute (also LFS).
3 Among women aged between 40 and 64, these increases have mainly occurred in public administration (92,800), social work and residential care (80,200), education (46,100), health (44,500) and retail trade activities (39,400).
4 This risk premium is defined as the difference between the average yield on German and Spanish ten-year bonds in the financial markets and in this case reflects investors' expectations about the Spanish financial evolution.
5 Several international institutions, among which ILO (2012), IMF (2012) and OECD (2012), have warned against the risk of such an approach in a context of economic recession, and have raised doubts about the feasibility of reaching the public deficit target in 2012.
6 According to a statement made by a high government official, http://politica.elpais.com/politica/2012/05/03/actualidad/1336042755_148092.html.
7 The severance pay for open-ended contracts has been practically reduced from 45 to 20 days per year worked, while temporary workers are entitled to receive 8 days per year worked.
8 Following the Equality Law 3/2007, all important legislative measures need a gender impact assessment report. The Ministry for Employment has provided a five-page report on the gender effects of the labour market reform and the Ministry for Economy and Public Finances a 480-page report on the general budget. However, both the quality of the reports and the positive assessment made on the gender impact of the labour reform and the 2012 General Budget are symptoms of the low sensitivity of both ministries to gender.

References

Acosta Ballesteros, J. and Osorno del Rosal, M.P. (2009) 'Transiciones laborales desde el empleo temporal y temporalidad regional', Santa Cruz de Tenerife, Instituto Universitario de Desarrollo Regional, Departamento de Análisis Económico, Universidad de la Laguna, (working paper). Available at: http://www.alde.es/encuentros/anteriores/xiieea/trabajos/pdf/106.pdf (accessed 11.05.2013).

Caparrós, A. and Navarro, M. (2006) 'Precariedad y transiciones laborales: un análisis con datos de panel', Granada, address delivered in the XV Workshop of the Education Economy Association, 18 and 19 September 2006. Available at: http://www.economic-sofeducation.com/wp-content/uploads/granada2006/24%20Precariedad%20y%20transiciones.pdf (accessed 11.05.2013).

Conde-Ruíz, J.I., Felgueroso, F., García Pérez, J.I. (2010) 'Las Reformas Laborales en España: un modelo agotado', ('Labour Market Reforms in Spain: an Exhausted Model'), *Papeles de Economía Española*, 124: 128–47. Available at: http://www.fedea.es/pub/est_economicos/2010/11-2010.pdf (accessed 11.05.2013).

FUNCAS (2013) 'Panel de previsiones de la economía española', Fundación Española de las Cajas de Ahorro, 16 May 2013. Available at: http://www.funcas.es/Indicadores/Indicadores.aspx?Id=1 (updated: 22 May 2013).

González Gago, E. and Castellanos Serrano C. (2011a) 'Spain: Pre-assessment of the 2011 National Reform Programme (SYSDEM experts)', European Employment Observatory (interim report).

—— (2011b) 'Adapting Unemployment Benefit Systems to the Economic Cycle. Spain', European Employment Observatory, Autumn Review 2011. Available at: http://www. eu-employment-observatory.net/resources/reviews/EEOReview-UB-2011-EN-OOPEC.pdf (accessed 11.05.2013).

—— (2011c) 'Crisis and Recovery in Europe. Labour Market Impact on Men and Women', National Report Spain. EGGE (Network of Experts in Gender Equality, Social Inclusion, Health and Long-term Care).

—— (2011d) 'The Socio-economic Impact of Pension Systems on the Respective Situations of Women and Men and the Effects of Recent Trends in Pension Reforms', National Report Spain, in Samek, M. *et al.* (2011) 'The Socio-economic Impact of Pension Systems on the Respective Situations of Women and Men and the Effects of Recent Trends in Pension Reforms Synthesis Report', EGGSI (Expert Group on Gender Equality, Social Inclusion, Health and Long-term Care Issues).

González Gago, E., Segales Kirzner, M. and Castellanos Serrano, C. (2011) 'The Impact of the Economic Crisis on the Situation of Women and Men and on Gender Equality Policies. National Report: Spain' in F. Bettio, M. Corsi, M. Samek, A. Verashchagina (2011) 'The Impact of the Economic Crisis on the Situation of Women and Men and on Gender Equality Policies', EGGE/ EGGSI networks.

Hidalgo Vega, A. (2007). La Discriminación Laboral de la Mujer: Una Década a Examen, Universidad de Castilla-La Mancha, Madrid: Studies and Researches Collection, Women's Institute, Equality Ministry. Available at: http://www.navarra.es/NR/rdonlyres/D91FE499-4898-4EDD-AA09-213A8AF122EA/192683/discriminacionlaboralmujer.pdf (accessed 11.05.2013).

IMF (2012) *World Economic Outlook April 2012: Growth Resuming, Danger Remain,* Washington DC: IMF. Available at: http://www.imf.org/external/pubs/ft/weo/2012/01/pdf/text.pdf (accessed 11.05.2013).

ILO (2012) *World of Work Report 2012: Better Jobs for a Better Economy*, Geneva: International Institute for Labour Studies, ILO.

OECD (2012) *OECD Economic Outlook 2012* (preliminary version), Paris: OECD, 22 May. Available at: http://www.oecd.org/finance/monetaryandfinancialissues/49995435.pdf (accessed 11.05.2013).

Toharía, L. and Cebrián, I. (2008) 'La Entrada en el Mercado de Trabajo: Un Análisis Basado en la MCLV', *Revista de Economía Aplicada*, E-1:16, 137–72.

13

LIVING THROUGH THE CRISIS IN ITALY

The labour market experiences of men and women

Alina Verashchagina and Marina Capparucci

Introduction

Italy is normally classified together with Greece, Portugal and Spain in a group of familialistic countries which adhere to a Southern European employment model (see for example Karamessini 2008; Ciccia 2010). In Italy the family serves as both an element of the production system (via small family firms and, sometimes, the hidden economy) and a source of support through sharing of income and care especially in hard times. But the reality is such that this family system cannot cope with the globalizing world or absorb the disruptive effects of a major crisis in employment and income. The crisis in Italy is also related to the accumulation of an excessive public debt of the range of 100 per cent of GDP, second highest in Europe after Greece. This is another complication which also renders managing the crisis rather difficult for the state.

Apart from a very low female employment rate compared to the EU average, the Italian labour market is also characterized by great regional disparities particularly evident in the case of women. Just before the eruption of the current crisis the female employment rate was almost twice as high in the North relative to the South, while female unemployment was three times higher in the South than in the North. Large regional disparities are also found in the availability of social care services and in the gender regime.

The first wave of the crisis was felt mainly by men involved in those sectors which were hit most by the recession but now that the second wave is gaining in strength, women may feel it more than men as budget cuts are reducing the provision of public services for which women are the main beneficiaries (e.g. education and health). This inevitably affects women's labour market position, both directly via cuts in women's jobs and indirectly via greater difficulties in reconciliation between paid and unpaid work at home.

The strategies which are being developed by families and women to cope with the crisis reveal both challenges and opportunities for a more egalitarian gendered division of labour. Italy has one of the highest shares of male-breadwinner couples in Europe, but the crisis may be eroding this model. When men are facing problems in the labour market, women are often forced into work in order to sustain the family. Whether newly mobilized women will remain in the labour market after the crisis depends largely on the policy actions that are being taken now. These need urgently to address the increasing gender segregation and gender pay gap, trends which are undermining the quality of female employment opportunities in Italy.

The chapter is structured as follows. We start by introducing the Italian context pre-crisis by describing the evolution of the gender regime. The following section explores: the labour market impact of the crisis; changes in employment, unemployment and inactivity by gender related to gender segregation; the gender pay gap; contractual arrangements; and persisting regional differences. Special attention is paid to vulnerable groups such as young workers, mothers and foreigners. This is followed by a discussion of the main policy initiatives expected to have an impact on gender equality, in particular the ongoing labour market reforms. The chapter concludes by considering prospects for gender equality.

The gender regime in Italy: the slow evolution towards equality

Traditional gender roles underpin the employment regime that is typical for Mediterranean countries (Karamessini 2008; Villa 2012). Men work full-time in secure jobs throughout their working life, while women provide the largest part of care and domestic work which reduces their presence in the labour market. This model is now becoming not only obsolete but also increasingly incoherent. One problem, 'the Mediterranean paradox' (Bettio and Villa 1998), was identified in the mid-1990s, whereby low female employment was associated with low fertility rates in a cross-country perspective. These effects are now aggravated by rising life expectancy, both resulting in an ageing population which calls into question the long-term sustainability of the Mediterranean model. Within Italy there has also been a growing gap in both participation rates and fertility rates between the Northern regions and the South (Picchi 2012: Fig. 1, p. 9), although the higher fertility rates (North-East 1.47, North-West 1.45 compared to 1.35 in the South) are primarily explained by the higher share of migrant women in the North, who have higher fertility rates than Italian women.

From the early 1970s to mid-1990s women's labour force participation has grown only slowly, starting from one of the lowest bases in Europe. Some scholars attributed the slow growth to supply side factors whereby being a housewife was still seen as a privilege;[1] others instead pointed to persistent problems on the demand side.[2]

From the mid-1990s and until the crisis the pace of female integration intensified due to the growing service sector, the increase in part-time jobs, and flexibilization of work hours. The change was also fuelled by an inflow of migrant women performing domestic and care jobs, freeing higher income women from part of the constraints of domestic work. The transformation has nevertheless been slow, partly because there has been little change in men's roles.

The evolution of the gender regime has not been homogeneous across the Italian regions; some of the Northern provinces (Bolzano, Emilia-Romagna, Valle d'Aosta) have levels of female employment above the European average while the South still lags far behind. This widening of the gap has occurred despite an apparent convergence of attitudes towards work among women living in the North and in the South of Italy (Andreotti and Mingione 2012). It reveals in fact the structural problems in the South, where poor investment, low productivity and scarce labour demand remain crucial.

Increasing educational attainments for women over recent decades has been one of the main factors driving the change in female labour market attachment (Simonazzi and Villa 2010). The percentage of women who were housewives halved between 1971 and 2001 (Andreotti and Mingione 2012, Tab. 3.2). This notwithstanding, every second working-age woman in Italy still does not work. This can be seen as a waste of human capital, especially in view of the fact that women nowadays outnumber men among the university students.

The growth in women's employment since mid-1990 occurred mainly via increases in the number employed in the Centre-North (+1.5m.), with only a marginal contribution from the South (+200k). Women in the South have been the main target group for employment policies (ISTAT 2012) as they have not been able to find viable jobs after the contraction in agricultural employment. Higher female attachment to the labour market has thus resulted in increasing unemployment rather than higher employment rates for women. Most new job opportunities in the South, especially for high-educated women, are in the public sector which is known to provide more possibilities for reconciling paid work with family care. Mainly for this reason those few women who manage to find a job in the South tend to remain in employment throughout their working life. Low-educated women are, however, often relegated to the home due to poor employment conditions and low pay. The North and the South also differ considerably in their care infrastructures but even in the better provided North, there is insufficient support considering the already high female labour force participation rendering the issue of reconciliation rather acute. The coverage rate of childcare services for children under three years of age is approaching 30 per cent in some Northern regions (Emilia-Romagna and Val d'Aosta), though the average is lower, but it remains at less than two per cent in Calabria and Campania. The most frequent alternatives include relying on grandmothers' help or the use of private facilities. With the increase in retirement age for women the availability of grandmothers is going to reduce, while the cost of private services is rather high, ranging from €600 per month for a nursery place to €1000 for a child minder (Andreotti and Mingione 2012) compared to €300 for a place at a public nursery (Picchi 2012). These figures should be compared to the net average wage of €1300 per month and only €900 for newly employed workers (ISTAT 2011).

Italy is moreover characterized by asymmetries in the distribution of time spent on housework between men and women of all social classes and regions. The time Italian women spend on unpaid family work remains the highest among the 14 European countries considered in the recent study by Francavilla *et al.* (2013). Time use surveys record little change in the distribution of roles within the family over the last 20 years. Having children is becoming ever more of a burden for women in addition to the paid job. Among couples where both partners are in paid work (and the female partner is aged 25–44), the total amount of working time, paid and unpaid, in 2008–9, was on average 53 minutes longer for a woman compared to male partner (ISTAT 2011: Fig. 3.20, p. 156). Where there are children the difference is 62 minutes and in the South the gap is even more pronounced, at 93 minutes. These gaps are quite atypical for developed countries, where the totals of paid and unpaid work for men and women, when both partners work, are in the same range (Miranda 2011: Fig. 7, p. 15).

Labour market impact of the crisis on men and women

The first signs of the crisis in Italy appeared in the second quarter of 2008, when GDP declined by 0.7 percentage points compared to the first quarter (EC 2010: Tab. 1, p. 22). It was thus among the first countries hit by the recession. The employment effects became more evident as the crisis turned from financial to fiscal: the worsening of the public accounts was in fact the result of state interventions aimed at supporting those sectors initially most hit by the crisis (banking and financial sector), coupled with reduced tax receipts due to both lower incomes and a smaller employment base.

Segregation initially protected female workers although the higher incidence of atypical (part-time and temporary) contracts among women made them more vulnerable as the crisis progressed. The delayed effects of the crisis on employment for women are now becoming even more evident, especially in view of the budget cuts. Implemented in order to reduce an excessive public debt, these affect women via two main channels: through the reduction of social services of which women are the main beneficiaries (such as health and education), rendering reconciliation of family and working life more complicated; and through the cuts in jobs in the public sector which remains the principal resort for women.

Employment and working conditions have become generally worse, with increased pressure on wages, lower work hours and less employment security. Moreover, high unemployment is leading to sharp competition for jobs and definitely does not help women's entry into the labour force. On the one hand it discourages entry into the labour force, on the other hand it keeps workers in a state of alert, compelling them to accept what they would otherwise not accept.

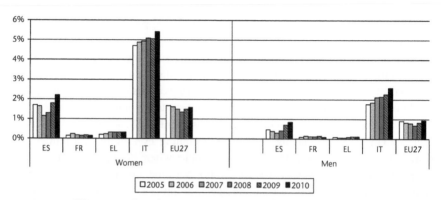

FIGURE 13.1 Discouraged workers as a percentage of the working age population in Italy 2005–2010

Note: Discouraged workers are persons who are not seeking work, because they believe that none is available, but would nevertheless like to have a job.

Source: own calculation using LFS data.

At the start of the crisis, the share of discouraged workers in Italy was in fact two to three times higher than the EU average, and it increased over the first three years for which the data is available (Figure 13.1). Importantly, the increase in discouragement rate during the crisis has been of the same range for both men and women, at about 1.5 percentage points.

Empirical research (Ghignoni and Verashchagina 2012) suggests that although the discouraged worker effect prevailed at the start of the crisis, there are now signs of the added worker effect but only in the Centre-South of Italy and for low-educated women. This means that the crisis has some (however small) potential to push forward change in the prevailing male-breadwinner model, but only once labour demand has begun to expand.

The next sections explore the most recent developments in the Italian labour market and their impact on gender equality in more detail.

Employment, unemployment and inactivity

The first wave of the crisis lasted until 2010Q1 and reduced the total employment rate from 59.2 per cent in 2008Q1 to 56.8 per cent. Afterwards there was a mild recovery but it did not last long. Already by the second half of 2011 the second wave of the crisis had hit and by 2012Q1 the employment rate had fallen to 56.5 per cent, comparable to that in 2003. It is also the lowest since the start of the crisis.

Table 13.1 shows that men lost (and continue losing) more jobs than women and also that male inactivity has increased a lot and is still on the rise. Conversely, after an initial fall in women's employment, there were some signs of improvement over 2010–11. In fact, female employment gains in 2010–11 of 106k exactly

TABLE 13.1 Changes in employment, unemployment and inactivity in Italy 2008–2011

	Men Δ 000s (Δ rates)	Women Δ 000s (Δ rates)
2008–2010		
Employment	−408 (−2.6%)	−106 (−1.1%)
Unemployment	+294 (+2.1%)	+119 (+1.2%)
Inactivity	+260 (+1.1%)	+206.2 (+0.6%)
2010–2011		
Employment	−20 (−0.2%)	+106.2. (+0.4%)
Unemployment	+1.2 (0%)	+4.6 (−0.1%)
Inactivity	+54.3 (+0.2%)	−33.5 (−0.4%)

Note: Δ rates = percentage point change.
Source: own elaboration using ISTAT data.

compensated for losses during the first three years of the crisis and female inactivity started to decline.

Segregation

As documented in earlier work (Bettio 1988; Rubery 1988) the behaviour of male and female employment over the cycle is largely affected by job segregation. The crisis was felt most in manufacturing and construction. While the former is catching up slowly again, the latter is continuing to shrink (Bank of Italy 2012). Manufacturing has seen a drop of approximately 450,000 jobs, which accounts for the majority of total net job losses; men lost about 299,000 jobs while women lost 151,000, but this represents a higher share of job losses than would be expected given their 21.3 per cent share of employment in manufacturing before the crisis.

The over-representation of women in the service sector, usually less sensitive to fluctuations in aggregate demand, tends to render women's employment also less sensitive to cyclical conditions – though, within any given workplace or particular job, female workers may still be more vulnerable than males, as the data concerning manufacturing appear to indicate. Women's segregation in services has not only sheltered women from higher job losses but even allowed them to benefit from net job creation in the service sector (+2.3 per cent) (see Figure 13.2). The gains are mainly in services to families and individuals, jobs which are often filled by migrant women. The increase may also reflect the better representation of migrant workers in the statistics due to a 2009 measure that facilitated the granting of work permits and incentivised the legalization of irregular immigrants.

The gender pay gap

Italy has a relatively low gender pay gap (GPG). But as econometric studies which take account of differences in both personal characteristics of male and female

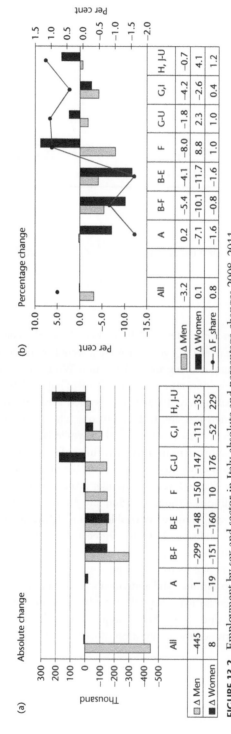

FIGURE 13.2 Employment by sex and sector in Italy, absolute and percentage changes 2008–2011

Note: A – Agriculture, forestry and fishing; B-F – Total industry; B-E – Manufacturing; F – Construction; F – Manufacturing; B-E – Total industry; G, I – Commerce, hotels and restaurants; H, J-U – Other services. Panel (b): Percentage change for Δ Men and Δ Women; percentage point change for Δ F_share.

Source: own elaboration using ISTAT data.

Panel (a) — Absolute change (Thousand)

	All	A	B-F	B-E	F	G-U	G,I	H,J-U
Δ Men	-445	1	-299	-148	-150	-147	-113	-35
Δ Women	8	-19	-151	-160	10	176	-52	229

Panel (b) — Percentage change (Per cent)

	All	A	B-F	B-E	F	G-U	G,I	H,J-U
Δ Men	-3.2	0.2	-5.4	-4.1	-8.0	-1.8	-4.2	-0.7
Δ Women	0.1	-7.1	-10.1	-11.7	8.8	2.3	-2.6	4.1
Δ F_share	0.8	-1.6	-0.8	-1.6	1.0	1.0	0.4	1.2

TABLE 13.2 Gender pay gap in unadjusted form in Italy 2007–2010

Country	2007	2008	2009	2010
Italy	5.1	4.9	5.5	5.5[P]
EU27	17.6	17.4	16.9[P]	16.4[P]

Note: P – provisional value.
Source: Eurostat, online database.

workers and the difference in male versus female employment rates make clear, this is primarily due to female workers having higher average educational achievement than male workers. If one takes this into account the GPG in Italy quadruples, rising above 20 percentage points (Mandrone 2012: 252). The unadjusted GPG actually increased over the first two years of the crisis contrary to the general tendency observed for the whole of the EU, but still remained at a relatively low level (Table 13.2). The widening of the unadjusted gap, coupled with the high adjusted GPG, is worrying in view of the general tendency for labour incomes to reduce during the crisis. This suggests that many more working women than men may end up below the poverty line.

Contractual arrangements

Another issue is security in employment. Atypical contracts may be used by employers to reduce both labour costs and risks; part-time and short-term contracts have grown over recent years and involve predominantly younger workers and women, together with workers of foreign origin. However, the incidence of part-time contracts in Italy is still lower than the European average for both men and women: 6.4 per cent and 30.8 per cent respectively in 2012Q1 versus 8.5 per cent and 32.1 per cent in the EU27 (9.2 and 37.8 in the EU15). The rise during the crisis mainly affected women (+2.7 percentage points over 2008Q2–2012Q1), while it was lower for male workers (+1.2 percentage points). It is worth noting that the percentage of involuntary part-time increased considerably for both men and women, by more than 10 percentage points over the period 2008–11, reaching the highest level in Europe for men (69.1 per cent out of the total part-time) and the fourth highest for women (50.6 per cent).

In 2011 temporary employees made up 12.3 per cent of all male employees and 14.7 per cent of all female employees. The percentage is higher than the pre-crisis value for men (11.2 per cent in 2007), but lower than for women (respectively 16.0). In the first years of the crisis the share of workers on temporary contracts went down, for both men and women, but then started to increase for men only. The explanation would be that temporary workers were the first to be laid off but men are being re-employed again on a temporary basis, while women often leave the scene once the temporary contract expires. The incidence of temporary contracts is higher in the South and among females with a university degree.

Women have a higher probability of holding a temporary contract in the age groups 25–29 and 30–34 (28 per cent and 18 per cent respectively), which also coincide with the fertile age. This increases the risk of non-renewal of the contract in case of pregnancy and may lead to postponement of maternity.

Employment risks for mothers

Employment risks for young mothers have also increased. In 2008–9 about 800,000 mothers who were employed, or had been in the past, declared that during their working life course they had been dismissed or they had been forced to quit due to pregnancy (ISTAT 2011: 154). This amounts to about 8.7 per cent of the total of working women aged 16–64 years. The highest percentage applies to young mothers, that is: 14.1 per cent left their job after the birth of a child, with almost all of them being forced to do so by an employer[3]. By comparison, of those aged 45–64 in 2008–9 about 15–16 per cent had left their job after the birth of a child, but only 7–8 per cent had done so against their will (ISTAT 2011: Fig. 3.19, p. 154). Living in the South and having low educational attainment are additional factors that increase the risk of losing a job for mothers.

The crisis is clearly not going to improve the situation, as emphasized in Picchi (2012). Also, ISTAT (2012) provides evidence that 64.7 per cent of mothers who gave birth in 2009/2010 were employed when they realized they were pregnant. About two years after the birth (in 2012) only 53.6 per cent of mothers were in paid employment and 10.1 per cent were looking for a job. Almost a quarter (22.7 per cent) of new mothers quit their job at the start of the pregnancy, 4.3 percentage points higher than in 2005 (ibid, Tab. 2, p. 120). The main reason was dismissal (23.8 per cent) or non-renewal of a temporary contract (19.6 per cent). Only about half (56.1 per cent) of women who quit declared that this happened on a voluntary basis, which is lower than the respective share in 2005 (68.1 per cent). The economic reasons for voluntary quits moreover increased to 13.5 per cent against 6.9 per cent seven years ago, due to increased dissatisfaction with the type of job or level of pay. Every third woman who had to interrupt their employment because of childbirth is aiming to return to work but in times of the crisis this is becoming ever more difficult, especially in the South.

Regional differences

Regional differences persist in the Italian labour market; the employment rate gap for men between the North and the South was at 15.1 percentage points in 2008, growing to 16.4 percentage points in 2011. For women it was 26.2 percentage points in 2008, remaining more or less in the same range (25.8 in 2011). A closer look reveals that in 2011 the employment rate of women in the North (56.6 per cent) was practically the same as that for men in the South (57.4 per cent), while that for women in the South was as low as 30.8 per cent (Table 13.3).

Unemployment rates have been increasing throughout Italy during the crisis years, the highest levels being reached in the South – 12.1 for men and 16.2 for

TABLE 13.3 Employment, unemployment and inactivity rates by sex and region in Italy 2008–2011

Region	2008		2009		2010		2011	
	Men	*Women*	*Men*	*Women*	*Men*	*Women*	*Men*	*Women*
Employment rate								
North	76.2	57.5	74.5	56.5	73.8	56.1	73.8	56.6
Centre	73.0	52.7	72.1	52.0	71.4	51.8	70.7	51.7
South	61.1	31.3	59.0	30.6	57.6	30.5	57.4	30.8
Total	**70.3**	**47.2**	**68.6**	**46.4**	**67.7**	**46.1**	**67.5**	**46.5**
Unemployment rate								
North	2.9	5.2	4.5	6.4	5.1	7.0	5.0	6.8
Centre	4.6	8.2	5.7	9.2	6.6	9.0	6.7	8.9
South	10.0	157	10.9	15.3	12.0	15.8	12.1	16.2
Total	**5.5**	**8.5**	**6.8**	**9.3**	**7.6**	**9.7**	**7.6**	**9.6**
Inactivity rate								
North	21.5	39.3	21.9	39.6	22.1	39.6	22.3	39.2
Centre	23.4	42.6	23.4	42.7	23.5	43.1	24.2	43.2
South	32.0	62.8	33.7	63.9	34.4	63.7	34.5	63.2
Total	**25.6**	**48.4**	**26.3**	**48.9**	**26.7**	**48.9**	**26.9**	**48.5**

Source: ISTAT (2011: Tab. 3.4, p. 112; 2012: Tab. 1.9, p. 44).

women in 2011. At the same time, the highest increase after the start of the crisis was observed in the North (although from lower values): +3.1 percentage points for men reaching 5 per cent in 2011, and +1.6 percentage points for women reaching 6.8 per cent in 2011.

Note that the measured unemployment rates do not capture the effect of the so-called *cassa integrazione guadagni* (CIG, wage supplementation fund) operating in Italy whereby some workers who face total or partial lay off still retain the status of employees. This allows firms to reduce capacity on a temporary basis without firing workers. The expansion of the CIG is estimated by ISTAT (2012) to have reduced the contraction of the employment rate by almost 4 percentage points.[4] The most affected sector was manufacturing (72 per cent of total hours lost), particularly the mechanical industry. Women only account for 30 per cent of workers under CIG.

Young workers

Young people under age 25 experienced the biggest increase in unemployment, a rise of +7.8 percentage points over the period 2008–11. The youth unemployment rate has been and has remained much higher in Italy compared to the EU average, although the gap reduced slightly over the last decade. As shown in Figure 13.3 the

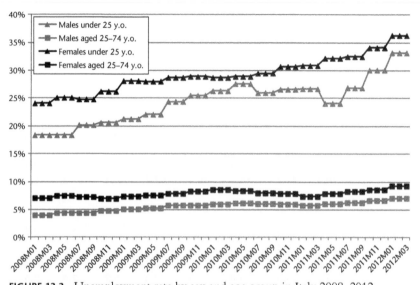

FIGURE 13.3 Unemployment rate by sex and age group in Italy 2008–2012
Note: Seasonally adjusted data.
Source: Eurostat online database.

unemployment rate for women under 25 exceeded that for men throughout the period but the gap varied from a low 1.3 percentage points to a high of 8.1, with the rate for women peaking at 36.3 per cent in the first months of 2012.

This increase in youth unemployment reflected the greater difficulties new entrants have experienced in securing a job after the crisis began. In addition, a much greater proportion than the rest of the labour force held short-term, atypical labour contracts and even those on permanent contracts were more vulnerable to employment loss.

Another worrying indicator is the high share of NEETs (*not in employment, education or training*) among the Italian youth: 22.1 per cent of the population aged 15–29 (equivalent to more than 2 million young people – 19.3 per cent for men and 24.9 per cent for women) compared to 15.3 per cent for the EU27 in 2010. Since 2007 the share of NEETs increased by 3.2 percentage points. The shares are particularly high in the South at 31.9 per cent compared to 16.1 per cent in the Centre-North (ISTAT 2012). Only one-third of NEETs are unemployed, others belonging to the category of inactive.

Foreign workers

Another important source of vulnerability is nationality. The incidence of under-employment, that is wishing to work more than in their current job, was higher for foreign workers at the onset of the crisis in 2008 and rose over the crisis from around 7 per cent to 10.1 per cent for men and 10.7 per cent for women of foreign origin in 2011. Education apparently has not helped as the incidence of overeducation is twice as high among the foreign origin male workers and almost three times as high among foreign origin female workers compared to those of national origin, reaching a high of 51.1 per cent for the foreign origin female workers (ISTAT 2011: Tab. 3.14, p. 135). This means that every second foreign woman working in Italy performs a job which does not require the level of education she has obtained.

Foreigners are also discriminated against in pay. Gaps for men of 20 per cent for full-timers and 10 per cent for part-timers were already found in 2008 and remained in the same range throughout the crisis years until 2010. The gaps for women were even bigger at 25 per cent for full-timers (20 per cent for part-timers) in 2008, increasing to 27 and 22 per cent respectively in 2010.

Despite the worsening of working conditions during the crisis, immigrant workers increased in numbers (+8.2 per cent) (ISTAT 2011: Tab. 1.8, p. 43) which may also be the result of their inclusion in the statistical database, as mentioned earlier. In turn we need to consider how the crisis has changed emigration patterns from Italy.

Spatial mobility

The lack of jobs is pushing more people to search for opportunities outside the country, in fact more women than men, which is different from the pre-crisis period 2002–8 (Table 13.4). As the educational attainments of Italian women have been rising over recent decades, so has their propensity to migrate in search of new jobs. This may be reinforcing the 'brain drain story' often told for Italy in view of the fact that 'the number of educated Italians leaving the country exceeds the number of educated foreigners entering it' (*The Economist* 2011).

There are also signs of increasing mobility of women with respect to men between Italian regions (Table 13.4). This may be a strategy not only to look for a job but also to find one more in line with educational qualifications. At the same time it may delay other lifetime decisions such as forming a family and having children.

Recent policy developments

The crisis in Italy initially started as a financial crisis but the support provided by the state to the banking and financial sectors turned it into a fiscal crisis with the public deficit growing rapidly. To address this deficit measures were taken to both increase fiscal revenues and selectively reduce public expenditure with negative implications for employment.

The increasing social tension brought about changes in the political arena with the new government led by Monti coming into power in November 2011. The new cabinet immediately initiated discussions about major labour market reform. Several critical objectives were identified including: regulating flexible contracts;

TABLE 13.4 Emigration and regional mobility by sex in Italy 2002–2010

Region	Men	Women	Men	Women	Men	Women	Female share (%)		
	2010		Δ 2002–2008		Δ 2008–2010		2002	2008	2010
Emigration									
North–West	11 203	9 689	4357	3577	1674	1866	45.1	45.1	46.4
North–East	10 673	9 348	5135	4516	1523	1653	44.2	45.7	46.7
Centre	6 756	6 294	1440	1374	823	985	46.7	47.2	48.2
South	4 848	3 907	149	473	-931	-579	41.6	43.7	44.6
Islands	2 684	2 099	-899	-207	-593	-591	41.0	45.1	43.9
Italy	36 164	31 337	10182	9733	2496	3334	43.8	45.4	46.4
Regional mobility									
North–West	218 749	216 181	22 180	21 402	-9 052	-1410	48.8	48.9	49.7
North–East	143 292	146 776	20 740	23 411	-2 311	3703	48.9	49.6	50.6
Centre	116 415	118 738	23 372	26 501	-9 498	-6253	49.0	49.8	50.5
South	131 962	132 210	6 897	10 523	-8 949	-5848	48.8	49.5	50.0
Islands	60 328	60 815	4 936	5 227	-3 002	-661	49.1	49.3	50.2
Italy	670 746	674 720	78 125	87 064	-32 812	-10469	48.9	49.3	50.1

Source: own elaboration on ISTAT data available at http://demo.istat.it

controlling illegal and discriminatory dismissal practices; introducing new forms of unemployment benefits and income support schemes; protecting older workers via either income support or guidance aimed at preventing early retirement; increasing female labour force participation; developing maternity and paternity leaves and enhancing reconciliation policies. Officially approved in June 2012 it was aimed not only at tackling the effects of the crisis, but also addressing the main deficiencies of the Italian labour market[5].

In what follows we concentrate on those policy measures which are either part of the ongoing reform or were introduced in recent years and expected to have a major impact on gender equality.

Increasing flexibility

According to pure market logic, wages have to fall to stimulate demand for labour. This approach was a guiding principle behind the contractual reforms implemented in Italy before the crisis, aimed at facilitating the integration of young, female and older workers. The results were modest in that the employment rates were on the rise, but this was accompanied by an increase in precarious and low-paid jobs which often became a trap. For women the increased uncertainty about future prospects often became the reason to postpone having children or not to have them at all.

There are numerous lessons from history that wage flexibility and laws (often counterproductive) cannot be the only way to deal with gender inequalities in the labour market (Villa 2007; Cappellari *et al.* 2009; Capparucci 2010). Instead they need to be coupled with social policies and investments in infrastructure and over-all economic growth, which are complementary to the policies aimed to reduce labour market rigidities.

What happened in Italy is that while contractual flexibility was increased, in particular by the 1997 Treu law and the 2003 Biagi law, no big changes were made in the social security system. This has increased the hardship faced by women in the crisis as many have only partially been able to take advantage of the income support schemes offered by the state as they are often employed in sectors or on temporary contracts where the main forms of benefits do not apply. However, some measures have been extended to cover categories of workers who were previously not eligible.[6] Coverage may now extend to small firms in the tertiary sector and temporary workers (provided they have an appropriate work history[7]).

The new government further recently announced a new system of unemployment benefits which will replace the forms of benefits other than CIG and will be extended to trainees and those on pseudo-self-employment contracts, as well as to other dependent workers in both public and private sectors who have at least two years of work experience. The maximum benefit duration will be 12 months (15 months for those over age 58) and will be paid at 75 per cent of the previous salary for the first 6 months, reducing over time. Women are expected to benefit from this measure in as much as they are more frequent among precarious workers previously not eligible for any form of unemployment benefits, but this will not benefit the most vulnerable group of young women, many of whom will not have reached the two-year benchmark for the work experience and will thus be ineligible.

The liberal philosophy and the labour market mechanisms embedded in the reforms strategy tend to reward male labour market attachment more than female. This is partly true also for policies which had an explicit gender equality motivation, such as the 2009 action programme (Programma 2020) put forward by the Ministers of Labour and Equal Opportunity with the aim of increasing female employment. The so-called entry contract was the main instrument designed to lower wage levels in order to provide an additional impetus for firms to employ new (especially young and female) workers.

Policies aimed at increasing contractual flexibility and reducing wages at the entry tend to increase female workers' vulnerability, especially during the economic downturns. They may improve chances to get into work, but render it unstable. Bruno *et al.* (2012) found temporary contracts had a positive impact on men's transition to permanent employment but not on women's. The latter often remain trapped in temporary contracts or exit the labour market altogether once the contract expires. In the short run the impact of the crisis on women appears to be limited to their holding a precarious job, but in the long run both the reduction of public services on offer and the difficulties of re-entry, often into unstable jobs, may generate discouragement effects.

The increased contractual flexibility could thus have had a positive effect where chances for employment are higher (e.g. in the North of Italy), but not where the gender division of roles is accentuated and induced by the structural lack of demand for labour (as in the South of Italy). Regional convergence was not helped by the decentralization of the implementation of activation and entry policies. Moreover, the recent monitoring study by ISFOL (2011) revealed how, during the years 2009–10, in practically all Italian regions there was a tendency to drift away from gender-related issues in the wake of the crisis. Most attention was paid to the use of European Social Fund monies for extending passive policies. Some regions have emphasized the importance of encouraging more women into work by financing specifically targeted programmes (positive examples are Lazio, Toscana and Campania), while others just mention the transversality of gender in all related policies (as in Emilia Romagna). In yet another case the recent actions have reduced gender equality actions to some conditions within the general labour market policies, such as training policies or providing fiscal incentives to enterprises which allow transitions from temporary to standard contracts.

Childcare support services

According to ISTAT, in 2010 about 15 million people in Italy (or 38 per cent of the reference population, mainly women) regularly take care of their family members (young children, elderly, disabled). At the same time there are about one million inactive persons involved in care activities who would be willing to work if they could reduce the time spent on care. The lack of child- and elderly care services represents an obstacle to full-time work for 14.3 per cent of women working part-time and for 11.6 per cent of non-working women who would otherwise be willing to enter the labour market.

Italian law establishes rights to a paid parental leave for both male and female workers, which can be taken even simultaneously and during the first eight years of the life of a child, with payment equal to 30 per cent of the previous salary. This low payment explains in part why in 2009 only 24,000 fathers against 253,000 mothers took parental leave, although notably the incidence is higher among men with higher levels of education (Del Boca *et al.* 2012). Only recently, within the ongoing labour market reform, has a three-day obligatory paternal leave been introduced, on an experimental basis for the period 2013–15. This is rather a symbolic action, and can hardly produce any significant effect on the distribution of gender roles.

The lack of childcare services is another obstacle that women face in Italy and the most important of recent initiatives was the so-called extraordinary plan for developing childcare services, launched in 2007 and initially planned for three years. It was expected to increase the coverage rate for children aged 0–3 years by up to 14–15 per cent (Villa 2011). The financial commitment was large by Italian standards, at around €730 million. The monitoring report (2011) nevertheless shows that little positive effect has been achieved, with only a modest increase in childcare service coverage from an initial 11.7 per cent in 2006 to 17.8 per cent at the end of 2009.

The recent budget cuts mean there are no chances for this initiative to continue and no big developments have been observed since 2010. If anything, the situation is getting worse, as it is becoming ever more difficult to sustain the level of provisions available pre-crisis, particularly in the South of Italy which is more dependent on central state funds for financing social policies, whereas Communes in the Centre-North often use their internal resources.

Pension reform: increasing the retirement age for women

One effect of the austerity plan on female employment has been to increase the minimum retirement age for female workers[8]. The pension reform launched in 2009 was the outcome of long-running debates but focused on the issue of increasing longevity rather than gender equality. There is no consensus about the gender effects of this measure. Some maintain that it could be advantageous if the related savings were redirected to fund care services (see e.g. Bettio 2009). Others argue that the savings would be insufficient to produce a significant effect and opt in favour of reintroducing the flexibility in retirement age[9] (Pizzuti and Raitano 2010).

As luck would have it, the reform was launched in the worst years of the crisis so that the saved funds (about €4 billion) instead of, as initially planned, being used to promote female employment, have been redistributed for general purpose actions. The side effect of the reform was to reduce the availability of grandmothers for child care, rendering it even more difficult for young women to get back to work after childbirth, especially in the South where childcare services are lacking.

Employment policies

Other interventions aimed at incentivizing the supply of female labour have so far been largely insufficient. In addition, some recent policy measures appear to be counterproductive including, for example, the reduction in taxes for overtime workers, introduced first in 2008 (L.93/2008) but recently extended (L.183/2011). This increases gender inequalities as women have fewer possibilities to go beyond standard work hours, especially those with children.

In December 2009 the Action Plan 'Italia 2020' for the inclusion of women in the labour market was announced, with a meagre budget of only €40m. The measures consisted mainly of childcare services for small children and only €16m were devoted to labour market policies (telework and training for women re-entering the job market). The Action Plan included measures to increase the employability of young people through the integration between learning and working experiences but a gender mainstreaming approach was completely lacking. This is a missed opportunity, as gender stereotypes in educational choices play a role in shaping employment opportunities open to women (hence occupational segregation and the gender pay gap).

One recent initiative, implemented in Tuscany only, aims at reducing educational segregation; girls who enroll in the faculty of engineering or science are offered a voucher equivalent to €1100. This symbolic sum can be an additional motivation for girls to overcome prejudice over non-traditional fields of study (Del Boca et al. 2012).

A new fund has, however, been established (the 'Salva Italia') to finance interventions in favour of qualitative and quantitative increases in youth and female employment for the period 2012–15. Also, the ongoing labour market reform includes several measures that should create additional incentives for employing older and female workers from disadvantaged areas. One of these is a 50 per cent cut in social security contributions for employers for 12 to 18 months (the longer entitlement if contracts are open ended) if they employ an older worker or a woman of any age who either has not been employed for at least 6 months and resides in regions supported by the ESF or who has not been employed for 24 months, independently of the region.

Public expenditure cuts and tax changes

Social policies have been very severely affected by the major budget cuts in ways that are undermining the very existence of minimum welfare services to people in need and families (Misiani 2010). The priorities of the Berlusconi government together with the critical situation of the public finances led to a considerable contraction in the total resources allocated to social policies over the first three years of the crisis: -78 per cent between 2008 and 2011. The cut of another 49.6 per cent is planned for the year 2013. A contraction of such huge proportions inevitably implies the cancellation or the drastic reduction in several types of services and initiatives. Many of those organized by local authorities have already been severely hit by the budget cuts (Misiani 2010).

The biggest cut concerns the National Fund for Social Policies which represents the largest contribution by the central government for the activities of assistance to individuals and families. It has been progressively reducing so that by 2013 it will be more than 20 times less compared to 2008 when the crisis set in. The other nine funds have also been hit by the budget cuts and three will have zero funding in 2011 including a fund for non-self-sufficient people, a fund for the social inclusion of migrants and the fund for childcare services. The remaining six funds will only have a symbolic budget. This applies to the fund for family policies (with only €51 million in 2011) and the fund for equal opportunities (only €17 million in 2011).

In August 2011, an *austerity plan* was announced that implied severe budget cuts and increases in tax rates. The manoeuvre was intended as a three-year plan to ensure financial stability, reduce public debt and balance the budget by 2014, now brought forward by the ECB to 2013. Two-thirds of the adjustment is to come from reductions in expenditure. The first cuts are expected for public services starting from public transportation, schools, street maintenance, etc. Public employees are also facing a reduction in real wages since they were frozen in 2010 until 2013.

In July 2012 the new Monti government presented a 'spending review', which implied further cuts in public expenditure, a reduction by 10 per cent in the number of public sector employees and by 20 per cent in the number of managers. It will mainly touch upon the health sector and local administrations, but also justice and universities. The measure concerns mergers of hospitals, local authorities, courts and universities. The impact on female employment will be significant, since these sectors are those with a traditionally high share of female employment.

Overall, the policies implemented since the onset of the crisis have not involved any *ex ante* gender impact assessment, and in many ways threaten the advancement in the labour market position of Italian women over recent decades.

Conclusion

The recent crisis is a challenging situation, which could be used to reduce the gender asymmetries typical for the Italian labour market. Since men were hit more by the crisis, some rebalancing in favour of women might have taken place. The analysis of the most recent trends in female and male employment patterns in Italy revealed still persistent gender gaps with the gender gap in employment rates, in particular, remaining rather stable at around 20 per cent, almost twice the European average (EC 2011). Both gender segregation and the gender pay gap are on the rise, again contrary to the average European pattern (see Bettio and Verashchagina, this volume).

Most of the policy initiatives implemented during the crisis are expected to reinforce the observed gender imbalances. In particular, the budget cuts and the income support schemes have been structured to reinforce the stereotyped gender roles within the family division of paid and unpaid work. By cutting childcare and elderly care, public transport, funds for disabled and immigrants the entire burden of missing welfare is shifted to women.

The positive effects, if any, are expected to come from the introduction of the new system of unemployment benefits which aims to provide a wider coverage. Women who are more frequently found among precarious workers who previously were not eligible for social security should benefit from this. More contradictory appears to be the ongoing pension reform, which aims to increase the retirement age for women. On the one hand, it should reduce the pension gap between men and women, thus alleviating the issue of poverty for women in older ages. On the other hand, it will increase problems of reconciliation for younger women who nowadays largely rely on the help of grandmothers for childcare. The youngest groups of women may be losing as a result.

Despite the political discussion on the need to stimulate female employment as a strategy to move out of the crisis, the announced labour market reforms have little to offer. Part-time and atypical contracts are still regarded by the government as sufficient measures to promote female employment. It is explicitly assumed that women employed under these atypical contracts would find it easier to reconcile work and family. The issues of job quality, career advancement, training, insecurity and low pay associated with these contracts are by and large ignored.

Despite many more Italian women now becoming active labour market participants, their opportunities are greatly affected by the familialist approach echoed in both individual behaviour and labour market policies, as well as the low emphasis placed on social policies (such as childcare and elderly care). The anti-crisis policy measures are too weak and fragmented to produce any substantial improvement, particularly as there is a lack of both gender mainstreaming and of gender-specific measures. As a result, the discouraged worker effect prevails in Italy and there is little space for rebalancing in gender roles.

To conclude, Italian policy makers are either unaware or unwilling to recognize the importance of gender issues. This has meant that the crisis has not provided the opportunity it should have to address persisting and severe gender inequalities.

Acknowledgements

We want to thank Francesca Bettio and Paola Villa for many useful suggestions which have helped us to improve the chapter. We feel also greatly obliged to the editors of the book for their guidance, especially at the final stage. All possible imperfections remain our own responsibility.

Notes

1   De Meo (1973) argued that the low female labour force participation in Italy was possible due to the general improvement in socio-economic conditions which meant that
female paid labour was not strictly necessary for household living standards.
2   La Malfa and Vinci (1973) considered the scarcity of jobs in Italy to be the main reason
for the low labour force participation by women.
3   This is often done on the basis of a blank resignation letter signed at the moment of
hiring (thus an Italian name *dimmissione in bianco* which literally means white dismissal).
This practice proliferated after the abolition in 2008 of the Act No.188/2007, which
required voluntary quits to be submitted by the worker to the employer only on the
paper prepared by the Ministry of Labour. The Labour Market Reform proposed by the
Monti Government in 2012 (Art. 4 L.92/2012) includes a requirement for voluntary
quits to be validated by authorized inspection services.
4   The request for lay off subsidies under the CIG increased by 300 per cent between 2009
and 2008 compared to only a 24 per cent rise between 2008 and 2007. A further increase
of 30 per cent occurred in 2010 but 2011 saw a reduction in total authorized hours by
19 per cent. At the peak in March 2010 the lost hours of work were equivalent to
717,000 full-time jobs and for the whole of 2010 the lost hours were equivalent to about
470,000 full-time jobs, with each worker experiencing on average a loss of €650 per
month (according to CGIL, the main Italian Union).
5   For   more   details   see: http://www.lavoro.gov.it/Lavoro/PrimoPiano/20120627_
riforma_mercato_lavoro.htm
6   The new government has passed some measures in order to temporarily extend the coverage rate of existing provisions (CIG, but also unemployment benefits) to groups of
workers normally excluded; the total resources made available for the 'social shock
absorbers' have been increased. Overall, the resources made available for 2009–10
amount to €32bln. (of which €8bln. for exceptional cases, so-called 'measures on dero-
gation') (Villa 2011).
7   For   more   details   see   http://www.cassaintegrazione.it/cassa-integrazione-in-deroga-
apprendisti-interinali-a-progetto
8   The retirement age for women was previously set at age 60. From 2010 women's
pensionable age was to increase by one year every second year to equalize with men in
2018. The 2011 reform increased the retirement age for men to 66 years starting from
2012. For women, it was fixed at 63.5/62 in the public/private sector due to be further
increased to 66 years by 2018 (CNEL 2012).
9   Already implemented back in 1995, but then cancelled in 2005.

References

Andreotti, A. and Mingione, E. (2012) 'The Modernization of Female Employment in Italy:
One Country, Two Patterns', in A. Buğra and Y. Özkan (eds) *Trajectories of Female
Employment in the Mediterranean,* Houndmills, Basingstoke: Palgrave Macmillan.
Bank of Italy (2012) *Economic Bulletin,* no. 64, April. Online. Available at: http://www.
bancaditalia.it/pubblicazioni/econo/bolleco/2012/bolleco68/en_bollec64/en_boleco_64.pdf
(accessed 12.12.2012).
Bettio, F. (1988) 'Women, the State and the Family in Italy: Problems of Female Participation
in Historical Perspective', in J. Rubery (ed.) *Women and Recession,* London and
New York: Routledge and Kegan Paul.
—— (2009) 'Donne in pensione più tardi? Voto sì purché…' Blog-entry. Online. Available
at: http://www.econ-pol.unisi.it/blog/?p=632&print=1 (accessed 12.12.2012).
Bettio, F. and Villa, P. (1998) 'A Mediterranean Perspective on the Breakdown of the Relationship
Between Participation and Fertility', *Cambridge Journal of Economics,* 22(2): 137–71.

Bruno, G.S.F., Caroleo, F.E. and Dessy, O. (2012) 'Stepping Stones Versus Dead End Jobs: Exits From Temporary Contracts in Italy After the 2003 Reform', IZA DP No. 6746. Online. Available at: http://ftp.iza.org/dp6746.pdf (accessed 12.12.2012).

Capparucci, M. (2010) *Politiche del Avoro e Politiche dei Redditi*. Modelli Teorici e Processi di Riforma, Milano: F. Angeli.

Cappellari, L., Naticchioni, P. and Staffolani, S. (2009) *L'Italia delle Disuguaglianze*, Roma: Carocci.

Ciccia, R. (2010) 'I regimi di impiego europei tra selettivita e regolamentazione', in M. Capparucci, *Politiche del Lavoro e Politiche dei Redditi. Modelli Teorici e Processi di Riforma*, Milano: Franco Angeli, 32–55.

CNEL (2012) *Rapporto sul mercato del lavoro 2011-2012*. Online. Available at: http://formazionelavoro.regione.emilia-romagna.it/lavoro-per-te/notizie/allegati/copy2_of_CNEL_Rapporto_20112012.pdf (accessed 03.01.2013).

Del Boca, D., Mencarini, L. and Pasqua, S. (2012) *Valorizzare le Donne Conviene*, Bologna: Il Mulino.

De Meo, G. (1973) 'Evoluzione e prospettive delle forze di lavoro in Italia', in P. Leon and M. Marocchi (eds) *Sviluppo Economico Italiano e Forza-lavoro*, Venezia: Marsilio Editori.

European Commission (2010) *Employment in Europe 2010*. Online. Available at: http://ec.europa.eu/social/BlobServlet?docId=6288&langId=en (accessed 12.12.2012).

European Commission (2011) *Labour Market Statistics*. Online. Available at: http://epp.eurostat.ec.europa.eu/cache/ITY_OFFPUB/KS-32-11-798/EN/KS-32-11-798-EN.PDF (accessed 12.12.2012).

Francavilla, F., Giannelli, G.C., Mangiavacchi, L. and Piccoli, L. (2013) 'Unpaid Family Work in Europe: Gender and Country Differences', in F. Bettio, J. Plantenga and M. Smith (eds) *Gender and the European Labour Market*, Routledge, forthcoming.

Ghignoni, E. and Verashchagina, A. (2012) 'Added Versus Discouraged Worker Effect During the Recent Crisis: Evidence from Italy'. Paper presented at the 5th ESPAnet Italia conference, 20–22 September, Rome. Online. Available at: http://www.espanet-italia.net/images/conferenza2012/PAPER%202012/Sessione_C/C_3_VERASHCHAGINA_GHIGNONI.pdf (accessed 12.12.2012).

ISFOL (2011) *Mercato del Lavoro e Politiche di Genere 2009-2010. Scenari di un Biennio di Crisi*. Online. Available at: http://annazavaritt.blog.ilsole24ore.com/files/isfol_mercato_del_lavoro_e_politiche_di_genere_2009-2010.pdf (accessed 12.12.2012).

ISTAT (2011) *Rapporto Annuale. La Situazione del Paese nel 2010*. Online. Available at: http://www3.istat.it/dati/catalogo/20110523_00/Avvio2010.pdf (accessed 12.12.2012).

—— (2012) *Rapporto Annuale 2012. La Situazione del Paese*. Online. Available at: http://www.istat.it/it/files/2012/05/Rapporto-annuale-2012.pdf (accessed 12.12.2012).

Mandrone, E. (2012) 'Partecipazione lavorativa femminile', in E. Mandrone and D. Radicchia (eds) *Indagine Plus. Il Mondo del Lavoro tra Forma e Sostanza*. Terza annualità/ ISFOL, Roma.

Karamessini, M. (2008) 'Still a Distinctive Southern European Employment Model?', *Industrial Relations Journal*, 39(6): 510–31.

La Malfa, G. and Vinci, S. (1973) 'Il saggio di partecipazione della forza-lavoro in Italia', in P. Leon and M. Marocchi (eds) *Sviluppo Economico Italiano e Forza-lavoro*, Venezia: Marsilio Editori.

Miranda, V. (2011) 'Cooking, Caring and Volunteering: Unpaid Work around the World', OECD Social, Employment and Migration Working Papers, No. 116, OECD Publishing. Online. Available at: http://dx.doi.org/10.1787/5kghrjm8s142-en (accessed 12.12.2012).

Misiani A. (2010) 'Finanziaria 2011: fine delle politiche sociali?'. Available at: http://www. nens.it/_public-file/Finanziaria%202011%20e%20politiche%20sociali%20-%20 aggiornamento%20approvazione%20definitiva:pdf (accessed 12.12.2012).

Picchi, S. (ed.) (2012) *Mamme Nella Crisi*, Roma: Save the Children. Italia ONLUS. Online. Available at: http://images.savethechildren.it/IT/f/img_pubblicazioni/img190_b.pdf (accessed 12.12.2012)

Pizzuti, F.R. and Raitano, M. (2010) 'Il sistema previdenziale Italiano', in F.R. Pizzuti (ed.) *Rapporto Sullo Stato Sociale 2010. La "Grande Crisi del 2008" e il Welfare State*, Milano: Academia UniversaPress.

Rubery, J. (1988) 'Women and Recession: A Comparative Perspective', in J. Rubery (ed.) *Women and Recession*. London and New York: Routledge and Kegan Paul.

Simonazzi, A. and Villa, P. (2010) '"La grande illusion": How Italy's "American Dream" Turned Sour', in D. Anxo, G. Bosch and J. Rubery (eds) *The Welfare State and Life Transitions: A European Perspective*, Cheltenham: Edward Elgar, 231–56.

The Economist (2011) 'No Italian Jobs: Why Italian graduates cannot wait to emigrate', 6 January. Online. Available at: http://www.economist.com/node/17862256 (accessed 12.12.2012).

Villa, P. (ed.) (2007) *Generazioni Flessibili. Nuove e Vecchie Forme di Esclusione Sociale*, Roma: Carocci.

—— (2011) *Gender Assessment of the National Reform Programme on Employment. Report on Italy. 2011*, External report commissioned by and presented to the European Commission Directorate-General for Employment, Social Affairs and Equal Opportunities, Unit G1 'Equality between women and men'.

—— (2012) '"Club Med" – Issues for Gender Equality and Intergenerational Solidarity in Mediterranean Countries', *European Women's Voice*, Spring, 16–18. Online. Available at: http://www.womenlobby.org/spip.php?action=acceder_document&arg=1515&cle=6d 18fbcaacc2a8af8da243ef8e128e403a8a91fc&file=pdf%2Feuropean_women_s_voice_ spring_2012_lr.pdf&lang=en (accessed 12.12.2012).

PART III

The policy challenges and the prospects for gender equality

14

POLICY IN THE TIME OF CRISIS

Employment policy and gender equality in Europe

Paola Villa and Mark Smith

Introduction

At its inception in 1997 the European Employment Strategy (EES) made the bold move of placing the goal of equality between women and men at the heart of its emerging employment policy for the European Union (EU). Gender equality was established as one of four pillars of the strategy during a period when political and institutional forces came together to strengthen commitment to equality goals (Stratigaki 2004). In retrospect, this early EES period can be regarded as at least a high point, if not quite a golden age for gender equality policy. The crisis has impacted on all aspects of the European project, calling into question the foundations, the membership and the goals of European integration. Coming at a time of significant policy reformulation, the crisis has also had important medium- to long-term effects on European and national policy agendas, as well as on the position of gender equality.

The EES represented a significant break in policy direction from that of previous decades where persistently high unemployment was met by policies to limit labour supply and protect incomes. This restrictive supply approach had a strong gender bias since it was men who were largely affected by measured unemployment, while inactive women represented a non-legitimate source of labour. By contrast, the EES promoted labour market participation and activation of labour supply as the sustainable solution to European economic and demographic challenges. As such, women, as a key source of unused labour supply, gained a new legitimacy in employment policy and gender equality and therefore became of interest to a wider group of policy makers. The position of gender equality goals came further to the fore with the setting of quantitative targets for female employment and childcare in 2000 and 2002.

The EES is not a policy tool developed at the EU level but a set of multinational mechanisms for persuading, recommending and reviewing employment policy developments at the member state level (Zeitlin 2005a). It was only in 1997 that the EU gained a competence in this area when a new Employment Chapter was added to the Amsterdam Treaty, and Commission and Council were charged with promoting a coordinated strategy for employment. This created a European-level role in employment policy, although not through direct influence, as in competition policy for example, but through a new governance instrument, the Open Method of Coordination (OMC). The core features of the OMC are iterative benchmarking of national progress towards common EU goals and targets, as well as organized mutual learning. The EES operates at three levels: at the European level the Commission and the Council are responsible for developing ideas, making hypotheses and shaping the policy discourse, as well as issuing country-specific recommendations (CSRs) on the implementation of the agreed guidelines for the employment policies of the member states;[1] at an inter-country level, peer review and dialogue shape processes for cross-national learning and the sharing of best practice; at the national level, EES priorities may influence policy debates and national policy formation. As Visser (2009) argues, the EES made a crucial contribution to changing policy makers' 'mental map', in particular from managing unemployment towards mobilizing for growth and jobs,[2] but also by increasing awareness of female employment and gender equality issues.

The visibility of the EU's commitment to gender equality in the early EES phase was strengthened further by the inclusion of gender mainstreaming as a horizontal guideline for employment policies from 1999, the establishment in 2000 of a specific target of 60 per cent for the EU's female employment rate by 2010,[3] and finally the adoption at the 2002 Barcelona summit of quantitative targets for childcare provision by 2010.[4] Certainly this EU level approach to gender equality has had a great influence on national policy developments, especially in the early years (Rubery 2005; Zeitlin 2005b: 452). Member states have of course differed in their receptiveness to this outside influence. Nevertheless, significant policy developments at the national level included improved access to active labour market policies and training schemes, individualization of tax systems, institutionalization of gender mainstreaming, as well as initiatives to reduce the gender pay gap and occupational segregation. However, the EES has been repeatedly reformulated, resulting in a progressive loss of visibility of gender equality goals at the EU level, with a parallel decline in gender priorities at the member state level (Smith and Villa 2010).

This chapter investigates the role for gender equality in the EES and its reformulations, using the crisis as benchmark. Drawing upon comparative policy analysis by the European Commission's expert group on gender and employment (EGGE), we examine EU policies towards employment over the period 2008–11 and highlight how during the Great Recession gender equality as a general goal was neglected. This neglect involved not only scant attention being paid to the gendered impact of the crisis on employment but also the implementation of gender blind policy measures. We identify two separate ways in which the crisis impacted upon the EES and the broader Lisbon strategy. First, we assess how the crisis affected progress under the Lisbon strategy towards not only female employment targets but also wider goals of gender equality. Second, as the formulation of the post-Lisbon agenda coincided with the crisis itself, we consider the major changes in the new EU agenda and identify the role assigned to gender equality. Next, we provide a brief overview of the mechanisms by which, in theory, supra-national employment polices impact upon national policy developments, focusing in particular on challenges to gender equality before examining how the crisis affected European employment policies under the umbrella of the EES. In the final section we explore the reasons for and implications of the withering role of gender equality in the EES.

The influence of EES on national policy environments and gender equality

One of the key debates on the EES has focused on the influence of this new regulatory governance approach on national level policy. The so-called 'soft law' approach of peer review and recommendations has been contrasted with 'hard law' that relies on directives that have to be translated into national legal frameworks (Mosher and Trubek 2003). Proponents of soft law point to its greater flexibility, allowing policy development to fit the wide variety of institutional and socio-economic arrangements across the EU. When it comes to gender equality the variety of starting points, measured by labour market participation, support for childcare and gender equality infrastructure, mean that there is rarely a one-size-fits-all policy.

Critiques of soft law point to the limited incentives for change where the prevailing priorities of the national administration do not fit the European initiative (Mailand 2008). Furthermore, member states may simply repackage existing national policies within broad European guidelines. However, the impact of hard laws may be overstated as studies show that their national application in the field of gender equality varies significantly (Falkner *et al.* 2007; Falkner 2010), casting doubt on the EU's capacity to implement common standards across member states. The Commission's own review of equal pay legislation reported considerable variety in the application of the principle of equal pay for work of equal value across the Union (EC 2009a).

OMC is one of the chief soft law processes. Despite much research on interactions between pan-national institutions and national policy making frameworks, in practice the direct influence of European-wide policies is very hard to measure. Heidenreich (2009) identifies three distinct channels of interaction: the structures of the EES and OMC which facilitate transnational learning and discursive diffusion of policies; 'adaptational' pressures that lead to reshaped policy trajectories as diffusion are limited by local institutional inertia (Scharpf 2002); and EU influences on domestic actors and their strategies and dynamics at the member state level.

In practice, evidence of first order/direct transfer from European policy agendas to member state policy is limited, although second order influences via modification of national policy trajectories may still occur (Zeitlin 2005a). Inertia at member state level, reinforced by domestic actors with interests in the status quo, limits the direct impact of international influences on the local (Heidenreich 2009). Such actors may actively defend gender relations that limit progress towards equality or protect privileges that disadvantage women. The potential for policy learning is bounded within a socially and historically determined problem space (Visser 2009) and these influences on gender relations are likely to be strong. This is evident in many of the post-socialist countries where refamilializing policies, based on traditional gender roles, were employed as an instrument to deal with high unemployment, a new phenomenon after 1989. For example, in the Czech Republic and Slovakia the government chose not to subsidize childcare services but to promote private care through long paid leaves (Szelewa and Polakowski 2008: 126). Likewise in Poland, many 'socialist' childcare centres were closed by local authorities once the central government ended their financing (Szelewa 2012: 13–14), with the outcome that the female employment rate is relatively low and declining. Though post-socialist welfare policies and the tools used to support working mothers differ (Szelewa and Polakowski 2008), there are similarities in outcomes: a reinforcement of traditional gender roles and a decline in female employment (especially in the Czech Republic, Poland and Romania), against the trend in most other member states.

Hard law initiatives face similar barriers at the national level although the scope for blocking such arrangements is more limited. Thus, according to Lopez-Santana (2009) there is a need for some kind of 'institutional and ideational fit' for policies to be established. Where there is a 'fit' European policies may be more readily adopted than where there is less congruence. For example, the contrasting use of national legislation based on the European Equal pay directive illustrates the difficulties of transposing a single legislative tool (EC 2009a). Furthermore, the resistance of the gender pay gap to such legislative measures, in almost all national contexts, highlights the difficulties of designing effective policy tools when existing gender inequalities are the outcome of a wide range of factors.

Some authors see the emphasis on soft law for social policy as part of a neo-liberal agenda to limit both the scope and centralized enforcement in these areas (Hermann 2007). For example, van Apeldoorn (2009: 30) contrasts the differing approaches of the European project to social and financial regulation:

> … with respect to the social policy areas bound up with the goal of 'social cohesion' – in particular employment – that EU governance indeed remains limited to policy co-ordination through benchmarking, whereas in the case of several policies deemed critical for achieving 'competitiveness', 'old-fashioned', 'hard' supranational law-making is still preferred, especially in the area of financial market integration.

Indeed, the Commission's own review of the Lisbon process suggested the OMC had been used more as a reporting device than a means to share good practice and develop policy (EC 2010a: 21).

Even when EU policy recommendations are relatively strong, their influence on national policy is at best uncertain but when policy priorities lose visibility, neglect by member states is even more likely. Two examples illustrate this risk: first, concern for quality of jobs in the EES framework has notably declined since 2004 (Davoine *et al.* 2008: 164–5; Begg 2010: 150); second, as Rubery *et al.* (2006) argue, a decline in gender priorities at the European level observed in the 2000s was quickly replicated at the member state level.

The way in which European institutions 'think' – i.e. choose among different hypotheses, develop ideas, frame the political discourse, choose the jargon to disseminate their policy recommendations, set targets – plays a role in shaping policy makers' 'mental map' (Visser 2009). Thus, the people working within (or for) European institutions – Commission and Council –[5] may be considered important actors with their own changing priorities in these cross-national interactions. The high priority accorded to gender equality in the late 1990s was the outcome of a particular set of institutional and political circumstances and the presence of key actors in the policy making process (Stratigaki 2004: 36; Walby 2004: 15), the constellations of actors, have since shifted. The priorities of the European Commission have evolved along with those of member states, who make up the European Council as well as being 'recipients' of EU priorities. In particular, the relaunch of the Lisbon strategy in 2005 which integrated the EES into a broader *Strategy for Growth and Jobs*, made more evident the subordination of the employment guidelines to the broad economic policy guidelines (BEPG), reinforcing the EU's hierarchy of priorities (backed by the historical domination of European Council Summits by finance ministers and the Commission's DG-Economic and Financial Affairs). Not least among these changing priorities has been the emphasis on the management and latterly the saving of the single currency, under the influence of the European Central Bank. However, even on the non-monetary side of European institutions the decline in the visibility of gender and increased emphasis on sustainability of member states' government debt, youth employability and raising skill levels upgrading is also evident.

The shifting position of gender equality in employment policy

We can identify four distinct phases of the EES characterized by significant changes in the relative position of gender equality (Smith and Villa 2012a: 5).

In the first phase, 1997 to 2002, equal opportunity was one of four pillars with three guidelines on gender issues (out of a total of between 18 to 22 guidelines). This was also the phase that introduced gender mainstreaming to the EES processes (in 1999). The principle of gender mainstreaming requires all policies to be tested for their gender impacts in design, development, implementation and evaluation

(Plantenga *et al.* 2008). The agreement on a ten-year plan and quantitative targets at the 2000 Lisbon Council further focused attention on the contribution gender equality could make to the aim of a high employment rate, with a target of 60 per cent for women and 70 per cent overall by 2010. By creating the EES, the EU significantly expanded its activities in the field of employment and social policies, with crucial implications for gender equality. Thus, the EU became a major proponent of gender equality and gender mainstreaming. The headline status of equal opportunities, accompanied by specific gender-related targets, provided a high point to the visibility of gender issues that with hindsight might even be considered a golden age for gender equality (Rubery 2002; Fagan *et al.* 2006; Smith and Villa 2010).

The second phase, 2003 to 2005, saw a streamlining of the EES: the pillar structure was abolished and replaced by three new overarching objectives (full employment, quality and productivity at work, social cohesion and an inclusive labour market) and only ten guidelines, with gender equality turned from a higher order principle into one of the guidelines (Rubery *et al.* 2003; Devetzi 2008: 5).

Phase three, 2005 to 2009, integrated previously separate reporting mechanisms on employment (National Action Plans) and economic policies (National Reform Programmes) (NRPs) (Rubery *et al.* 2006). This major reformulation led to gender falling out as a separate guideline and reliance was placed on gender mainstreaming of the employment chapters of NRPs, as the key monitor of gender equality. The loss of a specific guideline on gender equality, combined with the greater focus on creating more jobs, was a significant blow to the status of gender equality (Pfister 2008).

The fourth phase was marked by the end of the Lisbon process in 2010 and the beginnings of the formulation of a new strategy to take the EU to 2020. The new Europe 2020 strategy further marginalizes gender equality with none of the ten integrated guidelines related specifically to equal opportunities and only four related to employment. Moreover, gender mainstreaming is not mentioned. Furthermore, this reformulation occurred in the middle of the crisis, when policy makers' attention was focused on its immediate impact on male employment (Bettio and Verashchagina, this volume), a context in which the gains made in raising female employment during the Lisbon process were quickly overlooked.

In short, the evolution of the EES, as summarized in Table 14.1, shows that gender equality from its high profile in phase one progressively lost its position of centrality to the employment strategy and became sidelined into parallel initiatives. Thus, gender equality goals were increasingly focused on initiatives parallel to the EES, such as the Women's Charter (EC 2010b), the Commission's Gender Equality Strategies (EC 2010g), the gender equality Road Maps (EC 2006; EC 2011) and specific campaigns on pay gaps and work life balance (EC 2007; 2008b). Thus, gender equality is still on the EU agenda; however, it is now outside the disciplining mechanisms of European-wide targets and CSRs, as well as the process of monitoring, learning and diffusion between member states. Moreover, gender mainstreaming has been put aside in phase four. Once hailed as a means to push

TABLE 14.1 The changing position of gender in the European Employment Strategy

	The evolving structure of EES	Visibility of Equal Opportunities and gender	EU enlargement
Phase 1 1998–2002	4 Pillars; around 18-22 employment GLs	1 Pillar (out of 4) on Equal Opportunities; 3 GLs on gender issues; one horizontal GL on Gender Mainstreaming was added in 1999	15 Member States
Phase 2 2003–2005	3 overarching objectives; 10 employment GLs.	1 GL on equal opportunities, including the systematic Gender Mainstreaming of new policies	25 Member States in 2004
Phase 3 2005–2009	The employment GLs and the BEPGs are presented jointly in a single annual set on integrated GLs: 24 integrated GLs, *of which:* 8 employment GLs.	No GL (out of 8) on equal opportunities; there is a simple mention in the preamble stating *'Equal opportunities and combating discrimination are essential for progress. Gender mainstreaming and the promotion of gender equality should be ensured in all action taken'* (EC 2005: 29)	27 Member States in 2007
Phase 4 2010–2020	10 integrated GLs, *of which:* 4 employment GLs 3 EU targets	No GL (out of 4) on equal opportunities; there is a simple sentence in the preamble stating '... *visible gender equality perspective, integrated into all relevant policy areas*' (EC 2010f).	27 Member States in 2010

Notes: GL = Guideline; BEPG = Broad economic policy guideline.

forward equality goals, with hindsight some argue that gender mainstreaming has become a threat to equality goals (Meier and Celis 2011). In fact, this is what can be observed in the context of the recession: the weak institutionalization of gender mainstreaming, both at the EU and at the national level, meant, that as the crisis developed, mainstreaming mechanisms were easily dropped and gender equality goals lost their priority.

We can contextualize these shifts in policy and the position of gender equality by locating these four phases in relation to gender equality outcomes, in this case by examining trends in employment rates (Fig. 1). The underlying performance of European labour markets provides the context in which both short- and medium-term policy priorities are set. Phases 1 and 2 were marked by growth in employment rates driven almost exclusively by increased proportions of working age women in employment. Only in Phase 3, when gender equality had been mostly sidelined from the EES, do we see relatively strong employment growth for both men and women up until the latter part of 2008 when the crisis began to takes its toll on EU labour markets. In Phase 4, the backdrop for the new Europe 2020 strategy has been the loss of all the employment gains for men during the Lisbon process and the female employment rate receding from its 60 per cent Lisbon target.

The rapid falls in male employment in the crisis years have led to a loss of focus on the medium-term goal of raising overall employment rates, an aim that relies largely on boosting women's employment. To identify the *opportunity cost* of the downturn by gender requires a comparison of employment change against trends in male and female employment rates. Taking this approach, Smith and Villa (2012b) find that the employment rate falls measured against a simulated employment rate based on previous trends is much greater than actual employment rate falls for the EU27. This applies for both men and women, but for men the estimated fall against trend is 5.4 percentage points compared to an actual employment rate decline of 4.1 percentage points (2008 (q3) to 2010 (q1)) while for women, the estimated fall against trend was 3 percentage points, double the 1.5 percentage points actual fall. However, the fact that women faced a fall against trend of double the actual decline did not enter the policy debate and the EES

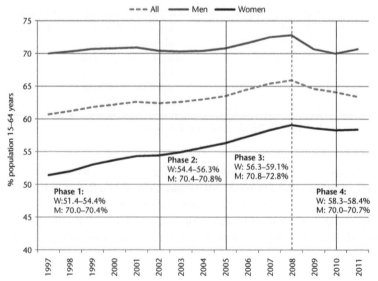

FIGURE 14.1 Four phases of the European Employment Strategy and trends in EU27 average employment rates

Source: European Labour Force Survey (Eurostat data online).

reform focused heavily on short-term trends in measured unemployment, losing sight of the longer-term gender equality goals embedded in the early EES.

The crisis and EU level employment strategy

The last days of Lisbon

The timing of the crisis was particularly unfortunate for the Lisbon process as it occurred shortly before the key milestones set for 2010 and determined the scenario in which the post-2010 strategy had to be formulated. The set of targets to be achieved by 2010 included not just 70 per cent for the overall employment rate but also 60 per cent for women and 50 per cent for older workers, as well as those for childcare coverage. The crisis jeopardized much of the progress made during the previous decade, initially in employment measured quantitatively but subsequently in more qualitative ways as gender-related priorities were eroded from policy formulation. Although most targets were not on track to be met in all member states, the female employment target had been surpassed in a number of countries and the EU rate was relatively close. The reversal of some previous gains during the crisis influenced the evaluation of the first phases of the EES.

The Lisbon strategy and feedback processes had not been established with notions of crisis in mind. Its goal of long-term structural reforms towards creating a globally competitive economy based on high levels of participation and knowledge work did not allow for short-term policy shifts. However, the various mechanisms for cross-national learning and sharing of good practices were used to address the changing employment situation and a series of European-level initiatives were triggered by the deteriorating economic conditions in the last months of 2008. However, the crisis responses uncovered the weak institutionalization of gender mainstreaming in member states and even in its previous champion, the Commission itself.

In November 2008, the Commission proposed a budgetary impulse of €200 billion (1.5 per cent of GDP), known as the European Economic Recovery Plan (EERP). Member states were encouraged to reach rapid agreement, requiring an unprecedented degree of cross-national coordination, on common initiatives to reduce social security contributions on lower incomes, to reduce indirect taxation on labour-intensive services and to accelerate investments in infrastructure, R&D, innovation and education. Despite previous Commission guidance to gender mainstream policies, the hastily prepared EERP made no mention of 'gender', 'women' or 'equality' (EC 2008a).

The European Parliament's response to the EERP did identify the need to use the crisis as a means to continue reform towards longer-term goals, such as sustainability, and also pointed out the plan's failure to consider the need to restructure labour markets and address gender inequalities (European Parliament 2009). However, the special Prague summit called to tackle the impact of the crisis on jobs in Europe in May 2009 (EC 2009b: 3) generated a response of ten points which emphasized the funding of short-time working schemes, promoting entrepreneurship, skills and training, as well as improved matching of labour supply and demand, but without reference to 'gender', 'women' or 'equality'.

In June 2009, the Commission did publish a Communication on *A Shared Commitment for Employment* in which 'gender' and 'women' were mentioned in its opening section (EC 2009c). However, there were few references to gender in the 11 key points or in the concrete measures proposed. Although the gendered impact of segmentation – with women more often on precarious contracts (op. cit: 9) – was recognized, no explicit mention was made of either the disproportionate impact of the first recession wave on men or of the potential gender effects from the subsequent reductions in public expenditure. No specific measures were identified for women or men, unlike for young people and older workers. The gender-blind approach was underlined by the encouragement for member states to promote work for 'low skilled labour' via service cheques for household and care services without recognition that this was likely to affect mainly women.

The ongoing crisis was in a state of flux when the formal review of the Lisbon process became due. In fact no systematic policy review of the Lisbon mechanisms, successes and failures, on the basis of which the proposal for a new strategy could be built, was undertaken. Pochet (2010: 142) argues that Lisbon reviews were 'essentially political' at each stage of the process prior to the crisis and describes the review during the crisis as 'non-existent'. Indeed the Commission's Lisbon evaluation (EC 2010a) was issued in February 2010, after the consultation on Europe 2020 started, further suggesting weak support for Lisbon-like mechanisms in the new strategy.

Furthermore, the Lisbon review made no mention of gender equality or gender mainstreaming and only mentioned women in relation to the unmet employment rate targets (EC 2010a). The positive outcomes of Lisbon – whereby the disciplining mechanisms of European-wide targets and the use of CSRs had contributed to discernible progress in female employment rates and childcare coverage (Plantenga and Remery 2009; Villa and Smith 2009; 2010) – went unacknowledged in both this review and the early Europe 2020 documents. Although the review placed considerable weight on the need for greater ownership of the policy at all levels and improved governance (EC 2010a: 6), this was not applied to gender equality even though the need for improved governance and greater involvement of stakeholders at all levels had been previously recommended by the Advisory Committee on Equal Opportunities for Women and Men (AC 2010: 23).

Lisbon becomes Europe 2020

In 2010 the whole strategy had to be rethought for the coming decade at a time of major economic crisis and in a context where gender equality goals had already been effectively sidelined from the EES and the short-term responses to the crisis. By 'reverting to type', and diverted by the rising levels of male unemployment, the new programme further excluded previously established gender equality priorities.

In addition, a number of new factors further undermined the broad commitment to the gender equality present at the inception of the EES. As well as being in a different economic situation, the composition and political orientation of the Union was quite different to that when the EES was initiated. In 1997 the EU was a group of 15 countries with two social-democratic countries, Sweden and Finland, recent members. Furthermore, there was a predominance of centre-left governments for whom gender equality was an accepted policy ambition.[6] By 2009 there were 27 member states, the incomers dominated by post-socialist countries where neo-liberal labour market policies prevailed and traditional family values were being reasserted. Only Slovenia could be regarded as a leader in gender equality policies. When these states joined in 2004 and 2007 the Lisbon process and its targets were policy priorities of the club they had joined, but not priorities to which they had contributed. There was also a difference in how unmet Lisbon milestones were judged by member states; some viewed the end of Lisbon as an opportunity to drop targets that were set by other actors – either because at that time they were not EU Members or because the political complexion of national governments had changed. The aspirations to develop a higher participation society were no longer underpinned by a commitment to an adult worker model family, where women and men are 'citizen workers' (Lewis and Giullari 2005) and gender equality is a broadly accepted principle. Instead, a competition-based neo-liberalism dominated political aspirations amongst much of the EU member states.

This major policy reformulation also came at a time of change in EU political machinery. The Barroso Commission came to an end in October 2009 and the incoming EU Commission was appointed late so that the first council meetings to discuss the Europe 2020 strategy were held in March 2010. As a result, the initial policy formulation occurred between commissions and was prepared primarily by the Commission's 'civil service' (DG Secretariat General) and with limited inputs from DG-Employment, which helps explain the limited consideration of labour markets and social inclusion. The consultation process, also coordinated from DG Secretariat General, was based on an EC document that maintained the focus on employment for women and men (EC 2009d), but the visibility previously given to gender equality and gender mainstreaming, for example evident in the preamble to the integrated guidelines in 2005 and 2008 (EC 2005; EC 2008c), was missing. Moreover, the Commission's working document was published late, leaving just seven weeks for stakeholders to submit responses. Following the 1500 submissions to the consultation process (EC 2010c), an EU summit agreed the broad direction of the new strategy (EC 2010d; 2010e) but in these early stages gender was almost completely absent.

Whereas in the early EES phase the Commission had been one of the drivers for a greater gender equality perspective in employment policy (Rubery 2002), this time the driver for a greater focus on gender gaps came from outside the Commission in the feedback process. Somewhat encouragingly for the position of gender among member states, 15 of them made some mention of women or gender equality in their responses (see Table 14.2). The Spanish went as far as to submit a separate

TABLE 14.2 Analysis of responses from Member States to the Commission's consultation on Europe 2020

Member State	Consideration given to gender issues	Comment
Belgium	Mention of need to promote equality between women and men	Gender equality included alongside social justice, intergenerational solidarity and children's rights as goals for Europe 2020
Bulgaria	None	n/a
Czech Republic	Women mentioned twice and equal opportunities once	A recognition of the need to unlock the 'economic potential of women' and 'non-discriminatory access to the labour market' also mentioned
Denmark	Gender mentioned once and women twice	In relation to the EU's demographic challenges the responses point out the need to raise employment rates for women and that 'mainstreaming of gender equality as well as a better work-life balance is crucial in this respect'
Germany	Gender equality mentioned once	Gender equality linked to opening up participation for social and economic goals and the need for 'effective progress should be made on gender equality – e.g. in terms of remuneration'
Estonia	None	n/a
Ireland	None	n/a
Greece	One sentence mentioning gender twice	Gender linked to the social and environmental dimension of EU2020 stating that 'with regards to gender inequalities, the new strategy should integrate the gender dimension (gender mainstreaming) in all relevant policies'
Spain	Separate report on gender equality	n/a
France	Three mentions for women, one for equality	The equality principle 'must' be included as a horizontal priority in active employment policies and women's employment quality needs to be raised.
Italy	Women mentioned twice and equality and gender once each	As well as mentions for female entrepreneurship, access to social protection and lifelong learning, the response states that 'the gender perspective should be better incorporated in the strategy'
Cyprus	Women mentioned twice	Women's employment linked to risks of precarious and flexible employment and as a vulnerable group alongside young, disabled and immigrants
Latvia	None	n/a
Lithuania	None	n/a

TABLE 14.2 (*Cont'd*)

Member State	Consideration given to gender issues	Comment
Luxembourg	None	n/a
Hungary	None	n/a
Malta	Two mentions for gender	One sentence underlining the need for gender mainstreaming 'in contributing towards gender balance in our societies'
The Netherlands	Three mentions for women	Women mentioned in relation to high participation societies, Lisbon targets and need to focus on women alongside other vulnerable groups
Austria	Section on Achieving gender equality (227 words) plus two other mentions of women	Mention of pay gap, Barcelona targets, job quality, childcare, division of unpaid work, training, 'Strengthening the dimension of gender equality in the future Europe 2020 strategy is crucial for achieving the goals of the strategy'
Poland	None	n/a
Portugal	None	n/a
Romania	None	n/a
Slovenia	One mention for gender equality	As part of the 'Vision of Europe in the next decade' gender equality and making work pay mentioned in relation to reducing social exclusion.
Slovakia	None	n/a
Finland	None	n/a
Sweden	Gender mentioned four times and women six.	The economic contribution of women underlined as well as the need to reconcile work and family, address the pay gap, promote entrepreneurship and equal access to science and education.
United Kingdom	Gender mentioned twice	To create more inclusive labour markets the response calls for 'greater participation and equality of women in the workplace by ensuring a new EU Gender Roadmap which includes agreement of targets to close the gender pay gap and increase the participation of women in public and private sector'

Source: EC (2010c).

document about gender equality; moreover, as holder of the EU presidency for the first six months of 2010 the Spanish Prime Minister made a number of high profile calls for a strong position for gender (Zapatero 2010).

A number of member states made the case for continuing policies that supported gender equality goals in the preceding decade. Austria called for continued commitment to the Barcelona target, the Dutch underlined the positive contribution from the Lisbon participation targets and 'particularly those for women and elder workers', while the UK suggested including targets for the gender pay gap and increased participation. Three countries (Denmark, Greece and Malta) called for gender mainstreaming for some or all of the new strategy while France, though not explicitly mentioning gender mainstreaming, called for 'women's rights and equality between men and women [as] a horizontal priority'. Another seven member states mentioned gender equality in their response (Belgium, the Czech Republic, Germany, Italy, Cyprus, Slovenia and Sweden) but in a more restricted way (see Table 14.2). Eight of the 12 countries not mentioning gender issues at all were new member states.

Beyond the member states' official responses a number of contributions to the consultation emphasized the need to raise the position of gender in the new strategy (EC 2010c). Recommended policy goals included closing the gender pay gap, individualization of social rights and support for female entrepreneurs; moreover, recommendations for policy mechanisms included specific targets – for example, for gender pay gaps – and also the reinstatement of the gender equality 'pillar' to raise the profile of gender in policy making. One of the most important recommendations was for consistent gender mainstreaming in the governance of the Europe 2020 strategy.

Few of these consultation responses were integrated into the next steps of the Europe 2020 Strategy. In March 2010 the Council of Ministers agreed to the Commission's proposed ten integrated guidelines (EC 2010d), Part I containing six broad economic guidelines and Part II four employment guidelines (EC 2010e). The key role for women's employment in previous phases of the EES had disappeared, with very low visibility accorded to women on the labour market, gender-specific targets and inequalities. Part I of the proposal only mentioned women once in its generic definition of inclusive growth, encouraging member states to 'ensure access and opportunities for all throughout the lifecycle, thus reducing poverty and social exclusion, through removing barriers to labour market participation *especially for women*, older workers, young people, disabled and legal migrants' (emphasis added) (EC 2010e, Part I: 5–6). The same quote appeared in Part II (p. 7) underlining the solely quantitative approach to women's employment at this point. Two further references to women and two references to gender were made in Part II, reinforcing the theme of freeing up female labour supply through reconciliation policies (p. 9). By contrast, the terms equity, equality and mainstreaming appeared in neither part. These outcomes might be surprising given the three consecutive pro-equality presidencies (Sweden, Spain and Belgium – from mid-2009 to end 2010) that had been seen as a force for progress in gender equity. Yet the inclusion of such goals in Europe 2020 was still resisted.

Over the course of 2010 the Europe 2020 was developed in further detail and resulted in some more emphasis on gender in the official documentation, driven by some member states who had called for a stronger gender dimension in their 2009 consultation responses (Smith and Villa 2012a for a detailed chronological analysis). However, the position of gender equality and gender-specific targets had become a contested terrain in comparison to the easier path to inclusion under Lisbon. The contested nature of the 'social' part of the new strategy is reflected in the delay in finalizing Part II (guidelines for the employment policies) in October 2010 while Part 1 (broad guidelines for the economic policies) was agreed in July.

The more tortuous passage for gender equality goals is also illustrated by the evolution of the employment rate target. The previous 60 per cent target for women aged 15–64 had provided a strong headline target for all member states and a basis for many CSRs (Villa 2013: Section 4). With the new working age population definition of 20–64, a proposal for a gender-neutral 75 per cent employment rate target was made in early March 2010. This became subject to considerable pressure to become a gender-disaggregated target but the outcome was only a symbolic change, with the target revised to an 'employment rate for women and men aged 20–64'. The EU27 employment rate at the time was 68.2 per cent (75.2 per cent for men, 62.3 per cent for women).[7] Although the Parliament argued for a 75 per cent target for women in May 2010 this was again resisted. By spring 2010, 13 member states had already achieved the target for men and of the remaining 14 just five were more than five percentage points below the target. By contrast, only Sweden had achieved the target rate for women, with just three member states being within five percentage points.

In October 2010 the final text was adopted which included an enhanced commitment to gender equality in the preamble with references to equal pay and conciliation measures, but retained the qualified statement 'gender equality perspective, integrated into all *relevant* policy areas' (emphasis added) (EC 2010f: 6). The final guidelines also contained a reminder of the gender equality provisions in the Treaty of the EU with one guideline (no. 9, on improving the quality and performance of education and training systems) remaining gender blind and all others making some mention of women or gender differences. Despite the higher profile for gender equality, the end result was far from a gender-mainstreamed document. This process contrasts with the principle of gender mainstreaming, supported by the Commission, that gender gaps should be considered at the outset of any policy-making process (Plantenga *et al.* 2008). To sum up, the greater emphasis on gender equality was largely the result of negotiated amendments to the original proposal rather than an ambitious plan from the Commission, in stark contrast to the outset of the EES and Lisbon process.

The low profile of gender equality issues in the Europe 2020 employment guidelines is perhaps not surprising, given the decline in the visibility of gender through the earlier stages, but the lack of any explicit reference to gender mainstreaming signals a further weakening of gender equality policy and perhaps a more widespread failure of gender mainstreaming as a strategy (Pfister 2008; Meier and Celis 2011). The European Parliament and other contributors to the 2020 consultation process had called upon the Commission to introduce more specific measures for gender equality *within* the main mechanisms of the Europe 2020 strategy. But in the end, the Commission's and member states' actions on gender equality are to be kept separate from the new employment and growth strategy, located in a series of specific mechanisms: the Women's Charter, the Gender Equality Strategy for 2010–15 and the Pact for Gender Equality 2011–20 (EC 2010b; EC 2010g; EC 2011). The very partial inclusion of gender issues within the Europe 2020 strategy seems to contradict the Commission's previous declarations and commitments for a gender perspective in all aspects of governance – it is rather a further stage in the visible decline in gender focus over the previous decade.

Discussion

The initial position of gender equality goals at the heart of the EES was a bold move and from the perspective of the aftermath of the Great Recession represented something even approaching a golden age within European-level policy development. In sharp contrast, in the 2008–10 period of European and member state policy making, gender equality policy faced more a *perfect storm*, with the combination of a major crisis and a major policy reformulation reinforcing trends towards weakening of commitments to gender equality.

While the timing of these events has proved negative for gender equality policy, hindsight underlines how policy formulation and policy goals are embedded in the temporal and institutional space in which they are developed. The end of the 1990s was a period in which policies focused on (male) unemployment had produced mostly limited results and the autonomous rise in female employment had served to bolster labour market performance across the then 15 member states of the European Union (Rubery et al. 1999). Furthermore, it was also a time when a social democratic model for Europe was being developed alongside a competition-based neo-liberal model (van Apeldoorn 2009). As discussed above, this reflected not only the particular constellation of actors (Stratigaki 2004; see Mazey 1998 for parallel in 1970s) but also the political complexion of the EU15, reinforced by the recent accession of Sweden and Finland characterized by dual breadwinner models and high gender equality.

By contrast, policy making in the Great Recession took place in a context where the position for gender equality in the EES had already been eroded (Rubery et al. 2004; Fagan et al. 2005; Smith and Villa 2010) and under quite different economic conditions that were undermining progress achieved under the Lisbon years. Perhaps more importantly, the key actors in favour of gender equality policy had been sidelined both internally in the Commission and externally among member states. The hiatus in Commission leadership at the end of 2009 might also be a factor putting equality policy on the back foot during this key period. Furthermore, the subsequent transfer of equal opportunities out of DG-Employment to DG-Justice distanced gender equality from employment policy and spread gender equality input thinly across the Commission. This is somewhat paradoxical given the apparent influence of the pro-equality, vice-President Redding during this period. The political complexion of most member states had also shifted to the right or at least right of centre reinforcing the neo-liberal hegemony (van Apeldoorn

2009; Hermann and Mahnkopf 2010). A significantly enlarged and changed composition of the EU marginalized gender equality and the social democratic model. In addition, the accession of 12 new member states, many of which were characterized by a more 'traditional' family orientation resulting from the fallout of socialist rule or a strong influence of the Catholic Church, challenged the prevailing notion of gender equality.

Exogenous to these changing dynamics among stakeholders, inside and outside the Commission, the financial crisis and weak regulation of the single currency highlighted how employment policy was subservient to the macroeconomic stability goals. Gender mainstreaming had rarely had any influence on macroeconomic policy and within the EES a gender perspective was only considered relevant, if at all, in employment policies. The ad hoc and short-term policy responses to the crisis can be characterized as a *reversion to type* and a rejection of a legitimate position for gender equality policy in the main portfolio of employment policy. More broadly, the absence of a gender perspective in key macroeconomic policy-making decisions is very clear in times of crisis but this was in fact the case during the benign economic period prior to 2008. The problem for Europe is that the deep-rooted challenges that inspired the high-profile position for gender equality at the end of the 1990s – demographic change, competitiveness, low employment rates and changing organization of households – remain just as pressing. The challenge is to make the case for gender equity goals to be more than a numerical count of the number of women and men in work in a more difficult political and economic climate than that at the turn of the century.

Notes

1   Since 1999, the Council in its annual review has identified some policy areas where developments are less than satisfactory, or where some member states should take action. These CSRs allow for a differentiated policy guidance to member states according to their situation and progress in implementation.
2   See Visser (2009: 42–44) on the role of ideas and international policy learning in the EES.
3   The so-called Lisbon strategy (or process) was launched in 2000 with the ambitious goal to make Europe the *most competitive and dynamic knowledge-based economy in the world* by 2010. The underlying philosophy was that the 'knowledge-based society' would require substantial structural reforms. Thus the Lisbon strategy incorporated the employed-focused policies of the EES (see Pochet and Boulin 2009).
4   The Barcelona childcare target was to provide services for 33 per cent of children aged under three and 90 per cent of children aged between three and mandatory school age.
5   Several important developments in the history of the EES confirm the influence of not only prevailing interest groups, the external experts providing advice to the Commission (for example, Ferrera in 2000, Esping-Andersen in 2001, Kok in 2003, Sapir in 2004) but also which EU institutions were taking the lead.
6   According to Tucker (2003: 14) the desire of the left-of-centre leaders to be seen to be doing something about social and employment issues was an important impetus for the creation of the EES (in 1998) and the Lisbon strategy when OMCs were extended to new issue areas and the annual Spring Economic and Social Summit was institutionalized (see also pp. 46–7).

7   See Eurostat labour force survey data base, quarterly data (variable code: lfsq_ergan). Annual average for 2010 shows a higher employment rate in the EU27 for the 20–64 age group (68.6 per cent) compared to the 15–64 age group (64.1 per cent), but also a slightly larger gender gap (five percentage points compared to 3.9). Although achieving the 75 per cent target requires women's greater integration into employment, member states may, in the short term, be able to focus on male employment rather than on closing gender gaps.

References

AC (Advisory Committee on Equal Opportunities for Women and Men) (2010) *Opinion on 'The Future of Gender Equality Policy after 2010'*, European Commission, Social Europe, January 2010. Available at: http://ec.europa.eu/justice/gender-equality/files/opinions_advisory_committee/2010_01_opinion_future_gender_equality_policy_after_2010_en.pdf (accessed 03.01.2013).

Apeldoorn van, B. (2009) 'The Contradictions of "Embedded Neoliberalism" and Europe's Multilevel Legitimacy Crisis: The European Project and its Limits', in B. van Apeldoorn, J. Drahokoupil and L. Horn (eds) *Contradictions and Limits of Neoliberal European Governance – From Lisbon to Lisbon,* London: Palgrave, 21–43.

Begg, I. (2010) 'Europe 2020 and Employment', *Intereconomics,* 3: 146–51.

Davoine, L., Erhel, C. and Guergoat, M. (2008) 'Monitoring Employment Quality in Europe: European Employment Strategy Indicators and Beyond', *International Labour Review,* 147(2–3): 163–98.

Devetzi, S. (2008) 'The European Employment Strategy', in S. Stendahl, T. Erhag and S. Devetzi (eds) *A European Work-First Welfare State,* Stockholm: Centrum för Europaforskning/Redaktörerna/Författarna, 31–48.

EC (2005) 'Guidelines for the Employment Policies of the Member States', Council Decision 10205/05, Brussels, 5 July 2005. Available at: www.cnel.gov.pt/document/council_decision_guidelines_employment_policies.pdf (accessed 20.05.2013).

—— (2006) 'Roadmap for Equality Between Women and Men, 2006–2010', Communication from the Commission to the Council, the European Parliament, the European Economic and Social Committee and the Committee of the Regions, COM (2006) 92 final, 1 March 2006. Available at: http://europa.eu/legislation_summaries/employment_and_social_policy/equality_between_men_and_women/c10404_en.htm (accessed 18.02.2013).

—— (2007) 'Tackling the Pay Gap Between Women and Men', Communication from the Commission to the Council, the European Parliament, the European Economic and Social Committee and the Committee of the Regions, COM(2007) 424 final, 18 July 2007. Available at: http://eur-lex.europa.eu/LexUriServ/LexUriServ.do?uri=COM:2007:0424:FIN:en:PDF (accessed 18.02.2013).

—— (2008a) 'A European Economic Recovery Plan', Communication from the Commission to the European Council, COM(2008) 800 Final, 26 November 2008. Available at: http://ec.europa.eu/economy_finance/publications/publication13504_en.pdf (accessed 18.02.2013).

—— (2008b) 'A Better Work-life Balance: Stronger Support for Reconciling Professional, Private and Family life', Commission of the European Communities COM(2008) 635, 3 October 2008. Available at: http://eur-lex.europa.eu/LexUriServ/LexUriServ.do?uri=COM:2008:0635:FIN:EN:PDF (accessed 18.02.2013).

—— (2008c) 'Employment Guidelines (2008). Indicators for Monitoring and Analysis, Endorsed by EMCO 25/06/08', Brussels: Commission of the European Communities.

Available at: http://130.203.133.150/showciting;jsessionid=67ED47A7AF05CCC236F
8015EBC381F84?cid=12003289 (accessed 18.02.2013).

—— (2009a) 'Evaluation of the Effectiveness of the Current Legal Framework on Equal
Pay for Equal Work or Work of Equal Value in Tackling the Gender Pay Gap. The
European Evaluation Consortium 2007 (version 19 July)'. Brussels: Commission of the
European Communities. Available at: ec.europa.eu/social/BlobServlet?docId=3893&lan
gId=en (accessed 18.02.2013).

—— (2009b) 'EU Employment Summit – questions and answers', Brussels, 7 May 2009,
MEMO/09/223. Available at: http://europa.eu/rapid/press-release_MEMO-09-223_
en.htm (accessed 18.02.2013).

—— (2009c) 'A Shared Commitment for Employment', Commission of the European
Communities, Communication from the Commission to the European Parliament, the
Council, the European Economic and Social Committee and the Committee of the
Regions, COM(2009) 257 final, 3 June 2009. Available at: http://europa.eu/legislation_
summaries/employment_and_social_policy/community_employment_policies/
em0021_en.htm (accessed 18.02.2013).

—— (2009d) 'Consultation on the Future "EU 2020" Strategy', Commission Staff Working Document, COM(2009) 647 final, 24 November 2009. Available at: http://www.
eucen.eu/sites/default/files/ConsultationET2020_ECommissionWorkingDocNov09.
pdf (accessed 18.02.2013).

—— (2010a) 'Lisbon Strategy Evaluation Document', Commission Staff Working
Document, SEC(2010) 114 final, 2 February 2010. Available at: http://ec.europa.eu/
europe2020/pdf/lisbon_strategy_evaluation_en.pdf (accessed 18.02.2013).

—— (2010b) 'A Women's Charter. A Strengthened Commitment to Equality between
Women and Men', Declaration by the European Commission on the occasion of
the 2010 International Women's Day, Communication from the Commission, COM
(2010) 78 final, 8 March 2010. Available at : http://europa.eu/legislation_summaries/
employment_and_social_policy/equality_between_men_and_women/em0033_en.htm
(accessed 18.02.2013).

—— (2010c) 'Europe 2020 Public Consultation. Overview of Responses', Commission
Staff Working Document, SEC(2010) 246 final, 4 March 2010. Available at: http://ec.
europa.eu/eu2020/pdf/overview_responses.pdf (accessed 18.02.2013).

—— (2010d) 'Europe 2020: Commission Proposes New Economic Strategy in Europe',
IP/10/225, 3 March 2010. Available at: http://europa.eu/rapid/press-release_IP-10-
225_en.htm (accessed 18.02.2013).

—— (2010e) 'Europe 2020: A New European Strategy for Jobs and Growth', in
"Conclusions". Council of the European Union, EUCO 7/10, 26 March 2010. Available
at: http://ec.europa.eu/research/era/docs/en/era-partnership-council-of-the-eu-03-2010.
pdf (accessed 18.02.2013).

—— (2010f) 'Council Decision of 21st October 2010 on Guidelines for Employment
Policies of the Member States', in *Official Journal of the European Union*, 2010/707/EU, 24
November 2010. Available at: http://europa.eu/legislation_summaries/employment_and_
social_policy/community_employment_policies/em0040_en.htm (accessed 18.02.2013).

—— (2010g) 'Strategy for Equality Between Women and Men, 2010–2015', Communication from the Commission to the European Parliament, the Council, the European
Economic and Social Committee and the Committee of the Regions, COM(2010)
491 final, 21 September 2010. Available at: http://europa.eu/legislation_summaries/
employment_and_social_policy/equality_between_men_and_women/em0037_en.htm
(accessed 18.02.2013).

—— (2011) 'Roadmap for Equality Between Women and Men (2006–2010). 2009–2010 Work Programme', Commission Staff Working Paper, SEC(2009) 1113 final, 31 July 2009. Available at: http://ec.europa.eu/justice/gender-equality/files/gender_roadmap_2009_2010_program_en.pdf (accessed 18.02.2013).

European Parliament (2009) 'European Parliament resolution of 11 March 2009 on a European Economic Recovery Plan', European Parliament, adopted text, P6_TA (2009)0123. Available at: http://www.europarl.europa.eu/sides/getDoc.do?pubRef=-//EP//TEXT+TA+P6-TA-2009-0121+0+DOC+XML+V0//EN (accessed 18.02.2013).

Fagan, C., Grimshaw, D. and Rubery, J. (2006) 'The Subordination of the Gender Equality Objective: the National Reform Programmes and "Making Work Pay" Policies', *Industrial Relations Journal*, 37(6): 571–92.

Fagan, C., Rubery, J., Grimshaw, D., Smith, M., Hebson, G. and Figueiredo, H. (2005) 'Gender Mainstreaming in the Enlarged European Union: Recent Developments in the European Employment Strategy and Social Inclusion Process', *Industrial Relations Journal*, 36(6): 568–91.

Falkner, G. (2010) 'Fighting Non-compliance with EU Equality and Social Policies: Which Remedies?', Harriet Taylor Mill Institute, *Discussion Paper*, 10/2010.

Falkner, G., Hartlapp, M. and Treib, O. (2007) 'World of Compliance: Why Leading Approaches to European Union Implementation are Only "Sometimes-true Theories"', *European Journal of Political Research*, 46: 395–416.

Heidenreich, M. (2009) 'The Open Method of Coordination. A Pathway to the Gradual Transformation of National Employment and Welfare Regimes?' in M. Heidenreich and J. Zeitlin (eds) *Changing European Employment and Welfare Regimes*, Abingdon: Routledge, 10–36.

Hermann, C. (2007) 'Neoliberalism in the European Union', *Studies in Political Economy*, 79, Spring: 61–89.

Hermann, C. and Mahnkopf, B. (2010) 'Still a Future for the European Social Model?', *Global Labour Journal*, 1(3): 314–30.

Lewis, J. and Giullari, S. (2005) 'The Adult Worker Model Family, Gender Equality and Care: The Search of New Principles and the Possibilities and Problems of a Capability Approach', *Economy and Society*, 34(1): 76–104.

Lopez-Santana, M. (2009) 'Soft Europeanization? The Differential Influence of the European Employment Strategy in Belgium, Spain and Sweden', in M. Heidenreich and J. Zeitlin (eds), *Changing European Employment and Welfare Regimes*, Abingdon: Routledge: 134–52.

Mailand, M. (2008) 'The Uneven Impact of the European Employment Strategy on Member States' Employment Policies: A Comparative Analysis', *Journal of European Social Policy*, 18(4): 353–65.

Mazey, S. (1998) 'The European Union and Women's Rights: from the Europeanization of National Agendas to the Nationalization of European Agenda', *Journal of European Social Policy*, 5(1): 131–52.

Meier, P. and Celis, K. (2011) 'Sowing the Seeds of Its Own Failure: Implementing the Concept of Gender Mainstreaming', *Social Politics*, 18 (4): 469–89.

Mosher, J.S. and Trubek, D. (2003) 'Alternative Approaches to Governance in the EU: EU Social Policy and the European Employment Strategy', *Journal of Common Market Studies*, 41(1): 63–88.

Pfister, T. (2008) 'Mainstreamed Away? Assessing the Gender Equality Dimension of the European Employment Strategy', *Policy and Politics*, 36(4): 521–8.

Plantenga, J. and Remery, C. (2009) *The Provision of Childcare Services. A Comparative Review of 30 European Countries*, Luxembourg: Office for Official Publications of the European Communities.

Plantenga, J., Remery, C. and Rubery, J. (2008) *Gender Mainstreaming of Employment Policies. A Comparative Review of 30 European Countries*, Luxembourg: Office for Official Publications of the European Communities.

Pochet, P. (2010) 'What's Wrong with EU2020?', in Forum 'Europe 2020 – A Promising Strategy?', *Intereconomics*, 3: 141–46.

Pochet, P. and Boulin, J. (2009) 'Introduction', *Transfer: European Review of Labour and Research*, 15(1): 21–32.

Rubery, J. (2002) 'Gender Mainstreaming and Gender Equality in the EU: The Impact of the EU Employment Strategy', *Industrial Relations Journal*, 33(5): 500–22.

Rubery, J. (2005) 'Gender Mainstreaming and the OMC. Is the Open Method Too Open for Gender Equality Policy?', in J. Zeitlin, P. Pochet and L. Magnum (eds) *The Open Method of Co-ordination in Action*, Brussels: Peter Lang, 391–415.

Rubery, J., Figueiredo, H., Smith, M., Fagan, C. and Grimshaw, D. (2004) 'The Ups and Downs of European Gender Equality Policy', *Industrial Relations Journal*, 35(6): 603–28.

Rubery, J., Grimshaw, D. and Fagan, C. (2003) 'Gender Equality Still on the European Agenda. But For How Long?', *Industrial Relations Journal*, 34(5): 477–97.

Rubery, J., Grimshaw, D., Smith, M. and Donnelly, R. (2006) 'The National Reform Programme 2006 and the Gender Aspects of the European Employment Strategy'. Synthesis Report Prepared for the Equality Unit, European Commission, European Work and Employment Research Centre (EWERC), University of Manchester, UK.

Rubery, J., Smith, M. and Fagan C. (1999), *Women's Employment in Europe: Trends and Prospects*, London: Routledge.

Scharpf, F.W. (2002) 'The European Social Model: Coping with the Challenges of Diversity', *Journal of Common Market Studies*, 40(6): 645–70.

Smith, M. and Villa, P. (2010) 'The Ever-declining Role of Gender Equality in the European Employment Strategy', *Industrial Relations Journal*, 41(6): 526–43.

—— (2012a) 'Gender Equality and the Evolution of the Europe 2020 strategy', *Bulletin of Comparative Labour Relations*, 80: 3–23.

—— (2012b) 'Recovery from the Great Recession: The Consequences for Gender Equality', paper submitted for the IAFFE conference, Barcelona, June 2012.

Stratigaki, M. (2004) 'The Cooptation of Gender Concepts in EU Policies: The Case of "Reconciliation of Work and Family"', *Social Politics*, 11(1): 30–56.

Szeelewa, D. (2012), 'Childcare Policies and Gender Relations in Eastern Europe: Hungary and Poland Compared', Harriet Taylor Mill-Institute, *Discussion Paper* 17, 03/2012.

Szeelewa, D. and Polakowski, M.P. (2008) 'Who Cares? Changing Patterns of Childcare in Central and Eastern Europe', *Journal of European Social Policy*, 18(2): 115–31.

Tucker, C.M. (2003) 'The Lisbon Strategy and the Open Method of Coordination: A New Vision and the Revolutionary Potential of Soft Governance in the European Union', University of California at Berkeley, Prepared for delivery at the 2003 Annual Meeting of the *American Political Science Association*, August 28–31, 2003.

Villa, P. (2013) 'The Role of the EES in the Promotion of Gender Equality in the Labour Market. A Critical Appraisal', in F. Bettio, J. Plantenga and M. Smith (eds) *Gender and the European Labour Market*, Abingdon: Routledge.

Villa, P. and Smith, M. (2009) *The National Reform Programme 2008 and the Gender Aspects of the European Employment Strategy*, The co-ordinators' synthesis report prepared for the Equality Unit, European Commission. Available at: http://ec.europa.eu/social/BlobSer vlet?docId=2479&langId=en (accessed 10.12.2012).

—— (2010) *Gender Equality, Employment Policies and the Crisis in EU Member States*, The co-ordinators' synthesis report prepared for the Equality Unit, European Commission.

Available at: ec.europa.eu/social/BlobServlet?docId=5630&langId=en (accessed 18.02. 2013).

Visser, J. (2009) 'Neither Convergence nor Frozen Paths', in M. Heidenreich and J. Zeitlin (eds) *Changing European Employment and Welfare Regimes*, Abingdon: Routledge, 37–60.

Walby, S. (2004) 'The European Union and Gender Equality: Emergent Varieties of Gender Regimes', *Social Politics*, 11(1): 4–29.

Zapatero, L.R. (2010) 'Making Women's equality a key target of the EU's "Europe 2020" strategy'. Available at http://www.eurostep.org/ (accessed 13.04.2012).

Zeitlin, J. (2005a) 'The Open Method of Coordination in Question', in J. Zeitlin, P. Pochet and L. Magnum (eds) *The Open Method of Co-ordination in Action*, Brussels: Peter Lang, 19–33.

—— (2005b) 'The Open Method of Coordination in Action', in J. Zeitlin, P. Pochet and L. Magnum (eds) *The Open Method of Co-ordination in Action*, Brussels: Peter Lang, 447–503.

15

GENDER, INEQUALITY AND THE CRISIS

Towards more equitable development

Diane Perrons and Ania Plomien

Introduction

The contemporary global economic crisis inspired many activist, policy and academic debates on the desirability and possibility of moving away from the prevailing neo-liberal model of capitalism. It thus provides an opportunity to articulate a call for a more inclusive model of development which, by definition, should integrate a gender perspective and so address questions of fairer access to resources and decision making power and consider the value of activities beyond narrow market concerns. As outlined in Chapter 1, the economic crisis was sparked by mismanagement of capital markets in the financial centres of the western world, but the underlying causes are complex and deeply rooted in rising economic inequalities associated with the neo-liberal model of global development. After the first financial phase of the crisis and initial expansionary policy responses,[1] a second phase ensued, as a consequence of policy reversal, in favour of fiscal consolidation and associated austerity measures including public spending cuts in the attempt to reduce government deficit and debt. Although the intensity and duration of the economic crisis has varied, many countries worldwide have been affected. With respect to its second phase – austerity – it is more accurately described as a European and North Atlantic phenomenon (Krugman 2012a) and associated with a sustained period of very low or negative growth, while elsewhere, especially in the emerging economies, growth has resumed.

In this chapter we argue that as the processes generating current inequalities are so profound and embedded it is necessary to challenge the intensifying neo-liberal policy orthodoxy and move towards a more inclusive model of development. Long-term resolution to the economic crisis depends on making fundamental adjustments to the neo-liberal model either by developing more equitable varieties of capitalism along the lines of, but not limited to, Keynesian social democratic policies, or, more radically but perhaps less realistically, by developing alternatives to capitalism altogether. The new paradigm would need to recognize connections between the economy and society, between growth and welfare, and between production and reproduction and by so doing, potentially secure more economically and socially sustainable and just societies. The central economic, social, political, and indeed conceptual problem is how to establish a relationship between the economy and society such that the economy serves society rather than the reverse. To address this question, we draw on the work of Karl Polanyi (1957), who analysed the tension between markets and states, between advocates insistent on self-regulating markets and those pressing for greater societal and state control, resulting in a double movement of capitalism between market liberalization and regulation. We also draw on the work of Nancy Fraser (2012), who argues that Polanyi's critique of market societies, although powerful, pits the economy against the society while failing to account for 'injustices within communities', including 'patriarchy', and thus obscures non-market related forms of domination (2012: 5, 13). As a consequence, Fraser argues, an emancipatory framework integrating economic, environmental and social reproduction concerns is required to secure equitable and inclusive development that would redress unequal power relations between countries as well as within communities, including gender hierarchies. Emancipatory analysis, politics and policies of such scope and scale depend on democratic, coordinated and systemic transformation and require continuous political engagement and strategy. Distinguishing between short- and long-term perspectives, we restrict our analysis to recent feminist economists' engagement with and critique of government responses to the crisis, in particular through gender responsive budgeting, highlighting the implications of austerity measures for socio-economic and gender inequalities. While these interventions aim to reform the state and its economic policy, at the same time, they derive from radically different understandings of the economy and so too can be considered emancipatory. As such, immediate and specific alternatives to current policies may serve as a link to the attainment of a just society pursued by wider social movements.

The chapter proceeds first by outlining the association between global neo-liberal economic growth and rising inequality, before identifying how inequality is implicated in the financial crisis. As the depth of the crisis and the subsequent policy responses vary between countries, we turn to the European Union (EU), particularly the United Kingdom (UK), and consider why, despite the failure to secure economic recovery, the UK coalition government persists with the oxymoronic policy of expansionary fiscal contraction,[2] which so far has failed to restore growth and is likely to exacerbate inequality. In these circumstances, as we discuss in the second section, rather than society reining in the economy, the UK government is instead intensifying neo-liberalism (Grimshaw and Rubery 2012) and attempting to make the self-regulating market the organizing principle of society. This is in contrast to expectations under Polanyi's (1957) double movement of capitalism or indeed as implied by EU dual objectives of attaining economic and social cohesion.

In the final section we turn to alternatives, specifically to gender-responsive budgets in the context of broader transformative politics.

Neo-liberal globalization, growth and inequality

The era of neo-liberalism has been associated with economic growth and rising affluence and in many ways society as a whole has never been more opulent (Sen 1999). Since the mid-1970s world income has doubled and for unprecedented numbers of people what Keynes (1931) termed 'the economic problem', namely the provision of basic needs including food, shelter and clothing, has been resolved. Whether this association is causal is more questionable, as China and India have both deviated from neo-liberalism yet fared significantly better than post-socialist Soviet countries that implemented radical neo-liberal reforms. These contrasting experiences led to the recognition that neo-liberal growth policies recommended, even enforced, by supra-national institutions from the 1980s, were not reflected in superior economic performances. In addition, neo-liberal growth is associated with rising inequality: labour's share of value added has fallen in a wide range of world regions, earnings inequalities have risen and while the gender wage gap has narrowed in the majority of OECD countries, it endures (UNCTAD 2012; OECD 2011; Seguino 2010).

In 'developed' OECD countries employee compensation as a share of GDP fell between 1970 and 2010. This decline is attributed to neo-liberal policies designed to deregulate and flexibilize labour markets in order to redress the 'downward stickiness of wages, overly tight social safety nets', and more generally, the social protection afforded by the welfare state (UNCTAD 2012: 143).[3] As demonstrated in the EU, inequality studies financed under the EU's research programme found that earnings rose more slowly than productivity for 48 per cent of EU workforce in the years 1996–99 widening to 61 per cent in the period between 2003 and 2006, and for 23 per cent of workers real hourly compensation fell while their productivity increased (Bogliacino 2009; INEQ 2009; Perrons and Plomien 2010). The decline in labour's share of output disproportionately affected low-income workers (IMF 2007), contributing to the rise in earnings inequality in 16 of 23 OECD countries (for which data was available) between 1980 and 2008 (OECD 2011). Largest increases in earnings inequality occurred in English-speaking countries (the USA, the UK, New Zealand, Australia and Canada) with the USA exemplifying the largest increase and highest absolute earnings gap between the ninth and the first decile of the income distribution from 3.8 to nearly 5 times, while the UK figure increased from 3 to 3.6. Large increases occurred also in several economies in Northern Europe (Denmark, Sweden and the Netherlands) albeit from a lower base, with Belgium, Germany, France and Ireland experiencing decreases (OECD 2012a).

As earnings inequality has increased, the gender pay gap has narrowed for all but two OECD countries, though it remains at an average of 16 per cent in 2010, with figures for the USA and the UK approximating this average (OECD 2012b; OECD 2012c). The decline results from women's increasing qualifications and labour market participation together with equalities policies. Less positively, the narrowing gender gap also stems from the decline in male wages at the lower end of the distribution. At the upper end women have moved into an expanding range of professional and managerial jobs, though rarely reaching the top. Meanwhile, many male-dominated jobs in manufacturing in the middle of the distribution have disappeared in favour of relatively low paid and more precarious personal services and elementary occupations, reflected in low pay among men relative to the male median. Precise patterns vary within countries, by age and position in the distribution, as well as between countries with the gender pay gap generally being lower where overall equality is higher (OECD 2012b). For the UK, when measured on an hourly basis, there is virtually no gender pay gap between women and men in the lowest decile, while a 16 percentage point difference exists in the top deciles, and 9 per cent at the median (ONS 2012). At the current rate of change the gender wage gap would not be eliminated for some 30–50 years for full-time workers and for female part-timers to achieve the same pay as male full-timers could take over 300 years. However, the factors shaping earnings differentials and the gender pay gap comprise only part of the processes generating and sustaining inequality, as the growing prevalence of single-parent households contrasted with high-income dual earner couples point to gender intersecting with other characteristics.

Rising inequality has generated some official concern, owing to the association between inequality and a wide range of social ills (Wilkinson and Pickett 2009), political instabilities (Alesina and Perotti 1996), and prospects for sustaining long-run economic growth (Perrons and Plomien 2010; Berg and Ostry 2011). More specifically, feminist and heterodox economists (Fitoussi and Saraceno 2009; Kumhof and Ranciére 2010; Rajan 2010; Reich 2010; Seguino 2010; Skidelsky 2012; Stiglitz 2011) argue that while the economic crisis began in the USA and the UK in the banking sector, as shown in Chapter 1, the underlying cause was rising inequality. Stating this position with reference to the USA Robert Reich (2010: 1) commented that:

> Wall Street's banditry was the proximate cause of the Great Recession, not its underlying cause. Even if the Street [Wall Street] is better controlled in the future (and I have my doubts), the structural reason for the Great Recession still haunts America. That reason is America's surging inequality.

Reich notes that the high level of inequality in 1928, when the top 1 per cent of the population held 23.9 per cent of income, was followed in 1929 by the Wall Street Crash. The introduction of Keynesian economic and welfare policies led to the 'great compression', when incomes and earnings inequalities fell. This decline continued until the mid-1970s when neo-liberal policies began to take effect and inequality widened once more (Krugman 2002). By 2007 the top 1 per cent accounted for 23.5 per cent of overall income,[4] very similar to the 1928 figure and to a crash the following year. The UK closely mirrors the USA pattern, although the degree of concentration, and thus inequality, is more moderate. Accordingly, in the UK in 1919 the top 1 per cent held 19.6 per cent of income, which in the period after World War II fell considerably to the lowest level of 5.7 per cent in 1978. In the following years, relatively steady year-on-year increases resulted in the top 1 per cent accounting for 15.4 per cent of wealth in 2007, prior to the crisis in 2008 (based on Alvaredo *et al.* 2012).

This association between inequality and the crisis suggests that in addition to the focus on banks and financial markets, attention needs to be given to the fundamental economic and political restructuring which took place in the decades of neo-liberal globalization preceding the financial crisis, particularly that associated with rising inequalities that resulted in low- and middle-income households having to rely on borrowing to maintain living standards (Seguino 2010) and in aggregate to unsustainable levels of individual and household debt. We focus on changes in the labour market fundamental to the widening inequality detailed above. The OECD (2008:116) shares the concern about rising inequality and points out that despite redistributive policies, significant levels of inequality remain and the taxes and social benefits necessary to effect redistribution are often very unpopular[5] so 'relying on taxing more and spending more as a response to inequality can only be a temporary measure. The only sustainable way to reduce inequality is to **stop** the underlying widening of wages' [our emphasis].

Understanding the underlying processes is clearly a prerequisite for 'stopping' rising earnings differentials and enduring gender inequalities. Orthodox explanations for rising wage inequality in OECD countries emphasize globalization, migration and trade on the one hand and skill-biased technological change on the other. The OECD (2011) re-estimates the significance of these differing explanations and identifies changes in labour market policies and institutions, specifically the weakening of labour market regulation, and technological change, which leads to a wage premium being paid for 'skill' as the two main factors responsible for rising inequality. It is important to note though that these factors still leave most of the increase in inequality unexplained. Additional explanations include those relating to the rising influence of the finance sector. David Rosnick and Dean Baker (2012) also using OECD data, found a strong positive correlation between the financial sector's share of GDP and rising inequality, which corresponds to data showing that finance workers are well represented among high earners.[6] Paul Krugman (2002) argues that the above explanations do not fully account for the dramatic widening of earnings inequality in the USA, especially in the top decile, and that it is important to recognize the significance of social norms that have become more tolerant of greater inequality. Clearly, if wages are determined by social norms rather than any notion of marginal productivity, then it is important to consider how they have been generated. Do they, for example, reflect social values and preferences, or do they reflect uneven power relations?

The argument that social norms are gendered, insofar as they privilege traditionally masculinized sectors linked with management and money over waged and unwaged labour linked with social reproduction, creating a set of circumstances not conducive to equitable or socially sustainable well-being, has been at the heart of feminist analysis and activism. Even in the twenty-first century, and across the globe, women continue to be over represented in the five Cs: cleaning, catering, caring, clerking and cashiering; while men are over represented in the four Ms: management, money, materials and machinery. These jobs are associated with different spheres of human activity, different economic properties and different rates of pay. In general terms, stereotypically women's jobs are more likely to be relational and concerned with caring and provisioning and are highly labour intensive with limited potential for productivity increases without changing the character of the work. These properties not only make it difficult to measure output but also mean that the relative costs will tend to rise over time.[7] What is less clear is why work in these sectors is not regarded as being more skilled and why the social value of this form of work is not recognized and better rewarded, especially as good quality care work creates positive social externalities. Specifically, care work provides the 'affective dispositions and value horizons that underpin social cooperation, while furnishing the appropriately socialized and skilled human beings who constitute "labour"'(Fraser 2012: 8; see also Elson 1998) and thereby contributes to sustaining the conditions necessary for the economy and market society.

Recognizing the social value of care work provides an economically rational argument for the workers employed in this sector to receive a larger share of social output. Arguably the social value is far higher than that arising from the work of highly paid workers in finance, where, in the UK, overall annual and hourly average earnings are approximately twice those of all other employees (Metcalf and Rolfe 2009). While the precise scale of this difference varies between locations, its gendered character does not. The fact that an executive from a failed UK bank was retained to advise on its restructuring at a monthly salary equivalent to three and a half times the annual salary of a childcare worker with twenty years' experience provides a telling illustration of comparative values, but whether the scale of the difference would be widely supported if known is more questionable[8] – the rise of the Occupy movement in the UK and USA and the *Indignados* (the outraged) in Spain suggest otherwise.[9] Even Adair Turner (2009: 5), Chair of the UK Financial Services Authority, argued with respect to the finance sector that high market returns and associated earnings 'can just as easily reflect market imperfections rather than proof of social value'. Joseph Stiglitz (2012: xiv) too comments on the lack of any relationship between private rewards and social returns, highlighting how the wealthy in the USA are not usually inventors who have contributed to productivity gains, but financiers who 'walked off with outsize bonuses, while those who suffered from the crisis brought on by these bankers went without a job'. Narrowing the differences in rewards through distributional changes would reduce inequality without necessarily affecting the overall level of economic activity. Indeed, it might even have a positive impact on the latter owing to the higher marginal propensity to consume among low-income earners compared to those on higher pay. From a feminist perspective, these comparative differences in pay also reflect the long-standing hierarchical dualism between productive and reproductive work and, in parallel, the separation between the economy linked with self-regulating markets and growth and society linked with redistribution. Feminists reject this separation and advocate a broader understanding of the economy as one of provisioning for human needs (Nelson 2006), which resonates with Polanyi's (1957) notion of re-embedding the economy in society and implicitly with the philosophy underlying the European social model.

Economy and society – changing the priorities

The European Union has consistently advocated economic growth and social cohesion and this concern with socio-economic inequalities and the ultimate goal of improving people's lives has evolved from the Treaty of Rome (1957) through the Lisbon Strategy (2000–2010) with economic, social and environmental pillars (Council of the EU 2000), to the current Europe 2020 agenda (2010–2020) for smart, sustainable and inclusive growth (CEC 2010). Particularly in the Lisbon and Europe 2020 policy cycles, the commitment of EU institutions – the Council, the Commission, or the Parliament – to employment and social issues has been not only explicit, but also presented as feasible and complementary, and indeed even critical to economic objectives, particularly where the objective is raising human capital and employment and articulating a social investment model (Jenson 2009). Furthermore, as they are now formally coordinated with fiscal and economic policies, social and employment matters seem to be increasingly central to European economic governance – reaffirming the synergy between social and economic goals. EU policy developments with respect to gender equality experienced similarly momentous landmarks, beginning with equal pay in the Treaty of Rome, and since then including numerous directives and policy innovations, such as gender mainstreaming. The pursuit of gender equality has featured strongly as key to the successful implementation of the economic agenda and growth, as highlighted during the Swedish presidency in 2009 (Council of the EU 2009; Löfström 2009). However, analysis of recent EU policy documents with respect to goals and instruments, and of the policy-making environment, suggest that social policies remain subordinate to economic objectives, and attention to gender issues has become much less prominent and less adequate than in the preceding decades (see, for example Daly 2008; Lewis 2006; Jenson 2009; Smith and Villa 2010, Villa and Smith this volume). This differential treatment rests on the neo-liberal assumptions that the economy and economic policies are wealth creating or productive while social policies – and employees within sectors such as health, education and welfare – are 'unproductive', concerned with redistributing rather than creating wealth, or even constitute a 'cost' and thereby stunt growth. The ideas that economic growth itself can be redistributive or that social policy can be economically productive are seemingly forgotten.

It was precisely this changing balance between economic and social priorities that Polanyi analysed in the *Great Transformation*, and in the context of the current crisis of neo-liberalism his analysis has renewed significance. Polanyi's key arguments are that self-regulating markets, that is, markets or economies that are free from the political sphere, are not natural phenomena but rather are consciously created and yet inherently unstable. Polanyi (1957: 3) maintains that without political control, self-regulating markets would create a 'stark utopia' and 'could not exist for any length of time without annihilating the human and natural substance of society [so] … society will inevitably take measures to protect itself'. Thus the movement to establish a self-regulating economy by disembedding the market from political control is met by counter movements to re-establish political control and re-embed the market into society. This tension or movement back and forth between economic freedom and social control represents the double movement of capitalism.[10] Looking back to the crisis conditions of the 1920s when economic liberalism reigned supreme, Polanyi (1957: 148) comments that:

> the repayment of foreign loans and the return of stable currencies were recognised as the touchstone of rationality in politics; and no private suffering, no restriction of sovereignty was deemed too great a sacrifice for the recovery of monetary integrity. The privations of the unemployed made jobless by deflation; the destitution of public servants dismissed without a pittance; even the relinquishment of national rights and the loss of constitutional liberties were judged a fair price to pay for the fulfilment of the requirement of sound budgets and sound currencies, these *a priori* of economic liberalism.

These themes resonate with contemporary politicians' statements advocating austerity. David Cameron (2010), the Conservative UK Prime Minister, continued to reiterate his faith in markets even after two years of austerity policies and low or zero growth, and similarly justified a series of public expenditure cuts and further liberalization of the economy:

> Getting our debt under control is necessary for growth. But it's not sufficient. Our responsible fiscal policy is being matched by active monetary policy… Fiscal responsibility and monetary activism is the right macroeconomic mix for our over-indebted economy. But the additional ingredient that government will deliver and needs to do even more of is a radical programme of microeconomic reform to make our economy more competitive – including competitive tax rates, planning reform and deregulation.

The values and beliefs stressing the efficacy of liberalization, self-regulating markets and balanced budgets were questioned in the 1930s and now by critics who promote Keynesian policies that were introduced in response to the depression of the mid-1930s. This turnaround led Polanyi (1957: 148) to remark that '[u]ndoubtedly, our age will be credited with having seen the end of the self-regulating market'. Eric Hobsbawm (2008) echoed these comments in relation to the current crisis in a radio interview:

> It's the end of this particular era. No question about it. There will be more talk about Keynes and less talk about Friedman and Hayek... We now know that the era has ended. [But] we don't know what's going to come.

When the economy seemed on the point of imminent collapse in 2008, Keynes was indeed once more on the agenda. Yet, not all commentators, in the 1930s or now, accept Polanyian or Keynesian theories that self-regulating markets are unsustainable. Rather, they attribute the problem to the 'incomplete application of its principles that was the reason for every and any difficulty laid to its charge' (Polanyi 1957: 149). Indeed, the UK government has been intensifying rather than countering neo-liberalism (Grimshaw and Rubery 2012), and called for more deregulation and cuts in public welfare expenditure to reduce the deficit, in the belief that this will establish financial stability and 'confidence', stimulate private sector expansion and compensate for job losses in the public sector stemming from expenditure cuts. That the policy is not working is clear.

The present (2012) shares all the hallmarks of a depression with either very low or zero growth and a clear lack of effective demand, along with high unemployment. Many people, especially those on low earnings, disproportionately women, are experiencing declining welfare as social benefits are cut even though the earnings of the top decile have continued to rise since the start of the financial crisis (OECD 2011). Even the IMF (2012a and 2012b: xv) identified fiscal consolidation among the 'forces pulling growth down' and called for more direct state activity to restore growth, pointing out that in the current environment, 'fiscal multipliers are large' such that a 1 per cent deficit reduction results in up to 1.7 percentage point reduction in growth. Lower growth also reduces tax revenues and increases spending on the unemployed, so preventing deficit and debt reduction (see also Batini *et al.* 2012; Krugman 2012a). Thus, the policy of expansionary fiscal contraction is in practice, as well as in language, oxymoronic and unlikely to lead to economic recovery. Indeed, Krugman (2012a: 2) maintains that 'the austerity programs that were supposed to restore confidence not only aborted any kind of recovery but produced renewed slumps and soaring unemployment.' While Krugman (2012a) is somewhat ambivalent about attributing the crisis to high levels of inequality, he demonstrates how inequality and the ensuing demand deficit is a major reason the economy is still so depressed and unemployment so high.

The need for neo-liberal policies to underpin growth is not supported by evidence. China and India, countries that least adhered to the neo-liberal model, experienced higher growth in the past three decades and a less serious economic crisis in 2008 (see Dunford and Yeung 2011; Quah 2011) although inequality also rose in both. In addition, European evidence shows that while inequality has increased in most countries (pre- and post-tax) there are significant cross-national variations, with lower levels of overall and gender inequality in social democratic countries especially Sweden and Norway, reflecting different welfare regimes or varieties of capitalism (Perrons and Plomien 2010). This contemporaneous spatial evidence together with the coexistence of growth and greater social inclusion in the period prior to neo-liberalism suggest that alternatives to current problems are not only desirable but also feasible.

Alternatives to capitalism or capitalist alternatives

Contemporary times are characterized by crisis and uncertainty. What is certain is that Polanyi (1957) and Hobsbawm (2008) were both wrong when they claimed to have seen the end of self-regulating markets. Nonetheless, heterodox economists (Krugman 2012a/b; Skildelsky 2012 and Stiglitz 2012) continue to advocate a Keynesian or Polanyian response. Feminist economists (Elson 1998 and 2010; Seguino 2010) and philosophers (Fraser 2012) recognize merit in these critiques, but note their shortcomings in terms of securing inclusive and sustainable growth and gender equitable outcomes. Heterodox and feminist economists agree that it is crucial to expand, rather than cut, public expenditure to boost demand and restore economic growth. Krugman (2012b), similar to Keynes, regards any form of expenditure sufficient, though in passing suggests that the re-employment of teachers dismissed with the cuts in the USA would significantly boost the economy. For the UK, Robert Skidelsky (2012: 2) is more specific; suggesting that investment in physical infrastructure would be preferable because it would result in a lasting product:

> In the short run, it doesn't matter whether the increase in aggregate demand takes the form of employing people to dig holes and fill them up again, giving every household a time-limited spending voucher or building a new railway. All that matters is that the overall level of spending in the economy is maintained − so that unemployment stops rising and with any luck, begins to fall again. But from any long term point of view, increasing aggregate demand by capital investment is better, because it creates identifiable future assets that promise to fund themselves and improve growth potential.

Skidelsky (2011 and 2012) implicitly assumes that social expenditure is less productive and, similar to Krugman (2012a/b) and Keynes (1933/1983), does not take gender into account. From a feminist perspective, therefore, these leading heterodox economists' resolutions miss an opportunity. Joseph Stiglitz (2012: 282) develops a different strategy; though he similarly backs public investment in technology and infrastructure to create employment, he also links ineffective demand to the scale of inequality and his agenda for change goes further by seeking to tackle excess earnings at the top (through tax reforms, banking and finance regulations) and reducing monopoly power by increasing competition, while developing support for the majority of the population through better education and social protection. And while Stiglitz (2012: 282) draws attention to gender (and racial) discrimination in the labour market and questions the disconnection between private rewards and social returns, he focuses on excessive incomes in finance rather than gender differentiated value of employment and the reproductive sectors.

Feminist economists, including Stephanie Seguino (2010) and Diane Elson (2010), similarly argue that policies to boost incomes and livelihood opportunities are necessary to redress the unequal distribution of income and demand deficit that led to the crisis, but integrate gender more fully into their analysis by highlighting the gender dimensions of the crisis. They suggest that the crisis provides an opportunity for rethinking macroeconomic policy, for promoting policies for greater equality by social class, gender and ethnicity and for transforming prevailing gendered social norms. Nancy Fraser (2012), likewise, brings gender dimensions to the fore by arguing that while Polanyi provides a powerful critique of market societies and their devastating impact on 'habitats, livelihoods and communities' he failed to consider how counter movements seeking to restore social protection led to solidifying 'hierarchies and exclusions' (Fraser 2012: 4–5). In particular, the social institutions that arose in response to the excesses of market society in the years following the Great Depression of the 1930s rested on hierarchical gender relations and uneven economic and geopolitical powers between states. Instead, she advocates a triple (rather than Polanyi's double) movement of capitalism to redress these concerns, and includes emancipatory politics to redress domination and attain more cohesive and egalitarian development. In this regard she looks towards non-mainstream political protests, such as feminist, environmentalist, anti-globalization or anti-capitalist movements such as Occupy and the *Indignados,* while acknowledging that not all support progressive politics.[11]

These social movement initiatives and subterranean politics expressed through protests and demonstrations, while heterogeneous and episodic, nonetheless resonate with aspects of mainstream public opinion that the current system is fundamentally unfair (Stiglitz 2012). In particular, there is a shared dissatisfaction with the way that contemporary democracy has intensified structural inequalities, allowed a minority to benefit disproportionately from past economic growth but now expects the majority, and especially low income groups, to pay disproportionately for the costs of austerity (Butler 2012; Kaldor and Selchow 2012; WBG 2012). Even so, while emphasizing the significance of inequality and the failure of orthodox politics to address the interests of the majority, these movements rarely acknowledge the specifically gendered dimensions of inequality. The general concerns are certainly important to articulate, as Judith Butler (2012) did in her support to Occupy Wall Street, focusing on issues such as the 'monopolization of wealth', the disposability of workers, the privatization of education, the inadequacy of health care, the dispossessions of housing, the expansion of poverty and 'economic racism'. Stressing that these issues are linked and that 'our politics depends on asking about the systemic and historical character of the economic system itself', she also urges tracking 'what is actually happening' and focusing on 'concrete instances where inequality takes place'. Arguably, this is precisely what feminist economists have done by tracing the gender implications of the crisis (Elson 2010) and by working with gender budgets (GB).

The purpose of GBs is to integrate a gender perspective into government (at all levels) revenue and spending decisions so that allocation of resources contributes to the attainment of gender equality. It requires identification of, and intervention, to redress gender gaps and inequalities. The practice of GB is spreading. In Poland it is increasingly applied at the local self-government commune level, while the Italian local level practice has established that it is a feasible and not necessarily an expensive strategy (Bettio and Rosselli 2008). In Iceland GB is a national policy introduced as part of the coalition platform of the Social Democratic Alliance and Left-Green Movement, and features in a parliamentary resolution on a gender equality action programme, according to which gender budgeting will be implemented by the Ministry of Finance incrementally, beginning with pilot projects to design procedures for the preparation of GBs, and will involve formal training (Ministry of Welfare 2012). The Scottish Women's Budget Group in coalition with other groups in the Equality and Budgetary Advisory Group has been able to ensure that the government commissioned and published an equalities impact statement, an analysis of the gendered impact of the recession, alongside the budget (Scottish Government Social Research 2010 and 2011). In the UK the Women's Budget Group regularly monitors the impact of national budgets and financial statements for their gendered implications and, in the context of contemporary austerity policies, has developed an 'alternative F' plan which makes the case for public investment in social and physical infrastructure, for increased expenditure on social reproduction including education, health and social care as well as public transport and green energy. The group argues that increased and redirected spending would boost consumer spending, provide the necessary increase in demand, and generate tax revenues that would in turn feed back into the government revenue and allow further rounds of spending consistent with the fiscal multiplier. Further, such expenditure is likely to create employment amongst relatively low income people, especially women, which would not only redress some of the adverse consequences and uneven impact of austerity policies to date but also have a more than proportionate impact on expenditure given the higher marginal propensity to consume among lower income earners. This approach would seek to establish a 'virtuous circle of expansion rather than the current [vicious] circle of decline' (WBG 2012: 17). The underlying rationale, here, is pure Keynes – that 'expenditure creates its own income … look after unemployment and the budget will look after itself' (Keynes 1933/1983: 80–1) – with the added value of the gendered focus. While the WBG regularly produces press releases and sends material to the Treasury they have no formal policy-making role.

On one level, the work of the WBG appears specific and detailed, and indeed it is. Yet the underlying principles rest on an emancipatory analysis of the economy that recognizes the significance of social reproduction not as a cost but as one of the 'conditions of possibility' for economic and social life (Fraser 2012) as well as a more equitable society. In this respect, gender budgets and the feminist economics from which they derive provide a link between small-scale adjustments and transformative change (Butler 2012). But, as the experience of gender budgeting elsewhere over a twenty-year period suggests, it is easier to conduct gender analyses and formulate alternative gender budgets than to secure their implementation. Rather dispiritingly, as one of the pioneers of gender budgeting, Debbie Budlender (2006: 324) noted: 'the more than fifty gender responsive budget initiatives around the world have probably produced relatively few budget changes.'

These approaches are difficult to implement not only because of continued adherence to neo-liberal policies, but also because resistance to neo-liberal policies is ineffective due to the fragmentation among the opposition and because of lock-in effects of successive political and legal decisions. With respect to the European Union, on one level, Europe as a political or a public space does not seem relevant and has few organized initiatives or actors aiming to transform it (Kaldor and Selchow 2012; Storey 2008). But even if a sufficient and organized opposition were to form, significant barriers have been built to protect against any challenge to the EU's neo-liberal character including a range of regulations, such as competition, liberalization, and fiscal monitoring, all of which limit the space for negotiation (Storey 2008). The institutionalization of such mechanisms is being ratcheted up further in the aftermath of the financial crisis with the introduction of a new macroeconomic regime. The new economic governance relies on rule-based fiscal policies focused on the reduction of deficit and debt, strengthens the liberalization and deregulation of markets, puts downward pressure on wages, transfers economic and budget decision-making power to bureaucrats without the involvement of European or national parliaments, and reinforces lack of transparency (Klatzer and Schlager 2012: 5). These recent shifts in the governance mechanism, policy goals, and state and public institutions reinforce an already existing economic policy gender bias with detrimental implications for equality (Klatzer and Schlager 2012: 6). The room for alternative policy developments within the currently engineered UK or the European context is thus increasingly constrained.

Conclusion

While it is possible to identify economic explanations for the crisis and why present government policies are not working, and to articulate alternative responses, the question of how to make these solutions politically acceptable is more challenging (Stiglitz 2012). Rising to the challenge requires participation of a wide range of social actors – scholars, activists and policymakers to name a few – and a wide range of social action – analysis and dissemination, protest, or direct engagement and reform are just some. Surely, if inequality is an underlying cause of the current crisis, as suggested by feminist and heterodox economists (Seguino 2010; Stiglitz 2012), then austerity policies of the kind pursued in the UK and elsewhere in the EU cannot provide an effective and long-term resolution. First, because the current strategy is unlikely to secure its stated objective of restoring adequate levels of economic growth, especially as demand will remain low. Second, because economic growth alone or the type of growth that disproportionately benefits the already privileged groups in society and perpetuates inequalities, is unsustainable in the long run. Keynesian-type policies offer alternative prescriptions that have worked in the past. But they did not resolve the problem of domination and inequality (Fraser 2012), especially with respect to gender relations and relations between states. Gendering and applying Keynesian ideas in today's global economy is complicated by the implications for competitiveness of increasing the labour's share of income and attending to the requirements of reproductive work. However, this argument is premised on the acceptance of a profit-led model of growth, whereas, as Stephanie Seguino and Caren Grown (2007: 306) have pointed out, the economy could equally be viewed as a 'closed wage-led economic system'. Working out what this means in practice combined with specifying more precisely the feminist alternative F plan for development is a task that requires urgent attention. The call for incorporation of feminist concerns of redistribution, recognition and representation (Fraser 2009) remains as relevant, if not more, as ever.

Notes

1 The initial round of responses to the crisis was expansionary and based on fiscal stimulus packages: the American Recovery and Reinvestment Act implemented by the Obama administration was 'the biggest job-creation program' in the country's history (Krugman, 2012a: 109) and the EU's Economic Recovery Plan committing €200 billion for member state responses around public works programmes and reduced VAT was unprecedented (CEC 2008).

2 Conventionally, government spending cuts and deficit reducing policies have negative effects on aggregate demand and output, although in two cases, Denmark in 1983–86 and Ireland in 1987–89, fiscal contractions were associated with economic recovery (see Giavazzi and Pagano, 1990, for the empirical studies, and Barry and Devereux, 2003, for theoretical exploration).

3 The UNCTAD (2012) point out that the precise patterns vary considerably between different countries, depending in part on the extent of labour market regulation and role of trade unions. Their figures exclude Eastern Europe. For a wider range of world regions see ILO 2008 and for a disaggregation between Japan, USA, other Anglo Saxon Countries (Australia, Canada and UK) and Europe (14 countries excluding Eastern Europe) see IMF 2007.

4 The extent of inequality based on these indicators is likely to be an underestimate, because, as Bastagli et al. (2012) note, they are typically based on tax-return data and omit unreported income and unrealized capital gains. Furthermore, the extent of inequality based on wealth is even more extreme – in the USA in 2007 the top 1 per cent controlled nearly 35 per cent of privately held wealth while the bottom 80 per cent was in possession of only 15 per cent (Dumhoff 2012).

5 Benefits can be regarded unpopular if seen as a disincentive to employment and a drain on the public purse; or if privileging particular social groups (e.g. public but not private sector workers, older but not younger generations).

6 In the UK high-income earners are more likely to be male, in their 40s, live in London or the South East and work in real estate, law or finance than the average tax payer (Brewer et al. 2008).

7 For a discussion of the contrasting economic properties of different kinds of work and care work in particular see Himmelweit (2007) and Folbre and Nelson (2000).

8 The bankers' salary information came from Treanor (2008) and the childcare workers pay from Payscale (2009).

9 The Occupy movement began in 2011, focusing on high levels of inequality – one slogan being 'we are the 99 per cent'. It is loosely organized and parallels the *indignados* (the outraged) in Spain.

10 One of the main reasons for this breakdown is because the corner stones of the market – land, labour and capital – are fictitious commodities, as labour relates to human beings, land to nature, and capital is 'merely a token of purchasing power' (Polanyi 1957: 75).

11 Social movements including Occupy are diverse and include anarchistic and libertarian elements as well as those pressing for progressive social change.

References

Alesina, A. and Perotti, R. (1996) 'Income Distribution, Political Instability, and Investment', *European Economic Review*, 40: 1206–228.

Alvaredo, F., Atkinson, A.B., Piketty, T. and Saez, E. (2012) The World Top Incomes Database. Available at: http://g-mond.parisschoolofeconomics.eu/topincomes (accessed 06.08.2012).

Barry, F. and Devereux, M.B. (2003) 'Expansionary Fiscal Contraction: A Theoretical Exploration', *Journal of Macroeconomics*, 25: 1–23.

Bastagli, F., Coady, D. and Gupta, S. (2012) 'Income Inequality and Fiscal Policy', IMF Staff Discussion Note 12/08. Available at: http://www.imf.org/external/pubs/ft/sdn/2012/sdn1208rev.pdf (accessed 12.12.2012).

Batini, N., Callegari, G. and Melina, G. (2012) 'Successful Austerity in the United States, Europe and Japan', IMF Working Paper WP/12/190. Available at: http://www.imf.org/external/pubs/ft/wp/2012/wp12190.pdf (accessed 12.12.2012).

Berg, A.C. and Ostry, J.D. (2011) 'Inequality and Unsustainable Growth: Two Sides of the Same Coin?' IMF Staff Discussion Note 11/08. Available at: http://www.un.org/millenniumgoals/pdf/Think%20Pieces/10_inequalities.pdf (accessed 12.12.2012).

Bettio, F., and Rosselli, A. (2008) 'Learning from Gender Budgeting for Small Administrations. The project BIG COSE in the province of Siena, Italy, European Gender Budgeting Network'. Paper presented at the conference, Public Budgeting Responsible to Gender Equality, Bilbao, 9–10 June.

Bogliacino, F. (2009) 'Poorer Workers. The Determinants of Wage Formation in Europe', *International Review of Applied Economics*, 23(3): 327–43.

Brewer, M., Sibieta, L. and Wren-Lewis, L. (2008) 'Racing Away? Income Inequality and the Evolution of High Incomes', IFS Briefing Note 76, London: Institute of Fiscal Studies. Available at: http://www.ifs.org.uk/bns/bn76.pdf (accessed 30.11.2012).

Budlender, D. (2006) 'Expectations versus Realities in Gender-responsive Budget Initiatives', in S. Razavi and S. Hassim (eds) *Gender and Social Policy in a Global Context Uncovering the Gendered Structure of 'The Social'*, Basingstoke: Palgrave Macmillan.

Butler, J. (2012) 'So, What Are the Demands? Occupy Wall Street'. Available at: http://www.scribd.com/doc/86333441/Butler-Judith-So-What-Are-the-Demands-Occupy-Wall-Street (accessed 30.11.2012).

Cameron, D. (2010) 'Transforming the British Economy: Coalition Strategy for Economic Growth'. A transcript of a speech given by Prime Minister David Cameron on 28 May 2010. Available at: http://www.number10.gov.uk/news/transforming-the-british-economy-coalition-strategy-for-economic-growth/ (accessed 06.08.2012).

Commission of the European Communities (CEC) (2008) 'Communication from the Commission to the European Council: A European Economic Recovery Plan', COM(2008) 800 final. Brussels, 26.11.2008. Available at: http://eur-lex.europa.eu/LexUriServ/LexUriServ.do?uri=COM:2008:0800:FIN:en:PDF (accessed 12.12.2012).

CEC (2010) 'Europe 2020: A European Strategy for Smart, Sustainable and Inclusive Growth', COM(2010) 2020 final. Brussels, 3.3.2010. Available at: http://eur-lex.europa.eu/LexUriServ/LexUriServ.do?uri=COM:2010:2020:FIN:EN:PDF (accessed 12.12.2012).

Council of the EU (2000) Lisbon European Council of 23–24 March 2000: Presidency Conclusions. Available at: http://consilium.europa.eu/ueDocs/cms_Data/docs/pressData/en/ec/00100-r1.en0.htm (accessed 12.12.2012).

Council of the EU (2009) 'Gender Equality: Strengthening Growth and Employment – Input to the post-2010: Lisbon Strategy – Draft Council Conclusions', Brussels, 10 November 2009 (SOC 662 -15488/09). Available at: http://www.consilium.europa.eu/uedocs/cms_data/docs/pressdata/en/lsa/111582.pdf (accessed 22.01.2013).

Daly, M. (2008) 'Whither EU Social Policy? An Account and Assessment of Developments in the Lisbon Social Inclusion Process', *Journal of Social Policy*, 37(1): 1–19.

Dumhoff, G.W. (2012) 'Wealth, Income, and Power', in *Who Rules America? Challenges to Corporate and Class Dominance*, University of California Santa Cruz Department of Sociology. Available at: http://www2.ucsc.edu/whorulesamerica/power/wealth.html (accessed 06.08.2012).

Dunford, M. and Yeung, G. (2011) 'Towards Global Convergence: Emerging Economies, the Rise of China and Western Sunset', *European Urban and Regional Studies*, 18 (1): 22–46.

Elson, D. (1998) 'The Economic, the Political and the Domestic: Business, States and Households in the Organisation of Production', *New Political Economy*, 3 (2): 189–208.

—— (2010) Gender and the Global Economic Crisis in Developing Countries: A Framework for Analysis, *Gender & Development*, 18 (2): 201–12.

Fitoussi, J-P. and Saraceno, F. (2009) 'How Deep Is a Crisis? Policy Responses and Structural Factors behind Diverging Performances', *OFCE Document de Travail 2009–31*, Paris: Centre for Economic Research. available at: http://www.ofce.sciences-po.fr/pdf/dtravail/WP2009-31.pdf (accessed 12.12.2012).

Folbre, N. and Nelson, J. (2000) 'For Love or Money – Or Both?', *Journal of Economic Perspectives,* 14 (4): 123–40.

Fraser, N. (2009) 'Feminism, Capitalism, and the Cunning of History', *New Left Review*, 56: 97–117.

—— (2012) 'Can Society be Commodities All the Way Down? Polanyian Reflections on Capitalist Crisis', Fondation Maison des Sciences de l'Homme. No 18, August 2012. Available at: http://www.msh-paris.fr/en/news/news/article/can-society-be-commodities-all-the-way-down-polanyian-reflections-on-capitalist-crisis/ (accessed 10.12.2012).

Giavazzi, F. and Pagano, M. (1990) 'Can Severe Fiscal Contractions be Expansionary? Tales From Two Small European Economies', in O.J. Blanchard and S. Fischer (Eds), *NBER Macroeconomics Annual.*

Grimshaw, D. and Rubery, J. (2012) 'The End of the UK's Liberal Collectivist Social Model? The Implications of the Coalition Government's Policy During the Austerity Crisis', *Cambridge Journal of Economics*, 36 (1): 105–26.

Himmelweit, S. (2007) 'The Prospects for Caring: Economic Theory and Policy Analysis', *Cambridge Journal of Economics*, 31 (4): 581–99.

Hobsbawm, E. (2008) 'Eric Hobsbawm says the free market has created great instability', *The Today Programme*, London: BBC. Available at: http://news.bbc.co.uk/today/hi/today/newsid_7677000/7677683.stm (accessed 6.08.2012).

ILO (2008) *World of Work Report 2008. Income Inequalities in the Age of Financial Globalisation*, Geneva: ILO. Available at: http://www.ilo.org/global/publications/books/WCMS_100354/lang--en/index.htm (accessed 30.11.2012).

IMF (2007) *World Economic Outlook Spillovers and Cycles in the Global Economy*, Washington DC: IMF. Available at: http://www.imf.org/external/pubs/ft/weo/2007/01/pdf/text.pdf (accessed 12.12.2012).

—— (2012a) United Kingdom 2012 Article IV Consultation, *IMF Country Report No. 12/190*. Available at: http://www.imf.org/external/pubs/ft/scr/2012/cr12190.pdf (accessed 12.12.2012).

—— (2012b) *World Economic Outlook: Coping with High Debt and Sluggish Growth*. October 2012, Washington DC: IMF. Available at: http://www.imf.org/external/pubs/ft/weo/2012/02/pdf/text.pdf (accessed 12.12.2012).

INEQ (2009) Europe's Inequality Challenge, *European Policy Brief*, No.4. Available at: http://ec.europa.eu/research/social-sciences/pdf/policy-briefs-inequality_en.pdf (accessed 20.05.2010).

Jenson, J. (2009) 'Lost in Translation: The Social Investment Perspective and Gender Equality', *Social Politics*, 16(4): 446–83.

Kaldor, M. and Selchow, S. with Deel, S. and Murray-Leach, T. (2012) 'The "Bubbling Up" of Subterranean Politics in Europe', Civil Society and Human Security Research Unit, London School of Economics and Political Science. Available at: http://www.subterraneanpolitics.eu (accessed 02.08. 2012).

Keynes, J. (1931) 'Economic Possibilities for our Grandchildren', in *Essays in Persuasion*, London: Macmillan.

—— (1933/1983) *The Collected Works of John Maynard Keynes: Volume 29*, London: Palgrave Macmillan.

Klatzer, E. and Schlager, C. (2012) 'New Gender Equality Challenges in the Context of the New Economic Governance in the European Union', Paper given at the IAFFE Annual Conference Facultat de Geografia i Historia, Universitat de Barcelona, Barcelona, 27–29. 06. 2012

Krugman, P. (2002) 'For Richer', *New York Times*, October 20th. Available at: http://www.pkarchive.org/economy/ForRicher.html (accessed 27.05.2012).

—— (2012a) *End this Depression Now!* New York: Norton.

—— (2012b) End this Depression Now! Public lecture, London School of Economics, 29 May. Available at: http://www2.lse.ac.uk/newsAndMedia/videoAndAudio/channels/publicLecturesAndEvents/player.aspx?id=1494 (accessed 05.06.2012).

Kumhof, M. and Rancière, R. (2010) 'Inequality, Leverage, and Crises', IMF Working Paper 10/268 Washington DC: IMF. Available at: http://www.imf.org/external/pubs/ft/wp/2010/wp10268.pdf (accessed 12.12.2012).

Lewis, J. (2006) 'Work/family Reconciliation, Equal Opportunities and Social Policies: The Interpretation of Policy Trajectories at the EU Level and the Meaning of Gender Equality', *Journal of European Public Policy*, 13 (3): 420–37.

Löfström, Å. (2009) *Gender Equality, Economic Growth and Employment*, Stockholm: Swedish Ministry of Integration and Gender Equality. Available at: http://www.se2009.eu/polopoly_fs/1.17994!menu/standard/file/EUstudie_sidvis.pdf (accessed 12.12.2012).

Metcalf, H. and Rolfe, H. (2009) *Employment and Earnings in the Finance Sector: A Gender Analysis*, EHRC Research Report 17, London: EHRC. Available at: http://www.equalityhumanrights.com/uploaded_files/download__finance_gender_analyis_research.pdf (accessed 12.12.2012).

Ministry of Welfare (2012) 'Parliamentary Resolution on a Four Year Gender Equality Action Programme'. Available at: http://eng.velferdarraduneyti.is/newsinenglish/nr/33182 (accessed 30.11.2012).

Nelson, J. (2006) *Economics for Humans*. Chicago: University of Chicago Press.

OECD (2008) *Growing Unequal. Income Distribution and Poverty in OECD Countries*. Paris: OECD. Available at: http://www.oecd.org/els/socialpoliciesanddata/growingunequal incomedistributionandpovertyinoecdcountries.htm (accessed 15.08.2012).

—— (2011) *Divided We Stand: Why Inequality Keeps Rising*, Paris: OECD. Available at: http://www.oecd.org/els/socialpoliciesanddata/dividedwestandwhyinequalitykeepsrising.htm (accessed 15.08.2012).

—— (2012a) OECD Earnings Database, Inter Decile Ratios. Available at: http://stats.oecd.org/Index.aspx?DatasetCode=DEC_I (accessed 09.12.12).

—— (2012b) *Gender Equality in Education, Employment and Entrepreneurship*: Final Report to the MCM, Paris: OECD. Available at: http://www.oecd.org/social/familiesandchildren/50423364.pdf (accessed 15.08.2012).

—— (2012c) Earnings Database, Gender Wage Gap. Available at: http://www.oecd.org/els/employmentpoliciesanddata/onlineoecdemploymentdatabasehtm (accessed 05.05.2012).

ONS (2012) Gross Domestic Product Estimates, Available at: http://www.ons.gov.uk/ons/dcp171778_264972.pdf (accessed 15.08.2012).

Payscale (2009) *Salary Survey Report for Job: Child Care/Day Care Worker*. Available at: http://www.payscale.com/research/UK/Job=Child_Care_%2F_Day_Care_Worker/Salary (accessed 05.05.2012).

Perrons, D. and Plomien, A. (2010) *Why Socio-economic Inequalities Increase? Facts and Policy Responses in Europe*. EUR 24471 EN. European Commission: Brussels.

Polanyi, K. (1957) *The Great Transformation. The Political and Economic Origins of our Time*, Boston: Beacon Press.

Quah, D. (2011) 'The Global Economy's Shifting Centre of Gravity', *Global Politics*, 2(1): 3–9.

Rajan, R. (2010) *Fault Lines: How Hidden Fractures Still Threaten the World Economy*, Princeton: Princeton University Press.

Reich, R. (2010) Recession caused by '*surging wealth inequality*', 8 July. Available at: http://coyoteprime-runningcauseicantfly.blogspot.com/2010/07/robert-reich-recession-cause-by-surging.html (accessed 08.08.2012).

Rosnick, D. and Baker, D. (2012) *Missing the Story, The OECD's Analysis of Inequality* (No. 2012-19), Washington DC: Centre for Economic Policy Research.

Scottish Government Social Research (2010) Coping with Change and Uncertainty: Scotland's Equalities Groups and The Recession. Available at: http://www.scotland.gov.uk/Resource/Doc/331394/0107863.pdf (accessed 08.08.2012).

—— (2011) The Position of Scotland's Equality Groups Revisiting Resilience in 2011. Available at: http://www.scotland.gov.uk/Resource/Doc/175356/0124251.pdf (accessed 08.08.2012).

Seguino, S. (2010) 'The Global Economic Crisis, Its Gender and Ethnic Implications, and Policy Responses', *Gender and Development*, 18 (2): 179–99.

Seguino, S. and Grown, C. (2007) 'Gender Equity and Globalization: Macroeconomic Policy for Developing Countries', in van Staveren, I., Elson, D., Grown, C. and Çagatay, N. (eds) *Feminist Economics of Trade*, London: Routledge.

Sen, A. (1999) *Development as Freedom*, Oxford: Oxford University Press.

Skidelsky, R. (2011) 'The Relevance of Keynes', *Cambridge Journal of Economics*, 35 (1): 1–13.

—— (2012) 'Printing Money and Tax Cuts Aren't Enough. We Need Real Investment', London: New Statesman, 1 March. Available at: http://www.newstatesman.com/economy/2012/03/investment-government-policy (accessed 27.05.2012).

Smith, M. and Villa, P. (2010) 'The Ever-declining Role of Gender Equality in the European Employment Strategy', *Industrial Relations Journal*, 41(6): 526–43.

Stiglitz, J. (2011) 'Of the 1%, by the 1%, for the 1%', *Vanity Fair*, May Issue. Available at: http://www.vanityfair.com/society/features/2011/05/top-one-percent-201105 (accessed 10.12.2012).

—— (2012) *The Price of Inequality: How Today's Divided Society Endangers Our Future*, London: W.W. Norton.

Storey, A. (2008) 'The Ambiguity of Resistance: Opposition to Neoliberalism in Europe', *Capital & Class*, 32: 55–85.

Treanor, J. (2008) 'Lloyds Offers Sidelined HBOS Head £60,000-A-Month Consultancy Role', *Guardian*, 5 November. Available at: http://www.guardian.co.uk/business/2008/nov/05/andy-hornby-lloyds-tsb-hbos (accessed 15.05.2012).

Turner, A. (2009) 'The Financial Crisis and the Future of Financial Regulation', Speech by Adair Turner, Chair, FSA, *The Economist*'s Inaugural City Lecture, 21 January 2009. Available at: http://www.fsa.gov.uk/library/communication/speeches/2009/0121_at.shtml (accessed 12.12.2012).

UNCTAD (2012) *Trade and Development Report, 2012, Report by the secretariat of the United Nations Conference on Trade and Development*, New York: UNCTAD. Available at: http://unctad.org/en/PublicationsLibrary/tdr2012_en.pdf (accessed 12.12.2012).

Wilkinson, R. and Pickett, K. (2009) *The Spirit Level. Why More Equal Societies Almost Always Do Better*, London: Allen Lane.

Women's Budget Group (WBG) (2012) 'The Impact on Women of Budget 2012'. Available at: http://wbg.org.uk/pdfs/The-Impact-on-Women-of-the-Budget-2012-FINAL.pdf (accessed 30.11.2012).

16

ECONOMIC CRISIS AND AUSTERITY

Challenges to gender equality

Maria Karamessini and Jill Rubery

To conclude this volume we apply the conceptual frameworks proposed in Part 1 to provide a comparative analysis of the immediate, unfurling and potential long-term impacts of the financial crisis and subsequent austerity policies on gender equality. To provide the context for understanding these effects we first explore the evolution of the gender regimes before the crisis in the case study countries. The second part summarizes how women and men have so far fared in the crisis and musters the evidence on both the emerging austerity policies and labour market trends to assess how they may fare in the future. The final section considers the longer-run implications of austerity policies and associated institutional changes for gender inequalities and the gender regimes. The key argument made is that although gender equality defined in the narrow sense of closing aggregate gender gaps in employment indicators may even have improved in the first phase of the recession, there are three core reasons why future prospects are bleak. First, much of the apparent progress in closing gender gaps has been achieved only by a levelling down of men's employment position and prospects; second, the full implementation of austerity plans is likely to harm women's employment position more than men's; and third, and most importantly, the pursuit of gender equality as a socially progressive agenda is being put into question by the reinforcement of neo-liberal policies that extend the market into all areas of activity and threaten to reverse pre-crisis trends towards greater social investment and de-familialization of care in the European country cases. These policies are affecting men as well as women. As such, not only does more common cause need to be made across the gender divide but gender equality has to be placed at the centre of any progressive plan for a route out of the crisis.

Trends in gender regimes pre-crisis: towards a universal adult worker model?

The characteristics of gender regimes can be expected to shape the impact of the crisis on gender inequalities. Particularly important are the degree to which women are integrated into the wage economy and the form of this integration, both embedded and reinforced by country-specific arrangements in life course and family organization, social and economic policies, labour market institutions and social norms. These reinforcing institutions may promote strong integration but also, alternatively, marginalization. The level and form of integration is likely to influence women's resistance to pressures to displace them from employment but recession in some contexts may also induce greater integration. The second key factor is the extent of continuing gender differences in employment. These gender differences in the distribution of employment by occupation and sector, employment forms and working conditions influence vulnerability to displacement by recession and austerity but also prospects for the future. While these factors influence the aggregate gender outcomes, there is increasing evidence of variation within genders by factors such as class, education, age or nationality. Our third sub-section thus briefly outlines some intra-gender differences of significance in studying recession and austerity impacts.

Gender regimes and women's integration into paid employment

In the pre-crisis period there was a clear case of converging divergences in the extent of women's integration into paid employment. Strong upward trends in female employment rates between 1994 and 2007 in eight of the nine case study countries still resulted in wide disparities in female employment rates even in 2007 (from 46.6 per cent in Italy to 81.7 per cent in Iceland). The rises were spectacular in Spain and Ireland (24 and 21.8 percentage points respectively) and impressive in Italy and Greece (11.2 and 10.8 percentage points respectively), all countries with employment rates below even 40 per cent in 1994. However, of these, only Ireland exceeded the 60 per cent Lisbon target for the female employment rate in 2007. Among the initial high employment rate countries (54 per cent or above), three – Portugal, Iceland and the UK – also experienced substantial rises (7.8, 7.1 and 4.2 percentage points respectively) but the USA registered only a small 0.7 percentage point increase. Nevertheless, all reached or substantially exceeded the Lisbon target. Hungary's employment rate had also started to rise before the crisis, up six percentage points by 2007 to 50.9 per cent from its low of 44.8 per cent in 1997, but this was still far below its socialist economy level of 80.7 per cent in 1988.

This high dispersion largely reflected differences in integration among the *low-educated* (Table 16.2), *younger* and *older* women (Table 16.1) and to some extent the *medium-educated* women (Table 16.2). In contrast, tertiary-educated women all had employment rates close to or above the new EU2020 employment rate target of 75 per cent already in 2007. Their universal high integration is significant as over recent decades previous educational gender gaps have reduced in all nine countries, and even reversed in seven, so that now more women have completed tertiary

TABLE 16.1 Female employment rates by age in selected European countries and the US 1994, 2007

	1994	2007	Δ1994–2007	2007		
	15–64 y.	15–64 y.	in p.p.	15–24 y.	25–54 y.	55–64 y.
Greece	37.1	47.9	10.8	18.7	60.8	26.9
Hungary	47.8	50.9	3.1	17.8	67.9	26.2
Iceland	74.6	81.7	7.1	75.0	84.1	80.0
Ireland	38.9	60.7	21.8	47.1	69.6	40.0
Italy	35.4	46.6	11.2	19.5	59.6	23.0
Portugal	54.1	61.9	7.8	30.6	74.9	44.0
Spain	31.5	55.5	24.0	37.0	65.6	30.0
UK	62.1	66.3	4.2	54.8	74.6	48.9
USA	65.2	65.9	0.7	51.8	72.5	56.6
EU-21 average	49.9	58.5	8.6	35.8	71.1	35.8
OECD average	52.9	57.2	4.3	39.2	66.3	43.6

y=years, p.p.=percentage points.

Source: OECD.Stat (data extracted on 28.12.2012).

education than men (see Table 16.3). The consequence is that younger cohorts of women in particular have developed aspirations for continuous employment over the lifecycle and gender equality in paid work.

TABLE 16.2 Female employment rates of 25–64 year-olds by educational attainment level in selected European countries and the US 2007

	Below upper secondary (1)	Upper secondary and post-secondary non-tertiary (2)	Tertiary education (3)	Difference (3)–(1)
Hungary	32.6	62.9	75.6	42.9
Italy	33.6	64.5	74.9	41.3
Greece	39.0	54.6	77.7	38.7
Ireland	40.8	65.5	82.5	41.7
Spain	42.8	66.6	79.7	36.9
USA	45.4	67.6	78.1	32.7
UK	57.5	75.9	85.8	28.4
Portugal	62.8	77.3	83.7	21.0
Iceland	77.9	80.9	89.3	11.4
EU-19 average	45.6	68.3	81.4	35.8
OECD average	47.6	66.7	79.2	31.6

Source: OECD, Education at a Glance 2010: OECD Indicators, Paris.

TABLE 16.3 Educational attainment of women and men aged 25–64 years in selected European countries and the US 2009

	Share (%) of population with at least upper secondary education		Share (%) of population with tertiary education	
	Women	Men	Women	Men
Greece	62.7	59.8	23.1	23.9
Hungary	77.5	83.8	22.1	17.5
Iceland	64.7	67.0	36.6	29.0
Ireland	74.7	68.4	38.7	33.0
Italy	55.1	53.5	16.0	13.0
Portugal	32.4	27.3	17.3	11.9
Spain	52.7	50.9	30.7	28.7
United Kingdom	70.4	77.0	37.0	36.7
United States	89.7	87.6	43.4	39.0
EU-21 average	74.0	75.3	42.5	33.7
OECD average	72.3	74.2	39.1	29.2

Source: OECD (2011), Education at a Glance 2011: OECD Indicators, Paris.

The variety in gender regimes covered by our sample of countries certainly reflects the history of women's integration in paid work in each country, shaped – as everywhere – by the specificities of the economy's industrialization and tertiarization pattern, welfare state development and evolution of family model and gender contract (Boserup 1970; Tilly and Scott 1978; Beneria and Sen 1981; Lewis 1992; Ostner 1994; Sainsbury 1994). The USA, the UK and Iceland were in the vanguard of tertiarization and concomitant feminization of the workforce while Portugal followed a different route to high female employment linked to colonial wars, mass male emigration and the growth of labour-intensive export industries (André 1996, Ferreira in this volume). In Italy, Spain, Greece and Ireland in the 1970s and 1980s employment demand failed to keep pace with rising female aspirations for employment, resulting in both the lowest female employment rates in the former EU12 and the highest female unemployment rates. Hungary, as already mentioned, moved from being a high to a relatively low female employment country, with the female employment rate plunging by around 36 percentage points between 1988 and 1997 before starting to rise slowly.

Notwithstanding historical legacies, there is evidence that these pre-crisis developments in female employment patterns were being embedded and supported by fairly radical reforms in labour market institutions and the welfare state in the 1990s and 2000s and by continuing changes in gender norms and values. Common trends in employment and social policy, especially in Europe, can be in part attributed to the core focus of EU employment and social policies, from the mid-1990s onwards, on mobilizing the potential labour supply of inactive people to counter demographic ageing. Under the EU's European Employment Strategy (Villa and

Smith this volume) promotion of women's employment and gender equality gained a new legitimacy, which pushed all EU member states to improve their parental leave systems and increase childcare services to assist in meeting the goal of higher maternal employment rates. The 'familialistic' care regimes of the southern European countries (Bettio and Plantenga 2004) made a considerable turn in family policy. In the pre-crisis decade all four improved childcare coverage (especially in Portugal and Spain (Gonzalez Gago and Segales Kirzner this volume; Ferreira this volume)) and Greece developed a generous and gender egalitarian parental leave system (Ray *et al.* 2010). The UK also made important changes in its care regime after the late 1990s including extended leaves, increased opportunities for flexible working, the first significant spread of childcare services and the uprating of child benefits and child tax credits (Rubery and Rafferty this volume). Ireland too uprated child benefits and other family support payments and extended entitlements to maternity leave but still left families dependent on very costly private market services for childcare (Barry and Conroy this volume). Finally, Hungary experienced the closing down of childcare centres and nurseries but to a lesser extent than in other ex-communist countries. Childcare coverage for children aged 0–2 dropped from 13.7 per cent in the early 1990s to around 9 per cent in the 2000s but enrolment rates for children aged 3–6 years remained stable at more than 80 per cent (Szikra and Szelewa 2010). The restructured leave arrangements reinforced previous patterns where mothers with young children were encouraged to take long leaves. Although little change took place in the care regimes of the US and Iceland from the early 1990s to the onset of the crisis, they nevertheless represented opposite ends of the spectrum of care regimes with the US providing only limited leave entitlements or public childcare and Iceland providing extensive childcare and flexible paid leaves for both parents, resulting in the highest take up of parental leave by fathers in Europe (Thorsdottir this volume).

Again, these common trends have not erased the large divergences among national care regimes. As Table 16.4 shows, with the exception of the US, the countries with the lowest enrolment rates of children aged 0–2 in formal care were those with the highest non-employment rates for mothers. In Hungary this is due to most mothers taking the three years paid parental leave. In Greece, a huge mobilization of informal carers – mainly grandparents and relatives – compensates for inadequate formal care services for all children up to age six while in Ireland, another country with high maternal non-employment rates, parents have only limited access to informal childcare arrangements. Interestingly, despite the absence of national paid leave policies and the availability of only means-tested child and elder care state supports, women in the USA record high full-time employment rates (Albelda this volume) while the employment rates of mothers are close to the OECD average. At the other extreme, in 2008 Iceland had the third highest coverage rate of formal childcare for ages 0–2 in the OECD.

Women's increasing integration in paid work has been reinforced by and is reinforcing changes in family models. Life courses have become more varied; there are now more single people and more lone parents with the share of lone-parent

TABLE 16.4 Childcare regimes and maternal non-employment in selected European countries and the US 2008

	Maternal non-employment rate (%)	Enrolment rates (%) of children in formal care and pre-schools		Coverage rate (%) of children by informal childcare arrangements	
	25–54 years	0–2 years	3–5 years	0–2 years	3–5 years
Hungary	45.6	8.8	87.1	31.6	38.7
Greece	41.2	15.7	46.6	52.5	38.7
Italy	44.8	29.2	97.4	31.5	37.0
Ireland	41.3	30.8	56.4	13.6	16.7
United States	33.3	31.4	55.7		
Spain	40.0	37.5	98.5	19.5	9.1
United Kingdom	32.9	40.8	92.7	31.7	36.9
Portugal	24.6	47.4	79.2	25.4	35.9
Iceland	15.2	55.0	95.9	2.2	0.1
EU-27 average		28.2	81.8	23.7	24.8
OECD average	33.8	30.1	77.3		

Source: OECD Education and family data bases.

families in all households with children among our nine countries ranging from a low of 15.8 per cent in Portugal to highs of 26.4 per cent and 28.3 per cent respectively in the UK and the USA. These changes in family structures encourage women to seek and secure economic independence. Another factor reinforcing women's integration is the importance of women's wages in family budgets. There has been an increase in dual-earner households in all case study countries except Hungary but there are still diverse working patterns at the household level. Dual-earner households are now the most common form in all nine countries but Iceland, Portugal and Hungary. The USA had the highest shares of couples with both partners working full time while in a very large share of dual-earner couples in the UK, Ireland and Italy the woman worked only part-time. Ireland, Italy, Spain and Greece had the largest shares of male-breadwinner families. These country differences are to some extent the outcome of the variety of gender contracts in the pre-crisis gender regimes (O'Reilly and Nazio this volume) and relate to four broad national models corresponding to different 'time policy' regimes (Anxo et al. 2007). Among our nine countries Iceland and Portugal come closest to the Nordic model exemplified by Sweden of continuous full-time or long part-time employment although Iceland has a higher share of short hour part-time jobs. The USA follows the 'modified breadwinner model' – typically represented by France – where some mothers withdraw from the labour market but those in employment work predominantly full time. The UK and Ireland fit the 'maternal part-time work model' where mothers normally work part-time even when children are older; and finally Greece, Italy, Spain plus now Hungary fit the

'Mediterranean exit or full-time work model' where fewer women are employed but when employed generally work full-time. However, this is changing as Italy and Spain now have high and medium female part-time work rates respectively, achieved after systematic state intervention in the 1990s and 2000s (Karamessini 2008) implying that, part-time work had become an option for increasing numbers of working mothers in these countries. Taking into account these differences in working hours would increase the gaps between employment rates of mothers with dependent children and other women in some countries, notably the UK and Ireland in our sample (Figure 16.1).

All these trends suggest a pattern prior to the recession of converging divergences. There are common upward trends in female employment, female aspirations for employment, support for working parents and diversity of household arrangements, including those where women's wages provide the sole or a joint source of income support. Yet within these upward trends there are also strong differences between the nine countries on each of these dimensions, suggesting different degrees of embeddedness of female integration in social norms and the wider social and economic system.

Gender differences within employment

A critical factor shaping whether women or men are more vulnerable to the crisis and austerity policy effects is their position within the labour market. Recession and austerity effects vary across sectors, firms, occupations and workforce groups;

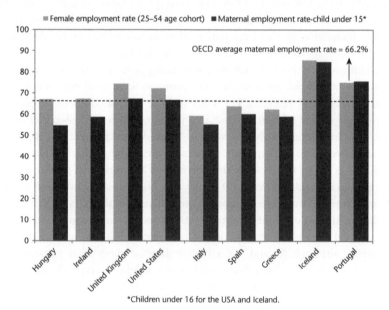

*Children under 16 for the USA and Iceland.

FIGURE 16.1 Maternal compared to female employment rates in selected European countries and the US 2009

these varying impacts are discussed and compared in Bettio and Verashchagina (this volume) and in the next section below. The key issue to note here is that despite the greater integration of women into paid work the form of work continues to be distinct from that carried out by men. This is found in continuing gender segregation by occupations and sector. According to an EU-wide report by Bettio and Verashchagina (2009), the degree of occupational segregation remained stable at an aggregate level for the EU27 and EU15 between 1992 and 2000 and then rose slightly up to 2007 while segregation by sector increased more strongly. As regards occupational segregation, the IP index[1] for our eight European countries, taking per cent values from 0 to 50, ranged from 22.4 per cent in Greece to 28.8 per cent in Hungary in 2007 (Table 16.5). In six countries the values of the index were higher in 2007 compared to 1997, with Iceland and the UK the exceptions. In 2007 the value of the IP index for the USA was 25 per cent (Alonso-Villar et al. 2010). Sectoral segregation, although somewhat lower than occupational – at 15.6 per cent in Greece and rising to a high of 23.3 in Ireland – also increased over this time period in all the European countries in our sample but the UK. Thus rising employment does not always lead to reduced gender segregation levels and may even increase them.

Another form of segregation, which makes women vulnerable to austerity in particular, is their greater reliance on the public sector. Measured by employment in public administration, education and health, which overstates the share of actual public sector employment, it accounts for 20 to 45 per cent of total female against 13 to 17 per cent of total male employment in our nine countries (Table 16.6). The

TABLE 16.5 Indicators of cross-country gender differences within employment in selected European countries and the US 2007

Countries	Segregation*		Part-time rate**		Temporary employment rate**	
	Occupational	Sectoral	Men	Women	Men	Women
Greece	22.4	15.6	5.0	13.7	9.3	13.1
Hungary	28.8	20.1	1.6	4.2	7.7	6.8
Iceland	27.5	23.0	7.8	24.8	11.2	13.6
Ireland	27.9	23.3	7.5	34.9	6.7	9.5
Italy	23.6	17.8	5.3	31.2	11.2	15.9
Portugal	26.5	20.6	2.0	8.7	21.8	23.0
Spain	27.5	20.7	3.4	20.8	30.6	33.1
UK	25.3	18.7	9.1	37.2	5.3	6.4
USA	25.0		7.6	17.9	4.2	4.2

* Measured by the IP index (per cent values from 0 to 50). ** Per cent of dependent employment.

Note: Segregation indices for Iceland refer to 2006; the temporary employment rates for the USA refer to 2005.

Sources: For segregation indices: Bettio and Verashchagina (2009) and Alonso-Villar et al. (2010); for part-time and temporary employment rates: OECD.stat (data extracted on 22.12.2012).

TABLE 16.6 Share of public sector employment* in total employment by sex in selected European countries and the US 2008

				%		
	All employed men	All employed women	High-educated women	Medium-educated women	Low-educated women	Female share of all employed
Iceland	14	45	62	37	39	74
UK	16	43	59	37	31	70
Ireland	15	38	49	28	30	73
Hungary	13	33	56	24	23	69
Italy	13	30	54	29	15	61
Greece	14	28	56	20	8	54
Portugal	17	28	59	27	18	65
Spain	15	26	44	20	11	61
USA	13 (18)	20 (40)				57 (66)

* Public administration, education, health and social work for European countries. Federal state and local government employment, including government-owned schools and hospitals and the Postal Service for the USA. **Figures in parentheses for the USA also include private education and health services and are comparable with those for the other eight countries.

Source: For European countries, European Labour Force Survey, special tabulations; for the USA, Current Population Survey (own elaboration of BLS online data extracted on 22.12.2012).

public sector also provides a very high share of female university graduate employment in all the European countries, making these women particularly vulnerable to austerity policies. It accounts for a lower share of medium- and low-educated women with the public sector only an important employer for this latter group in Iceland, the UK and Ireland. However, for this group the quality of jobs on offer compared to equivalent private sector jobs tends to be higher (Rubery 2013). US women, both high and low educated, are more concentrated in the private sector than in Europe, relying both on the greater opportunities for the more advantaged to enter high level private sector jobs and the growth of a low-wage labour market staffed by the less advantaged groups, including women, to provide personal services to the higher paid women and men (Mandel and Shalev 2009). The same services are today provided by large numbers of migrant women in southern European countries (Bettio et al. 2006), frequently working informally.

Women may also be more vulnerable to recession due to their greater involvement in part-time and temporary jobs that are more easily eliminated through redundancies. However, although there is a significant gender gap in part-time work in all nine countries there are major differences in the concentration of women in part-time work, reflecting national differences in working time regimes and forms of flexible working (O'Reilly and Fagan 1998; Rubery et al. 1998; Rubery et al. 1999; Gornick and Heron 2008; Plantenga and Remery 2010).

There was also a gender gap to women's disadvantage in the incidence of temporary employment in 2007 in seven of the nine countries, even if much smaller than that in part-time work and insignificant in the UK, non-existent in the USA and to men's disadvantage in Hungary (Table 16.5). Some self-employed workers are also potentially vulnerable to recession. This mainly applies to those categories in which women are most commonly found including: unpaid female workers in family businesses and farms particularly in Greece (Karamessini this volume); dependent workers classified as self-employed, particularly in Portugal and Greece (Ferreira this volume, Karamessini this volume); and informal workers, most numerous in Southern but also Eastern Europe countries such as Hungary (Frey this volume). These different examples point to the importance of interactions between the employment regime and the form of gender integration in shaping vulnerability to recession.

Intra-gender differences

Reduced aggregate gender differences in employment patterns have been accompanied almost everywhere by persistence or even growth in intra-gender differences, albeit with considerable variation across countries. Regional disparities in women's employment rates are strong in many countries but huge in Italy; with female employment rates in the North almost twice those in the South and female unemployment rates only a third as high even pre-crisis (Verashchagina and Capparucci this volume). These patterns reflect the stagnation of the Southern economy compared to the more dynamic North (Andreotti and Mingione 2012).

In all EU countries migrant women tend to experience in many areas of their lives a 'double disadvantage' by being both female and a migrant (Rubin *et al.* 2008). In some EU member states non-EU born women's employment rates exceeded those of EU-born women while in others the opposite was the case. The former applies mainly to the Southern and Eastern European member states including those studied here, that is to 'new' immigration countries, while the latter applies to the Northern EU member states, in particular the 'old' immigration countries.

There are also differences in female employment patterns over the life course. Female employment rates are particularly low for young women in Greece, Italy and Hungary, reflecting not only their investment in education but also difficulties in integrating into employment even before the crisis. These same countries also have very low female employment rates for older workers, reflecting the low activity of these older cohorts in prime age (European Commission 2007). Low legal ages of retirement for women in Italy and Greece and various early retirement options exerted a further dampening effect. In Hungary, older women who faced job loss and unemployment in the transition to capitalism made massive use of the early retirement options (Frey this volume). Conversely, the high official age of retirement in Spain has had limited effect due to the low activity rates in prime age of current older cohorts of women. Iceland stands out at the other end of the spectrum with a long-standing retirement age at 67 for both women and men and an employment rate of 80 per cent reflecting integration across a long working life (Thorsdottir this volume). Older women are now everywhere facing rising retirement ages due to both equalization of retirement ages with men and other policies to postpone retirement or reduce incentives to retire early. Thus maintaining integration for older women is turning into an economic necessity such that older women are less likely to act as a labour force buffer in economic downturns or indeed as a source of informal care support as early withdrawal from the labour force is now very costly for women and their families.

From he-cession to sh(e)austerity

Assessing labour market developments

The key patterns to emerge from a cross country and gender analysis of the immediate and unfurling effects of crisis are fourfold: women and men have shared the falls in employment, ending the long-run upward trend in women's employment, but the immediate effects on men have been stronger, leading to reductions in gender gaps; segregation by sector is the main cause of these gender effects but while segregation protected women in the recession, under austerity they face greater risks; these risks vary within genders, with young people of both genders facing the most severe problems but the impact on other forms of inequality varies by country; finally, women's response to the demand downturn has been primarily to reinforce their commitment to the labour market through added worker effects. Women are thus not acting as a buffer either in protecting men against job loss or acting as a labour reserve in voluntarily withdrawing from the labour market.

Table 16.7 shows that the 'Great Recession' has reversed the long-term upward trend in female employment rates in Europe and the USA and pushed up female unemployment rates. In mid-2012, when the EU was entering a second recessionary dip, the employment rates of both women and men were much lower and their unemployment rates much higher than pre-crisis in all nine case study countries (Table 16.7), even though about half experienced growth in 2010 and 2011. The most dramatic employment effects were in Greece, Spain and Ireland where male employment rates dropped by 14 to 15 percentage points and female rates by 4 to 7 since mid-2008. Only in Italy and Hungary did the female employment rate return to or exceed respectively the mid-2008 level by mid-2012.

The impact of the crisis on gender inequalities in the labour market has been a downward levelling of gender gaps in employment, unemployment, economic activity and pay, as demonstrated by Bettio and Verashchagina's (this volume) comparative study of EU countries. This is due to faster declines in men's employment in the initial years of the crisis, a pattern largely followed by our nine countries. The 'he-cession' was followed by 'he-recovery' in the USA where male employment

TABLE 16.7 Employment and unemployment rates in selected European countries and the US 2008, 2012

	Employment rate %				Unemployment rate %			
	Men		Women		Men		Women	
	2008q2	2012q2	2008q2	2012q2	2008q2	2012q2	2008q2	2012q2
Italy	70.5	66.5	47.2	47.2	5.6	10.1	9.0	11.8
Hungary	63.1	62.2	50.2	52.2	7.6	11.6	8.1	10.5
Greece	75.3	60.6	48.8	42.0	4.9	21.7	11.4	28.0
Spain	74.3	60.4	55.2	50.9	9.1	24.7	12.4	25.0
Ireland	75.7	62.4	60.7	54.8	6.4	18.5	4.0	11.2
Portugal	74.3	65.6	62.8	59.0	6.7	16.1	9.2	16.0
USA	76.9	72.1	65.7	62.2	5.6	8.5	5.2	8.0
UK	77.6	75.2	66.0	64.8	5.8	8.6	4.9	7.5
Iceland	88.7	81.9	79.7	78.3	2.6	5.8	2.3	6.1
EU-27	72.9	69.8	58.8	58.6	6.5	10.5	9.2	16.0

Note: Employment and unemployment rates refer respectively to the population and active population aged 15–64 years.
Source: OECD.Stat (data extracted on 24.12.2012).

rose more strongly than female from 2009 onwards (Albelda this volume) and in the UK where it increased against further declines for women after late 2009 (Rubery and Rafferty this volume). In Italy and Hungary – the other two countries with positive GDP growth in both 2010 and 2011 – the recovery of female employment was stronger than male. This has been also the case in Iceland since 2011 (Table 16.8).

The rise in men's unemployment rate was also higher in all countries except Iceland but between mid-2008 and 2012 the increase in percentage points was roughly equal in Greece, the USA and the UK (93 to 99 per cent of the male increase) and not far behind in Spain and Portugal (81 and 72 per cent of the male increase respectively), implying relatively equal increased misery in all six countries. In contrast in Italy, Hungary and Ireland the increase for women was only around three-fifths that experienced by men. By mid-2012 only Italy and Greece had significant gender gaps in favour of men although even here the size of the gender gap in Italy had halved to 1.7 percentage points. Spain and Portugal had also seen sizeable pre-crisis gaps in favour of men disappear as unemployment rates roughly equalized for the two genders. In Iceland the unemployment rates of men and women remained roughly equal but men's slight disadvantage had been turned into a slight advantage. In Hungary the gender gap switched from a small disadvantage for women to a more sizeable disadvantage for men. The UK, the USA and Ireland started with a disadvantage for men but, while this increased slightly in the former two cases in Ireland, it increased from a gap of 2.4 to 7.3 percentage points over the four years.

TABLE 16.8 Change in employment by total and in public sector services in selected European countries and the US 2008–2010, 2010–2012

	Total	(Total female)	Public administration	Education	Health	All public sector	(All public sector female)
	End year – initial year change (%)						
	All NACE		NACE O*	NACE P	NACE Q**	NACE O+P+Q	
	2008q2–2010q2						
Ireland	−12.0	(−6.5)	5.3	3.0	6.4	5.1	(3.9)
Greece	−3.4	(−0.8)	−2.2	2.8	7.4	1.9	(5.2)
Spain	−9.6	(−5.1)	7.2	3.7	7.9	6.3	(7.3)
Italy	−2.4	(−1.0)	−2.0	−4.4	1.4	−1.6	(−0.7)
Hungary	−2.3	(0.3)	8.1	3.8	0.2	4.1	(4.8)
Portugal	−4.7	(−3.0)	−10.6	7.5	16.5	3.8	(8.1)
UK	−2.4	(−1.5)	−8.3	14.2	5.3	4.8	(5.2)
Iceland	−8.0	(−2.6)	−3.3	−4.5	9.8	1.3	(−2.3)
USA	−4.6	(−3.4)	1.1	3.7	3.7	2.4	(2.1)
	2010q2–2012q2						
Ireland	−1.5	(−0.5)	−8.1	−1.5	4.2	−0.2	(−0.5)
Greece	−14.1	(−13.5)	−13.2	−7.8	−7.1	−9.8	(−14.8)
Spain	−5.8	(−2.8)	−3.6	0.9	2.6	−0.1	(2.7)
Italy	0.1	(2.5)	−2.9	−0.7	3.0	0.0	(0.5)
Hungary	2.4	(2.2)	1.8	1.1	2.5	1.8	(0.5)
Portugal	−5.9	(−4.6)	−5.3	3.8	8.9	2.7	(2.2)
UK	1.3	(0.9)	−7.0	−1.8	0.9	−1.8	(−1.0)
Iceland	1.7	(2.6)	−4.6	−3.7	−9.5	−6.3	(−6.4)
USA	2.1	(1.6)	−3.7	5.6	3.7	−0.1	(0.2)

* In the EU and Iceland it refers to public adminstration, defence and compulsory social security while in the USA to federal, state and local government employment, including government-owned schools and hospitals and the US Postal Service. ** In all countries the sector also includes social care and social assistance work.

Sources: Own elaboration of data from the European Labour Force Survey (Eurostat online) and the US Current Population Survey (BLS online) - data extracted on 22.12.2012.

Sectoral and occupational segregation by sex provides the main explanation for the less steep fall in female employment rates during recession in all nine countries. Bettio and Verashchagina (this volume) found that the cross-country comparative vulnerability of male and female employment to recession in the EU is correlated with cross-country differences in the degree of sectoral and occupational segregation. In fact, sectoral segregation appears as the main determinant of the pattern of job loss in recession and under austerity, with the initial recession blasts hitting mainly male-dominated construction and manufacturing in all nine countries together with finance in the USA, UK, Iceland and Ireland. Only later did the recession spread to the more mixed private services where women became more vulnerable to job loss. It is, however the timing, severity and form of austerity policies and their direct effects on public sector employment that have mostly differentiated the pattern of job loss across countries along the different phases of the crisis and the size of its negative employment impact on women.

Table 16.8 shows that aggregate employment in public administration, education and health and social care grew during the first phase of the crisis except in Italy. This exerted a strong positive influence on overall female employment due to women's high representation, except in Iceland and again Italy where in both cases women's employment fell. During the next phase this protection effect effectively disappeared; only two countries, Portugal and Hungary, recorded positive growth, in four countries public employment stagnated (Italy, USA, Spain, Ireland) while in the UK, Iceland and Greece employment fell by 1.8, 6.4 and 9.8 per cent respectively. The fall in Greece is the joint outcome of huge reductions in temporary jobs, hiring restrictions and mass take-up of early retirement in anticipation of pension reforms while redundancies of permanent public sector employees have just started (Karamessini this volume).

These aggregate second stage developments reduced protection for women but the pattern of change was quite diverse. Female employment fell in four countries, at above the rate for men in Ireland and Greece (with the latter recording a fall of nearly 15 per cent) while in Iceland the fall was roughly equal and in the UK male employment fell faster. In the remaining countries female employment rose but only marginally in the USA, Italy and Hungary. In this last case the increase for men and women combined was more substantial (1.8 compared to 0.5 per cent rise for women), suggesting that men mainly benefited from the public work schemes that swelled public sector employment in Hungary after 2009. Portugal and Spain recorded significant – above 2 per cent – increases for women against a background of even higher growth for men in Portugal but declines for men in Spain. Future job cuts can be expected in both countries where public sector recruitment is now frozen and job cuts expected (Gonzalez Gago and Segales Kirzner this volume; Ferreira this volume).

Patterns of change between the subsectors were mixed. Employment in public administration declined in five countries even in the first phase of the crisis and in all but Hungary in the second phase. Health provided the main source of growth in the first phase with positive growth everywhere, even if almost stagnant in Hungary, but in the second phase growth went into dramatic reverse in Greece and Iceland and growth rates reduced in Spain, the UK, Portugal and Ireland by between 2 and 7 percentage points. Only Hungary and Italy recorded higher growth but from low growth or a decline respectively in phase one, while growth remained stable in the US where health is in any case primarily private. Employment in education increased in the first phase in all nine countries but Italy and Iceland, who also experienced declines in the second phase along with Greece, the UK and Ireland. Only Greece and Iceland recorded falls in each area of the public sector in the second phase.

The above-described gendered effects of the crisis on public sector employment are undoubtedly provisional. With fiscal consolidation plans in the Eurozone's periphery countries and the UK ongoing, just started or tightening and in the face of an imminent turn towards more restrictive fiscal policy in the US, it is too early to assess the full gender impact of austerity on employment and anticipate whether the austerity will be a 'he' or 'she' in terms of job loss. It is, however, seriously compromising job opportunities for women, including the higher educated.

Another longer-term consequence of the crisis may be further growth in non-standard forms of employment for both men and women. In the immediate crisis the flexibility these employment forms offer may, however, lead to more rapid employment reductions and women's greater concentration in temporary jobs pre-crisis resulted in women facing greater loss of temporary jobs in eight of the nine countries, the exception being Spain. They have also benefited less than men from new hires on such contracts – except in Hungary (Table 16.9). Net changes in part-time work for women have so far been limited but it should be noted that the share of involuntary part-time has risen for both men and women in all our countries (Bettio *et al.* 2012, figure 1.8). The most striking change is the masculinization of part-time work, with male part-time jobs growing at a much faster rate than female, although they still have a way to go to catch up (Table 16.9). This development is probably related to the conversion of full-time jobs into part-time to reduce redundancies. The spectacular rise in both male and female part-time jobs in Hungary, though from a very low starting point, is not only due to

TABLE 16.9 Change in part-time and temporary employment in selected European countries and the US 2008–2011

	End – initial year change (%)			
	Part-time		*Temporary*	
	Men	*Women*	*Men*	*Women*
Greece	16.6	–4.7	–8.7	–13.1
Hungary	65.5	45.4	6.5	18.8
Iceland	16.7	0.6	20.4	18.4
Ireland	28.0	1.5	8.6	–3.1
Italy	5.4	3.1	3.1	–4.7
Portugal	37.0	–5.9	–5.8	–6.3
Spain	25.8	–0.8	–24.4	–18.6
UK	12.0	3.8	17.7	6.5
USA	1.1	–7.3		

Source: OECD.Stat (data extracted on 24.12.2012).

employer adjustment policies but also to the large-scale public works jobs scheme (Frey this volume).

The differentiated impact of the crisis on groups of women has in some countries increased pre-crisis inequalities in paid work among women but in others led to a compression of inequalities, although often in a downward direction. In the USA women of colour, single mothers and younger women were hit the hardest by recession, feeding long-term inequality among women (Albelda this volume). Greece provides an opposite example of downward compression of inequalities as the employment rate of high-educated women has declined much more than those of the low and medium educated, thereby narrowing pre-crisis inequalities (Karamessini this volume).

The great increase in youth unemployment rates of both sexes across Europe has increased inequalities between younger and older women in our eight European countries. In Ireland, in particular, women aged 45 to 59 have seen their employment rates rise until 2010 and stabilize since then, in stark contrast with the dramatic reduction in job opportunities for young women who have started emigrating in increasing numbers. Intergenerational inequality is also evident in public sector employment where young teachers, doctors and nurses (majority women) are being employed after 2010 on terms and conditions estimated as up to 30 per cent lower than those employed pre-2010 (Barry and Conroy this volume).

A key issue is whether the demand deflation has led to any signs of women acting as a flexible labour reserve. In practice it has been men who have been more likely to withdraw from the labour market as men's activity rates dropped in all countries while female activity rates rose except in the USA and Ireland, indicating that the 'added-worker effect' has dominated over the 'discouraged worker effect' in the other seven countries, although this applied to all women, not just married women who have been the focus of most studies of added-worker effects. In the exceptions, the female activity rate in the USA fell for the first time in the history of recessions (Albelda this volume). In Ireland the fall may be partly due to an untargeted early retirement scheme in the public sector (Barry and Conroy this volume). In Italy the female activity rate slightly decreased during the initial phase of the crisis but registered a significant increase in the subsequent phase (Verashchagina and Capparucci this volume).

Women's commitment to employment is also demonstrated by the significantly rising share of female-breadwinner couples between 2007 and 2009 in the seven countries for which we have data (Bettio and Verashchagina this volume, Table 4.2). The parallel considerable reduction in dual-earner couples in the same countries over the same period implies that when male partners lose their jobs women remain in or even (re)enter the labour force. It also suggests that the crisis has interrupted trends towards a universal adult worker family model where both partners contribute to household budgets. Now both male and female sole breadwinners are facing the strain of losing their partners' income in managing household budgets. However, this strain is likely to be greater on women who not only still face reduced earnings opportunities but who may also still take on the main responsibility for care.

Employment policy trends under austerity

The crisis has also been the time for policy action aimed at changing labour market systems. Political justifications for these rapid changes in policy include increasing labour market flexibility and responsiveness, bringing about internal devaluation in indebted Eurozone countries and reducing public deficit. In some cases these pragmatic justifications for crisis measures are extended into more far-reaching objectives such as removing privileges for labour market insiders or reducing reliance on the state for care to facilitate women's employment. These policies have tended to take three different even if often interrelated forms: (i) specific changes to employment conditions in the public sector; (ii) reforms to collective bargaining arrangements in the private sector; (iii) changes to legal employment rights and protections. These developments have potential to lead to long-run changes in social models and gender regimes, as discussed in the next section, but also have immediate short-term effects on particular groups of men and women including the unemployed, the low paid, lone parents and public sector employees.

In implementing austerity policies all the countries considered here either sought to reduce public sector employment or change public sector employment and working conditions or both (Table 16.10). Governments are not only reducing pay but also increasing the work intensity through, in some cases, longer hours and in all cases, except Hungary, reduced staffing to meet the same or rising social needs. Reductions in public sector employment may be the outcome of budget cuts (for example in the UK, the USA, Iceland) or of specific employment reduction policies such as early retirement schemes (non-targeted in Ireland, for mothers in Greece) and hiring freezes and rules limiting the ratio of hires to exits (for example in Greece, Spain, Ireland, Portugal and Italy) or according to fixed targets (either agreed with the troika as in Greece and Portugal or self-imposed as in Italy). Changes to public sector pay and conditions have been by and large imposed by the state even where there are collective bargaining rights in the public sector[2] (for example in Greece, the UK, Ireland, Spain (see Vaughan-Whitehead 2013 for country details) and Italy[3]) but, in addition, collective bargaining rights have been removed from various categories of public sector workers in the USA, Greece and Hungary.

Reforms to private sector collective bargaining have been sought in Greece, Spain, Portugal and Ireland. These are aimed at decentralizing collective bargaining, including derogations from sector minima at the company level, individualizing bargaining in low-paid sectors with weak unionization and introducing more flexibility of working hours and schedules. Reforms are also aimed at reducing legal protections including establishing lower than minimum entry-level wages for young people (for example in Italy and Greece) reducing the minimum wage (in nominal terms in Greece) or freezing it elsewhere (for example Ireland, Portugal)

TABLE 16.10 Changes to pay and working conditions in the public sector in selected European countries and the US during the crisis and austerity

Greece	2010 pay cuts according to salary level plus cuts to 13th and 14th month salaries amounting to an average 15% cut (civil service) and 25% (public utilities and undertakings); 2011 reform of public sector salary grid (further reduction in pay by c. 20%); 2012 further cuts (17% on average) for employees under special wage regimes and in state-owned enterprises. Working time increased from 37.5 to 40 hours. Recruitment freeze in 2010, one hire for every 10 in 2011, one in five from 2012 onwards.
Hungary	Freezing of pay scale plus abolition of 13th month salary (8.2% average cut in gross average pay between 2008 and 2010) but lower paid partially protected by increase in national minimum wage. Employment in public sector boosted by those on public works programmes but at only around 70% of the minimum wage.
Iceland	Fiscal consolidation plan included nominal salary cuts for many government employees.
Ireland	Lower pay rates (-10%), pension entitlements and working conditions for new entrants from 2010 onwards (two-tier structure). Pay cuts in 2010 of 5% to 15% according to salary level (average cut 13.5% over 2009–10). Increase in teaching hours. Recruitment freeze until 2013 and non-targeted early retirement scheme from 2010 to 2012 reducing employment.
Italy	Pay freeze and a 20% replacement rate of retiring staff from 2010 to 2013 plus cuts of 5 to 10% in 2010 for higher paid civil servants. Plan for 10% cut in public sector employment announced July 2012.
Spain	Salary cuts of 3–8% in 2010 (5% on average); a base salary freeze for 2012, with one of two bonus payments cut. No replacement of retiring staff (10% replacement rate only in education, health and the armed forces). Increase in civil servants' and teachers' working time.
Portugal	Cuts in pay in 2011 (3.5% above a threshold to a maximum of 10.5%) plus suspension of 13th and 14th month salaries in 2012 (subsequently annulled by the Constitutional Court), a recruitment freeze since 2011 (substituting for the previous 50% replacement rate) and personnel cuts of 2% per year until 2014. Increase in teaching hours in education.
UK	Imposed two year wage freeze 2010–2012 to be followed by two years of 1% pay rises. Budget cuts imply a 16% cut in public sector employment by 2018.
USA	Federal government wages have been frozen since 2010; federal government workforce declined by 0.5% in 2011, with some agencies (e.g. the Social Security Administration and the Internal Revenue Service) with cuts of 6%. States, led by Ohio and Wisconsin have taken action to reduce public sector employees' collective bargaining rights despite evidence that they are paid less than in the private sector.

Source: country case studies this volume, Grimshaw et al. (2012), Vaughan-Whitehead (2013) and OECD Human Resources Management: Country Profiles (updated in December 2012) http://www.oecd.org/governance/publicemploymentandmanagement/hrpractices.htm.

or uprating it by less than inflation (Spain, UK). In the USA one of the rare increases in the federal minimum wage occurred in 2009, but this had the result of reducing the number of workers covered by higher state minimum wages (Mishel *et al.* 2012, table 4.AF). Policies have also been aimed in some countries at easing dismissals of employees on permanent contracts (Greece, Spain, Italy, Portugal and the UK) and in easing the use of atypical contracts (for example Greece).

Italy has, however, taken some steps to improve the regulation of those on atypical contracts and to extend rights, from a low starting point, for workers on such contracts to unemployment benefits. In the US, too, new federal support for unemployment costs for states were made contingent on extensions to low income, part-time and irregular workers, of direct benefit to women, although at the same time the full problems of the welfare reforms in the 1990s became evident as the reformed programmes provided very limited support despite the intense recession (Albelda this volume).

Many of these policy reforms are legitimized as efforts to reduce the 'privileges' of the best-protected, mostly male workforce. The benefits for women are supposed to come simply from evidence of everyone being all in it together rather than from any tangible likely improvements in women's own situation. While women may not have benefited as much as men from collective bargaining and employment protections, they are even more exposed when the only protections are through individual negotiations with employers. Furthermore, measures targeting both the public sector and the lower end of the wage distribution are more deleterious for women given that both public sector and low-paid workers represent a higher share of female than male employment. Moreover, the next phase involving the full implementation of austerity measures may have further and longer-term implications for gender equality and for the related social fabric of societies. It is to these questions that we now turn.

Austerity as a critical juncture for gender and social regimes

A key question that we have sought to explore in this volume was whether the consequences of this current crisis and associated austerity might mark a critical juncture in the development of gender relations in advanced countries. A critical juncture could imply a process of reversal in improvements in women's labour market position and economic and social independence, which have been evident for much of the post-Second World War period but also strengthened in the 1990s and 2000s. Any sustained tendency to reversal would be likely to be associated with a revitalization of traditional gender ideologies. The critical juncture could, however, take different forms, involving a critical change in men's opportunities on the labour market and a further but more decisive move away from the notion of the male breadwinner and provider. Even more likely is the further delineation of different paths for men and women according to social class, reinforced by unresolved struggles between the state and the family (in practice women) as to who should provide care, with both those in need of care and women from lower social classes the most likely losers. In this context we explore the key findings so far on these issues while remaining mindful of the difficulties at this stage in the austerity era in assessing or theorizing on the long-term effects. This is because no one knows how long the austerity era will last or what the path out of the current crisis might be. The long-term consequences of current policy directions are hard to predict as there may yet be several changes of course. Furthermore, the impacts clearly differ across countries and social classes, reflecting differences both in starting points and in the severity of the experience of the crisis. Finally, while policymakers in some countries, under influence from capital, may be taking advantage of current conditions to pursue long-term radical change, these policies may yet be met by active resistance, requiring perhaps a reinvention of social models. This potential for reinvention must be kept in mind even though the outlook in the current climate is towards erosion and destruction of social support systems vital for a positive form of gender equality.

We evaluate the evidence for and against the critical juncture hypothesis from a range of dimensions, taking into account that gender relations may be both an influence on policy choices as well as affected by the impact of policy developments. Firstly, we look for changes to commitments towards gender equality as a policy objective at an international and a national level. Secondly, we assess the extent to which austerity policies are intended or likely to lead to longer-term changes in social and economic models with implications for gender equality. Thirdly, we consider evidence related to changes in the gender regime or form of gender relations. To conclude we consider the essential ingredients for, and prospects of, a path to recovery that would deliver a more gender equal society. Important amongst these ingredients is the future role for a public space and for the maintenance of values that cannot be reduced to market relations.

How fragile are commitments to gender equality as a social goal?

The EU provides the most striking example of a U-turn in the importance attached to gender equality as a social goal. As Villa and Smith detail in this volume, the EU has shifted from being a leader in promoting gender equality, not only as a social goal but also as an integral part of its employment strategy, to a position where not only are gender equality issues almost invisible in their policy agendas but any significant references have had to be reinserted into EU documents as a consequence of objections from individual member states. Before the economic crisis it was widely believed that gender equality issues had become firmly embedded in EU social and employment policies, even if despite general commitments to gender mainstreaming EU economic policymaking had remained gender blind. The embedding of gender equality goals in the employment strategy and perhaps even more importantly in the social funds' evaluation criteria had assured that even member states that had no track record of national concerns with gender equality would pay this issue some attention. In this context it is thus even more shocking that gender equality should have disappeared almost completely from the

EU2020 vision until some minor amendments were made at the last stage of drafting. However, this U-turn also demonstrates the weakness of the commitments to gender equality, which were bound to the business or economic case. The European Employment strategy was formulated in a context where it was assumed there would be no overall limit on employment opportunities so that the key employment problem was to address supply-side barriers, including problems of childcare for women returners and lack of motivation for the unemployed. In the crisis this assumption of full employment has had to be rethought and the imperative of improving women's access to the labour market has fizzled out. All attention became focused on the employment losses experienced by men and there was little recognition of the decline in female employment, particularly viewed against predictions of a rising trend towards greater equality (Bettio and Verashchagina this volume). The commitment to women's employment was thus a commitment to a high overall employment rate and not fundamentally to gender equality as a goal in its own right.

As the EU switched its focus so too did many member states (Villa and Smith this volume), with gender issues allowed to slip to the back or even off the agenda altogether. Among our sample of countries those where there has been most explicit backsliding from gender equality commitments include Spain where the Equality Ministry was abolished and commitments to assist with elderly care needs (otherwise undertaken by women) abandoned almost before they had really been implemented (see Table 16.11). Likewise, Ireland has abolished most of its gender mainstreaming machinery. The UK has cut its budget for the Equality and Human Rights Commission by two-thirds, leading to a warning from the UN about its status in relation to human rights enforcement, and it is bringing forward a review of the duty on public sector organizations to promote gender equality (Rubery and Rafferty this volume). In all three cases where the machinery of gender equality policy was closed or severely cut back the implied message is that such policies in the current crisis are at best a distraction. Although presented as cost-cutting measures, the savings are sufficiently small for a more ideological rationale to be mooted. It is also the case that social policy in all three countries has historically taken the male breadwinner model as the policy norm and only recent strides have been taken to improve care and leave arrangements, such that commitments to gender equality are only weakly embedded in the societal model. This may explain in part these developments, coupled with the political changes that have come about in response to the recession which have in all three cases involved the election of more fiscally conservative governments. Hungary provides a fourth somewhat different example of retreat from gender equality policy, which in any case was never firmly established on the policy agenda. The government is now, however, actively promoting a family policy, which is seen to be contrary to notions of gender equality and endorsing traditional gender roles. This focus on a strong family policy to boost fertility is consistent with a nationalist policy response to recession (Walby 2009) as adopted by the new right-wing government elected in 2010. However, the policy towards women's employment is far from coherent:

TABLE 16.11 Changes to equality policies in selected European countries and the US during the crisis and austerity

Greece	National Programme for Substantive Gender Equality 2010-2013 involving gender mainstreaming, plus counselling centres, shelters from domestic violence, support for childcare costs and integration programmes for vulnerable women; the programme is funded by the ESF.
Hungary	New emphasis on family policy which is seen as in contrast to gender equality. Cut from three to two years' paid leave by previous government restored and new incentives for part-time work for parents of children under 3.
Iceland	New positive gender equality laws providing for 40% quotas on boards, regulation of prostitution and domestic violence, development of an equal pay standard and new gender mainstreaming/gender data gathering but alongside major cuts in parental leave pay which reduced fathers' take up (but some reversal of cuts in 2013).
Ireland	Dismantlement of gender mainstreaming system plus major budget cuts, closures and mergers of gender equality bodies.
Italy	Symbolic introduction of 3 day paternity leave and new €300 voucher for women returning to work after 5 months maternity leave, both for a 3 year experiment.
Spain	Equality Ministry abolished in 2010 after opening 2008 and some gender monitoring institutes at the regional level also closed. Extension of paternity leave postponed.
Portugal	New gender equality policies introduced in 2011 have been suspended by new right wing government at end of 2011.
UK	Two third budget cut for Equality and Human Rights Commission plus early review of gender duty on public sector organisations. Failure to implement parts of 2010 Equality Act.
USA	Equal pay rights restored by Lily Ledbetter Fair Pay Act which reverses curtailment of time period for equal pay cases. Improvements to women's healthcare coverage including maternity through health care reforms.

Source: country case studies this volume plus Center for American Progress (2009) http://www.americanprogress.org/issues/women/news/2009/01/29/5500/president-obama-signs-lilly-ledbetter-fair-pay-act/ and J. Arons (2012) *Women and Obamacare*, http://www.americanprogress.org/wp-content/uploads/issues/2012/05/pdf/women_obamacare.pdf

the new government has reversed cuts to the long three-year paid leave that were made to encourage women to make an earlier return to work but at the same time is increasing part-time work options (Frey this volume).

In Italy commitments to gender equality are weak; this is indicated by the decision to introduce paternity leave but only as a three-day leave and for a three-year experiment.

Among the European countries it is only Greece, Portugal and Iceland where there have been positive moves towards stronger gender equality policies during the recession. However, in the first two cases there has already been backsliding. In Greece a new gender equality programme involving gender mainstreaming and support for women's employment was launched in 2010 but implementation has already been slowed by the June 2012 new coalition government. Likewise, in Portugal, the election of a new conservative coalition in mid-2011 led to the suspension of new gender equality policy instruments introduced in the beginning of 2011. Iceland thus provides the only positive example where women have increased their representation in government as a consequence of the recession and once in power have maintained and increased the visibility of gender equality issues, even if these are pursued within a framework of declining real income and employment opportunities. Even here there were some negative developments, in particular, the cuts to parental leaves which reduced the take up by fathers but in 2013 these cuts are due to be largely restored.

In the USA there has been no explicit national policy of fostering female employment growth for macroeconomic reasons and, in fact, the EU policy was aimed more at catching up with the USA where employment among women has been high for a long time, even if driven in part by declining wages among men (Mishel *et al.* 2012, figure 4C) and by lack of alternatives to support via the market due to family fragility and lack of welfare even now for single parents. There have been no major explicit gender equality policies under Obama but his election and re-election, achieved through a much higher share of the female vote, saw off further threats to gender equality under the influence of the Tea Party, ensured, through the signing of the Lily Ledbetter Fair Pay Act, that equal pay legislation would not be weakened by a supreme court ruling and delivered prospects of more comprehensive health care coverage with more limited scope for discrimination against women's health concerns (Arons 2012).

Austerity policies and social and economic models

One of the many unknowns in the current context is whether the policies adopted ostensibly to deal with the current debt crisis will have intended or unintended long-term implications for the kind of society in which we live, as a consequence of changes not only in competitiveness or the world economic order but also through fundamental changes in social and political arrangements. If social models are being fundamentally restructured it is also more likely that we will face a critical juncture in gender relations. Although social models and, in particular, welfare systems may perpetuate aspects of gender inequalities, it is also through social interventions that much of the progress in reducing gender inequality has taken place.

Walby (2009) has suggested there may be three types of responses to the crisis: the neo-liberal; the social democratic; and the nationalist with differing implications for democracy. Within the countries considered here the most common response has been an intensification of neo-liberalism, either voluntarily adopted by national governments – as in the case of the UK – or involuntarily imposed by international institutions and markets as in the case of the southern European countries and Ireland. This reinforcement of the neo-liberal experiment in the face of its clear failure in the 2008/9 financial crises – neo-liberalism's 'Berlin wall moment' according to commentators such as Hobsbawm and Stiglitz (Peck 2010) – is the most ironic outcome of the crisis, where the recipe offered to address the aftermath of the financial collapse is simply more of the same – a clear example of the 'triumph of failed ideas' (Lehndorff 2012). In almost all countries the initial enthusiasm for positive intervention to offset the market collapse has given way to a policy agenda of restricting state intervention and reasserting the need for more supply-side reform to let markets work more freely even when the origin of the crisis was to be found in the most 'free' country, that of the USA. Crouch's (2011) volume on the strange non-death of neo-liberalism attributes the survival of the market model to the fact that the endorsement of markets is but a thin disguise for the increasing political as well as economic power of corporate capitalism. Other explanations may lie in part in the absence of appropriate alternative political and economic mechanisms to resolve the specific problems of the Eurozone; the lack of political union to provide the basis for a more solidaristic policy in the Eurozone, coupled with the removal of devaluation as an adjustment mechanism, narrowed the range of possible economic and political options under current Eurozone rules. A lack of political imagination and innovation has contributed to the continued reliance on these failed ideas of free markets, reduced welfare states and deregulated employment.

However, the resurgence of neo-liberalism cannot be mainly laid at the door of inertia and sterility of political ideas. The swelling of public debt in response to the financial crisis provided an opportunity for the blame for the current crisis to be diverted from the banks and the market deregulation to the apparent profligacy of the modern welfare state, thereby opening up a space for pursuing radical change in employment and welfare systems that would probably not be tolerated in less turbulent times. Enthusiasm for a forward push in changing the role of the state and regulation of employment can be seen perhaps most clearly in the UK, Spanish and Portuguese cases, spurred on by an apparent political mandate when right-wing governments were elected to replace the more left-wing governments in power at the time the crisis hit. In the UK the big society of volunteer labour is being promoted as an alternative to public sector employment, in Spain public services are to be cut if they are not deemed 'profitable' and the Portuguese government has launched a debate on the 'refoundation of the social state' along 'minimum state' neo-liberal principles calling into question even free compulsory education. In Italy the right-wing Berlusconi government only adopted an austerity plan in August 2011 in order to calm down financial markets but it had already drastically curtailed expenditure on social policy since the very beginning of the crisis. In Greece and Ireland it is still unclear how far these reforms have been actively pursued and embraced by internal political forces as politicians are using the troika's imposition of draconian reforms as cover for the fallout from unpopular measures. One of the reasons why the USA perhaps did not move further in this direction was that a right-wing president was in power when the crisis came, so that the beneficiaries of the electoral revolt were initially the Democrats and Obama, which provided space for the important stimulus package in a country with weak automatic stabilizers.

In two of the countries in the sample the responses to the crises have taken a somewhat different turn. In Hungary the response, at least since 2010, has been more nationalistic and populist, with the focus on increasing the role for Hungarian rather than foreign companies, increasing the birth rate to defend the long-term interests of the country and its culture and recentralizing the public sector under direct central government control. Iceland in contrast has taken the third route, in line with its long-standing position within the group of social democratic Nordic states with its foray into international finance as its core economic model perhaps more a deviation from its historical path. However, this return to a more social democratic path was brought about through greater female involvement in the political process as an immediate response to the bankruptcy of the previous model. The sustainability of the political change is not yet assured since the result of the April 2013 parliamentary election is yet unknown.

Two of the key differences in the way in which Iceland adjusted to the crisis compared to Ireland, a country with a similar overextended financial system, was first that Iceland did not socialize the debts of the banks and second, in asking for contributions from citizens, it took into account ability to pay. In contrast Ireland has introduced a highly regressive universal social charge. Benefit reforms are also taking their toll in other countries, for women are often more reliant on benefits in general due to low pay and the problems of being lone parents. Many of the policies hit the poorest groups hardest and have disproportionate effects on women: in Greece there has been a 22 per cent cut to the minimum wage; in the UK expenditure cuts are higher in the most deprived areas and benefits have been cut or upgraded by less than inflation; in Spain low income pensioners, many of whom are women, will have to pay more for their healthcare and non-contributory benefits on which more women rely are being downgraded in value due to the low uprating of the minimum wage on which they are based; in Hungary a flat rate tax has been introduced providing major benefits to the better off and general cuts to unemployment and social benefits in Hungary are affecting more women than men due to higher inactivity rates; in Portugal pensions have been frozen and a wide range of social benefits have been substantially reduced; in Italy it is funds for social policies which assist individuals and families in distress that have been hit hardest; and in the USA states have been cutting back on health care and social services, with most impact on low income women. Only in Iceland is a coherent policy of protecting the poor from the impact of austerity evident.

The particular form of cuts is also having a gender impact. In Portugal increasing use of means testing for entitlement to many benefits is reducing women's economic autonomy. Likewise, in the UK, incapacity benefits are also to be subject to means testing after one year, again affecting more women claimants. Major reforms are also being made to lone parents' benefits, for example requiring even those with young children to engage in active job search in the UK, while in Ireland the drastic cut in the earnings disregard for lone mothers before loss of welfare payments will discourage many from joining the labour force (Barry and Conroy this volume).

There are only very few examples of new policies that specifically benefit women and most are found in countries with poor overall female integration: for example, in Italy, there are incentives for employers to hire unemployed women and unemployment benefits have been extended to those on non-standard contracts, many of whom are women (Verashchagina and Capparuci this volume), and in Portugal, the self-employed who are mainly dependent on one client will also become entitled to unemployment benefit from 2013 onwards. The USA has also extended unemployment benefits to non-standard workers (Hartmann et al. 2013) but again these are from a low welfare base. Hungary has introduced a special retirement opportunity for older women.

These overall regressive changes to benefit systems have clear negative impacts on women and indicate a trend towards more unequal societies in which women are likely to be the losers. In addition, in most countries there is evidence of a reversal in state support for de-familialization of care. Here we find evidence of cutbacks in often only fledgling support schemes: for example, new programmes for childcare in Italy and for eldercare in Spain have been cut back before they have even really been fully implemented. Likewise, the relatively newly established framework for childcare and after school care in both Greece and the UK have been partially dismantled through budget cuts and quality standards reduced. Social investment plans in Portugal for developing social care have been halted, although current projects continue. Services for low-income families are being cut back in the US even though already limited in provisions. There is less change in Hungary as support is primarily through paid leaves or in Ireland where services are already low. In Iceland childcare services have been maintained although costs to parents have increased and reduced incentives for fathers to take leave have cut total childcare support. These cuts to existing or to plans for childcare and elder care services (see Table 16.12) not only reduce support for working families but also deprive children of early education and limit independence for elderly adults. There is also a retreat from supporting the costs of raising children and providing independent incomes to the disabled, all of which threaten a general retreat from the role of the state in supporting and securing social reproduction. Eight of the nine countries record temporary or longer-term cutbacks with only the US moving to providing more generous support particularly for those with low wage income. These changes to European care regimes have major effects on women, through squeezing mothers' budgets, increasing demands for unpaid domestic work and reducing demand for paid work as care staff. However, these changes reflect above all a shift in the political agenda in now treating care as a low national priority in sharp contrast with the pre-crisis situation.

TABLE 16.12 Changes to care regimes in selected European countries and the US during the crisis and austerity

	Family support	Childcare	Eldercare
Greece	Abolition of child tax credits	Reduced provision and understaffing	Future of 'home help' programme after 2013 not secure
Hungary	Family allowance frozen since 2009 but generous tax reductions for families within regressive flat rate tax system	Modest expansion of nursery facilities	Municipalities reducing provision of elder care [1]
Iceland	Freeze in child benefits plus more means testing; restoration of some cuts 2013	Rise in childcare costs	
Ireland	Reduced child benefits	No change from low base	Cuts to domiciliary care and to carers' allowances
Italy	Major reductions in funds for family policies due to a general 92% reduction in social expenditure	Policy to expand childcare from 2007 only partially implemented before halted	Budget cuts reducing social care
Spain	New 2007 policy of giving €2500 to new parents abolished		Suspension of new rights to domiciliary care and ending of opportunities for non-professional carers to be covered by social security
Portugal	Means-testing of social benefits including family support	Investment in social care programme halted but existing projects being implemented	Investment in social care programme halted but existing projects being implemented
UK	Cuts in child tax credits and freezes to child benefits plus abolition for higher rate tax payers	Scaling down of subsidised childcare services plus reduction in support through child tax credits	Budget cuts leading to cutbacks in care provision
USA	More generous support for children through child tax credits and Earned Income Tax Credit due to lowering of minimum earnings thresholds before payments can be made[2]	Reduced state funding for childcare services	Reduced state funding for eldercare services

Source: country case studies this volume plus 1) Berki et al. (2012) and 2) Hartmann and Hayes (2013).

All current changes in political direction and in social and economic models are as yet only tendencies which may be halted or reversed as the implications of the changes become clearer to the electorates. However, it is also the case that it is easier to elect a different government than for that government to be able to rebuild the social model where the institutional arrangements and also the tax base may have been partially destroyed.

One of the reasons why the current policy directions are not necessarily indicative of longer-term trends is that in no cases have we found examples where policy is directed at resolving longer-term structural problems with their national models. As Lehndorff (2012) has argued, it would not be sufficient – although absolutely necessary – for the EU to find a new policy path out of the crisis. In addition each country needs to address their long-term structural problems – that is do their own homework – but there is little evidence of that happening. The structural problems vary and have divergent impacts by gender. The US needs to find a new position in the new world order and address its structural deficits with China. The Eurozone countries need to deal with the problems of divergent growth paths within the currency union, which cannot be resolved through devaluation. Ireland and Hungary need to become less reliant on inward FDI. However, the problems are not only ones of monetary policy and the European periphery countries need to develop distinctive comparative advantages compatible with global markets; this means in some countries – particularly Portugal – finding a way out of their specialization in the female-dominated textile sector, with likely implications for the demand for female labour. Likewise, southern Italy in particular needs to find a new economic model to overcome long-term stagnation. The UK, US, Ireland and Spain still need to not only deal with the hangover toxic assets related to their ill-founded construction and finance booms but also find new sources of work for the displaced male labour. The UK, Iceland and Ireland need to reduce reliance on financial services and fill the large hole left by the collapse of their international finance adventures. Southern European countries in particular have to address their weak domestic tax bases and all advanced countries need to work together to ensure a higher tax take from international companies. Without serious attention to these rebalancing issues the current policy programmes will not solve underlying economic problems while ensuring a downgrading and dismantlement of the social model, which is likely to intensify the economic pressures. However, even though the long-term future for European economies remains unclear, there is little evidence that the future will not be both reliant upon and involve the economic activity of women as much as men. Any return to a male first employment model would require the establishment of traditional family structures, founded on strong family ties and secure male employment in family wage jobs. None of the trends point in that direction and even in a context of continuing scarcity of work it is clear that women are as much the preferred employees of companies as men. The key issue for the future is likely to be the terms on which women and indeed men are employed rather than a move towards a predominantly male employment system.

Austerity policies and gender relations

To assess whether the current crisis and associated policies are inducing a critical change in gender relations or gender contracts we need to look at four dimensions, namely at: gender roles in the private and the public spheres; gender positions within the public or labour market sphere; gender in public policy and wider societal values; and gendered ideologies and social norms.

Debates on gender contracts have focused on men's and women's different positions within the public and the private spheres (O'Reilly and Nazio this volume). While women have been accepted into the public spheres, their integration is more partial and more dependent upon their specific historical role in the private sphere than is the case for men. As their integration is less complete, prolonged recession could be expected to induce some retreat into the private spheres. However, as already documented above, the main change has been in the opposite direction with evidence of what is known as added worker effects in all nine countries studied in this volume except the US and Ireland. Women with limited past histories of integration are moving into the public sphere to seek work. The only evidence of a resurgence of women's domestic roles is in the level of work that now may have to be performed in addition to wage work, due to cutbacks in social services. Besides, in spite of the opportunities granted to women in order to withdraw from employment in a few countries during the crisis (new early retirement schemes in Ireland and Greece), recent pension reforms (Table 16.13) have repeated the main policy directions of all pre-crisis reforms in the 1990s and 2000s. These include raising retirement ages, incorporating financial penalties for early retirement and equalizing the legal retirement age of women and men as well as increasing qualifying periods for full pension entitlements, a measure which fails to recognize women's more interrupted careers due to care responsibilities. The high public deficits and rising sovereign debts generated during the crisis have thus maintained and even heightened the interest in keeping older women as well as men in employment – hence in the public sphere – for more years to improve the health of public finances.

The second dimension is the position of women relative to men in the public spheres. Again, gender contract debates have looked at how women's relatively disadvantaged position within the labour market, even once integrated, is influenced by their subordinate position in the private sphere and by the policies of social actors in regulating labour markets. A change in gender contract or gender relations in this field might include a trend towards relatively lower pay or greater employment insecurity amongst women. The evidence from this volume suggests that the crisis is leading to job losses, unemployment and real and even nominal wage cuts for women workers but the differences between men and women in these respects may have narrowed rather than widened. Indeed, what we may be witnessing is the use of conditions in the largely female and unregulated sectors as an increasing benchmark for acceptable conditions in sectors or occupations undertaken by now relatively disadvantaged men. The widening flexibilization of

TABLE 16.13 Pension reforms in selected European countries during the crisis and austerity

Greece	2010 and 2012 reforms: pensionable age of women and men equalised (for insured before 1993) and raised for both from 65 to 67 from 2013 onwards; full pension to require 40 years contributions and be based on lifetime earnings; new early-retirement disincentives but new entitlement for mothers born before 1977.
Ireland	2010 reform of public service pensions: pension age raised from 65 to 66 years and maximum retirement age from 65 to 70 years; pensions to be based on career average earnings; non-targeted early retirement scheme.
Italy	2010 and 2011 reforms: women's retirement age raised from 60 to 66 and seven months 2010–2018 to equalize with that of men. By 2021, retirement age of both sexes to be 67 years and two months. From 2012 compulsory defined-contribution system plus additional qualifying conditions for pension: a contribution record of at least 20 years and sufficient amount of contributions to qualify for at least 1.5 times the social pension.
Spain	2010 reform: retirement age raised from 65 to 67; minimum contribution period for full pension extended from 35 to 38.5 years, pensions now based on the last 25 instead of last 15 years of working life.
UK	2010 reforms: retirement age to increase to 66 and 67 for both sexes by 2026 to 2028 instead of 2036 plus widespread reforms of public sector pensions. Improved basic pension from 2016.

Source: country case studies this volume, OECD, *Pensions at a Glance 2011*, Paris and EIRO online.

the labour market and the more rapid growth of precarious or part-time employ-ment among men in the majority of the countries examined in this volume may herald a less gender-differentiated public sphere as poor conditions in women's work become established as the new norm for flexible European labour markets. The immediate and potentially short-term effects of the crisis, whereby for example lower wages and more flexible or part-time work may be accepted as an alternative to unemployment, are also being reinforced by further institutional changes in the form of labour market deregulation and longer-run cuts to pay and conditions in the public sector. This is creating downward homogenization of pay and conditions within women's work as the public sector is the area where women are most likely to have been protected against discrimination and also the sector where many women with higher education find employment (Table 16.10).

These changes within the female labour market co-exist with downward pres-sures on men's wages, particularly the low and medium educated, due to recession and changes in employment regulation and collective bargaining in the private sector. The joint outcome of the above trends in the private and public sector on these gender gaps is unknown but will certainly reflect downward pressures on both women's and men's wages and employment conditions.

We should also note the process of conversion of the public sector as an institutional form that could be expected to provide an example of good practice, defined as good and fair employment conditions for the workforce, to an institution where employment conditions should in principle be based more on providing good value to the taxpayer than ensuring it operates as a 'good employer'. This institutional conversion reinforced by rhetoric on public profligacy may be helped by the specific nature of the public sector – such that many staff are trapped in long-term relationships due to non-transferable expertise and commitment to public service. It may also be questioned whether the predominance of women and their limited alternative opportunities may also have reduced concerns among policy-makers over the fairness and the sustainability of the changes introduced.

This discussion of the changes in states' public sector policies brings us to the third area where we may look for a change in public policy. Although most EU governments had not gone as far as the Swedish state in developing a clear commitment to gender equality – including both similarity of treatment and greater equality of status (Hirdman, cited by O'Reilly and Nazio this volume) – under the influence of the EU most had started down the path of providing more support for women to enter work and of promoting female employment as the means of resolving the low employment rate problem in Europe. What we find in the crisis is a cut back in support for working parents and for elderly care. In some cases, for example Iceland, Greece and Portugal, this is more the consequence of a general across the board cut in public expenditure although in the latter case the intensification of means-testing as the means of cutbacks may have longer-term consequences. In others, notably the UK, Spain, and Portugal, there is a more explicit repudiation of the state's role in providing such support. Work and care choices are being redefined a private matter for the individual family and indeed for employers in deciding how to organize work, a situation that already exists in the USA. Even where no strong ideological stance against supporting working parents has been enunciated by governments, by their actions they are often distancing the state from a responsibility for ensuring a better match between the organization of the labour market and the needs of the now more gender diverse labour supply with continuing care commitments. For example, in the public sector working hours for teachers and public sector employees more generally have been increased without concern for the effect on the work-life balance possibilities for the staff. This increased freedom for employers to set their own terms of employment engagement is also evident in new opportunities in Spain for employers to opt out of collective agreements where they face financial problems. Clauses that they may decide to derogate from include support for working parents (Gonzalez Gago and Segales Kirzner this volume). Thus the setting free of employers from responsibilities for reconciliation is one way by which the state may be trying to step back from addressing the new challenges and social needs thrown up by changes to gender relations and social reproduction. Yet full abdication from these challenges is not necessarily an option for the state. In many advanced countries more and more households are single-parent households and the state may not be willing to provide the support of the normally male absent partner. Thus pressure on those with the highest care commitments – single parents – to enter employment is increasing even alongside another discourse that work and care decisions are a private matter to be made in the best interests of the child. This narrowing of the focus on higher employment integration for women to single parents can be considered a conversion of an emancipatory into a coercive policy, where women's right to employment is turned into a policy of a requirement to work without a right to care.

These apparently confused signals and conflicting ideologies existing side by side within government policy brings us to the final area to consider and that is the issue of gender ideologies and gendered social norms. O'Reilly and Nazio (this volume) have already shown that attitudes towards maternal employment vary considerably both within and across societies. There is thus not one gendered ideology or one social norm and in the crisis there is evidence of a resurgence of conservative gendered norms alongside continuing equality norms. The most obvious case of growing divergent ideologies can be found in the US where the rise of the Tea Party and the conservative gender social ideology, including the anti-abortion campaigns, coexist not only with gender equality norms in employment but also with the emergence of alternative ideologies such as the Occupy movement. The decisive female vote for Obama in 2012 suggests that the hankering after conservative gender roles may be stronger among the male population but this has not stopped individual states introducing more restrictive abortion policies. In the UK there is a much weaker connection between politics and religion, which may preclude the equivalent of a Tea Party movement but for the first time for decades there are government ministers advocating halving the time limit on abortions. In Spain, the recently introduced right to abortion on demand up to 14 weeks is being discussed by the new government with the prospect of very limited rights to abortion in the future. Hungary has also experienced a resurgence of a family ideology, which is seen to be in conflict with the notion of gender equality as promoted through the EU. These developments in Hungary could well presage wider divides within the EU, led by some eastern European member states against the individualist gender equality ideology that has infused EU policy over past decades. The argument to be made here is not that the conservative or traditional gender ideology will necessarily reassert itself and become dominant but that despite the trend towards a more egalitarian approach in Europe and the US over recent decades, the conservative gender ideology has remained ever present and could underpin a revival of such social norms and expectations at least within certain countries or classes. One factor that may keep the policies at bay, however, is simply the increasing economic necessity of women working, even in socially conservative regions or countries.

If we look at these four areas together we can imagine the potential for the current crisis to constitute a critical juncture or turning point in gender relations, but the form this will take is likely to be highly variable and subject to conflicting trends. It is probable, for example, that there may be increasing convergence in the fortunes of men and women in the lower skilled/lower educated groups if Europe moves towards the model already found in the US of a highly polarized society where the main divides are by class and race rather than by gender. We may, however, still find an increasing divide between more advantaged or higher educated men and their female counterparts if the latter are faced by long-term deterioration in conditions in the public sector for professional groups. We have also found some move away from policies that require employers to take actions to reconcile work and care issues and to begin to recognize that employees do not arrive free of care commitments. In this context the issue is whether the outcome may be both a decline in the quality and extent of care provided an increasing tendency social needs such as desires for children to be increasingly subordinated to the needs of the market.

Conclusions and future prospects for a more gender equal society

The comparative analysis of labour market, welfare state and policy developments during the crisis and up to mid/late 2012 in our nine selected countries of Europe and North America has identified several common trends. First, in spite of significant falls in female employment, women's labour market participation increased nearly everywhere; far from quitting the labour market, women who lost jobs continued to seek work and were counted as unemployed, more became sole breadwinners as their partners lost employment and some inactive women were entering the labour market for the first time. Their growing attachment to careers for reasons of economic independence, personal fulfillment or economic necessity (to secure the family income or improve living standards), thus seems irreversible in advanced economies even in the context of a major economic crisis such as the one we are living through. Second, gender inequalities in employment and incidence of part-time and temporary work have narrowed because of greater job loss and spread of flexible forms of employment among men. Third, austerity and fiscal consolidation policies – more widespread in the second phase of the crisis – have been accompanied by employment contraction, pay freezes and cuts and deterioration of working conditions in the public sector which is a major employer for women, especially for the high educated. These same policies have also been responsible for the retrenchment of state support for working parents and the rights to long-term care of the elderly and the disabled, arousing fears about a longer-term retreat of the state from social reproduction, a key field of state intervention for the promotion of women's employment integration in previous decades. Austerity thus represents a threat to the full integration of women into economic life and gender equality in employment and professional achievement. It is though hard to predict the full gendered effects of austerity, given that most fiscal consolidation programmes are still in progress. In the US the president is indeed still trying to avoid austerity in order to maintain economic growth and job recovery. We are thus in the middle, not the end of the austerity phase of the crisis in the advanced economies.

Comparative analysis has also revealed that those countries that have been implementing in recent years the most far-reaching fiscal consolidation under the auspices of the troika (Greece, Portugal, Ireland) or on a voluntary basis (Spain, UK) have also engaged in more or less sweeping changes in employment regulation, wage determination and social benefit systems. These are aimed at both reducing the 'privileges' and power of labour market insiders, by bringing public sector employment conditions in line with those prevailing in the private sector and further deregulating the lower labour market segment. They are also freeing employers from responsibilities towards their employees for enabling reconciliation of work with family responsibilities and personal life. It is in these countries that the neo-liberal model of capitalism has intensified the most during the crisis while Iceland has followed a social-democratic route and Hungary a nationalist route out of the crisis. The US, the most neo-liberal country before the crisis, has avoided a further movement to deregulation and has even reinforced some income guarantees and social rights (e.g. unemployment benefits, health reform) and refrained from austerity at the federal level.

Several important issues for further discussion emerge from these general trends up to this stage of the current global economic crisis. To start with, the narrowing gender gaps in labour market performance are misleading indicators of progress towards gender equality in paid work when women's employment participation and conditions are deteriorating (Bettio and Verashchagina this volume) or in national contexts of extensive social regression that affects the lives of both women and men (Karamessini this volume). The gendered effects of the current economic crisis and austerity thus represent a challenge for rethinking the notion of gender equality as a social goal, even when applied in particular areas of human activity such as work, and point to the need for associating it with those of social progress, social justice and improvement of the quality of life of citizens in order to keep intact its liberating potential.

Another important issue is whether the current crisis is proving to be a critical juncture for gender relations (Rubery this volume). Our comparative analysis has shown that the ongoing austerity experience has created the potential for the current crisis to become a turning point although the scale, duration and policy-mix of fiscal consolidation and the sharing of its financial and social costs among genders, social classes and other social groups has differed between the countries studied here, depending on the internal political situation and external pressures by international creditors. In all nine countries though austerity policies have interrupted the steady expansion of the role of the state in promoting gender equality both through the de-familialization of care and through providing good quality employment as a direct employer of female labour. The coming years will show whether and in which countries this interruption will be only temporary or initiate a longer-term reversal of trend that confirms the hypothesis of the current crisis as a critical juncture for gender relations and contracts.

If current trends towards intensification of neo-liberalism continue, we anticipate a move towards more polarized societies according to class and ethnicity, an equalization of financial and employment conditions between the lower educated/lower skilled women and men and the widening of gender gaps in the situation and prospects among the higher educated/higher skilled. At the same time, failures to develop state support for care or reductions in existing provision may lead to different reactions by class and gender. Lower-educated women may increase time spent on unpaid work or increase their involvement in part-time jobs; higher-educated women may rely more on paid domestic care or on more equal sharing of unpaid care with their partner. The outcomes may also include reduced fertility, and an increasing tendency for persons needing care to be left without adequate support. The potential diversity of such 'arrangements' could lead to a further 'balkanization' of gender contracts and labour market trajectories of women than that observed before the crisis across a spectrum from work-poor to work-rich households, while the immediate consequence of austerity and rising levels of unemployment is the increase in the share of jobless households (O'Reilly and Nazio this volume).

The capacity of the above trends to destroy the social institutions that promoted gender equality in the pre-crisis period depends on social and political resistance to the dominant neo-liberal responses to the crisis and support for alternative models of socio-economic development. These need not only to be inclusive and equitable (Perrons and Plomien this volume) but also to provide solutions to the main structural problems faced by each national economy and society, and by regional entities such as the EU and the Eurozone. Resistance to the erosion and destruction of social institutions supporting positive forms of gender equality also depends on keeping gender equality as a goal high on the political agenda. Unfortunately, the perception of the economic crisis as primarily a crisis for men has meant that gender equality considerations have been absent from policy making during both the initial and second phase of the crisis in all the nine countries with the exception of Iceland. Most have even witnessed a retreat in gender equality commitments and policy under austerity. Gender equality has been also downgraded among EU policy priorities, especially in the field of employment, reflecting in part a weaker commitment to gender equality among member states joining in the 2000s. Such developments are worrisome given the resurfacing of conservative ideas on gender roles in Europe next to the dominant equality norms that are though losing ground. Fortunately, in the US, the (re)election of Obama has put some brakes on the rising ideological influence of the Tea Party in recent years.

It is clear that long-term progress towards gender equality as a socially progressive goal requires fundamental adjustments to the neo-liberal model as Perrons and Plomien point out. Within this new form of capitalism there is a need to retain and develop a public space that provides for an alternative calculus to the market and which values activities outside the market, in particular, care. This requires the recapturing of the state from the clutches of international capital and the development of a more progressive politics in which gender equality is accepted as a core goal by men as well as women. This implies also the implementation of innovative gender equality policy approaches and tools such as gender mainstreaming of macro-economic policy and gender budgeting. The need for men and women to make common cause against the mix of austerity and deregulation currently on offer becomes clearer the more that men are themselves increasingly faced with low paid, insecure employment and unemployment and the more that the state is acting against the interests of both male and female citizens. The next phase of gender equality policy and politics thus requires a more integrated approach which allows for renewed and more equal gender contracts and for new social models which facilitate both men and women to fulfil their aspirations under conditions of economic security. The pursuit of gender equality needs to be considered part of the solution to the current endemic crisis and not treated as a luxury policy to be pursued only once growth has returned.

Notes

1 It can be interpreted as the share of the employed population that would need to change occupation (sector) in order to bring about an even distribution of men and women among occupations or sectors. In percentage terms the index ranges from 0 to 50, the maximum value being reached when there are as many women as men in employment working in completely segregated occupations/sectors.
2 According to the ICTWSS database in 2010 four of the nine countries have rights to collective bargaining in the government sector (Greece, Iceland, Spain, UK) and three more with minor restrictions (Ireland, Italy, USA) while Hungary has major restrictions on the right to collective bargaining and Portugal has no collective bargaining.
3 Collective bargaining suspended in Italy for public sector workers 2010–2012 http://www.eurofound.europa.eu/eiro/2011/02/articles/it1102049i.htm

References

Alonso-Villar, O., del Río, C. and Gradín, C. (2010) 'The Extent of Occupational Segregation in the US: Differences by Race, Ethnicity and Gender', *ECINEQ Working Paper*, No. 2010–180. Available at: http://www.ecineq.org/milano/WP/ECINEQ2010-180.pdf (accessed 13.01.2013).

André, I.M. (1996) 'At the Centre of the Periphery? Women in the Portuguese Labour Market', in M.D. García-Ramon and J. Monk (eds) *Women of the European Union. The Politics of Work and Daily Life*, London: Routledge, 138–55.

Andreotti, A. and Mingione, E. (2012) 'The Modernization of Female Employment in Italy: One Country, Two Patterns', in A. Buğra and Y. Özkan (eds) *Trajectories of Female Employment in the Mediterranean*, Houndmills, Basingstoke: Palgrave MacMillan, 38–64.

Anxo, D., Fagan, C., Cebrian, I. and Moreno, G. (2007) 'Patterns of Labour Market Integration in Europe – A Lifecourse Perspective on Time Policies', *Socio-Economic Review*, 5(2): 233–60.

Beneria, L. and Sen, G. (1981) 'Accumulation, Reproduction and Women's Role in Economic Development: Boserup Revisited', *Signs*, 7(2): 279–98.

Berki, B., Neumann, L., Edelényi, M. and Varadovics, K. (2012) *Public Sector Pay and Procurement in Hungary: National Report*, EWERC working paper, Manchester Business School. Available at: https://research.mbs.ac.uk/european-employment/Portals/0/docs/Hungary-national%20report.pdf (accessed 15.01.2013).

Bettio, F. and Plantenga, J. (2004) 'Comparing Care Regimes in Europe', *Feminist Economics*, 10(1): 85–113.

Bettio, F. and Verashchagina, A. (2009) *Gender Segregation in the Labour Market. Root Causes, Implications and Policy Responses in the EU*, Report by the European Commission's Expert Group on Gender and Employment Issues, European Communities, Luxembourg: Publications Office of the European Union. Also available at: http://ec.europa.eu/justice/gender-equality/document/index_en.htm (accessed 13.01.2013).

Bettio, F., Simonazzi, A. and Villa, P. (2006) 'Change in Care Regimes and Female Migration: The "Care Drain" in the Mediterranean', *Journal of European Social Policy*, 16(3): 271–85.

Bettio, F., Corsi, M., Lyberaki, A., Samek Lodovici, M. and Verashchagina, A. (2012) *The Impact of the Economic Crisis on the Situation of Women and Men and on Gender Equality Policies*, Report by the European Commission's Expert Groups on Gender and Employment (EGGE) and Gender Equality and Social Inclusion, Health and Long-Term Care (EGGSI). Available at: http://ec.europa.eu/justice/gender-equality/document/index_en.htm (accessed 13.01.2013).

Boserup, E. (1970), *Women's Role in Economic Development*, London: George Allen & Unwin.

Crouch, C. (2011) *The Strange Non-death of Neo-liberalism*, Oxford: Polity Press.

European Commission (2007) 'Active Ageing and Labour Market Trends for Older Workers', in *Employment in Europe 2007*, Luxembourg: Office for Official Publications of the European Communities.

Eurostat (2008) *The Life of Women and Men in the EU. A Statistical Portrait – 2008 edition*, Luxembourg: Office of the Official Publications of the European Communities.

Gornick, J.C. and Heron, A. (2006) 'Working Time Regulation as Work-Family Reconciliation Policy: Comparing Europe, Japan, and the United States', *Journal of Comparative Policy Analysis: Research and Practice*, 8(2): 149–66.

Grimshaw, D., Rubery, J. and Marino, S. (2012) *Public Sector Pay and Procurement in Europe During the Crisis*. EWERC working paper, Manchester Business School. Available at: https://research.mbs.ac.uk/european-employment/Portals/0/docs/Comparative%20report%20final.pdf. (accessed 14.05.13).

Hartmann, H. and Hayes, J. (2013) 'Single Mothers in the Great Recession: How Well Did the Safety Net Work?' Paper presented at joint URPE/IAFFE session ASSA conference San Diego, January 6th.

Karamessini, M. (2008) 'Still a Distinctive Southern European Employment Model?', *Industrial Relations Journal*, 39(6): 510–31.

Lehndorff, S. (2012) 'Introduction – The triumph of Failed Ideas', in S. Lehndorff (ed.) *A Triumph of Failed Ideas. European Models of Capitalism in the Crisis*, Brussels: ETUI.

Lewis, J. (1992) 'Gender and Development of Welfare Regimes', *Journal of European Social Policy*, 2(3): 159–73.

Mandel, H. and Shalev, M. (2009) 'Gender, Class and Varieties of Capitalism', *Social Politics*, 16: 161–81.

Mishel, L., Bivens, J., Gould, E. and H. Shierholz, H. (2012). *The State of Working America, 12th Edition*. Economic Policy Institute. Ithaca, N.Y.: Cornell University Press. Available at: http://stateofworkingamerica.org/subjects/overview/?reader (accessed 31.12.2012).

O'Reilly, J. and Fagan, C. (1998) *Part-time Prospects: An International Comparison of Part-time Work in Europe, North America and the Pacific Rim*, London: Routledge.

Ostner, I. (1994) 'Independence and Dependence. Options and Constraints for Women Over the Life Course', *Women's Studies International Forum*, 17(2/3): 129–39.

Peck, J. (2010) *Constructions of Neoliberal Reason*, Oxford: Oxford University Press.

Plantenga, J. and Remery, C. (2009) 'The Provision of Childcare Services. A Comparative Review of 30 European Countries', Report by the European Commission's Expert Group on Gender and Employment Issues, European Communities, Luxembourg:

Office for Official Publications of the European Communities. Also available at: http://ec.europa.eu/justice/gender-equality/document/index_en.htm (accessed 13.01.2013)

Plantenga, J. and Remery, C. (2010) 'Flexible Working Time Arrangements and Gender Equality. A Comparative Review of 30 European Countries', Report by the European Commission's Expert Group on Gender and Employment Issues, European Communities, Luxembourg: Office for Official Publications of the European Communities. Also available at: http://ec.europa.eu/justice/gender-equality/document/index_en.htm (accessed 13.01.2013)

Ray, R., Gornick, J.C. and Schmitt, J. (2010) 'Who Cares? Assessing Generosity and Gender Equality in Parental Leave Policy Designs in 21 Countries', *Journal of European Social Policy*, 20(3): 196–216.

Rubery, J. (2013) 'Public Sector Adjustment and the Threat to Gender Equality', in D. Vaughan-Whitehead (ed.) *The Public Sector Shock. The Impact of Policy Retrenchment in Europe*, Geneva, Switzerland: International Labour Office, 23–43.

Rubery, J., Smith, M. and Fagan, C. (1998) 'National Working-Time Regimes and Equal Opportunities', *Feminist Economics*, 4(1): 71–101.

Rubery, J., Smith, M. and Fagan, C. (1999) *Women's Employment in Europe. Trends and Prospects*, London: Routledge.

Rubin, J., Rendall, M.S., Rabinovich, L., Tsang, F., van Oranje-Nassau, C. and Janta, B. (2008) *Migrant Women in the European Labour Force. Current Situation and Future prospects*, Rand Europe, Technical Report prepared for the European Commission. Available at: http://www.rand.org/pubs/technical_reports/TR591.html (accessed 13.01.2013).

Sainsbury, D. (1994) *Gendering Welfare States*, London: Sage.

Szikra, D. and Szelewa, D. (2010) 'Do Central and Eastern European Countries fit the "Western" picture? The Example of Family Policies in Hungary and Poland', in C. Klemmer and S. Leiber (eds) *Welfare States and Gender Inequality in Central and Eastern Europe. Continuity and Post-socialist Transformation in the EU Member States*, Brussels: ETUI.

Tilly, L. and Scott, J. (1978) *Women, Work and Family*, New York: Holt, Rinehart & Wilson.

Vaughan-Whitehead, D. (ed.) (2013) *The Public Sector Shock. The Impact of Policy Retrenchment in Europe*, Geneva, Switzerland: International Labour Office and Cheltenham: Edward Elgar.

Walby, S. (2009) *Globalization and Inequalities: Complexity and Contested Modernities*, London: Sage.

INDEX